MW01242937

CHINA'S ECONOMIC FOOTPRINT IN SOUTH AND SOUTHEAST ASIA
A Futuristic Perspective

Case Studies of Pakistan, Sri Lanka, Myanmar and Thailand

CHINA'S ECONOMIC FOOTPRINT IN SOUTH AND SOUTHEAST ASIA
A Futuristic Perspective

Case Studies of Pakistan, Sri Lanka, Myanmar and Thailand

Reena Marwah
University of Delhi, India

Sanika Sulochani Ramanayake
University of Kelaniya, Sri Lanka

World Scientific

NEW JERSEY · LONDON · SINGAPORE · BEIJING · SHANGHAI · HONG KONG · TAIPEI · CHENNAI · TOKYO

Published by

World Scientific Publishing Co. Pte. Ltd.
5 Toh Tuck Link, Singapore 596224
USA office: 27 Warren Street, Suite 401-402, Hackensack, NJ 07601
UK office: 57 Shelton Street, Covent Garden, London WC2H 9HE

Library of Congress Cataloging-in-Publication Data
Names: Marwah, Reena, 1960–   author. | Ramanayake, Sanika Sulochani, author.
Title: China's economic footprint in South and Southeast Asia : a futuristic perspective :
    case studies of Pakistan, Sri Lanka, Myanmar and Thailand / Reena Marwah,
    University of Delhi, India, Sanika Sulochani Ramanayake, University of Kelaniya, Sri Lanka.
Description: New Jersey : World Scientific, [2022] | Includes bibliographical references and index.
Identifiers: LCCN 2021022920 (print) | LCCN 2021022921 (ebook) |
    ISBN 9789811236372 (hardcover) | ISBN 9789811236389 (ebook) |
    ISBN 9789811236396 (ebook other)
Subjects: LCSH: China--Foreign economic relations--Southeast Asia. | Southeast Asia--
    Foreign economic relations--China. | China--Foreign economic relations--South Asia. |
    South Asia--Foreign economic relations--China. | Southeast Asia--Economic conditions |
    South Asia--Economic conditions
Classification: LCC HF1604.Z4 A785625 2022 (print) | LCC HF1604.Z4 (ebook) |
    DDC 337.5105--dc23
LC record available at https://lccn.loc.gov/2021022920
LC ebook record available at https://lccn.loc.gov/2021022921

British Library Cataloguing-in-Publication Data
A catalogue record for this book is available from the British Library.

For any available supplementary material, please visit
https://www.worldscientific.com/worldscibooks/10.1142/12259#t=suppl

Desk Editors: Jayanthi Muthuswamy/Sandhya Venkatesh

Typeset by Stallion Press
Email: enquiries@stallionpress.com

Dedicated with Affection and Gratitude to our Families

Preface

"The fact of the matter is that our China must be regarded as the root of all other countries".

Li Ruzhen, 1827

In the early nineteenth century, the novelist Li Ruzhen wrote the above statement in his novel *Flowers in the Mirror*, exhibiting the confidence of the people against the British trade missions. However, China has never in history been as confident, muscular, and belligerent as in 2020. The aura of superiority it radiates has its resonance with the notion of *"tianxia"* (*all-under Heaven*).

China's proximity with Central Asia, Southeast Asia, and South Asia, has ensured that these three subregions of Asia are transformed, even as China seeks to regain its Middle Kingdom status. John Fairbank writes that the formalities of the tributary system constituted a mechanism by which formerly barbarous regions outside the empire were given their place in the all-embracing Sinocentric cosmos. However, according to Zhou Fangyin, China's primary interest is in stabilizing its relationships with neighbors through concessions. The narrative from Zhou's exposition is that China is at the disadvantaged side of tributary relationships: frustrated in conflicts and conceding to neighbors in order to pacify its borders (Womack, 2012).

The purpose of writing *China's Economic Footprint in South and Southeast Asia* is to place the above contrasting views in perspective and provide readers with an understanding of the extent of China's economic influence in these two subregions of Asia. The rapid growth of the

Chinese economy, especially since 2001, has stunned the world. China not only seeks super power status, it also desires to unseat the United States as the number one global economy.

Xi Jinping's articulation of the Chinese Dream is without a parallel, encompassing smaller countries in its embrace. This penchant for influence is well-conceived by China as the supplier of physical infrastructure. The recipient countries' demand for physical assets to buttress and fortify their growth is synchronized with China's pursuit for water, mines, energy, connectivity, territory, and maritime supremacy. It is the alacrity and speed with which China pens agreements, commits funds, and executes that has resulted in over 2,200 projects being commissioned in over 130 countries. The Maritime Silk Road, the Silk Road Economic Belt (SREB), have been subsumed in the Belt and Road Initiative (BRI), which has been compared to China's erstwhile tributary system.

BRI is a natural offshoot of China's breakneck growth at home. After three decades of phenomenal annual growth, in double digits for many years, overcapacity issues came to confront the Chinese economy, even as its rate of growth slowed to the 6% range. This resulted in overtures of Chinese funding for projects, which sometimes ill-conceived or unviable, have become a strain on the host economies. To be fair to China, it is also true that smaller states tend to gravitate toward a country they consider a development partner.

China's expanding economic influence buttressed by projects streamed through the BRI is not driven by legal structures, however formal or loose, but by an implicit desire to put the law at the service of commerce to achieve operational results. Hence, ASEAN's informal nature concurs with the fact that there is no Belt and Road charter. It suits the countries of South and Southeast Asia, especially those with authoritarian regimes and low levels of development, like Cambodia and Laos, to accept connectivity projects and commercial and cultural exchanges for integration with a powerful neighbor. This initiative is slowly being built by specific, bilateral project investment undertakings and an interconnected network of "soft-law" memoranda of understanding (Wang, 2019).

Economic aspirations must be shielded and protected by security umbrellas, thus making these countries partners of the China-dominated security architecture in South and Southeast Asia. Nowhere is this more evident than in the countries of Sri Lanka and Pakistan in South Asia.

Despite Southeast Asian nations being viewed as within the ambit of China's historical sphere of influence, Myanmar and Thailand provide experiences different from their neighbors. The authors also navigate China's policies at home and abroad, providing a futuristic perspective of China's path to victory.

Choice of Countries

Pakistan, Sri Lanka (South Asia); Myanmar, Thailand (Southeast Asia)

In South Asia, the salient motivation for China to strengthen its partnership with Pakistan and Sri Lanka has been to contain India. Moreover, with both these countries, China has the patronage of historical connections — comprising trade and travelers. The geo-strategic location of these two countries cannot be understated either. Pakistan provides a conduit for expansion of its ties with Middle East and beyond. The Indian Ocean's supremacy requires an acquiescent Sri Lanka. Another factor of significance is the strong military. In Pakistan, the nexus between the politicians and generals is well-established. The military was strengthened in Sri Lanka to deal with the issue of the Liberation Tigers of Tamil Eelam (LTTE). The longstanding ethnic narrative of the Tamils was rebranded by Rajapaksha, with the help of China into one of terrorism, post which the Rajapakshas entered into several agreements with their benefactor under the BRI. In terms of economic fragility and access to aid, China was a willing donor to both Pakistan and Sri Lanka. Hence, the justification for the countries chosen in South Asia.

In Southeast Asia, Myanmar and Thailand were selected for our book for the following reasons. First, while these countries are in China's immediate neighborhood on the mainland, they are not in the category of Laos and Cambodia, who rarely contradict their gargantuan neighbor. Second, these two countries have a strong military (Myanmar) or have experienced a strengthening of the military (Thailand). Third, it is these countries which have a "kith and kin" relationship, given that they host a large population of ethnic Chinese. Fourth, these two countries are recipients of BRI projects. Fifth, China's strategy of "non'-interference" and prioritizing long-term economic development over human rights and freedom of expression are manifested in both countries.

With respect to the four countries case studies discussed in this book, while Myanmar and Thailand do seek to maintain some elements of hedging and balancing in their economic engagement and foreign policy, Sri Lanka and Pakistan are completely under the sway of China. In fact, Thailand, due to its strategic nodal location, and Myanmar as it moves toward democratization, do exhibit agency in pushing back Chinese investment.

Some of the questions the authors seek to address are:

➢ If the path to growth-led development for the developing countries of Asia is indeed to be defined and articulated by the country's political leadership, then to what extent can external investment stimulate the impulses of growth?

➢ How have strengthened economic relations of Pakistan, Sri Lanka, Myanmar, and Thailand with China impacted their economies?

➢ Are the BRI projects and the debt burden they entail sustainable in the future, especially as economies are battered due to the pandemic?

➢ Could these countries afford to rethink their economic relations with China, given that there is a potential wariness of China's growing economic footprint and possession of their key resources?

➢ Could there be any roadblocks to China's emergence as the leading power in the Asia-Pacific region and globally? What will be the fallout for global geopolitics?

Outline of Chapters

The book comprises 10 chapters. The contents of each are briefly described as follows:

1. Rise of China

Much has been written about the rise of China, especially since it embraced the forces of globalization since 1979. This chapter focuses on the review of relevant literature, given that several authors from all over the world have tried to analyze the rapid transformation in the Chinese economy that has made it the factory of the world. Authors include Jonathan Ward (*China's vision of victory, 2019*), Bertil Lintner (*The Costliest Pearl*, 2019, *China's India war, 2018*), Bruno Macaes (*China's Belt and Road: A Chinese world order*, 2019) among several others. The economic transformation of China including a detailed analysis of data over the period 1980–2020 is discussed.

2. The Chinese Dream and Vision
The persona of Chinese Premier Xi Jinping and his vision of the Chinese Dream to replace the existing international order is challenging the United States' supremacy in various ways. This chapter analyzes the manifestations and contours of Belt and Road Initiative in the context of the Chinese Dream. Xi's Chinese Dream is programmatic and tied to goals, targets, and planning; it was seen as highly pragmatic by recipient partners. However, the contours of the "Dream" continue to transverse across the economic, cultural, social to the political and strategic arenas, too. These have ramifications for other countries as well.

3. China in South Asia: History Informs but Geography Governs
China and India share colonial connections through historical times, during the British rule in the Indian subcontinent. During the cold war, South Asia was one of the most important regions in China's international relations and foreign policy. The 1962 Sino-India war resulted in a breakdown of the *Panchsheel Agreement*; ever since, bilateral relations between the two countries have been replete with distrust. Despite the effort toward regional integration by India through South Asian Association for Regional Cooperation (SAARC) since 1985, the constant fear of Indian domination by other member countries, severe institutional weaknesses, and deficiency in acceptable and visionary regional leadership have added to its laggardness. China's motivations to contain India have resulted in it engaging bilaterally with each country in South Asia. This chapter provides insights into the bilateral engagement, to contextualize the detailed country experiences of Pakistan and Sri Lanka.

4. China and Pakistan: "Iron Brothers"
Pakistan has always viewed China as a guarantor of its security, even when it was and continues to be seen by India and the United States as an exporter of terrorism. While China continues to give Pakistan constant support at international forums, it refrains from commenting on its internal challenges. Over the years, the relationship has blossomed into an "All-Weather Strategic Cooperative Partnership", with the China Pakistan Economic Corridor at its core. Pakistan considers China as one of its closest friends and partners and China considers Pakistan as its "Iron Brother". Moreover, the relationship has forged ahead through economic, cultural, political, and strategic engagement. This bilateral partnership comprises several facets; however, the focus of this chapter is on the economic

impact of the BRI projects, given that Pakistan's frail economy has become overdependent on China.

5.   China in Sri Lanka: A Small Island Syndrome

China's Sri Lankan relationship has a long history, though more contemporary ties can be traced to the Rubber-Rice Pact of 1952. The Presidency of Mahinda Rajapaksha witnessed a greatly strengthened partnership, with several infrastructure projects being commenced and completed. China and Sri Lanka also share a military relationship, with China selling a range of modern armaments to the latter. This chapter assesses the impact of Chinese investment through BRI projects and trade relations on the Sri Lankan economy and articulates the economic and strategic implications for the future.

6.   China's Visible Influence in Southeast Asia: People, Polity, and Prowess

China's historical relations with Southeast Asia are well-documented (Wang, 1995, *The Chinese way*; Skinner 1957, *Chinese Society in Thailand: An Analytical History*; Reid, 1993, *Southeast Asia in the Age of Commerce, 1450–1680*, etc.). In the 1990s, China was perceived as a threat to its Southeast Asian neighbors in part due to its conflicting territorial claims over the South China Sea as well as support of communist insurgency. This perception began to change during the Asian financial crisis of 1997/1998, and after China's economic rise became more perceptible. In the present times, China's "charm offensive" and economic diplomacy as well as its proximity to authoritarian regimes has downplayed territorial disputes while focusing on economic relations, through both trade and investment in BRI projects. China is also beginning to develop bilateral and multilateral security relationships with Southeast Asian states. A brief overview of China's bilateral relations with each country of ASEAN is discussed to contextualize the case studies of Myanmar and Thailand.

7.   China and Myanmar: The "Pauk-phaw" (Fraternal) Relationship

China and Myanmar (formerly Burma) reflect elements of their traditional pauk phaw (siblings from the same mother) relationship that accorded China seniority. This chapter discusses China–Myanmar relations, particularly Chinese investments and BRI projects. The evidence of pushback of certain projects and the reasons thereof are delineated.

8.   China and Thailand: "Kith and Kin" Relations
Thailand and China have a long historical connection. This is evident not only through the visibility of Chinese ownership of more than a third of businesses in Thailand, but also from the diaspora. In the Xi Jinping era, since 2013, the comprehensive strategic cooperative partnership between the People's Republic of China and the Kingdom of Thailand continued to deepen. The two countries signed cooperation documents in economy and trade, science and technology, education, maritime cooperation, energy, and other sectors. Bilateral trade and investment has continued to grow. Thailand's economic policy planners and government leaders remain supportive of BRI, although there are local concerns about a potential debt trap and a raw deal with disadvantageous terms. China's economic footprint, though substantial, is not without thorns. Thailand must engage with this gigantic partner, but not exclusively!

9.   China in South and Southeast Asia: Pursuit vs. Proximity
This chapter discusses the manifestations of China's footprint in economic, strategic, and security spheres through a comparative macro analysis of South and Southeast Asia. A comparative quantitative analysis (costs and benefits) of the impact of China's economic engagement (trade and investment) on the economies of the four countries is also presented.

10. China: A Futuristic Perspective
The pandemic has witnessed China striving to salvage its reputation, from being viewed as the source of the outbreak of COVID-19, to being the benevolent power; a power which is not only capable of controlling the pandemic within its boundaries, but also providing aid and assistance, coupled with vaccine diplomacy to BRI partner countries. There are several emerging issues on the landscape of the global order that the book has sought to address. Hence, policy goals articulated within China and perspectives in external engagement are elucidated in the last chapter through two sections:

➢   China's Prowess, Pathways, and Progress: Internal Dimensions
➢   China's External Engagement: Cooperation and Competition

About the Authors

Reena Marwah, M.Phil, PhD, International Business, is an Associate Professor at Jesus and Mary College, University of Delhi. She is the recipient of several prestigious fellowships including the ICSSR, Government of India Senior fellowship, McNamara fellowship of the World Bank, 1999–2000, and the Asia fellowship of the Asian Scholarship Foundation, 2002–2003. She is also a Senior Fellow of the Institute of National Security Studies Sri Lanka (INSSSL). She has been a Consultant for the World Bank and UN Women. In addition to several chapters and articles published in books/journals, she is author/co-author/co-editor of 15 books and monographs including *The Global Rise of Asian Transformation*, (Palgrave Macmillan) 2014. Her latest co-edited book is *China Studies in South and Southeast Asia: Pro-China, Objectivism, and Balance*, (2018). Her most recent book, titled *Re-imagining India Thailand Relations: A multilateral and bilateral perspective*, World Scientific Publishers, Singapore, has been published in March 2020.

Sanika Sulochani Ramanayake is working as a Senior Lecturer at the Department of Social Statistics in the University of Kelaniya. Prior to this appointment she was a senior researcher at Hector Kobbekaduwa Agrarian Research Institute, and a visiting lecturer at General Sir John Kottelawela Defence University, University of Colombo, and University of Vocational Technologies in Sri Lanka. Earlier, she was a Post-Doctoral researcher at International Development Research Centre (IDRC), Canada, affiliated to the Indira Gandhi Institute of Development Research (IGIDR), Mumbai (From 2016–2018), and a Post-Doctoral researcher at Seoul National University and Inha University, which was funded by the Social Science Korea (SSK) program in South Korea (from 2013–2016). She obtained her PhD degree from Seoul National University and received the Brain Korea scholarship for her PhD studies. Her recent publications have appeared in *International Journal of Finance & Economics, European Journal of Development Research, Journal of the Asia Pacific Economy, Millennial Asia,* and *South Asia Research Journal.* She has also published a book chapter in *Innovation Policy, System and Management* by Cambridge University Press, UK. She was the recipient of Vice Chancellor's Award 2020 — 1st place — Early Career Researcher in the Faculty of Social Sciences, University of Kelaniya, Sri Lanka.

Acknowledgments

This volume, titled *China's Economic Footprint in South and Southeast Asia: A Futuristic Perspective*, could not have become a reality without the valuable cooperation of several scholars, officials, and diplomats from countries in the region. Our endeavor to document the trajectory of China's Belt and Road projects in the four countries, viz. Pakistan, Sri Lanka, Myanmar, and Thailand, required us to seek out various official records and utilize past interviews of an oral history project undertaken by the Association of Asia Scholars in collaboration with Taiwan National University; in particular, we are grateful to Prof. Chih-yu Shih and Prof. Swaran Singh. We sincerely acknowledge and thank all our interviewees for their candid sharing of views and experiences from their own country.

Despite the inability to conduct face-to-face interviews due to the pandemic, we have been fortunate to have received the valuable guidance, mentoring, and knowledge from several senior experts, policymakers, officials, members of the Indian diaspora, and friends. We are particularly thankful to Prof. Keun Lee from South Korea, Dr. Khin Maung Soe from Myanmar, Dr. Piyanat Soikham from Thailand, Mr. Prasanna Liyanage from Sri Lanka as well as Dr. Furrukh Khan and Dr. Pervaiz Mahesar from Pakistan. Discussions and candid sharing of views helped to enrich our understanding of the subject. We are grateful to each one mentioned in our list of interviewees.

We are grateful to our heads of institutions viz. Dr. Sandra Joseph, Principal, Jesus and Mary College, University of Delhi, India, and

Professor Nilanthi de Silva, Vice-Chancellor, University of Kelaniya, Sri Lanka, for their kind encouragement.

Our families have been our constant strength and have encouraged us in every way to complete this seminal work. This volume also acknowledges the pivotal contribution of several authors, who have contributed to enriching our knowledge and understanding of the subject.

This book would not have been possible without the kind cooperation of the production and editorial teams of World Scientific Publishers, Singapore. Each one deserves our sincere appreciation and gratitude.

Contents

Preface   vii

About the Authors   xv

Acknowledgments   xvii

List of Figures   xxv

List of Tables   xxix

List of Maps   xxxi

List of Abbreviations   xxxiii

List of Interviewees: Unpublished Interviews   xxxvii

Chapter 1   Rise of China   1
    1.1 Introduction   1
    1.2 Literature Review   2
        1.2.1 Reform-led growth   2
    1.3 The Growth of the Chinese Economy Since the 1960s:
         In Numbers   6
        1.3.1 GDP, GDP Growth, & GDP per capita in China   6
        1.3.2 Sectoral change in China   10
        1.3.3 Global trade expansion   13
        1.3.4 China's overseas investments   16
        1.3.5 Chinese investments in R&D   20
        1.3.6 Outbound Chinese tourism   23
        1.3.7 Internationalization of the Renminbi (RMB)   25
        1.3.8 A rising China, a declining America   26
    1.4 Conclusion   28

Chapter 2   The Chinese Dream and Vision   29
   2.1 The Context — Economic Reforms (1980s to 2012)   29
   2.2 President Xi Jinping and the Chinese Dream   32
   2.3 The Belt and Road Initiative: A Sino-globalization
        that is Programmatic and All-Encompassing   35
   2.4 The Key Routes   37
        2.4.1 Speed breakers encountered by BRI projects   38
        2.4.2 BRI benefitting whom?   39
   2.5 China's Soft Power Projection: Some Aspects   40
        2.5.1 Confucius institutes and centers in BRI countries 41
   2.6 Development Assistance: China's Footprint as an
        Aid Giver   42
   2.7 BRI: Crafting New Institutions   44
        2.7.1 Asian Infrastructure Investment Bank (AIIB)   45
        2.7.2 Regional Comprehensive Economic Partnership
              (RCEP)   48
   2.8 Conclusion — "Quantity has a Quality of its Own"   49

Chapter 3   China in South Asia: History Informs
             but Geography Governs   53
   3.1 Introduction   53
   3.2 The Idea of South Asia   54
        3.2.1 China's forays into South Asia: Increasing
              influence, expanding ambitions   56
   3.3 Subregional Cooperation in South Asia   58
        3.3.1 China-led BCIM   58
   3.4 South Asia: Contrasting Economic Indicators   59
   3.5 China's Bilateral Connections in South Asia   63
        3.5.1 Afghanistan   63
        3.5.2 Bangladesh   64
        3.5.3 Bhutan   67
        3.5.4 India   68
        3.5.5 Maldives   70
        3.5.6 Nepal and China: Handshake across the Himalayas 71
        3.5.7 Pakistan   76
        3.5.8 Sri Lanka   77
   3.6 China in South Asia: A Tighter Embrace in 2020   79
   3.7 Conclusion   79

Chapter 4   China and Pakistan: "Iron Brothers"   83
4.1 A Brief History of Pakistan   83
4.2 Pakistan's Economy: A Brief Overview   84
4.3 China — Pakistan Relations: All Weather Friendship   85
4.4 China — Pakistan Economic Engagement   87
    4.4.1 Pakistan and China: Trade   87
4.5 Chinese Investments in Pakistan   89
    4.5.1 CPEC (2017–2030)   90
4.6 BRI Projects   92
    4.6.1 Port city of Gwadar   92
    4.6.2 Karakoram Highway (Upgraded)   98
    4.6.3 Railway projects   98
    4.6.4 Energy projects   99
4.7 Costs & Benefits of BRI Initiatives in Pakistan   102
    4.7.1 Benefits of BRI   103
    4.7.2 Costs of BRI   104
    4.7.3 Other economic aspects   109
4.8 Conclusion   111

Chapter 5   China in Sri Lanka: A Small Island Syndrome   113
5.1 The Context: *When the West Chides, China
Commends*   113
5.2 A Brief History of Sri Lanka   114
5.3 The Sri Lankan Economy: In Brief   114
5.4 China–Sri Lanka Relationship   116
5.5 China–Sri Lanka Economic Engagement   117
    5.5.1 Contemporary trade data   118
5.6 Chinese Investments & BRI Projects in Sri Lanka   119
    5.6.1 BRI projects   120
5.7 BRI Projects: Authors 2020 Survey and Analysis   128
5.8 Costs & Benefits of BRI Initiatives in Sri Lanka   131
    5.8.1 Benefits of BRI   132
    5.8.2 Costs of BRI   133
    5.8.3 Other external impacts of BRI on Sri Lanka   138
5.9 Conclusion   143
Appendix   145

Chapter 6   China's Visible Influence in Southeast Asia:
             People, Polity, and Prowess   147
    6.1 The Context: Southeast Asian Historical Connections
         with China   147
    6.2 ASEAN Countries: An Economic Profile   150
    6.3 ASEAN–China Free Trade Area (ACFTA)   152
    6.4 RCEP and ASEAN   155
         6.4.1 Inward FDI flows from China to ASEAN
                (2010–2018)   156
         6.4.2 Tourism   157
    6.5 Economic and Political Indicators of ASEAN
         Countries and China   158
    6.6 China's Water Diplomacy: Lancang–Mekong
         Cooperation   160
    6.7 China and Southeast Asian Countries: A Brief Overview
         of Bilateral Relations   162
         6.7.1 Brunei   163
         6.7.2 Cambodia and Laos: Political twins   164
         6.7.3 Indonesia   165
         6.7.4 Malaysia   166
         6.7.5 Myanmar   168
         6.7.6 Philippines   169
         6.7.7 Singapore   171
         6.7.8 Thailand   172
         6.7.9 Vietnam   173
    6.8 Summary and Conclusion   174

Chapter 7   China and Myanmar: The "Pauk-phaw" (Fraternal)
             Relationship   179
    7.1 A Brief History of Myanmar   179
    7.2 Myanmar's Economy: A Brief Overview   181
    7.3 China–Myanmar Relationship   182
         7.3.1 President Aung San Suu Kyi & relations
                with major powers   184
    7.4 China–Myanmar Economic Engagement   185
         7.4.1 Myanmar and China: Bilateral trade   185
         7.4.2 Chinese investments   188
         7.4.3 BRI projects   189

7.5 Costs & Benefits of BRI Projects in Myanmar   199
  7.5.1 Expected benefits of BRI projects   199
  7.5.2 Costs of BRI   201
7.6 November 2020: Elections   207
7.7 Conclusion   208

Chapter 8   China and Thailand: "Kith and Kin" Relations   211
8.1 Introduction   211
8.2 A Brief History of Thailand   212
8.3 Thailand's Economy: A Brief Overview   212
8.4 China–Thailand Relations   215
  8.4.1 Thailand China: The military relationship   216
8.5 China–Thailand Economic Engagement   217
  8.5.1 Thailand and China: Trade   217
  8.5.2 Chinese investments in Thailand   220
  8.5.3 BRI projects   221
  8.5.4 Status of the Sino-Thai rail project   223
8.6 Benefits and Costs of BRI Initiatives in Thailand   228
  8.6.1 Benefits of BRI   229
  8.6.2 Costs of BRI   230
8.7 Impact of Pandemic on Thai Tourism   234
  8.7.1 Alipay in Thailand   235
8.8 Conclusion   235

Chapter 9   China in South and Southeast Asia: Pursuit vs.
             Proximity   239
9.1 Introduction   239
9.2 China's Trade Relations   240
  9.2.1 SAARC countries and China   240
9.3 China's Investment: Recipient Countries   243
9.4 Country-Specific Analysis: Pakistan, Sri Lanka,
     Myanmar, and Thailand   244
9.5 Human Development Index (HDI)   244
9.6 Government Debt   245
9.7 Bilateral Trade with China: Pakistan, Sri Lanka,
     Myanmar, and Thailand   247
9.8 China's Investment in the Four Countries   249
9.9 The Xi Jinping Era: Chinese Investment in South
     and Southeast Asia   251

9.10 China in South vs. Southeast Asia: A Macro Perspective   254
9.11 Comparing CPEC of Pakistan with CMEC of Myanmar   259
9.12 Limits to Chinese Checkers   260
    9.12.1 Evidence and lessons learnt   260
9.13 Conclusion   264

Chapter 10   China: A Futuristic Perspective   267
10.1 Introduction   267
10.2 China's Prowess, Pathways, and Progress: Internal
    Dimensions   268
    10.2.1 BRI: Sustainability during and after the pandemic   269
    10.2.2 China's demographic challenge: The silver
        economy   270
    10.2.3 China's internal reset: Dual circulation strategy   271
    10.2.4 Thousand talents program: Bringing world-class
        research teams to China   272
    10.2.5 China's money matters   273
    10.2.6 China's private sector: Reined in   275
    10.2.7 China's economic miracle: Are there constraints
        to future growth?   276
10.3 China's External Engagement: Cooperation and
    Competition   277
    10.3.1 Collective response of big powers: Will
        China change?   278
    10.3.2 US — China rivalry: The way forward   279
    10.3.3 The tryst with technology   283
    10.3.4 Global governance: China secures seats on
        many high tables   284
10.4 Conclusion   286

References   291
Index   311

List of Figures

Figure 1.1:   China's GDP growth: 1978–2014.   3
Figure 1.2:   China's BRI.   7
Figure 1.3:   Real vs. nominal GDP in China (1960–2019).   8
Figure 1.4:   China's annual GDP growth (1961–2019).   9
Figure 1.5:   GDP per capita in China (1960–2019).   10
Figure 1.6:   Sectoral contribution as a share of GDP.   11
Figure 1.7:   Exports & imports of goods, top five economies
               (2019).   14
Figure 1.8:   China's exports and imports — 1982–2019
               (Constant 2010 US$).   15
Figure 1.9:   Chinese investment by sector: 2005–2019.   17
Figure 1.10:   China: FDI net inflows and outflows (1980–2019).   19
Figure 1.11:   FDI net inflow and outflow as share of China's
               GDP (%).   19
Figure 1.12:   China's school enrollment, tertiary (% gross).   20
Figure 1.13:   China's researchers in R&D (per million people).   22
Figure 1.14:   Patents by select countries.   23
Figure 1.15:   Chinese tourists: Annual overseas visits (millions). 24
Figure 1.16:   RMB exchange rate trends.   26
Figure 1.17:   China and USA's share of GDP to World GDP.   27
Figure 2.1:   Projects approved by AIIB (2016–2020).   47
Figure 2.2:   AIIB: Types of approved project investments.   47
Figure 3.1:   China and South Asia.   56
Figure 4.1:   Pakistan's top 5 export partners (US$ Billion).   88
Figure 4.2:   Pakistan's top 6 import partners (US$).   88

Figure 4.3:   China's ambitious plan for Pakistan.   93
Figure 4.4:   Bilateral trade between China and Pakistan
               (2009–2019).   105
Figure 4.5:   Pakistan's total external debt (2009–2018).   107
Figure 5.1:   Sri Lanka's top six import partners (US$).   118
Figure 5.2:   Sri Lanka's top six export partners (US$).   118
Figure 5.3:   Chinese Development Finance to Sri Lanka
               (US$ million).   121
Figure 5.4:   Occupation of respondents.   129
Figure 5.5:   Respondents view of China.   129
Figure 5.6:   Chinese Projects considered successful in ·
               Sri Lanka.   130
Figure 5.7:   Rajapaksha Government's relations with China
               in the future.   131
Figure 5.8:   Bilateral trade between China and Sri Lanka (US$).   134
Figure 6.1:   Tourist arrivals in ASEAN by country
               (Year 2018 — in millions).   157
Figure 6.2:   China and Southeast Asia.   163
Figure 7.1:   Myanmar's top five export partners (US$ Billion).   186
Figure 7.2:   Myanmar's top five import partners (US$ Billion).   187
Figure 7.3:   Myanmar's Kyaukphyu Port.   190
Figure 7.4:   Muse to Mandalay railway.   195
Figure 7.5:   New Yangon City project.   195
Figure 7.6:   Kyaukphyu-Kunming Railway.   196
Figure 7.7:   China's investment in Myanmar (US$ Millions).   200
Figure 7.8:   Bilateral trade between China and Myanmar.   202
Figure 7.9:   Government debt as a share of GDP in
               Myanmar (%) (2010–2019).   203
Figure 8.1:   Thailand's top five export partners (US$).   219
Figure 8.2:   Thailand's top five import partners (US$).   220
Figure 8.3:   Thailand's bilateral trade with China (2010–2019).   231
Figure 8.4:   Government debt to GDP in Thailand
               (2010–2019) (%).   232
Figure 9.1:   SAARC countries trade with China (2001–2019).   241
Figure 9.2:   ASEAN countries trade with China (2001–2019).   243
Figure 9.3:   China's investment in South Asia and Southeast
               Asia (2019).   244
Figure 9.4:   Total Chinese investment as a % of the
               destination country's GDP (2018).   245

Figure 9.5:   Real GDP per capita (2009–2019): Four countries.   245
Figure 9.6:   Human Development Index of 4 countries
              (2010–2019).   246
Figure 9.7:   Government debt to GDP (in %) (2010–2019).   247
Figure 9.8:   Sri Lanka–China trade (2010–2019).   248
Figure 9.9:   Pakistan–China trade.   249
Figure 9.10: Myanmar–China trade (2010–2019).   249
Figure 9.11: Thailand–China trade.   250
Figure 9.12: Investment by China in Sri Lanka.   250
Figure 9.13: Investment by China in Pakistan.   251
Figure 9.14: Investment by China in Myanmar.   252
Figure 9.15: Investment by China in Thailand.   253

List of Tables

Table 1.1:   China's exports and imports growth difference (1982–2019).   15

Table 1.2:   Patent by selected countries — All patent types pre-2002 and post-2002.   23

Table 3.1:   South Asian Countries: GDP, debt, HDI in 2019.   60

Table 3.2:   South Asia: Economic indicators (2019).   61

Table 3.3:   Political situation: Some key indicators.   62

Table 4.1:   Pakistan: GDP, GDP per capita, debt, & HDI in 2019.   84

Table 4.2:   Pakistan's leading export industries (2019).   88

Table 4.3:   Pakistan's imports from China and growth rate of imports (2010–2018).   89

Table 4.4:   Financial terms and expected economic benefits of major Chinese projects.   94

Table 4.5:   Details of Gwadar project.   96

Table 4.6:   CPEC–Energy priority projects.   100

Table 4.7:   CPEC–Energy actively promoted projects.   101

Table 4.8:   CPEC–Potential energy projects.   101

Table 4.9:   Pakistan's external public debt.   106

Table 5.1:   Trends in human development and income.   115

Table 5.2:   Financial terms and expected economic benefits of major Chinese projects.   122

Table 5.3:   Top five BRI projects in Sri Lanka: Respondents' Assessment.   130

Table 5.4:   Sri Lanka's external public debt.   135

Table 5.5:	Top three nations for tourist arrivals in Sri Lanka (2018 and 2019).	139
Table 5.6:	Bilateral Trade between China and Sri Lanka	145
Table 6.1:	ASEAN: Demographic and economic indicators.	151
Table 6.2:	China's trade in goods with ASEAN (US$ Million).	154
Table 6.3:	Inward FDI to ASEAN from China (2010–2018).	156
Table 6.4:	Key indicators of ASEAN countries and China.	159
Table 6.5:	ISEAS survey results: 2019 and 2020.	175
Table 7.1:	Myanmar: GDP, GDP per capita, debt, and HDI in 2019.	181
Table 7.2:	The top 10 export-oriented industries in Myanmar (2019).	187
Table 7.3:	Financial terms and expected economic benefits of major Chinese projects in Myanmar.	198
Table 8.1:	Thailand: GDP, GDP per capita, and debt.	214
Table 8.2:	HDI in Thailand.	214
Table 8.3:	International trade of Thailand in 2019.	218
Table 9.1:	Trade in goods: South Asian Association for Regional Cooperation (SAARC) and China (2001–2019).	240
Table 9.2:	Trade in goods: Association of Southeast Asian Nations (ASEAN) and China.	242
Table 9.3:	China's investment in South and Southeast Asia in 2019.	243
Table 9.4:	China's investment in four countries (2015–2019).	253

List of Maps

Map 8.1:   China–Thailand HSR.   222
Map 8.2:   Kra Isthmus Canal in Thailand.   225
Map 8.3:   U-Tapao–Pattaya International Airport
            development project.   227

List of Abbreviations

ACFTA	ASEAN–China Free Trade Area
ADB	Asian Development Bank
AEC	ASEAN Economic Community
AEI	American Enterprise Institute
AFTA	ASEAN Free Trade Area
ADMM	ASEAN Defense Ministers Meeting
AIIB	Asian Infrastructure Investment Bank
ASEAN	Association of Southeast Asian Nations
APEC	Asia-Pacific Economic Cooperation
ARE	Academy-Run Enterprises
ARF	ASEAN Regional Forum
APT	ASEAN Plus Three
BA	Bangkok Airways
BBIN	Bangladesh, Bhutan, India, Nepal
BCB	Building Cities Beyond
BCE	Before the Common Era
BCIM	Bangladesh, China, India, Myanmar
BSA	Bilateral Swap Arrangements
BIMSTEC	Bay of Bengal Initiative for Multisectoral Technical and Economic Co-operation
BoI	Board of Investment
BOT	Build–Operate–Transfer
BRI	Belt and Road Initiative
BRF	Belt and Road Forum
CBMs	Confidence-building measures

CI	Confucius Institutes
CC	Confucius Classrooms
CCP	Chinese Communist Party
CGIT	China Global Investment Tracker
CCP	China's Communist Party
CCCC	China Communications Construction Company, Ltd
CCCPC	Central Committee of the Communist Party of China
CECA	Comprehensive Economic Co-operation Agreement
CGGC	China Gezhouba Group Company
CGTN	China Global Television Network
CHEC	China Harbour Engineering Company
CIPEC	China–Indochina Peninsula Economic Corridor
CLMV	Cambodia Lao PDR Myanmar Vietnam
CMB	Central Bank of Myanmar
CMIM	Chiang Mai Initiative Multilateralization
CMEC	China–Myanmar Economic Corridor
CPEC	China–Pakistan Economic Corridor
CPCC	CHEC Port City Colombo
CPI	China Power International
CORPATs	Coordinated Patrols
COTRI	China Outbound Tourism Research Institute
CAFTA	China–ASEAN Free Trade Area
CSIS	Centre for Strategic and International Studies
CSOs	Civil Society Organizations
CSR	Corporate social responsibility
DAC	Development Assistance Committee
DFTZ	Digital Free Trade Zone Initiative
DMK	Don Muang Airport
EAS	East Asia Summit
ECNEC	Executive Committee of National Economic Council
EEC	Eastern Economic Corridor
EIA	Environmental Impact Assessment
EU	European Union
EXIM Bank China	Export–Import Bank of China
FDI	Foreign Direct Investment

FTA	Free Trade Agreement
GCI	Global Competitiveness Index
GDP	Gross Domestic Product
GAME	Guidelines for Air Military Encounters
HDI	Human Development Index
HSR	High-speed rail
IT	Information Technology
IFC	International Finance Corporation
IMF	International Monetary Fund
KKH	Karakoram Highway
KIO	Kachin Independence Organization
LoC	Lines of Credit
LTTE	Liberation Tamil Tigers of Tamil Eelam
LNG	Liquefied natural gas
MAI	Market Access Initiative
MANPADS	Man-Portable Air Defense Systems
MDA	Market Development Assistance
MEA	Ministry of External Affairs
MERICS	Mercator Institute for China Studies
MoU	Memorandum of Understanding
MRIA	Mattala Rajapaksa International Airport
MRC	Mekong River Commission
MSR	Maritime Silk Road
NCPO	National Council for Peace and Order
NDRC	National Development and Reform Commission
NLD	National League for Democracy
NORINCO	North Industries Corporation
NPL	National Poverty Line
NYDC	New Yangon Development Company
OBOR	One Belt, One Road
ODI	Overseas Direct Investment
ODA	Official Development Assistance
OOF	Other Official Flows
PBOC	People's Bank of China
PCT	Patent Cooperation Treaty
PLA	People's Liberation Army
PoK	Pakistan occupied Kashmir
PPP	Public Private Partnership
Ppp	Purchasing power parity

PRC	People's Republic of China
ReCAAP	Regional Cooperation Agreement on Combating Piracy and Armed Robbery against Ships in Asia
R&D	Research and Development
RIMPAC	Rim of the Asia Pacific
RCEP	Regional Comprehensive Economic Partnership
RIS	Research and Information System for Developing Countries
RMB	Renminbi
RTA	Royal Thai Army
RTAF	Royal Thai Air Force
SAARC	South Asian Association for Regional Cooperation
SCO	Shanghai Cooperation Organization
SDG	Sustainable Development Goals
SEA	Southeast Asia
SEATO	South East Asia Treaty Organization
SEZ	Special Economic Zone
SIA	Social Impact Assessments
SOE	State-Owned Enterprises
SRT	State Railway of Thailand
SREB	Silk Road Economic Belt
STEC	Sino-Thai Engineering and Construction
TAC	Treaty of Amity and Cooperation
TFP	Total Factor Productivity
TEU	Twenty-foot-equivalent-unit
THCN	Trans-Himalayan Connectivity network
TPP	Trans-Pacific Partnership
ULCC	Ultra-large container carriers
USA	United States of America
UNCLOS	United Nations Convention on Law of the Seas
UNCTAD	United Nations Conference on Trade and Development
UNWTO	United Nations World Tourism Organization
WB	World Bank
WDI	World Development Indicator
WHO	World Health Organization
WIPO	World Intellectual Property Organization
WTO	World Trade Organization
WW2	World War Two

List of Interviewees: Unpublished Interviews

Country	Name	Designation	Date
Pakistan	Dr. Furrukh Khan, Interview to RM	Professor in Lahore University of Management Studies	August 28, 2020
Pakistan	Dr. Pervaiz Ali Mahesar, Interview to RM	Teaches at University of Sindh Jamshoro	September 20, 2020
Sri Lanka	Mr. Prasanna Liyanage to Dr. SSR	Senior Vice President of Colombo Chamber of Commerce (CCC) & an Executive Committee member of Society for International Development (SID) Sri Lanka Chapter.	August 20, 2020
Sri Lanka	Dr. Dushni Weerakoon to RM	Executive Director of the Institute of Policy Studies of Sri Lanka (IPS) and Head of its Macroeconomic Policy research	March 26, 2019
Myanmar	Mr. Khin Maung Soe to RM	Advisor, MISIS	September 26, 2020

(Continued)

(*Continued*)

Country	Name	Designation	Date
Myanmar	Diplomat (Anonymity)		
Myanmar	Dr. Am Yu, through Mr. Soe	Japanese Professor	September 27, 2020
Thailand	Mr. Satish Sehgal, Mr. D.K. Bakshi, Mr. Subash Bajaj	Indian businesspeople	July 21–31, 2014
Thailand	Prof. Chayan Vaddhanaputhi to RM	Chiang Mai University	May 21, 2018
Thailand	Dr. Piyanat Soikham to RM	Ubon Ratchathani University	September 2, 2020

Interviews Published (2012–2016)

- Marwah, R. and Singh, S. (2013). Interview, http://www.china-studies.taipei/act02.php, March 2, 2013: Dhaka.
- Interview on January 27, 2012 Interviewer: Dr. Reena Marwah Interview of Mr. Ramesh Nath Pandey, http://www.china-studies.taipei/act02.php.
- Marwah, R. and Singh, S. (2013). Interview, http://www.china-studies.taipei/act02.php, March 2, 2013: Dhaka.
- Setiono, B. (2016). Interviewee: Matsumuro — February 29, 2016, http://www.china-studies.taipei/act02.php.
- Singh, S. (2016). Interview: Ms. Lily Wangchuk, Bhutan, in an interview on June 4, 2016, http://www.china-studies.taipei/act02.php.
- SinhaRaja, (2012). Interviewee: Dr. SinhaRaja Tammita-Delgoda Interviewer: Dr. Sharad Soni Date: March 22, 2012, http://www.china-studies.taipei/act02.php.
- Soni, S. (2016). Interviewee: Ehsanul Haque, Bangladesh by Prof. Sharad Soni, March 24, 2016, http://www.china-studies.taipei/act02.php.
- Interviewee: Dr. SinhaRaja Tammita-Delgoda Interviewer: Dr. Sharad Soni Date: March 22, 2012, http://www.china-studies.taipei/act02.php.

Chapter 1

Rise of China

1.1 Introduction

In 1975, Mao Zedong had lamented that China was one of the poorest countries in the world.

> *Poverty gives rise to the desire for changes, the desire for action, and the desire for revolution. On a blank sheet of paper free from any mark, the freshest and most beautiful characters can be written; the freshest and most beautiful pictures can be painted.* — **Mao Zedong.**

Much has been written about the rise of China, especially since it embraced the forces of globalization since 1979 and transformed into the factory of the world. This chapter focuses on the review of relevant literature, given that several authors from all over the world have tried to analyze the rapid transformation in the Chinese economy. Authors include Jonathan Ward (*China's Vision of Victory*, 2019), Bertil Lintner (*The Costliest Pearl*, 2019, *China's India war*, 2018), Bruno Macaes (*China's Belt and Road: A Chinese world order*, 2018), among several others.

According to Kristof (1992), China is the fastest-growing economy in the world with a rapidly growing military budget. Xuetong (2001) states that China's rise will create a huge market that will contribute to scientific progress, and the rise of China will benefit both the domestic constituency and the rest of the world. The economic transformation of China will also be reviewed within the chapter, including a detailed analysis of data over the period 1980–2020.

As a result of its membership in the World Trade Organization in 2001, China has benefitted tremendously through its manufactured exports and its status has catapulted to the second-largest economy in the world, displacing Japan in 2011. During the 18th Communist Party Congress (CPC) in November 2012, President Xi Jinping and Premier Li Keqiang, along with their new members of the Politburo Standing Committee, were officially elected. A year later, at the CPC's 3rd Plenum President Xi revealed the most ambitious and detailed roadmap to structurally reform China, to grow more sustainably and domestically oriented (Hoontrakul *et al.*, 2014).

1.2 Literature Review

There is a substantial difference between a country that takes 30 years to rise and one that takes 300 years, and China is named one of the miracle countries with rapid economic growth within a short time period. Ikenberry (2008) wrote that the rise of China would undoubtedly be one of the great dramas of the twenty-first century. Without a doubt, China's persistent economic growth in the 1980s and 1990s indicated its emergence as a great power in world politics, too. Brown (2000) had visualized China being poised to become the second-largest economy in the world. China did overtake Japan to become the second largest; simultaneously, it also modernized its military and adopted a more assertive diplomatic posture.

1.2.1 *Reform-led growth*

In 2008, Brandt and Rawski (2008) had written about how China's gross domestic product (GDP) growth lagged dramatically behind that of Japan. They were proved wrong in barely three years, when China's GDP of US$10 trillion helped it surpass Japan as the second-largest economy in 2011.[1] Ever since, China has been referred to as one of the emerging countries with the fastest economic growth with high competitiveness. However, this growth has been achieved through a gradual process of opening-up and reforms, beginning with the rural areas with the house-

---

[1]China overtakes Japan as the world's second-biggest economy, https://www.bbc.com/news/business-12427321, accessed on July 12, 2020.

Figure 1.1:   China's GDP growth: 1978–2014.

Sources: Wind database: Hofman, Bert, and Jinglian Wu (2007) by Pleter Botteller, forthcoming, China's economic policies 1940–2016, Julian Gewirtz, 2017 unlikely partners, various official documents and publications.

hold responsibility system and township and village enterprises. It was in the 1990s that the economy was opened to foreign trade and investment. The financial sector and State-Owned Enterprises (SOE) reforms also gained momentum only in the 1990s.

Figure 1.1 provides the trends of opening-up and reform over the period from 1978 to 2014. There are three distinct periods according to Bert Hofman,[2] comprising market seeking reforms, market building reforms, and market enhancing reforms.

Hu and Mathews (2008) have asserted that China is transforming itself into the workshop of the world by building an export-oriented national production system linked by global value chains to the world's leading economies. Others predict that China will be the leading Global country in 2030; because they are investing on R&D, new innovation, and institutions.

---

[2] Hofman, Bert, Reflections on forty years of China's reforms, http://blogs.worldbank.org/eastasiapacific/reflections-on-forty-years-of-china-reforms, accessed on April 12, 2019.

Political legitimacy vs. Revisionist power: Feigenbaum (2020); Kagen (1997); Larson and Shevchenko (2010, p. 84); Mead (2014); Nelson (2011); Shambaugh (2001, p. 76; 2005); and Zhao (2016, 2018) consider China as a revisionist power which does not accept existing liberal values and norms of individualism, human rights, political freedom, the rule of law, transparency, democracy, and humanitarian intervention. Some others have cited it as a status quo power that has integrated into and benefited from the existing global order, and therefore, it is an active "participant", "contributor", and "defender" of the current order (Kumar, 2020).

The Economic Miracle: Wang and Yao (1999) indicate that China's performance in economic growth and poverty reduction has been remarkable. Wu (2004) explains that economic growth was extremely volatile in the pre-reform period (1954–1977), with the rate of growth ranging from 21.3% in 1958 to −27.3% in 1961. Li (1998) has written that China has created an economic miracle since the late 1970s with the beginning of economic reforms and became the fastest growing economy in the world. China's GDP has grown at almost 10% annually for 18 years (1950 to 1978), and personal income and living standards have improved significantly. Zhu (2012) also highlighted the 10% growth rate achieved by China during 1952 to 1978 and the period since 1978; however, sources of growth were defined as capital deepening, labor deepening, and productivity growth. He also argued that China's rapid growth over the three decades (1979–2009) had been driven by productivity growth rather than by capital investment.

China's export-oriented strategy helped the Chinese economic Miracle (Lee, 2013; Nayar, 2004). Wu (2004) underlines that China followed the East Asian model of development by encouraging foreign trade, particularly exports. China's high-speed growth coupled with a rise of capabilities in manufacturing as well as in research and development ensured economic success (Brandt and Rawski, 2008).

According to Yang and Zhao (2015), the success of the Chinese economy relies not just on the State's economic policy but also on its social policies. They further highlight the State's innate capacity to make a policy shift whenever it confronts unintended negative consequences of earlier policies. The Chinese State is compelled to make policy shifts quickly because performance constitutes the primary base of its legitimacy; given the fact that the State enjoys a high level of autonomy.

Belt and Road Initiative (BRI) in China: In 2013, President Xi Jinping first announced the BRI project. It is widely considered to be Xi's flagship project. China's BRI is a planned multi-trillion-dollar infrastructure program that was intended to link China with more than 100 countries through railroad, shipping, and energy projects. The BRI has endeavored to recreate the Silk Road, an old network of trading routes between the East and the West, by investing billions of dollars in other countries for building infrastructure projects.

The historical perspective of the Silk Road has been explained by Ge (2018). He states that,

> *It is generally understood that the Silk Road started from Luoyang and Chang'an of ancient China, went all the way through the Hexi Corridor to its terminal of Dunhuang before trifurcating: the north route to the Tianshan Mountains and Urumqi; the middle route from Turpan to the West, through the southern edge of Xinjiang, Hotan to Central Asia, then through Central Asia to Persia (Iran) and finally to Europe; and the southern route along the Pamir plateau today into Pakistan and India.* (Ge, 2018, p. 1).

Hu (2018) writes about the BRI as follows:

> *It is a grand-scale revolution of economic geography, a revolution that reshapes economic geography of China and countries along the routes as well as the world as a whole. Second of all, in terms of international relations, it gives birth to an era of win–win, which is neither similar to colonialism and imperialism a few centuries ago nor the post-WW2 hegemonism. The Belt and Road Initiative is the first-ever non-zero-sum game of mutual-benefit and win–win cooperation* (Hu, 2018, p. 15).

In 2017, a speech about BRI by President Xi, "In doing so, we hope to achieve policy, infrastructure, trade, financial, and people-to-people connectivity and thus build a new platform for international cooperation to create new drivers of shared development", envisioned the BRI as the "belt" that will consist of land routes connecting economies in Asia, Africa, and Europe. And the "road" — while not actually a road — will connect various ocean routes through these areas.[3] China's BRI

---

[3] What is China's Belt and Road Initiative? https://www.foxnews.com/world/what-is-chinas-belt-road-initiative, accessed on July 14, 2020.

projects through the New Silk Road, Maritime Silk Road, and the China Pakistan corridor are shown in Figure 1.2.

1.3   The Growth of the Chinese Economy Since the 1960s: In Numbers

In 2020, China is an upper-middle-income country and the world's second-largest economy. However, per capita income is only about a quarter of that of high-income countries. Moreover, 373 million Chinese subsist below the upper-middle-income poverty line of US$5.50 a day. This section discusses Chinese economic advancement through diverse economic indicators over the period of 1960s to 2020; the focus, however, is on the more recent decades of China's momentous growth.

1.3.1   *GDP, GDP Growth, & GDP per capita in China*

Gross domestic product is a commonly used economic indicator for measuring the state of a country's economy. The real nominal GDP in China from 1960 to 2019 is presented.[4] As is evident from Figure 1.3, it was the shift to an open-door economic policy of Deng Xiaoping that ushered in a period of high economic growth in the first half of the 1980s. Tisdell (2009) has written about Deng Xiaoping's decision to craft the new development path. The vision of Deng Xiaoping (1984) was to develop socialism with Chinese characteristics.

> *Since 1978, China has experienced extraordinary institutional change which has proven to be effective in promoting its economic growth and is advancing its international status* (Tisdell, 2009, p. 271).

Additionally, the promotion of economic openness through international economic cooperation, investment, trade, and exchange helped China increase its pace of growth. At the same time, the introduction of the one-child policy in 1979 by Deng Xiaoping enabled control of China's

---

[4]Nominal GDP is the measure of the annual production of goods or services at the current price, whereas real GDP is the measure of the annual production of goods or services calculated at the actual price without considering the effect of inflation and hence nominal GDP is considered a more apt measure of GDP.

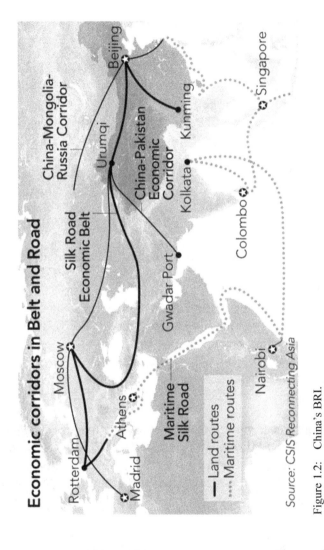

Figure 1.2: China's BRI.

Source: Center for Strategic and International studies, https://www.csis.org/analysis/chinas-belt-and-roller-coaster, accessed on July 7, 2021.

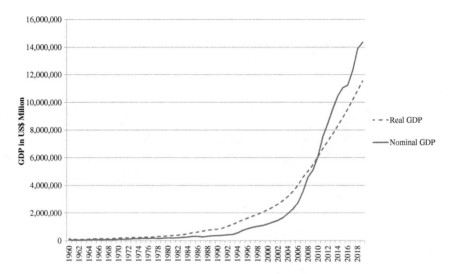

Figure 1.3:   Real vs. nominal GDP in China (1960–2019).

Source: Authors' formations using World Bank — World Development Indicator's (WDI) data.

rapidly growing population.[5] Deng Xiaoping's four modernizations deserve mention here. These visionary policies included Modernizing Agriculture, Expanding Industry, Developing Science and Technology, and Upgrading China's Defense Forces. GDP, trade, and industrial output rose due to the automation of manufacturing processes.[6] This underlined the usefulness of the four modernizations.

China's economic growth rose significantly since the 1990s, with even faster growth rates recorded post-2005. This was a result of China's increasing engagement and integration with the world economy.

Figure 1.4 shows the annual GDP growth from 1961–2019. The average GDP rate of growth rose from approximately 4% prior to the reforms to 9.5% during 1978–2005. According to the World Bank — WDI data, in 1961 and 1962, China had negative growth, of −27.27 and −5.58%, respectively. Negative growth rates were a result of adverse weather patterns, droughts, and floods. Hence, crop production declined from 200 million

---

[5] When introduced, the policy mandated that Han Chinese, the ethnic majority, could only have one child per family.

[6] Deng Xiaoping, https://dengxiaopingproject.weebly.com/four-modernizations.html, accessed on July 23, 2020.

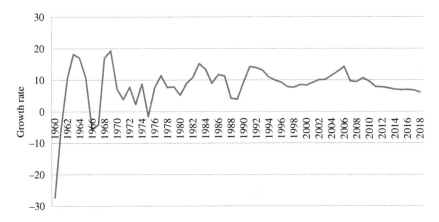

Figure 1.4:   China's annual GDP growth (1961–2019).

Source: Authors' formations using World Bank — WDI data.

tons in 1958 to 143.5 million tons in 1960. However, under Mao, high growth rates were attained only in 1964 and 1965, these being 18.18% and 17%, respectively. In 1969, the growth rate was 17%. The Cultural Revolution from 1966–1976 resulted in a plummeting of the economy.

Figure 1.4 points to the steep rise in growth rates post the death of Mao in 1976. However, it is the high rates of growth achieved by China over the period 2009 to 2019 (average growth rate being 7.85%) that has catapulted it into a world leader, with an overall GDP exceeding US$13 trillion in 2019 (authors' own calculations using World Bank — WDI data). In 2019 the annual growth rate of the Chinese economy was 6.11% (according to the World Bank — WDI data).

1.3.1.1 *China: Per capita GDP*

In the 1960s, China's GDP per capita was less than US$150. In 1975, Mao Zedong had alluded to China's per capita being about US$140. China is a middle-income country, and its income per capita is equivalent to 65% of the world's average.[7] Given the size of China's population of over 1.3 billion people, in 2014, per capita GDP was only about one-seventh as large

---

[7] Per capita GDP is defined as the GDP divided by the total number of people in the country. This indicator is generally used to compare the economic prosperity of countries with varying population sizes.

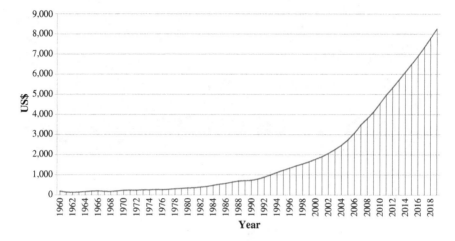

Figure 1.5: GDP per capita in China (1960–2019).

Source: Authors' formations using World Bank — WDI data.

as that of main industrialized countries. When compared to other emerging markets, China ranked third among BRICS countries in terms of GDP per capita, followed only by India. In 2019, per capita income was US$8,254 (World Bank data) (see Figure 1.5).

To further understand China's growth story, it is significant to view the sectoral contribution to GDP.

1.3.2 *Sectoral change in China*

Sectoral change, that is, the reallocation of economic activities across different sectors, is a common feature among most countries that have embarked on the road to industrialization. The economic development since China's reform and opening-up was also in line with this trend (Guo *et al.*, 2018). China's transformation from a vast, rural, agricultural giant to a manufacturing and service sector hub was a result of infrastructure development, urbanization, rising per capita income, and a big shift in the composition of its GDP.

According to the National Bureau of Statistics of China (2008), China was number one in Agriculture. China ranked first in worldwide farm output, primarily producing rice, wheat, potatoes, peanuts, tea, millet, barley, cotton, oilseed, corn, and soybeans. The development of the agriculture sector played a major role in supporting the growth of what is now the largest population in the world.

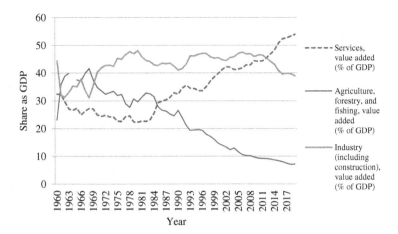

Figure 1.6: Sectoral contribution as a share of GDP.

Source: Authors' formations using World Bank — WDI data.

Figure 1.6 presents China's growth story. It points to the relative decline in the share of the agricultural sector in late 1970s with a synchronized upward movement and growth of the manufacturing and services sectors. While the manufacturing sector has consistently contributed 40 to 50% of China's GDP, the service sector growth trajectory is consistently rising. Brandt, Hsieh, and Zhu (2008), in their study, have shown that the economic development process required a large-scale reallocation of labor from agriculture to manufacturing and services, which reduced the share of agriculture in total employment from 69 to 32% between 1978 and 2004. According to Kwan (2007), there were approximately 150 million surplus laborers in the rural areas during 2004–2005, and it was the movement of abundant surplus labor from the rural areas to the industrial sector that was an enabler for growth.

At the same time, China makes and sells more manufactured goods than any other country. The range of manufactured goods includes iron, steel, aluminum, textiles, cement, chemicals, toys, electronics, rail cars, ships, aircraft, and many other products. In 2015, manufacturing was the largest and most diverse sector in the country. China is a world leader in many types of goods. For example, almost 80% of all air conditioners are manufactured here. The country manufactures more than 45 times as many personal computers per person as the rest of the world combined. It is also the biggest producer of solar cells, shoes, cellphones, and ships (Ross, 2015).

Construction and industry (including mining, manufacturing, electricity, water, and gas) accounted for 44% of China's GDP in 2013, with over four-fifth of the contribution being from the latter. China also has a growing automobile manufacturing industry, being the third-largest globally. The service sector contributes almost 50% of its GDP. This sector includes trade, retail, post, and many other industries. Liao (2020) highlights the role of the service sector in China's achievement of unprecedented growth.

However, the service sector contribution in other high-income economies, in comparison to China, has been higher at around 70%. In China, this was about 55% in 2019 (see Figure 1.6). The services sector's share of GDP in China is much lower than in countries like the US (79%), Japan (73%), Brazil (69%), and India (57%). Over time, and as China shifts to high-tech services, it is expected that this share will grow.

1.3.2.1 *Employment and employment share by sectors*

Brandt *et al.* (2008) indicate that between 1978 and 2004, total employment increased from 401.52 million to 752.00 million in China. However, from 1978 to 2015, the agricultural sector's employment share fell from 70.5 to 28.3%, with the share of value-added decreasing from 27.7 to 8.9%; the industrial sector's employment share rose from 17.3 to 29.3%, with the share of added value decreasing from 47.7 to 40.9%; the service sector's employment share increased from 12.2 to 42.4%, with the share of added value increasing from 24.6 to 50.2% (Guo *et al.*, 2018). Bloom *et al.* (2009) stated that trade, an intervening factor in impacting the demand for skilled labor, is affecting technology. The latest International Labor Organization (ILO) report stated that Chinese enterprises are facing shortages of skilled workers. Ironically, university graduates are having difficulty getting jobs due to technological mismatch.[8] Therefore, in recent times there is a surplus of Chinese labor. It is this unskilled and semi-skilled surplus Chinese labor that is being diverted to work in BRI projects of host countries.

However, in recent years, China has fast been moving away from a situation of having a large surplus labor force toward a stage of labor

---

[8] Skills, and employability in China and Mongolia, https://www.ilo.org/beijing/areas-of-work/skills-and-employability/lang--en/index.htm, accessed on July 23, 2020.

shortage, as symbolized by the tightening supply of migrant workers in the coastal areas. Cai Fang, director of the Institute of Population and Labor Economics, Chinese Academy of Social Sciences (CASS), predicted over a decade and half ago that China's labor demand has been increasing at a more rapid pace than the workforce since 2004, and rural surplus labor will run out completely by around 2009.

The next section provides an overview of China's expanding global footprint.

1.3.3 *Global trade expansion*

The global trade landscape has been greatly altered in the past few decades. The expansion in trade is mostly accounted for by growth in non-commodity exports, especially of high-technology products such as computers and electronics. These developments in global trade have important implications for trade patterns, especially in response to relative price changes. Bloom *et al.* (2009) indicate that a major benefit of Chinese trade had been lower prices for consumers in the developed world, and the country benefited with high-paced technological changes coupled with innovation.

China's total trade is US$4.5 trillion; with BRI partner countries this was US$1.34 trillion in January 2020. In comparison, total trade of USA is US$5.6 trillion. It is evident that while the US has a deficit in trade, China secures huge surpluses.

Figure 1.7 shows global trade expansion, with a focus on the world's top five exporters and importers.

According to IMF Trade Statistics, 2020, China was leading in exports of goods in 2019; the export value was US$2,501.33 billion. The USA ranked second, and Germany ranked third as global exporters. In rankings as importers, USA ranked first, with China ranked second with an amount of US$2,134.03 billion. The stupendous pace of China's global positioning in trade is evident if we highlight that in the 1980s, China accounted for about 1% of total imports to the US and EU. By 1991, this was still only 2%, but by 2007, China accounted for almost 11% of all imports.

Between 1987 and 1996, Chinese exports increased by an average of 14% each year, boosting Chinese exports (Breslin, 2011). See Figure 1.8. It is véry evident that with China's entry into the WTO in 2001 (its entry was supported by the US), the country has grown as a global leader.

Exports of Goods, Top 5 Economies, Billion US$

Goods, Value of Exports, Free on Board (FOB), US Dollars

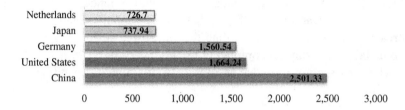

Imports of Goods, Top 5 Economies, Billion US$

Goods, Value of Imports, Cost, Insurance and Freight (CIF), US Dollars

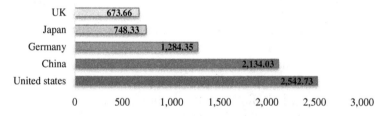

Figure 1.7:   Exports & imports of goods, top five economies (2019).

Source: International Monetary Fund, "Direction of Trade Statistics".

Figure 1.8 also reveals that the two main global economic crises in this century, in 2008 and in 2013/2014, caused a decline in both Chinese imports and exports. The East Asian financial crisis in 1997 & 1998 created a new window of opportunity for China to enter the global market.

Amiti and Freund (2008) explain that China's export structure changed dramatically, with growing export shares in electronics and machinery and a decline in agriculture and apparel. At the same time, Chinese manufacturing and exports shifted to advanced, high-tech products. This was because Chinese export growth was accompanied by increasing specialization. Eichengreen *et al.* (2004) point to the impact of China on the exports of other Asian countries; they confirm the tendency for China's exports to crowd out the exports of other Asian countries.

Table 1.1 shows China's exports and imports growth differential in ten-year periods from 1982 to 2019.[9] This data provides evidence with a

---

[9]This data was calculated by the authors using World Bank — WDI imports and exports data.

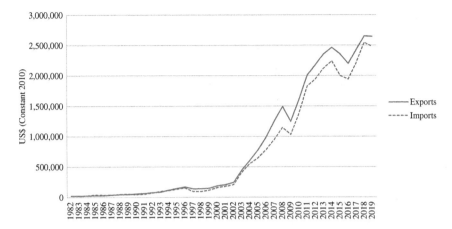

Figure 1.8: China's exports and imports — 1982–2019 (Constant 2010 US$).
Source: Authors' formations using World Bank — WDI data.

Table 1.1: China's exports and imports growth difference (1982–2019).

Long-term growth difference	1982–1989 (%)	1990–1999 (%)	2000–2009 (%)	2010–2019 (%)
Increase in Exports	51	62	85	39
Increase in Imports	61	61	84	44

Source: Authors' calculations using World Bank — WDI data.

comparison of the pre-WTO and post-WTO period. China had achieved significant price competitiveness and could take advantage of the world markets to increase its exports. However, long-run growth shows some slowdown between 2010–2019 of both imports and exports.

Bloom *et al.* (2016) examine the impact of Chinese import competition on broad measures of technical change — patenting, Information technology (IT), and Total Factor Productivity (TFP). Their study also shows that rising Chinese import competition also led to a fall in employment and the share of unskilled workers. Bloom *et al.* (2009) find that Chinese import competition led to both within-firm technology

---

Note: (10 years growth difference = (exports amount 1989 – exports amount in 1982)/ exports amount in 1989).

up-gradation and between firm reallocation of employment toward more technologically intensive plants. These effects are growing over time with rising Chinese trade volumes. As of 2020, China has 24 FTAs, among which 16 agreements have been signed and implemented already.[10] It is important to add here that the China-led Regional Comprehensive Economic Partnership (RCEP) has been signed by 15 member countries in November 2020, making this the largest trade deal in the world.

1.3.4 *China's overseas investments*

Overseas investment has enabled China to leverage its economic strength to increase its influence abroad. The value of China's overseas committed investment since 2005 exceeds US$2 trillion.

Chinese firms have actively expanded their overseas footprint, particularly from 2005–2017, and explored investment opportunities in a range of sectors.[11]

According to the UNCTAD Report (2007), China became a major player in the global market for foreign direct investment (FDI), receiving annual inflows of almost US$70 billion during 2004–2006 and generating moderate, but rapidly increasing, outflows of direct overseas investment (US$16.1 billion in 2006). This was driven in part by Beijing's "Going Global" strategy,[12] which encouraged investment in foreign markets. China Global Investment Tracker (CGIT) data indicates that from 2005 to 2017, low and middle-income economies received 83.9% of the US$734 billion spent by China on construction projects across the globe. In contrast, high-income countries, mainly those in North America and Europe,

---

[10] China FTA network, http://fta.mofcom.gov.cn/english/index.shtml, accessed on December 10, 2020.

[11] China power, https://chinapower.csis.org/china-foreign-direct-investment/, accessed on July 24, 2020.

[12] Since the mid-1990s, China has attempted to do this through the "Going Global" (G.G.) strategy, a foreign policy framework designed to direct Chinese firms and their investment to foreign markets, http://www.futuredirections.org.au/publication/chinese-overseas-agricultural-investment-beijings-dream-new-economic-world-order/, accessed on July 24, 2020.

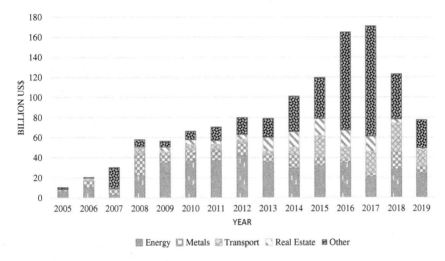

Figure 1.9:   China's investment by sector: 2005–2019.

Source: CGIT (Total in $ Billion), https://chinapower.csis.org/china-foreign-direct-investment/, accessed on December 30, 2020.

attracted 65.6% of Chinese FDI outflows. Chinese investment in Asia and Oceania rose steadily from US$5.68 billion in 2005 to US$38.01 billion in 2017. Of the total US$307.7 billion invested in the region, US$90.9 billion (29.6%) had been channelized to Australia and US$90.9 billion (29.5%) into Southeast Asia.[13]

Figure 1.9 shows China's Investment Breakdown by Sector over the period 2006 to 2018. These calculations in subsequent sections are derived from data provided by the American Enterprise Institute (AEI), and the Heritage Foundation's CGIT.[14]

---

[13] Chinese Renminbi Internationalization: Guide to recent developments, https://www.pnc.com/insights/corporate-institutional/go-international/chinese-renminbi-internationalization-guide-to-recent-developments.html, accessed on July 26, 2020.

[14] CGIT is the only comprehensive public data set covering China's global investment and construction, which are documented both separately and together. Inaugurated in 2005, the CGIT now includes over 3,300 large transactions across energy, transportation, real estate, and other industries, as well as 300 troubled transactions. The tracker is published by the American Enterprise Institute.

Interestingly, post 2013, the rise in China's investment in agriculture and technology (others category), as well as real estate has grown substantially. According to the CGIT data of China's overseas investment, in 2005 energy investment was US$6,360 million; this increased to US$29,500 million in 2017. Agricultural investments increased from US$1,580 million in 2010 to US$45,870 million in 2017. China's investment in transport is also significant as this increased from US$100 million in 2005 to US$28,680 million in 2017. Investment in real-estate increased from US$ 1300 million in 2006 to US$12,420 million in 2017. Overall, during the period of 2006 to 2018, the energy investment grew 78%, investment in transportation rose by 100%, investment in real-estate increased by 90%, and investment in logistics grew by 100%. Australia had been the second-largest recipient country of Chinese FDI after the US. Despite this, China's investment stock constitutes a mere 2% of Australia's total inward FDI. Outbound Chinese FDI in Asia has been significant. Of all investment in Southeast Asia, China's share is 38.4%; in Western Asia (60.4%), Central Asia (93.8%), and Southern Asia (47.3%). The largest of these investments are concentrated in Southeast and Western Asia. Even as energy has remained China's primary sector for investment in the region, Chinese capital has also diversified into sectors such as transportation, real estate, technology, and tourism.[15] Zhuhai Port Holdings' US$1.62 billion investment in the Gwadar port in Pakistan is especially notable, as it is the first foreign port investment in the BRI. In Southeast Asia, Chinese investment has begun to flow into real estate and finance (CGIT).

Figure 1.10 presents the FDI inflows and outflows to and from China. To take advantage of Chinese cheap labor supply, several foreign companies including American, European, Japanese, and Korean, moved to China. Figure 1.11 highlights that at the beginning of the 1990s, FDI inflow as a share of GDP increased by about 6% in China. However, post-2010, the adverse effects of the financial crisis and the rising labor costs reduced the inflows to China.

China's wave of reforms in the late 1990s and early 2000s transformed it into a middle-income country. When China became an upper-middle-income country, a number of foreign companies moved out

---

[15] Chinese Renminbi Internationalization: Guide to recent developments, https://www.pnc.com/insights/corporate-institutional/go-international/chinese-enminbi-internationalization-guide-to-recent-developments.html, accessed on July 26, 2020.

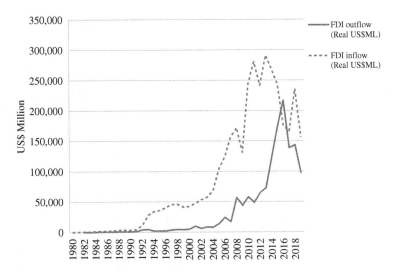

Figure 1.10:   China: FDI net inflows and outflows (1980–2019).
Source: Authors' formations using World Bank — WDI data.

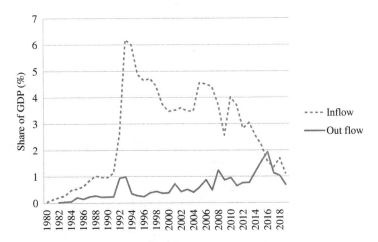

Figure 1.11:   FDI net inflow and outflow as share of China's GDP (%).
Source: Authors' formations using World Bank — WDI data.

of China and invested in countries like Bangladesh, Myanmar, and Cambodia, among others. Post-2010, however, there were significant Chinese investment outflows into the developing countries in Africa and Asia; however there is a significant decline in FDI outflows after 2015.

Even as China emerged as a major investor in the developing world, it sought to take a bold step, demonstrating its resolve to secure a dominant role in the world. China's leadership in the Asian Infrastructure Investment Bank (AIIB), which it established in December 2015, validated Beijing's desire to create its own development lending platforms. There is an expectation that it will also launch an SCO Bank for the partner countries of the Shanghai Cooperation Organization in 2021.

1.3.5 *Chinese investments in R&D*

This higher expenditure on R&D enabled an economic catch-up for the Chinese people, with an increasing income level and standard of living. China has been able to achieve a large number of patents based on the results of R&D and technological innovations. China has continuously increased its expenditure on R&D as percentage of GDP from 0.563% in 1996 to 1.991% in 2013 and further to 2.4% in 2020. Figure 1.12 indicates how China increased enrollment in tertiary education since the late 1990s. The growth of tertiary school enrollment from 1970–2016 was 99%. Tertiary school enrollment increased to 48% over 2000–2017. This was possible because China considerably enhanced the scope of university

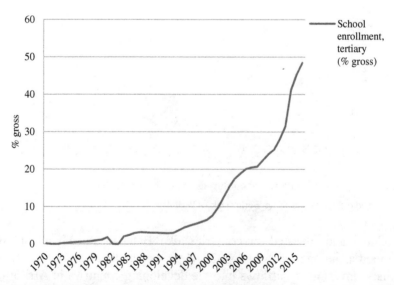

Figure 1.12:   China's school enrollment, tertiary (% gross).

Sources: Using World Bank — WDI data, created by the author.

education, resulting in increasing the size of its skilled workforce. This is one significant factor in the Chinese growth model.

Chinese President Xi Jinping has underlined the role of higher education and knowledge as vital inputs for economic growth. The Chinese government provides opportunities for foreign education; scholarships are provided for Chinese students to study in the USA, UK, Japan, Korea, and so on. Chinese academic institutions are incentivized to contribute to the real-world economy. Gu *et al.* (2018) indicate that China has received huge investments in knowledge resources. They also elucidate how China has nurtured some national champions in the high-tech sector by exploiting universities' scientific knowledge, known as Academy-run enterprises (ARE), namely Lenovo, Founder, Tsinghua Tongfang, and Dongruan. Gu and Lundvall (2006) explain that China's research expenditure as a share of GDP exceeds not only that of many emerging economies (such as Brazil, India, Malaysia, Indonesia, Mexico, South Africa) but also the EU average of public expenditure on education as a share of GDP. Schwaag Serger *et al.* (2015) explain that Chinese depth and world-leading excellence in frontier research at a few increasingly elite institutions could be at the expense of an inclusive base for research and education. The authors also point out that, while China had a number of medium and long-term plans on science and technology starting in the 1950s, the first medium- and long-term plan for education was only presented in 2010. Figure 1.13 indicates China's researchers in R&D per million people.

1.3.5.1 *China's patent applications*

China emerged as the world leader in international patent filings in 2019, with 58,990 applications, overtaking the United States. World Intellectual Property Organization (WIPO) annual report indicates that in 2018 China filed 265,800 international patent applications. WIPO's complex system of registering international patents involves multiple categories. However, in the main category, the Patent Cooperation Treaty, or PCT China, topped the ranking for the first time in 2019, with 58,990 applications.[16]

WIPO Director General Francis Gurry said in a statement that "China's rapid growth to become the top filer of international patent applications via WIPO underlines a long-term shift in the locus of innovation

---

[16] China overtook the US with most patent filings in 2019: UN, https://news.cgtn.com/news/2020-04-07/China-overtakes-U-S-with-most-patent-filings-in-2019-UN-Pv5rx0R1v2/index.html, accessed on July 24, 2020.

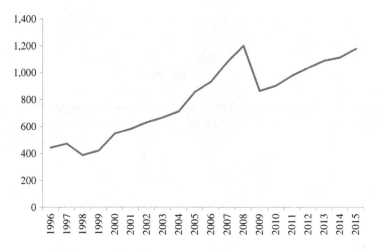

Figure 1.13:   China's researchers in R&D (per million people).

Sources: Using World Bank — WDI data, created by the author.

toward the East, with Asia-based applicants accounting for more than half of all PCT applications".[17]

Figure 1.14 shows the number of patents of some selected countries, including China. It shows the rapid rise of Chinese patents since 2005. While in the period prior to 2002, China had 1,140 patents, over the twelve years, from 2003 to 2015, China had filed a total of 44,226 patents, with almost 9,000 patents having been filed in 2015 alone. Refer to Table 1.2. The patent growth rate during this period was 96%. Compared to most middle-income countries, this is significant.

According to WIPO's report, Asian-based applicants account for 52.4% of all filings, while Europe and North America accounted for less than a quarter each. Interestingly, China-based telecom giant Huawei Technologies topped the global ranking in 2019 with 4,411 PCT applications.[18]

---

[17]China rolls out "one of the world's largest" 5G networks, https://www.bbc.com/news/business-50258287, accessed on July 26, 2020.
[18]*Ibid.*

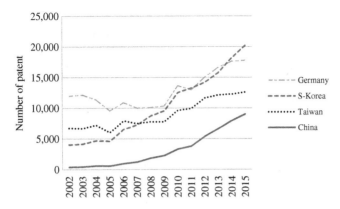

Figure 1.14: Patents by select countries.

Source: A patent technology monitoring team report: US Patent and Trademark Office (granted: 01/01/1977–12/31/2015).

Table 1.2: Patent by selected countries — All patent types pre-2002 and post-2002.

Origin	Pre 2002	2002	2005	2008	2011	2014	2015	All Years
Japan	464,244	36,339	31,833	36,679	48,256	56,005	54,422	1,069,394
Germany	185,657	11,957	9,575	10,085	12,967	17,595	17,752	365,627
South Korea	22,860	4,009	4,590	8,730	13,239	18,161	20,201	166,353
Taiwan	37,034	6,730	5,995	7,781	9,907	12,255	12,575	162,732
China	1,140	390	565	1,851	3,786	7,921	9,004	45,366

Source: A patent technology monitoring team report: US Patent and Trademark Office (granted: 01/01/1977–12/31/2015).

1.3.6 *Outbound Chinese tourism*

With a rising middle class and rising income-levels, data from the China National Tourism Administration showed that Chinese tourists traveled overseas on 131 million occasions in 2017, an increase of 7.0% from the previous year. Data from the International Association of Tour Managers shows that overseas travel spending by Chinese tourists reached US$261.1 billion in 2016, an increase of 4.5% year-on-year, and ranking first worldwide (Outbound Chinese Tourism and Consumption Trends, 2017). Figure 1.15 indicates the increasing number of Chinese tourists from 2000 to 2018.

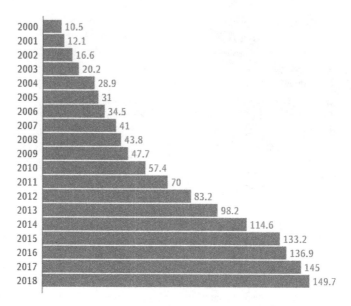

Year	Value
2000	10.5
2001	12.1
2002	16.6
2003	20.2
2004	28.9
2005	31
2006	34.5
2007	41
2008	43.8
2009	47.7
2010	57.4
2011	70
2012	83.2
2013	98.2
2014	114.6
2015	133.2
2016	136.9
2017	145
2018	149.7

Figure 1.15:   Chinese tourists: Annual overseas visits (millions).

Source: China Outbound Tourism Research Institute (COTRI). Taken from the website of https://www.telegraph.co.uk/travel/comment/rise-of-the-chinese-tourist/, accessed on July 24, 2020.

In less than two decades, China has grown from travel minnows to the world's most powerful outbound market. According to the United Nations World Tourism Organization (UNWTO), Chinese tourists overseas spent US$277.3 billion in 2018, up from around US$10 billion in the year 2000.

According to the Outbound Chinese Tourism and Consumption Trends, 2017 Survey, jointly issued by Nielsen and Alipay in 2017, Chinese tourists are exhibiting stronger purchasing power than non-Chinese tourists. As an example, Chinese tourists spent an average of US$762 per person toward shopping on their most recent overseas trip, while non-Chinese tourists average spend was about US$486. Moreover, among all Chinese tourists who traveled overseas in 2017, 67% had traveled to other Asian countries or regions and 51% to Hong Kong, Macao, or Taiwan, while 38% had been to Europe, 25% to North America, and 20% to Australia/New Zealand. In Asia, the top three choices were Japan, Thailand, and South Korea, followed closely by Singapore, Malaysia, and the Maldives (Outbound Chinese Tourism and Consumption Trends, 2017).

1.3.7 *Internationalization of the Renminbi (RMB)*

There has been an effort to internationalize the official currency, the Renminbi (RMB). RMB Internationalization accelerated in 2009 when China established the dim sum bond market and expanded the Cross-Border Trade RMB Settlement Pilot Project, which helps establish pools of offshore RMB liquidity.[19,20] In 2013, the RMB was the 8th most traded currency in the world and the 7th most traded in early 2014. By the end of 2014, RMB ranked 5th.[21] In 2020, RMB is once again in the 8th position.

Over the last few years, the Chinese government has undertaken other measures to liberalize and internationalize its currency, the RMB, relaxing some rules to move toward allowing its currency to become more freely usable and tradable. The People's Bank of China (PBOC) is laying the groundwork to ensure that the RMB becomes a global currency in a three-step process: first, to pitch RMB as a global trade currency, second, RMB as a global investment currency, and third, to build RMB as a global reserve currency, respectively.[22] Figure 1.16 shows the RMB exchange rate trends from 2014 to 2019. There are several fluctuations during this period. However, as of 2019, RMB's share of international transactions is only 4.3%, compared to 88% for the USD.

The RMB has experienced greater volatility since 2016, driven mainly by PBOC intervention and US–China trade disputes. Soon after President Trump took office in 2017, the PBOC discouraged speculators from betting against the RMB. Throughout 2017, the RMB appreciated not only due to PBOC actions but also due to stronger economic data and a broadly weaker dollar. The RMB appreciation came to a halt at the end of 1Q18 as trade discussions between the US and China escalated. In May 2019, the US imposed 25% tariffs on US$200 billion worth of Chinese goods (up from 10% previously), which drove the RMB back to 2018 lows near 7.0%. At the G-20 Summit in August 2019, the two countries

---

[19] RMB Settlement, Kasikorn Research Center, Bangkok, February 8, 2011.

[20] Chan, Norman T.L. (2014). Hong Kong as Offshore Renminbi Centre — Past and Prospects. HKMA. Retrieved July 24, 2014.

[21] RMB now eighth most widely traded currency in the world. Society for Worldwide Interbank Financial Telecommunication. Retrieved October 10, 2013.

[22] Chinese Renminbi Internationalization: Guide to recent developments, https://www.pnc.com/insights/corporate-institutional/go-international/chinese-renminbi-internationalization-guide-to-recent-developments.html, accessed on July 26, 2020.

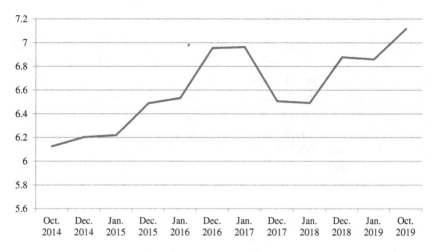

Figure 1.16:   RMB exchange rate trends.

Source: Using data from website and some modification, https://www.pnc.com/insights/corporate-institutional/go-international/chinese-renminbi-internationalization-guide-to-recent-developments.html, accessed on July 25, 2020.

were yet unable to come to an agreement on trade.[23] The China–USA trade war has had magnified adverse implications not only for the functioning of the World Trade Organization but also the trading arrangements between other countries.

1.3.8 *A rising China, a declining America*

China reached the middle-income group within a short span of time and has consistently recorded high rates of growth; hence, it now seeks to occupy the number one position in terms of the highest overall GDP. This would further embolden its muscular influence. Here, a comparison of China's and the USA's GDP as a share of World GDP is merited. To derive this figure, we took world GDP as the benchmark of 100. It shows how the performance of the US economy is declining against China's GDP progression. In the 1980s, share of China's GDP in the world GDP was 1.7%; however, this increased to 16.5% in 2019. In contrast, the USA's

---

[23] Chinese Renminbi Internationalization: Guide to Recent Developments, https://www.pnc.com/insights/corporate-institutional/go-international/chinese-renminbi-internationalization-guide-to-recent-developments.html, accessed on July 26, 2020.

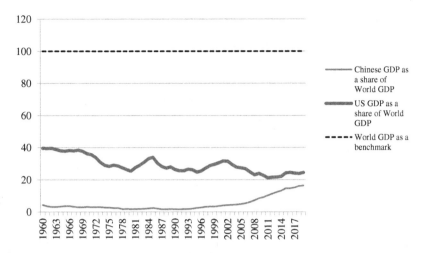

Figure 1.17: China and USA's share of GDP to World GDP.

Source: Authors' formations using World Bank — WDI data.

was 25.1% in the 1980s and 24.5% in 2019. It is evident that the gap between the share of US and China's GDP as a share of World GDP is steadily narrowing (see Figure 1.17).

With respect to the future, China is investing in new technologies. As a result, it achieved the vast capability of new technological advancement. The introduction of 5G[24] technology is one example of China's capability, where it is gaining influence in several countries, barely slowed down by a pandemic that has ravaged the world.[25] China's government stated that more than 130,000 5G base stations had been activated by the end of 2019 to support the 5G network. Beijing and Washington, joined by Norway, Canada, and Germany have been embroiled in a power struggle over technology.[26] The pandemic has further exacerbated tensions, even as China leads in global technology, global tourism, political power, and world trade in the 21st century. This is discussed in greater detail in Chapter 10 of this book.

---

[24] The next generation of wireless technology rolling out across the world, promises to deliver much faster wireless service and a more responsive network.

[25] 5G will change the world and China wants to lead the way, https://www.cnet.com/news/5g-will-change-the-world-and-china-wants-to-lead-the-way/, accessed on July 26, 2020.

[26] China rolls out of "one of the world's largest" 5G networks, https://www.bbc.com/news/business-50258287, accessed on July 26, 2020.

1.4 Conclusion

The above discussion amplifies China's rise and its transformation from one of the poorest countries in the world to one that is challenging the existing world order. Its global outreach through investment outflows and economic footprint is unparalleled, eclipsing the rise of Japan and challenging the United States in more ways than one. The technological superiority that it has achieved, both through innovations and adoption of the best available techniques, acquired by merit or otherwise, has placed it firmly on the path of becoming a dominant geo-economic powerhouse.

The globalized world is more interdependent in 2020 and over 130 countries are now critically linked to China's Belt and Road Initiative. Several among them, which will be discussed in the succeeding pages, are in China's apron fold. In Asia, China is the most powerful and formidable power, with its ambitions galloping on the strength of hundreds of infrastructure projects in the three subregions of Asia in its vicinity — Central, Southeast, and South Asia.

The scope of this book focuses on countries in South and Southeast Asia, which are engaging with their giant neighbor in areas as high-tech industrialization, quality manufacturing, building employment-generating supply-side capacities, as well as greater participation in international supply chains. With growth rates impacted adversely in most countries due to the onslaught of the pandemic, there is rising resentment against Chinese products, as well as investments from China in the USA. China's wolf warrior diplomats with their diatribes have only exacerbated the already hostile climate. Hence, even as the debate on economic decoupling from China continues to engage several countries, the fact that China is their largest trading and investment partner will be a challenge not only for the rise of China but also those embedded in its economic grip.

Chapter 2

The Chinese Dream and Vision

Joseph Nye, "…the essence of power lies in the conversion of resources into influence" (Nye, 2015).

This chapter analyzes how the BRI took shape within the Chinese Dream articulated by Chinese President Xi Jinping. However, before discussing the OBOR and its later manifestation as the BRI, it is crucial to contextualize Xi's ascent and the contribution to the economic reform of his predecessors since Deng Xiaoping. The previous chapter has provided insights on the manifestations of China's rise.

2.1 The Context — Economic Reforms (1980s to 2012)

There were mainly three favorable conditions that resulted in the reforms in China in the 1970s. According to Howe and Robert (2003, pp. 26–27), these conditions included a stagnation in living standards, inadequate levels of industrial technologies, and a favorable external environment. Moreover, the CCP recognized that China's problems were qualitative and institutional. The economy had huge structural excess capacity in several industries of significance, coupled with bankrupt public sector enterprises, a corrupt bureaucracy, and several other inefficiencies.

During the Third Plenum of the 11th CCCPC Central Committee of the Communist Party of China (CCCPC) held from December 18 to 22,

1978, Deng admitted errors of the past years (Cultural Revolution, Great Leap Forward in the period of Mao Tse Tung), and initiated the process of economic reforms. This meeting of 1978 was when Deng Xiaoping — who had emerged as China's new leader after the passing away of Mao Zedong — opened a top leadership meeting that would put China on a new pathway to unalterably change the contours of global geopolitics.[1] The significance of this event for the 21st Century is likened to the fall of the Berlin Wall in the 20th Century.

According to Cable (2017), Deng Xiaoping pursued a policy of reforms and opening-up, beginning with the acceptance of foreign investment in Guandong and special economic zones to facilitate exports, increasingly linked to Hong Kong, followed by Fujian, Shanghai, and 14 coastal cities. With Deng's philosophical aura, soothing critics of liberalization (when you open the window some flies come in), while also focusing on the impoverished peasants, his reforms picked pace. With the ending of Communes, there was the emergence of township and village enterprises (TVEs), which resulted in a build-up of the manufacturing and export capacity. While millions came out of poverty, employment in the TVEs increased from 28 million in 1978 to 106 million in 1992, i.e. in about 14 years; moreover, production grew 50 times in value. Deng Xiaoping's policy of opening up the economy also achieved spectacular results. In 1978, China's trade was vastly limited — exports were $10 bn, under 1% of world trade, but this had grown to US$25 bn by 1985. After continued rapid growth, by 2014, China was the world's largest trading nation in goods (US$4.3 trillion). Hence, Deng laid the foundations and created political and administrative structures within which his successors could operate.

Jiang Zemin, who was to succeed Deng, had urged reform of State-Owned Enterprises (SOEs) since mid-1994. After assuming leadership post the death of Deng on February 19, 1997, he advocated central SOEs to be transformed into joint-stock entities with modern corporate governance (Howe *et al.*, 2003, p. 52). Soon after his taking over, the Asian financial crisis struck most of East Asia, resulting in a decline in China's rate of growth of foreign trade from 15.3% to 0.3%. In December 2001, China and Taiwan formally entered the WTO. Bill Clinton, the then

---

[1]Abraham Denmark, "40 years ago Deng Xiaoping transformed China and the world", *Washington Post*, https://www.washingtonpost.com/news/monkey-cage/wp/2018/12/19/40-years-ago-deng-xiaoping-changed-china-and-the-world/, December 19, 2018, accessed on July 18, 2020.

President of the United States, favored China's entry, confident that the world economy would benefit from trade with China. Twenty years later, the world and the USA are unsure it was the right move.

While Deng Xiaoping made the development of the productive forces of the very essence of socialism a priority, Jiang Zemin, during his two five-year terms as President, shared the concerns of the last of the Party elders and their idealistic views of Chinese socialism. Additionally, what differentiated him from his predecessors was that he also accommodated the younger generation of economic reformers who helped China achieve staggering growth in its domestic economy and foreign trade. According to Gilley (1998), Jiang's ability to either satisfy his allies and adversaries or ruthlessly exploit their weaknesses stood the country well as he maneuvered China on the world stage.

According to Mulvad (2019, p. 455), Jiang's "Three Representatives" theory in 2000, which allowed capitalists into the Party by ensuring that the CCP represented the most advanced productive forces in China, helped the country to become much wealthier but not without unequal distribution of wealth. While his successor Hu Jintao complied with the new tradition, he also laid the foundation for an equitable and socially stable "harmonious socialist society", organized on the technocratic basis of "scientific development".

Hu Jintao realized that the Chinese economy could not thrive forever on the growth model of low-wage export and investments. In 2007, premier Wen Jiabao declared that the Chinese economy was becoming increasingly "unstable, unbalanced, uncoordinated, and [ultimately] unsustainable". Hence, he sought a consensus to bring in supply-side reforms to create a growth model that would be secured through domestic consumption. This led to the "walking on two legs" approach, that is, adoption of both, a people-centered approach and a GDP-centered approach. Externally, the harmonious world theory, which projected a non-threatening philosophy, underscored the notion of harmony without uniformity.

In the sphere of foreign policy, according to Mulvad (2019), the Hu Jintao administration continued with its system of "laying low" (except in terms of establishing Confucius Institutes in other countries), just as his predecessor Deng Xiaoping had emphasized. The focus of foreign policy was on soft power outreach initiatives and the push for a harmonious world. The pitch for a "harmonious world" with its vision of stable world order became more China-centric, with the accession of Xi Jinping as the Party Secretary. This concept is discussed in the next section.

The rest of the chapter is divided into the following sections: Xi Jinping and the Chinese Dream, the Belt and Road Initiative and its various manifestations, and China's bid to build new institutions and establish its position as a donor through aid and development assistance to developing countries.

2.2 President Xi Jinping and the Chinese Dream

The son of a Communist revolutionary, and with more than four decades of experience as a grassroots worker, Xi Jinping was not well known in the Western world before being appointed to the Party's top post in November 2012. Xi replaced Hu Jintao as China's President. He has undoubtedly become the country's most powerful leader even as his tenure has stamped out dissent with his signature anti-corruption campaign, with almost 1.5 million officials punished or eliminated. It was in 2012 that the slogan of the "Chinese Dream of National Rejuvenation" was first used by Xi in his November 2012 speech at the "The Road to Rejuvenation" exhibition at the National Museum in Beijing.

Xi defined the "dream" as follows:

I firmly believe that the goal of bringing about a moderately prosperous society in all respects can be achieved by 2021 when the CCP celebrates its centenary; the goal of building China into a modern socialist country that is prosperous, strong, democratic, culturally advanced and harmonious can be achieved by 2049; that is when the People's Republic of China marks its centenary, and the dream of rejuvenation of the Chinese nation will then be realized (Mulvad, 2019, pp. 449–460).

In speeches and official documents outlining the China Dream, Xi has also indicated that it incorporates the "rejuvenation of China", or the Chinese "renaissance". In the official narrative, this rejuvenation is highly nationalistic and will provide a "restoration of dignity" for the Chinese state following China's Century of Humiliation (Hayes, 2020).

The persona of Chinese Premier Xi Jinping has also been written about extensively. His vision of the Chinese Dream to replace the existing international order with one led by China is challenging the United States's supremacy in various ways. Mohanty (2013), in an essay, delineates President Xi Jinping's initiatives on various political, economic, and international issues. Xi's Chinese Dream is programmatic and tied to goals, targets, and planning; and is viewed as highly pragmatic. However, the contours of the "Dream" continue to transverse across the economic, cultural, social to the political and strategic arenas, too, with the strategic footprint outdoing the economic.

The CCP National Congress of the 19th Communist Party of China held from October 18–24, 2017, has been described as "historic" even as the achievements of five years were articulated. At that time, China had entered a new era, even as it was in the stage of rejuvenation for the first time since the 19th Century, explained Xie Chuntao, a Professor of CPC Affairs.[2]

During his Speech (in October 2017), Xi Jinping's confidence and focus on the economic achievements of five years was palpable, *With the GDP rising from 54 trillion to 80 trillion yuan, China has maintained its position as the world's second-largest economy and contributed more than 30% of global economic growth.* He also referred to the supply-side structural reforms, the building of infrastructure, and the digital economy.[3]

This October 2017 speech also brought in an additional stipulation, raising the stature of Xi Jinping to that of Mao. President Xi Jinping and his political philosophy would be included to the country's constitution. "Xi Jinping's Thought on Socialism with Chinese Characteristics for a New Era" was enshrined just as that of Mao Zedong's. The unusual step highlights the speed and enthusiasm with which Xi consolidated power since his ascension in 2012.

Even as Xi Jinping began his second five-year term in October 2017, he had acquired power and influence more than any Chinese leader since Mao Zedong. Although the Constitution of Communist Party of China [Chapter II, Article 10] "forbids all forms of personality cult", the Chinese Communist Party's Central Committee proposal of February 25, 2018, deleted the condition that "a president shall serve no more than two consecutive terms" from the constitution. The annual sitting of Parliament, the National People's Congress in mid-March 2018, passed this.[4] The proposal also covered the vice president's position. Given that young minds

---

[2] https://www.globalsecurity.org/military/world/china/xi-jinping-cult.htm, accessed on August 29, 2019.

[3] Cited from Xi Jinping, "Speech at the 19th National Congress of the Communist Party of China" (October 18, 2017), accessed on July 17, 2020.

[4] Read more: "The Chinese Dream" and Xi Jinping's power politics, https://www.dw.com/en/the-chinese-dream-and-xi-jinpings-power-politics/a-41941966, accessed on August 29, 2019.

are easiest to influence, Universities and colleges across the country were encouraged to establish research centers for "Xi Jinping Thought".

Evidently, Xi Jinping does not believe in the ancient Chinese philosopher Lao Tzu's advice to leaders,

> "A leader is best when people barely know that he exists, not so good when people obey and acclaim him, worst when they despise him. Fail to honor people, they fail to honor you. But of a good leader, who talks little, when his work is done, his aims fulfilled, they will all say, "We did this ourselves". (Lao Tzu)

On the issue of Xi Jinping's consolidation of power, Western experts have several critical views. Elizabeth C. Economy, a China scholar from Stanford University, is of the view that the excessive control of the Party by Xi Jinping has contributed to economic stagnation. Additionally, Xi's predilection for State control has also resulted in the private sector being deprived of capital. There is increasing suspicion of Chinese enterprises located in other countries. She further cites the intensifying penetration of the Party into Chinese businesses has caused all Chinese companies to be viewed as extended arms of the Communist Party.

Others as David Bandurski, co-director of the China Media Project, a research program affiliated with the University of Hong Kong, asserted that Xi even claims historic greatness when the President added a modern twist to the rural imagery exhibition. This was done with farming harvesters placed in the background to showcase China's technological advancements. Though Xi Jinping continues to project China's invincibility, Bandurski expresses his view of the importance assigned to China's rise by referring to a quote by the President, i.e. when he frequently states, *The great rejuvenation of the Chinese nation depends on our economic competitiveness.*[5]

Given China's Belt and Road Initiative's expanse and outreach, a signature campaign of Xi Jinping, it is important to delineate this.

---

[5] *The New York Times*, https://www.nytimes.com/2018/09/28/world/asia/xi-jinping-china-propaganda.htmlXi Jinping, accessed on August 29, 2019.

2.3 The Belt and Road Initiative: A Sino-globalization that is Programmatic and All-Encompassing

The BRI is certainly more than roads and ports. It now envelops locations from outer space to the depth of the seas, even as Beijing develops a space-based Silk Road to undersea Internet cables and satellite navigation. The digital and health Silk Roads have already taken shape, with the latter having encompassed over 110 countries till 2020.

The genesis of Xi Jinping's vision was to build the "Silk Road Economic Belt" and broaden the sites of cooperation between and with the Eurasian countries. President Xi Jinping officially launched the One Belt, One Road (OBOR) initiative in September 2013, intending to revive the Silk Road linking Asia, Europe, and Africa. This project, known as the One Belt, One Road, was announced by President Xi during his visits to Kazakhstan and Indonesia in 2013. The plan included: the overland Silk Road Economic Belt and the Maritime Silk Road. The two initially referred to the first as the One Belt, One Road initiative, but eventually became the Belt and Road Initiative in 2016.

Xi's vision of OBOR included creating a vast network of railways, energy pipelines, highways, and border crossings, both on the westward side — through the former Soviet republics and to Pakistan, India, and the rest of Southeast Asia. Such a network would expand the international use of Chinese currency, the renminbi, and "break the bottleneck in Asian connectivity". In addition to physical infrastructure, China had plans to build fifty special economic zones, modeled after the Shenzhen Special Economic Zone, credit for which went to economic reforms under leader Deng Xiaoping.[6]

Given the scope for outreach, a step-by-step approach was envisaged: First, to strengthen policy communication and consultations.

Second, to improve road connectivity by opening up the transportation channel from the Pacific to the Baltic Sea, initiating a transportation network that could connect East Asia, West Asia, and South Asia.

Third, to promote trade facilitation.

---

[6] Andrew Chatzky and James McBride, https://www.cfr.org/backgrounder/chinas-massive-belt-and-road-initiative, January 28, 2020, accessed on July 22, 2020.

Fourth, to enhance monetary circulation, to reduce financial risks, and enhance competitiveness. Fifth, to strengthen people-to-people exchanges.

This new approach got enshrined in Xi's pronouncement of the "new normal" philosophy in May 2014 to describe China's next economic growth period.[7]

The OBOR of 2013 and BRI of 2016 (given that there were multiple Belts and Roads) were motivated by the Asian Development Bank's (ADB) indication of the existence of a massive infrastructure gap. A 2009 ADB report highlighted that the Asian region requires approximately US$750 billion in annual financing to develop its infrastructure (Bhattacharyay, 2010). The year 2009, i.e. post the 2008 financial crisis, was also the exact point when China's overseas direct investment (ODI) began to burgeon. This was an inflection point for the global order. The decline of the West was imminent and this was not an opportunity an ascendant power would miss!

Another motivation to speed up the process of outward expansion of investment was that when Xi Jinping assumed leadership, China was in the grip of an economic slowdown. This slowdown majorly affected its industries, particularly steel. China produces half of the world's steel, but in 2014, steel consumption declined for the first time in 20 years. With contracting demands at home, China needed to shift its focus outward to solve the issue of overcapacity. Therefore, China's funding of transport, energy, and telecommunications infrastructure all along the Belt and Road was to create demand for Chinese steel products and spur Chinese production capacities abroad. According to Bhattacharya (2016), the BRI initially covered 60 emerging market countries and developing countries with a total population of over 4 billion and an aggregate GDP of about US$21 trillion, accounting for about 65% and 30% of the global totals in land-based and maritime-based economic production values, respectively.

A key policy document that details the scope and ambition of BRI (titled "Vision and Actions on Jointly Building Silk Road Economic Belt and 21st Century Maritime Silk Road") also mentions "connectivity" more than a dozen times (NDRC, 2015). Additionally, while the word "maintain" has been used once, "upkeep" is not used at all. On the other

---

[7]Pratibha MS, (2018). East Asia Strategic Review: China's rising ambitions in Asia, Pentagon Press LLP and Institute for Defence Studies and Analyses, New Delhi.

hand, "construct"/"construction" is used fourteen times, and "build"/ "building" thirty-two times. What does China hope to achieve?

2.4 The Key Routes

The BRI comprises three main routes, combining existing infrastructure with planned future infrastructural development (both immediate and long-term).

These are:

i. The Northern Route, which has been referred to as the "Eurasian Land Bridge", linking Beijing with Russia, Germany, and Northern Europe.
ii. The Middle Route, which refers to existing and proposed oil and gas pipelines linking Beijing, Xi'an, Urumqi, Afghanistan, Kazakhstan, Hungary, and Paris.
iii. The Southern Route, which refers to the development of transnational highways linking Beijing with Southern XUAR, Pakistan, Iran, Iraq, Turkey, Italy, and Spain.

In addition to the above trading routes, the following proposed economic corridors are in progress:

a. The China–Pakistan Economic Corridor (CPEC), which focuses on the trade of commodities
b. The Bangladesh–China–India–Burma Economic Corridor, to facilitate trade with ASEAN states
c. The China–Mongolia–Russia Economic Corridor, to serve an essential role in national security and energy and
d. The New Eurasian Land Bridge, which will be "the main logistics route between China and Europe".

China's BRI, by 2021, has expanded to more than 130 countries, with ever-growing influence and footprint. However, the core of the policy is centered around diplomatic efforts in its complex neighborhood. Chinese leaders initiate an interlocking set of foreign affairs activities they group under the umbrella of "periphery diplomacy", to enhance their influence. China's strategic rationales for working more closely with its neighbors include managing the security of its border, expanding trade and investment networks, and preventing a geopolitical balancing coalition.

Beijing uses a range of tools for peripheral diplomacy, including deepening economic integration, engaging significant neighboring powers, and using coercion to achieve its aims. China has, since ancient times, employed the carrot and stick approach to deal with erring states, requiring them to pay tribute and behave as ordered to (French, 2017).

It has been estimated that China has already invested over half a trillion dollars in over 2200 BRI projects worldwide. Given the impact of COVID-19 on China's rate of growth in 2020, China's non-financial ODI declined 1.6% (year on year) in the first five months of 2020, according to its Ministry of Commerce. The ODI in 157 countries and regions was 296.27 billion yuan (about 42.2 billion US dollars) during the period. However, it is interesting to note that Chinese companies increased investment in BRI countries during the first five months of 2020, with new acquisitions up 16% year on year to reach 6.53 billion US dollars. The country's ODI mainly went to sectors such as leasing and business services, wholesale and retail, and manufacturing. The value of new projects abroad reached 601.88 billion yuan, up 14.4% year on year. During the period, projects with a value of more than 50 million US dollars was 319, an increase of 32 from the same period a year earlier. Those projects' total contract value amounted to 70.57 billion US dollars, accounting for 82.3% of the total of the newly signed contracts.[8]

This implies that BRI countries continue to be in the grip of Chinese companies even as they coped with the pandemic's economic consequences. Therefore, it is not out of place for Hayes (2020) to state that the BRI represents a bold plan for Chinese development domestically. It also can have a significant impact on twenty-first century globalization, or rather, China's robustly-entrenched "Sino-globalization".

2.4.1   *Speed breakers encountered by BRI projects*

What are the potential roadblocks? Given that the Belt and Road Initiative has also stoked opposition, according to Careem (2017), for some countries that take on large amounts of debt to fund infrastructure upgrades, BRI money is seen as a potential poisoned chalice. BRI projects are undertaken not through aid but low-interest funds. Several BRI

---

[8]http://www.xinhuanet.com/english/2020-06/18/c_139149626.html.

investments have less than transparent bidding processes and require the use of Chinese firms. As a result, contractors have inflated costs, resulting in canceled projects and political backlash. Examples of such criticisms abound.

Some examples of opaque and predatory project funding from recent years in Asian countries are cited here. In Malaysia, Mahathir bin Mohamad, elected prime minister in 2018, campaigned against over-priced BRI initiatives, which he alleged were partially redirected to funds controlled by his predecessor. Once in office, he canceled US$22 billion worth of BRI projects, although he later announced his "full support" for the initiative in 2019. It is well known that several countries in South and Southeast Asia, as in Malaysia, have run — and won — campaigns on anti-BRI platforms. In Kazakhstan, mass protests against the construction of Chinese factories in 2019 were an outcome of concerns about costs and rage over the Chinese government's treatment of Uighur Muslims in it's Xinjiang Province. A 2018 report by the Center for Global Development refers to several such instances, which note that at least eight BRI countries are vulnerable to debt crises.

The Council for Foreign Relations' (CFR) Belt and Road Tracker shows that overall debt to China has soared since 2013, surpassing 20 percent of GDP in some countries. Some governments, for example, Kenya and Zambia, are carefully studying BRI investments before they sign up. Chinese leaders were reportedly surprised by such pushback, and BRI investment began to slow in late 2018. Yet, by the end of 2019, BRI contracts again saw a significant uptick. However, Dudarenok, quoted by Careem (2017) (a Russian who spent five years in China, based now in Hong Kong), says she has yet to see the initiative's real effect, which is aimed at fostering a labyrinthine connectivity and cooperation in Eurasia.

2.4.2 *BRI benefitting whom?*

Is Beijing's grand strategy benefiting smaller companies? When it comes to the extent to which the "Belt and Road Initiative" generates opportunities for small- and medium-sized outfits across the route, opinions are divided.

According to Dudarenok, "Contract for tenders are often acquired through corrupt practices, as a result of which small businesses rarely have opportunities for benefiting; it is largely the big companies which secure the deals. I deal with a lot of companies in Russia and other countries that are supposed to be part of the OBOR initiative, and I have yet to see small businesses having meaningful and beneficial participation", she added. In her opinion, the small businesses that benefit from some projects in the informal sector are roadside eateries catering to construction workers, especially in countries like Laos and Cambodia.

However, Yukon Huang, senior fellow, Asia Program at Carnegie Endowment for International Peace, believes otherwise. In his view, the massive scale of the initiative implies that small businesses would benefit. "It depends on the nature of the project", Huang says. "Also, on who is managing the project and the source of financing. If financing is coming from China, this may well mean the involvement of its large SOEs, but they will also need local partners, and these could be smaller companies".

The narrative of project finance and the projects themselves is thus clearly oriented toward construction and not at the maintenance of what already exists or is currently under construction. It is essential to draw attention to the "on-the-ground" vulnerability of the infrastructures being built. Chinese border regions abound in ruins, the legacy of earlier developmental campaigns: villages to which people never moved, urban neighborhoods that stand empty, development zones that have not attracted businesses, and bombastic museums that do not house any exhibitions. These modern ruins suggest that China's construction is often linked to speculation, corruption, and short-sighted megalomania (Kobi, 2016; Woodworth, 2018, cited in Luthi, 2020), with infrastructures not to help the ordinary but to generate revenue and special doles for politicians. Thus, the question that must be asked is: How many of the projects pursued in the name of the New Silk Road, as the Economic Belt is sometimes referred to, will turn into similar modern ruins when the major thrust of the BRI is over?

The case studies from specific country analyses in this book will shed more light on the above.

2.5 China's Soft Power Projection: Some Aspects

This section includes China's outreach initiatives in establishing Confucius Institutes and Confucius Centers in BRI partner countries, providing aid, and establishing the AIIB.

2.5.1 *Confucius institutes and centers in BRI countries*

Concurrent with its policy of establishing brand "China", Beijing continued to promote the establishment of Confucian centers and China study programs, especially in BRI partner countries. It is worth noting that between 2004 and 2018, 548 institutes and nearly 2,000 Confucius classrooms in 154 countries, most of them at foreign universities or institutions, have been established with Chinese funding.

Confucius Institutes (C.I.s) and Confucius Classrooms (C.C.s) have been growing in numbers in Africa with China's increasing economic presence in the continent. In South Asia, they have acquired a firm foothold in Pakistan, Bangladesh, and Nepal. Sri Lanka has two C.I.s — at the Colombo and Kelaniya Universities. They have only a marginal presence in India because of New Delhi's entrenched suspicions about Chinese initiatives. The Chinese government funds the C.I.s and C.C.s and also sends and pays the teachers. Each CI or CC is attached to a Chinese university. Each CI has two Directors, one from China and the other from the host country.

As Ms. Pang Chunxue, Charge de' Affaires at the Chinese Embassy in Colombo said, "most of the C.I.s are in countries which are on the BRI route. The C.I.s' goal of bringing people together matches the goals of the BRI, which are to narrow gaps in development between countries".

The C.I.s and C.C.s are developed at the Confucius Institute Headquarters in China called "Hanban". But in response to demands from the host countries, the courses have been expanded beyond language and culture to include subjects of local interest. For example, in Pakistan, the C.I. at the Agriculture University in Faisalabad has tied up with an engineering and an agricultural university in Lahore to teach Chinese useful to agriculture and engineering students.

According to Balachandran (2018), "in Nepal, locals are taught vehicle maintenance not only to learn the trade but to be able to work in Chinese infrastructure projects", said Professor Wang Shengli of the CI in Kathmandu University.

However, C.I.s and C.C.s have become controversial in some countries. They are suspected of having ulterior aims of weaning people of the host countries away from their entrenched beliefs and make them think and act like the Chinese. The burgeoning of the Confucius Institutes and Centers is being viewed increasingly in several countries with suspicion and integral to China's expansionist vision entrenched with the power of money and muscle.

Hence, after a global pushback due to host countries' censorship, China is abandoning its Confucius Institute brand, switching to a new format as a center for "language exchange and cooperation". In a directive to lower-level agencies, the Ministry of Education said the Hanban had changed its name to the Ministry of Education Centre for Language Education and Cooperation.

In addition to the above, it is crucial to understand the establishment of institutions to provide funding for BRI partner countries, many of whom do not have the capacity for generating their own resources for the mega projects they seek to build.

2.6 Development Assistance: China's Footprint as an Aid Giver

The Asian Survey (2020) states that the enormous investment figures and the inclusion of the BRI in the Party's constitution in October 2017 show that development assistance has become the mainstay of China's future economic and foreign policy. Approximately, development assistance does not meet the DAC definition of ODA (which included a 25% grant element) due to the low concessional feature of its loans.

The research by AidData (2019), undertaken over five years for the period 2000–2014, provides interesting insights on China's motivation for extending aid as well as the nature and quantum of aid itself. Over the period 2000–2014, China provided US$354.4 billion of official funding globally and spent an amount almost similar to that by the United States in the same period, this being US$394.6 billion. In fact, to some countries, China's aid surpassed that of the United States.[9]

Over the period 2000 to 2014, Sri Lanka in South Asia and Cambodia in Southeast Asia were countries to receive more than US$2 bn in aid from China, more than what they had received from the United States. 45% of Chinese BRI projects in 2017 were assigned to Southeast Asia (Lubin *et al.*, 2018: 44).

---

[9]Brad Parks, the executive director of AidData, (a research lab at the College of William & Mary), said it took five years for a team of nearly 100 scholars and research assistants from all over the world to collate the data from 15,000 distinct information sources covering 4,300 projects in 140 different countries.

Some specific insights from the AidData Survey are as follows:

a. Chinese data on aid is difficult to access due to secrecy in the provision of Other Official Flows (OOF).[10]
b. Data accessed for Chinese government-financed projects (by AidData) in 138 countries revealed that Chinese projects are densely concentrated in African and Asian countries. This is probably due to the high need level of the recipient countries.
c. Governance is not a criterion: "China is well known for funding several governments with poor governance such as Venezuela, Angola, Iran, and Pakistan", said David Dollar, a senior fellow at the Brookings Institution who was the US. Treasury's economic and financial emissary to China between 2009 and 2013. "[However,] these are balanced by large amounts of lending to countries with relatively good governance: Brazil, India, Indonesia, and the East African states. China's lending seems to be indifferent to governance".
d. Convergence with Chinese interests: AidData noted that African nations that vote with China at the United Nations get an average of 86% in aid from Beijing.
    "The criteria for China to provide foreign aid is not the nature of the government, but the convergence of interests", said Yun Sun, an expert on Chinese funding who is with the Stimson Center in Washington. "That need could be political, commercial, or even reputational".
e. Other factors: Recipients of Chinese aid were also those countries that are well endowed with natural resources, were considered creditworthy, or were significant trade partners.
f. The major share of China's global development spending is not official aid but rather distributed via "other official flows", or OOF.

Research by AidData suggests that China's commitment to building connective infrastructure has far-reaching distributional consequences in low-income and middle-income countries, which have positive spin-offs as well. When Chinese funding, however, is similar to ODA, it boosts economic growth in recipient countries just like aid from another

---

[10] https://www.washingtonpost.com/news/worldviews/wp/2017/10/11/china-treats-its-foreign-aid-like-a-state-secret-new-research-aims-to-reveal-it/, accessed on July 23, 2020.

government or institution. This is about a 0.4% average increase in the rate of growth, two years after the project has been committed.[11]

Among these are those that help reduce inter-spatial inequalities, including the development projects in general and Chinese transportation projects. Chinese Government-financed transportation projects were underway at 1,331 locations in 86 countries worldwide over the 2000–2014 period. The total financial value of these projects amounts to US$69.5 billion. 61% of these projects were fully complete by 2014.

However, the flip side is provided by Blum *et al.* (2018), who states that China's "aid on-demand" approach is vulnerable to domestic political manipulation, primarily because government officials often direct Chinese aid to their home regions. Others have also shown that Chinese development projects, including infrastructure projects, produce several negative externalities, including loss of trade unionism, local corruption, and environmental degradation. Hurley *et al.* (2018) indicate that countries may have huge unsustainable debt burdens heaped on them. This discussion is considered pertinent in understanding the deeper nuances of aid provided by China in countries selected for further research by us.[12]

2.7 BRI: Crafting New Institutions

The construction of megaprojects require huge investments, which several host countries have been unable to provide. Hence, China created numerous new institutions to finance development projects. In addition to the Export–Import Bank of China and the China Development Bank, China's BRI projects are supported by the Silk Road Fund (worth US$40 billion), the China ASEAN Investment Cooperation Fund (US$10 billion), and the multilateral AIIB, with the capital of US$100 billion. Although the plans are not very lucid or well-publicized, it is estimated that the total infrastructure investments under the BRI will require at least US$1 trillion (Hillman, 2018).

---

[11] http://docs.aiddata.org/ad4/pdfs/WPS64_Connective_Financing_Chinese_Infrastructure_Projects_and_the_Diffusion_of_Economic_Activity_in_Developing_Countries.pdf, accessed on August 12, 2020.

[12] http://docs.aiddata.org/ad4/pdfs/WPS64_Connective_Financing_Chinese_Infrastructure_Projects_and_the_Diffusion_of_Economic_Activity_in_Developing_Countries.pdfKING PAPER 64, accessed on August 12, 2020

How is China reaching out to the multilateral system or changing the world order? First, China, as it appeared in 2020, has been re-working its positioning and policy impetus concerning international institutions, including enhancing its influence within the existing multilateral institutions such as the World Trade Organization, World Health Organization, among others. Second, a key component of China's newfound commitment to be a "keeper of international order" has been the construction of new multilateral institutions. These include the BRICS New Development Bank (NDB, created in 2014), the Chiang Mai Initiative Multilateralization Agreement (CMIM, signed in 2014), the expansion of the Shanghai Cooperation Organization (SCO, founded 2001), the RCEP in 2020, and most prominently the AIIB, with a capital of US$100 bn.[13]

To further understand China's logic of institutional statecraft, it would be appropriate to seek answers through the following:

First, the new institution may represent a substitute node of regional cooperation to create mutual benefits.

Second, founding an institution offers a new instrument of statecraft and governance mechanism to build bilateral and multilateral influence within a grouping or across the global arrangement.

A third purpose is to use the new institution to challenge and replace the prevailing substantive rules and norms within the policy domain in which it operates.

Repeated over the longer term, new institutions could subvert and ultimately replace existing institutions and enable the sponsor to write or rewrite the rules.

A final option is to directly oppose or refuse to comply with the existing institutional framework.

While all the institutions mentioned above would merit discussion, those discussed here (AIIB and RCEP), are especially relevant for this chapter.

2.7.1 *Asian Infrastructure Investment Bank (AIIB)*

The AIIB's creation resulted from more than a decade of deliberations among East Asian governments on institutional innovation to meet

---

[13] https://www.brookings.edu/wp-content/uploads/2017/04/chinas-emerging-institutional-statecraft.pdf.

regional infrastructure needs and provide alternatives to the Bretton Woods institutions. A key objective for China is to bring the domestic order in sync with global norms and reflect its commitment to following established guidelines. The AIIB signals a potential "international order with Chinese characteristics" that links both liberal and non-liberal elements. AIIB has its headquarters in Beijing.

This China-led institution is a multilateral development bank proposed by Xi Jinping in 2013, with 21 countries signing an initial MOU in October 2014. By the time of the AIIB's official launch and the release of its Articles of Agreement in June 2015, 57 countries had signed, including several non-Asian states such as the United Kingdom, Germany, and Brazil as well. The United States and Japan have, to date, declined to join. Chinese officials maintain that the AIIB intends to complement rather than compete with or upend the existing multilateral institutions providing development financing in the region — principally the World Bank and ADB. These existing institutions offer loans for a broad spectrum of purposes, including infrastructure construction and projects targeting health, education, and the environment. In contrast, the AIIB is focusing on building infrastructure that enhances connectivity between economies.

With a contribution of one-third of the initial capital (33.4%), China's voting weight is 28.5%. Like the World Bank, the AIIB is not funding its lending program directly from member states' cash contributions, but from capital raised on international financial markets backed by the collateral of member contributions (Mathew and Skidmore, 2019).

Therefore, the AIIB must earn a greater return from its loans than it initially pays to borrow the funds.

No existing multilateral development bank has had a borrower default on its loan. If an AIIB project were to fail, in addition to making a loss, the institution's borrowing costs would rise. Accordingly, the AIIB is adopting a cautious approach in its early lending to focus on securing an AAA credit rating for its bonds. AIIB partnered with the ADB, World Bank, and European Bank of Reconstruction and Development for the first four projects announced in 2016. With such a policy, AIIB would be able to build up a portfolio of low-risk projects more quickly and build a positive reputation in financial markets.

By 2020, there were 87 approved projects, 43 proposed projects, and project preparation special fund approvals by AIIB. Figure 2.1 shows a summary of all approved projects. According to AIIB data, the approved financing amount was US$19.60 billion.

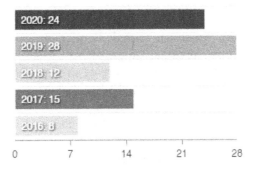

Figure 2.1: Projects approved by AIIB (2016–2020).

Source: AIIB home page, https://www.aiib.org/en/projects/summary/index.html, accessed on July 24, 2020.

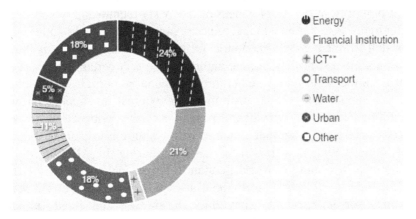

Figure 2.2: AIIB: Types of approved project investments.

Source: AIIB home page ** Information and communications technology.

There are seven main types of project investments funded by AIIB. Figure 2.2 provides details: Energy (24%), Financial institutions (21%), Transport (18%), Water, Urban development, and Others, respectively. It is well known that hydro and wind energy investments give higher returns. The International Renewable Energy Agency's (IRENA) new 2020 Global Renewables Outlook confirms that clean energy yields an economic return 3 to 8 times higher than the initial investment.[14]

---

[14] Jennifer Layke and Norma Hutchinson, https://www.renewableenergyworld.com/2020/05/06/3-reasons-to-invest-in-renewable-energy-now/#gref, accessed on December 27, 2020.

2.7.2 *Regional Comprehensive Economic Partnership (RCEP)*

The Regional Comprehensive Economic Partnership (RCEP), comprising ASEAN plus six other regional states: China, Japan, Korea, Australia, New Zealand, and India, endeavors to create a free-trade zone comprising almost half the world's population and 30% of global trade by value, with a year-end target for a broad consensus on the deal. The negotiations for the 15 country RCEP commenced in 2013, and were finally signed in November 2020.

The fact that Trump walked out of the Trans-Pacific Partnership (TPP) in 2017, five years after having started negotiations, created a new urgency for China to see RCEP through. The geostrategic logic is the one that looms large (Marwah, 2018).

Particularly in the international trade realm, China has benefitted handsomely from the development of the WTO regime and would likely suffer major losses from a global return to protectionism or any other policies that harmed global economic growth. Accordingly, it may be in Beijing's interest to play a more significant role in certain underwriting aspects of the status quo, whether through enhanced participation, authority, and support of existing institutions or external innovation via new institutions consistent with liberal principles. Early evidence of this has already emerged in the trade domain, with Chinese President Xi Jinping positioning China as a free-trade champion during the APEC forum in November 2016 and the World Economic Forum in January 2017 (Kim, 2020). Indeed, while it's more about a trade deal for China as it seeks conduits for its goods to flow through its Belt and Road Initiated Infrastructure, critics say that China has been the key driver for furthering this pact in response to the "fast track" status that was given to the TPP by Barack Obama. When the Obama administration proposed the TPP, the logic was again based on gaining strategic influence in global matters: Evidently, "If the United States did not write the rules on trade, China would". In particular, Beijing hopes to oversee the successful completion of the China-led RCEP.

China's hopes were belied in November 2019, in Bangkok, Thailand, when India announced its decision to withdraw from the China-led grouping. India made this announcement during the 3rd Regional Comprehensive Economic Partnership Summit, which brought together the 16 participating countries' leaders to review developments in the negotiations. Fifteen participating countries concluded text-based negotiations. The other participating countries also reaffirmed their commitment to continue working with India on these issues.[15] Despite the pandemic, China scored a significant victory when 15 countries signed the RCEP in November 2020. India stayed out of the grouping.

2.8 Conclusion — "Quantity has a Quality of its Own"[16]

Many policymakers and scholars believe that President Xi's foreign policy has been more proactive and dynamic than his predecessors'. Under his leadership, China embarked on the ambitious One Belt, One Road Initiative (OBORI) and launched such proactive diplomatic concepts as a "New Type of Great Power Relations". AidData shows that China's ODI reached US$27 billion in 2002 and skyrocketed more than 20-fold in 2009, reaching US$565 billion. It reached US$1.961 trillion in 2016, followed only by the US.

The short- and long-run consequences of China's infrastructure financing activities — including the US$1 trillion Belt and Road Initiative — are sources of growing speculation and debate (e.g. Perlez and Huang, 2017). Several Western politicians and public intellectuals claim that China prioritizes quantity and speed over quality and often funds "white elephant" projects. However, many developing countries have huge infrastructure financing needs. These countries' leaders are quick to point out that China is willing and able to finance roads, bridges, railways, and ports when Western donors and lenders are not (Dollar, 2018).

For Xi, the BRI serves as pushback against the US "pivot to Asia", as well as a way for China to harness new investment opportunities, develop export markets, and boost incomes and domestic consumption within the country. "Under Xi, China now actively seeks to shape international norms and institutions and forcefully asserts its presence on the global

---

[15] https://unctad.org/en/PublicationsLibrary/diaepcbinf2020d4.pdf, accessed on July 29, 2020.

[16] "Quantity has a quality all its own" source? http://h-net.msu.edu/cgi-bin/logbrowse.pl?trx=vx&list=h-russia&month=1004&week=a&msg=ljEwsM4dMrpmUGVfl7EGqg, Tim Davenport, h-russia https://nctworks.h-net.org/h-russia, April 5, 2010. *Source*: https://quotepark.com/quotes/699033-joseph-stalin-quantity-has-a-quality-all-its-own/, accessed on July 25, 2020.

stage", writes Elizabeth C. Economy (2019). At the same time, China desires to boost global economic links to its western regions. Promoting economic development in the western province of Xinjiang, as well as securing long-term energy supplies from Central Asia and the Middle East, are critical for China.

COVID-19 has tested the regime of Xi Jinping in more than one way, though the responses have left the international community quite shocked. While the world battles the pandemic, China finds time not only to help the domestic industry but also stretch its resources on potential battlegrounds from the Himalayas in South Asia to the South China Sea as well as unleash its wolf-warrior diplomats across the continents, from Asia to Australia, USA, and Europe. Its public health outreach has also not been nixed; in fact, its partner countries of the BRI have been helped with vaccines, masks, PPE kits, as well as equipment including ventilators, etc. A few analysts speculate that the COVID-19 pandemic will inevitably, seriously slowdown the BRI.

The current crisis has also exposed shortcomings in South Asia's public healthcare capacities. According to the World Development Indicators, South Asian countries perform poorly in most essential healthcare parameters. Pakistan only has 0.1 health workers, 0.6 nurses, and one physician per 1,000 citizens, while Bangladesh spends only 2.3% of its GDP on healthcare. These deficiencies imply that when these countries talk about infrastructure next, they will mean hospitals and laboratories along with ports and highways. As they seek to fill crucial gaps in their weak healthcare systems, the Health Silk Road will become a significant component of the BRI in South Asia and globally, at least in the immediate aftermath of the pandemic. According to Henry Tillman, the Health Silk Road has brought in its fold almost 120 countries by the end of 2020.[17]

China hopes that HSR will allow it to find newer markets. BRI partner countries will be willing recipients for China's healthcare systems and technology. The country's National Health Commission has a detailed plan for the HSR since 2017. This includes offers of infrastructure development, capacity building, and identification, prevention, and control of diseases. Beijing can also share research in biomedical technology or synthetic biology and collaborate on telemedicine. These will require

---

[17]Henry Tillman, in response to R. Marwah, one of the authors of this book, during his lecture at the Association of Asia Scholars webinar on December 9, 2020.

real-time communication, which ensures opportunities for Chinese companies offering 5G services.

South Asian countries will also need to adapt to China's new "wolf-warrior" diplomacy, which comes as inflexible political and economic strings attached to aid.[18]

Hornby and Zhang (2019) write about how nations, like Malaysia, have pushed back China-led investments, resulting in the East Coast Railway Link project's renegotiation with Malaysia. Suspicions in the region are further fueled by China's assertive actions in the South China Sea, based on a 1947 map of disputed relevance and validity, wherein it asserts dominion over this strategic body of water through which roughly 20% of sea-borne commerce passes. Thus, the BRI can be best understood as an unprecedented commercial opportunity and a strategic platform designed to reshuffle the geopolitical deck. It is, therefore, a "dual-purpose" initiative (Dezenski, 2020).

China's nosediving relations with neighboring countries and more so with the United States has led the world to believe that another Cold War is unfolding; only the War has several ramifications on multiple fronts — from trade and technology to military alliances and disintegrating world order. While it would not be fair to lay all the blame on China (the USA also has to bear its share), their greatest folly has been to suppress the voices of the troubleshooters who warned the Chinese government of the outbreak of the pandemic in early December 2019. While the Chinese economy has partially revived in Q3 and Q4 of 2020, the rest of the world continues to face the worse downturns and recessions since the past 100 years, with rampant joblessness, shutting down of businesses, and ravaged societies.

In these attenuating circumstances, can China continue to hold political and economic sway over the BRI countries? We will address this question and more in the next chapters.

---

[18] https://theprint.in/opinion/health-silk-road-how-china-plans-to-make-bri-essential-in-covid-hit-south-Asia/439603/, accessed on July 23, 2020.

Chapter 3

China in South Asia: History Informs but Geography Governs

China's phenomenal rise has been the subject of global attention for over 40 years, ever since the country commenced reforms and opening-up in 1979. Undoubtedly, as Basu stated, "China's success is the outcome of an intelligent and hugely powerful government" (Basu, 2013, p. 29).

3.1 Introduction

This chapter provides a panoramic glimpse of China's presence in the region of South Asia. With China's rise, its influence globally has increased consistently, not only through its economic outreach and prowess but also through a rising consciousness of China watching. According to Shi *et al.* (2019, p. xii), "China represents a real threat and a real opportunity, a component of the self and a constituent of alterity, and a bygone nostalgia and an inspiring future simultaneously". It is China's geographical proximity to South Asia that makes an understanding of China particularly relevant. Hence, this chapter seeks to contextualize China's linkages with this region, and given that each country has a differentiated understanding, engagement, and vision of China, there must be an attempt to present the bilateral as well. As China's economic footprint imbues it with political influence, it is also important to underline that, as Jacques (2009) stated, "China's rise has been seen in almost exclusively economic terms, failing to grasp the full meaning of China's rise. Its political and cultural impact will be at least as great".

Given the concurrence between economic weight and geopolitical influence, it merits questioning why China and India remained self-centric till the 1980s. As has been explained by Marwah (2020, p. 25), Asia's grand failure was a result of the complacency of the East, its tendency to look within, its devotion to past ideals and methods, respect for those in authority, and being suspicious of new ideas. Asia lacked the excitement of Europe. Both China and India were self-satisfied, the former believing that they had nothing to learn from outsiders, whom they considered barbarians.

Regions, as is well known, are fundamental to the structure of world politics and may even provide solutions to some global dilemmas (Katzenstein, 2002). Hence, a discussion on the role of history and geography in deciphering China's interest and engagement becomes pertinent.

To further explain China's engagement with this sub-region of Asia, this chapter has two main sections; the first provides South Asia's idea and importance for China. The second provides a profile of the countries, and the third comprises a brief outline of China's outreach to each of the countries.

3.2 The Idea of South Asia

The region of South Asia warrants special attention in this context, considering the region's colonial origin. There are mainly two views on how the region of South Asia came into being. One group of scholars argues that the common colonial history binds South Asian nations together and provides them with regional bonding. On the other hand, scholars have argued that this subcontinent was largely known as British India, which leads to an "imperial" imagination of South Asia (Yasmin, 2019, p. 324). When the British finally left in 1947, it was evident that the Indian subcontinent would become a theater of the Cold War. Once India and Pakistan gained independence, the state of Kashmir became riveted on both sides staking claims. The contentious issue of the India–Pakistan border continues till the present, due to which limited wars and subversive activities continue.

After India's independence from the British in 1947 and with the beginning of the Cold War post-World War II, the USA's interest in South Asia grew. Ali (2019) notes that US policy toward South Asia during the 1950s was based on the perception that China and the Soviet Union posed a united Communist threat to American influence in the region. Hence, although India preferred to remain Non-Aligned, the USA was keen to develop partnerships with both India and Pakistan to prevent the spread of

Communism. Moreover, the China–India border issue hinged on the McMahon Line, which was rejected by the Chinese due to the issue of Tibet. South Asia has been one of the most critical regions for China's international relations and foreign policy. The fleeing of His Holiness Dalai lama in 1959, with thousands of followers, and the boundary issue, resulted in the 1962 Sino-India war. The war resulted in a breakdown of the Panchsheel Agreement, post which bilateral relations nosedived for over two decades. In the 1980s, Sino-Indian relations received a fillip with the visit of Rajiv Gandhi in 1988, after which engagement between the two countries increased. At this time, the South Asian Association for Regional Cooperation (SAARC) was launched in 1985. SAARC was viewed as an India-centric regional grouping comprising the eight countries of Afghanistan (included in 2007), Bangladesh, Bhutan, India, the Maldives, Nepal, Pakistan, and Sri Lanka (Ahmed, 2012, p. 286).

At this stage, it is important to understand the raison d'etre for China to engage countries in South Asia. While for China, with its accumulated surpluses, its deep pockets have replaced Maoism as the tool for gaining global influence, there is no other country where this strategic tool has been better deployed, uniquely as it engineered to keep India, a rising neighbor, in check. A prime factor has been the India-led SAARC grouping's slow progress, held hostage by the difficult India–Pakistan relations. Despite efforts for expanding cultural, economic, and strategic partnerships, through 18 summit meetings, the grouping continued to experience weaknesses. Among these, the constant fear of Indian domination by other member countries, severe institutional weaknesses, poor alignment of the SAARC issues with national priorities, absence of monitoring and evaluation, and deficiency in acceptable and visionary regional leadership have added to its laggardness. Activities were initiated as summit rituals (Lama, 2017). In South Asia, the China–Pakistan axis and its growing interface with all countries in India's neighborhood have meant India's distrust of China continues. This is even though China's economic relations with India have been growing (Deshpande, 2010). The idea driving the twenty-first century relations is not the traditional view of politics in a zero-sum game but "connectivity" that Khanna (2016, p. 6) develops his framework in Connectography, bringing out the compulsions of competitive geographical connectivity.

This is also underlined by Tangredi *et al.* (2019), "Zheng He's fleet was actually an armada, in the sense that it carried a powerful Army that could be disembarked, and its purpose was to awe the rulers of Southeast Asia and the Indian Ocean into sending tribute to China".

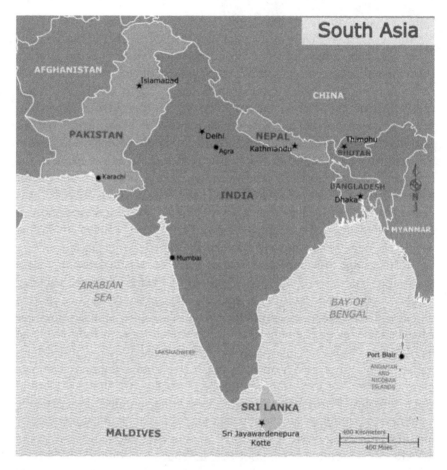

Figure 3.1:   China and South Asia.

Source: Wikimedia Commons, accessed on April 13, 2021.

3.2.1 *China's forays into South Asia: Increasing influence, expanding ambitions*

While it is evident that China's strong position can be attributed to the radical changes in China since 1978, especially the reforms initiated by Deng Xiaoping, there are other aspects of its strategy which must be highlighted (Desai, 2005). The strategic motive for expanding China's economic engagement is critically linked to checking India's rise by exploiting the India–Pakistan rivalry, enhancing access to the Indian Ocean, and countering terrorism and religious extremism (Bartholomew *et al.*, 2019). With these strategic calculations emboldened with its economic capabilities, as explained in Chapter two, China has sought to diminish the influence of the United States in this region while at the same time keeping India engaged in its anti-terrorist operations with Pakistan. Consequently, SAARC has not made much headway in regional integration, and thus remains globally one of the least integrated regions. Through China's "string of pearls" strategy, the encirclement of India is not without reason. In South Asia, these comprise Chinese investment in port facilities in strategic locations in the Indian Ocean (including Chittagong in Bangladesh, Gwadar in Pakistan, Colombo and Hambantota in Sri Lanka, Marao in the Maldives). These are inevitably for surreptitious strategic leverage. Over the last few years, India's concerns have grown, even as its traditional sphere of influence has been compromised.

As China grew economically, its interests grew, too. Given its historical gaze and interest in South Asia, and its special "all-weather partnership" with Pakistan, especially since the 1980s, China has continued to expand its influence.

According to Wagner (2016), China's forays into South Asia have been based on its increasing power and stature. To justify China's smooth entry into the region, it is important to underline here that, firstly, the baggage of history does not weigh heavily. Second, China, with its deep pockets has a higher economic attraction for most these countries. China's core interests center around Tibet and Xinjiang. However, under its "OBOR" initiative, the maritime space, and continental South Asia gain strategic importance (Wagner, 2016, p. 310).

China shares a border with four South Asian nations — India, Pakistan, Nepal, and Bhutan. The last two are landlocked countries of the region, making them highly dependent on India for sea access. Bangladesh, Sri Lanka, Maldives, and Pakistan are important for China's maneuvering in the Indian Ocean, the Bay of Bengal, and the Arabian Sea. Hence, China has consistently pursued these countries, with overtures of checkbook diplomacy, scholarships for students, infrastructure development, and more. Despite India's consistent opposition to China's BRI, especially the China–Pakistan Economic Corridor, which passes through Pakistan Occupied Kashmir (Disputed territory, according to India), China's connectivity projects gain momentum.

Inexorably, New Delhi has been watchful of China's relentless courting of India's maritime neighbors, i.e. Sri Lanka and Maldives through the building of infrastructure, including ports, airports, and other infrastructure.

3.3 Subregional Cooperation in South Asia

While SAARC, the India-led grouping, has had its limitations, China did not lose much time in presenting its own "neighborhood-first" policy, comprising an outreach for filling in infrastructure gaps. Given that most of these countries, viz. Nepal, Pakistan, and Afghanistan have low levels of development, the engagement by China at all levels has been appreciated and welcomed. China has acted swiftly from the provision of railways to waterways, gas pipelines, and electricity connections. This has been in contrast to India's slower response, especially in terms of implementation of projects. Given the issues in reinvigorating SAARC, India hoped to create regional groupings minus Pakistan. India initiated the Bangladesh, Bhutan, India, Nepal (BBIN) initiative in 2015, essentially to smoothen the flow of goods through a Motor Vehicles Agreement and the Bay of Bengal Initiative for Multi-Sectoral Technical and Economic Cooperation (BIMSTEC in 1997). The urgency of promoting BIMSTEC and BBIN is the compelling strategic test for India posed by China's muscular geo-economic and geopolitical interventions in South Asia.

3.3.1 *China-led BCIM*

The Bangladesh, China, India, Myanmar (BCIM) Forum for the Regional Cooperation project, which was initially known as the "Kunming Initiative", was founded in 1999, with its Secretariat in Kunming, China. The objective of the four countries, was to initiate a Track II dialogue for the creation of a subregional "cooperation zone" linking the relatively backward regions stretching from landlocked areas of Southwest China to Eastern India, along with the adjoining least developed countries (LDCs). BCIM had been initiated to assume that the project would be activated at the intergovernmental level, known as Track I, to promote trade and connectivity from Kunming to Kolkata. Bangladesh and Myanmar proposed several initiatives for enhancing regional cooperation, connecting the Western Region of China with Myanmar and Bangladesh. However, major issues were still under constant debate, such as the Indian Government's disinclination to get engaged in multilateral, regional forums with China, considering the long-standing sensitivity of India's insurgency-prone northeast region. In 2013, a car rally from Kunming (China) to Kolkata (India) known as the K2K rally was organized to ensure the corridor's road transportability of almost 2800 km that would connect the four countries resulting in an economic corridor. Hence, the BCIM-EC was expected to develop overland transport linkages and manufacturing zones between India and southern China, running through Bangladesh and Myanmar (Karim and Islam, 2018). While China was quick to build the roads leading to the border areas and even organized various academic exchanges and initiatives for their successful implementation, India has been cautious, especially after China's BRI corridor with Pakistan. India, which is not a signatory to the BRI, believes that BCIM predates the concept of BRI and, therefore, cannot be included in BRI. At a BCIM Meeting in mid-2019, all four countries agreed that it was necessary to widen the partnership to build this corridor. India also viewed this corridor as bringing business opportunities for its Northeast region. However, given the altered circumstances between India and China post-June 2020, a result of the tensions in the border areas and the unprecedented impact of the pandemic, India–China subregional cooperation has been stalled.

At this stage, it is important to understand the levels of development and vulnerability of most countries in South Asia, through their GDP, per capita incomes, debt, trade, global indices to measure fragility, corruption, and competitiveness.

3.4 South Asia: Contrasting Economic Indicators

The region of South Asia presents country experiences of varied hues and lessons. These present themselves in terms of post-colonial struggles for developing much-needed infrastructure with limited financial capabilities. Hence, despite the geographical proximity, India, the largest neighbor, has been found wanting in the development of roads, railways, and ports. This lacuna China identified and leveraged. Moreover, countries in the region have seen frail polities, weak governments, low human development levels, and amenability to manipulation by international donors and multilateral institutions.

Additionally, South Asian countries have rising populations, which exert a strain on available resources. Bangladesh has a high population density, with an average of 950 persons per square kilometer. Most countries struggle with high levels of debt, low levels of human development, and low per capita incomes. See Table 3.1. Compared to Sri Lanka, other South Asian countries are lagging in the Human Development

Table 3.1:   South Asian Countries: GDP, debt, HDI in 2019.

Countries	Population	Annual GDP USD (Million)	GDP per capita USD	HDI	Debt	Government Debt (% GDP)
Afghanistan	37,172,386	19,630	528	0.498	1,353	6.89
Bangladesh	161,356,039	288,424	1,788	0.608	91,524	33.99
Bhutan	754,394	2,582	3,423	0.612	2,642	102.38
India	1,352,617,328	2,718,732	2,010	0.640	1,849,402	68.05
Maldives	515,696	5,328	10,332	0.717	3,623	68.03
Nepal	28,087,871	29,040	1,034	0.574	8,766	30.20
Pakistan	200,960,000	314,588	1,565	0.562	225,435	71.69
Sri Lanka	21,670,000	88,901	4,102	0.770	74,008	83.28
Total SAARC	1,803,133,714	3,467,225	1,923	—	2,256,755	63.94

Source: Country Reports, https://countryeconomy.com/countries/groups/south-asian-association-regional-cooperation, accessed on August 4, 2020.

index. Sri Lanka's expected years of schooling is 14 years, employment to population ratio (15 years and older) is 50.2%, per-capita Carbon dioxide emissions is 1.0 tonnes, and 34.1% of the country's population uses the Internet. India has a ranking of 129, Bhutan is at 134, Bangladesh at 135, Nepal at 147, Pakistan at 152, Myanmar at 145, and Afghanistan at 170 in the latest HDI report.[1]

It is also important to assess countries' economic situation in South Asia concerning their trade volumes and other indicators. Table 3.2 shows that the trade imbalances in absolute terms and in terms of percent of GDP are serious in Afghanistan, Maldives, Nepal, and Pakistan. It is interesting to note that Nepal's export earnings are less than 10% of its import expenditure; for Afghanistan, this is about 15%, while for Pakistan, this is about 50%. Moreover, the 2019 Global Competitiveness Index (GCI) 4.0 indicates that most South Asian countries are ranked among the lower half of the world except for India, which held the 68th position out of

---

[1] Sri Lanka improves ranking in human development index 2019, https://www.onlanka.com/news/sri-lanka-improves-ranking-in-human-development-index-2019.html#, accessed on August 7, 2020.

Table 3.2:   South Asia: Economic indicators (2019).

Countries	Global Competitiveness Index 2019	Doing Business Index 2018	Exports USD Mn 2019	Imports USD Mn 2019	Trade Balance (% GDP)
Afghanistan	n.a	167	1050.0	7310.0	−33.23
Bangladesh	105	176	37,943.2	60144.0	−7.37
Bhutan	n.a	81	590.0	960.0	−17.12
India	68	77	324,162.8	483,863.9	−6.82
Maldives	n.a	139	350.0	2900.0	−49.19
Nepal	108	110	900.0	12,140	−41.07
Pakistan	110	136	23,352.0	50,463.0	−11.65
Sri Lanka	84	100	11,973.2	19846.1	−11.63

Source: Data compiled by the Authors from www.countryeconomy.com.

141 countries (these 141 countries account for 99% of the world's GDP).[2] This justifies India having low incentive for trade and investment in South Asia.

In South Asia, India, in the 68th position, loses ground in the rankings despite a relatively stable score, mostly due to faster improvements of several countries previously ranked lower. It is followed by Sri Lanka (the most improved country in the region at 84th), Bangladesh (105th), Nepal (108th), and Pakistan (110th).[3]

The Ease of Doing Business Index 2018 also points to the difficulty of doing business with most South Asian countries. India has consistently sought to improve its rankings, providing much impetus to Chinese investment in the Indian industry, financial services, and unicorns.

While the USA, Russia, and China occupy the first, second, and third place in the most powerful countries rankings of the US. News and World Report, five out of eight countries in South Asia do not even find a place

---

[2]The GCI 4.0 is the product of an aggregation of 103 individual indicators, derived from a combination of data from international organizations and the World Economic Forum's Executive Opinion Survey. Indicators are organized into 12 "pillars": Institutions; Infrastructure; ICT adoption; Macroeconomic stability; Health; Skills; Product market; Labour market; Financial system; Market size; Business dynamism; and Innovation capability.

[3]http://www3.weforum.org/docs/WEF_TheGlobalCompetitivenessReport2019.pdf.

Table 3.3:   Political situation: Some key indicators.

Countries	Fragile State Rank 2018 1=Most fragile)	Democracy Index-Score/10	Rank/	EI. Process & Pluralism/10	Civil Liberties/10	Corruption Index 2018 (100=very clean) (0=highly corrupt)* (180 countries)	CPI* Rank/ 180 countries 2019 Rank1= least corrupt
Afghanistan	9	2.85	141	3.42	3.82	16	173/180
Bangladesh	32	5.88	80	7.83	5.00	26	146
Bhutan	81	5.30	91	8.75	3.82	68	25
India	72	6.90	51	8.67	6.76	41	80
Maldives	89	—	—	—	—	31	130
Nepal	39	5.28	92	4.83	5.59	31	113
Pakistan	20	4.25	108	6.08	4.71	33	120
Sri Lanka	50	6.27	69	7.00	6.47	38	93

Note: *The Corruption Perception Index (CPI) scores and ranks countries/territories based on how corrupt experts and business executives perceive a country's public sector to be. It is a composite index, of 13 surveys and corruption assessments, collected by various reputable institutions. The perceived levels of public sector corruption in 180 countries/territories around the world are studied. (100 is very clean, and 0 is highly corrupt). https://images. transparencycdn.org/images/2019_CPI_Report_EN_200331_141425.pdf.

Source: http://www.eiu.com/public/thankyou_download.aspx?activity=download&campaignid=democracyindex2019.

among the 80 countries included in the study.[4] Three countries whose rankings figure among the 80 countries include: India–17, Pakistan–22, and Sri Lanka–60.[5] Table 3.3 provides a glimpse of the political situation in South Asian countries.

According to the Economist Intelligence Unit 2019 report on Democracy, India and Sri Lanka are flawed democracies, Bangladesh, Bhutan, Nepal, and Pakistan are hybrid regimes, whereas Afghanistan is authoritarian.

The Fragility States Index studied 178 nations based on cohesion, economic, political, and social factors to identify the most vulnerable countries globally. States with the highest scores were identified as the most fragile. Afghanistan is one of the most fragile countries politically, while Bangladesh and Pakistan also have low rankings.

3.5 China's Bilateral Connections in South Asia

China prefers to deal with countries bilaterally, especially with authoritarian regimes or single-party polities. China's democracy score dropped from 3.32 to 2.26 from 2018 to 2019; a result of its increasing surveillance activities and restrictions on freedom of speech. The evidence of this is also palpable in its neighborhood, especially in Tibet and among Tibetans in South Asian countries. A brief discussion of each country's bilateral relations with South Asian countries and their geopolitical and geostrategic importance for China is discussed here.

3.5.1 *Afghanistan*

Historically, China has considered Afghanistan as a neighbor of less strategic significance. The inception of the provisional government, led by President Hamid Karzai in 2001, developed bilateral ties between the two countries. Since then, China has considered undertaking commercial opportunities in resource-rich Afghanistan. It had no interest in being

---

[4] The report surveyed over 20,000 people from four regions around the world. Respondents were asked to associate 80 countries with five attributes: Military alliances, international alliances, political influence, economic influence, and leadership. China was 3rd after the USA and Russia in 2019.

[5] https://worldpopulationreview.com/country-rankings/most-powerful-countries.

involved in the country's politics, even though it did provide some assistance to the United States, Pakistan, and Saudi Arabia in the 1980s in arming the Afghan Mujahideen to wage jihad against the Soviets. It did not, however, get involved in the war against terror post-2001.[6]

Given that China's restive Xinjiang shares a 47 miles border with Afghanistan, China's fundamental interest in Afghanistan is stability in its western region. Islamic fundamentalism is entirely intolerable to China, which it perceives as a threat to its domestic security, particularly in Xinjiang. Hence, while the United States was engaged in wars in Afghanistan and Iraq, China focused on building its strength. Although China did portray commercial interests in a copper mine in 2008 and oil exploration in the Amu Darya in 2011, its total investments in Afghanistan have been around US$2.5 million, minuscule compared to its investment in neighboring Pakistan.

On June 8, 2012, China and Afghanistan signed a strategic partnership agreement highlighting the mutual economic benefits that could accrue to them and their shared security interests (Wishnick, 2012). Given the high costs for the United States in maintaining peace in Afghanistan, the Trump administration has reduced American troops' presence. This might result in Beijing enhancing its military and economic assistance and development aid to the country. However, according to Siegfried Wolf, "China will not put boots on the ground".[7] Nevertheless, whether the US will completely withdraw from its engagement of almost 20 years is yet to be fully witnessed.[8] Evidently, Beijing will be measured in its engagement with this strife-torn country.

3.5.2 *Bangladesh*

Bangladesh's (formerly known as East Pakistan) independence in 1971 and state formation was with India's cooperation. The two countries share close linguistic, cultural, and historical ties, with significant economic cooperation levels. Moreover, Bangladesh is critical for India's

---

[6] http://diplomatist.com/2020/04/17/chinese-interests-in-afghanistan-from-indifference-to-strategic-involvement/, accessed on July 12, 2020.
[7] Siegfried Wolf, in response to a question by the author, Reena Marwah, in his lecture at the Association of Asia Scholars webinar on August 5, 2020.
[8] https://warontherocks.com/2020/04/chinas-strategic-assessment-of-afghanistan/ China's Strategic Assessment of Afghanistan, Yun Sun, April 8, 2020, accessed on July 12, 2020.

connectivity with its states in its Northeast and India's Act East policy also hinges on Bangladesh's key Bay of Bengal location.

China's economic relations with Bangladesh have been strengthened, especially in the Xi Jinping period. China has been consistently increasing its share in Bangladesh's total exports in several commodities, including textile and textiles articles, machinery, chemical products, and transportation equipment industries. Contrarily, India is losing market shares. Apart from economic reasons, the negative impacts of non-tariff barriers are mainly responsible for slowing trade with India (Sahoo, 2013). China's outreach initiatives are helping to bridge the gap in the understanding of China in Bangladesh through educational and cultural exchanges, organizing visits of media and political parties' delegations, establishing Chinese language institutes, organizing interactions among the trade bodies, think tanks, and many other activities (Yasmin, 2019).

During the interview, Ambassador Harun ur Rashid shared, "There was a 180-degree turn in Bangladesh's foreign policy after August 1975. The country became friendly with China, US, and other Islamic countries" (Marwah and Singh, 2013). Ehsanul Haque also underlined, "Bilateral relations between Bangladesh and China are driven mainly by trade and investment linkages. China is also a major development assistance partner for Bangladesh" (Soni, 2016).

A member of the BRI since 2016, Bangladesh has received vast amounts of funding from China for infrastructure projects. The two countries signed 27 agreements for investments and loans worth around US$24 billion during Chinese President Xi Jinping's 2016 visit to Dhaka. With the US$13.6 billion invested in joint ventures earlier, Chinese investment in Bangladesh is worth over US$42 billion, making Bangladesh the second-largest recipient (after Pakistan) of Chinese loans under BRI in South Asia. Bangladesh has allocated two special economic zones for Chinese investors in Chittagong around a major port, and near Dhaka. India has also been uneasy as it witnesses China's rising investments in Bangladesh's port infrastructure along the Bay of Bengal. China helped upgrade Chittagong port and had been pursuing a port project at Sonadia Island. In February 2016, however, Bangladesh decided to shelve the Sonadia project and opted to develop another deep seaport with Indian investment. Given the Sheikh Hasina's Government's favorable relations with India, Bangladesh also permitted Indian cargo ships to access Chittagong Port. China continues to woo Bangladesh for expansion in economic ties, even as voices of debt trap concerns are being voiced occasionally.

The sister-city arrangement allows China to penetrate deep inside Bangladesh's society locally. Bangladeshi Prime Minister Sheikh Hasina's July 2019 visit to China saw the two countries sign nine instruments — these included five agreements, three memorandums of understanding (MoUs), and a document — covering a range of sectors, including power, investment, culture, tourism, and technology. China has also agreed to provide Bangladesh with 2,500 metric tons of rice as aid for Rohingya refugees. Two agreements related to China's extension of loans worth US$1.7 billion for Bangladesh's power sector have also been signed.

China is also Bangladesh's largest trade partner, and trade is growing rapidly. Two-way trade, which was worth US$12 billion in 2014, is expected to exceed US$30 billion by 2021. While trade is booming, there is a strong imbalance in favor of China.[9] Despite a huge trade imbalance with China, the issue is hardly highlighted and recognized as a problem in bilateral relations. Given that Bangladesh is a major exporter of ready-made garments and textiles, it seeks to build port capacity. But like other countries in the region, Bangladesh needs major investments in ports. No new ports have been developed since the country gained independence in 1971.[10]

Given China's strategic engagement with all countries in South Asia, it is evident that Bangladesh is a recipient of Chinese aid and investment. The major projects are (i) 6.5-kilometer road/rail bridge over the massive Padma river, (ii) An industrial park in Chittagong, (iii) the Payra port in which Chinese companies were granted the majority of contracts to develop a new deep-sea port at Payra, which will include an LNG terminal, an oil refinery, a coal terminal to service a power plant, and a container terminal, and (iv) A Karnaphuli River tunnel project has also been initiated.

3.5.2.1 *Issues in BRI projects*

Several concerns are emanating from Chinese investments in Bangladesh. While it is well known that a project, viz. a US$1.2 billion credit for the Padma Multipurpose Bridge project, was canceled by the World Bank, citing high-level corruption, China readily agreed to fund it.

---

[9] https://asiatimes.com/2019/07/chinese-investment-in-bangladesh-has-sometimes-violent-implications/, accessed on July 12, 2020.

[10] https://www.lowyinstitute.org/the-interpreter/bangladesh-road-bri, accessed on July 14, 2020

Specific issues that have arisen are:

a. **Chinese debt:** Bangladesh is aware of the hazards of being caught in the web of Chinese debt. The country understands that it has a limited capacity to absorb and service the debt, even though, as shown in Table 3.1, this is about 34% of its total debt. Bangladesh's total external debt (owed to all lenders) is around US$33 billion, placing it in a low-risk category.

b. **Clash of workers:** Bangladeshi and Chinese workers at the Payra power plant site clashed violently in June 2020, resulting in the death of a Chinese worker and injuries to dozens of others. As in other BRI member countries, Chinese personnel comprise a significant propor- tion of the labor on project sites in Bangladesh. Tensions among workers is often a cause for delays in project execution.

c. **The slow pace of funding:** Bangladesh is concerned over China's slow pace of reimbursement. China has disbursed just US$981.36 million, less than 5% of the funding promised since the preliminary agreements were signed in 2016. Concerning the US$689.35 million-Karnaphuli River tunnel project, only US$194.81 million was released by the Chinese by the end of 2019; the deal was signed in October 2016.

If Sri Lanka and Pakistan have become examples of how the BRI can drag countries into debt traps, Bangladesh provides lessons for how to do business with the Chinese. Bangladesh's Prime Minister Sheikh Hasina, in her visit to Beijing in mid-2019, stressed the need for funds for the committed projects. Beijing is also keen to see the progress of the project as envisaged. However, at least Bangladesh is aware of the nuances of over-dependence on China, both in its mounting trade deficit and debt. Whether and for how long Bangladesh can continue to avoid the BRI's downsides remains to be seen.[11]

3.5.3 *Bhutan*

A landlocked country, Bhutan shares a special relationship with India, through cultural linkages, peaceful historical relations, close cooperation in all fields as well as cordial people-to-people ties. In comparison, Bhutan and China have yet to establish official diplomatic ties. It was only after the

---

[11] Sudha Ramachandran https://thediplomat.com/2019/07/how-bangladesh-learned-to-love-the-belt-and-road/.

Chinese annexation of Tibet in 1951 that Bhutan and China became neighbors. The border issue (Bhutan–China share a border of 290 miles with two tri-points with India) results in unease and tensions. China's soft-power overtures toward Bhutan have been witnessed in the dispatch of circus artists, acrobats, and footballers to the tiny kingdom state of less than a million people. Beijing has also granted a limited but growing number of scholarships for Bhutanese students to study in China. According to Lintner, the virus crisis has provided China with an opportunity: create trouble for India along the border, make new offers of cultural exchanges — and perhaps even suggest establishing some kind of more formal diplomatic relations.[12]

Ms. Lily Wangchuk, Bhutan, to Prof. Swaran Singh, stated, "There was sympathy for Tibet in Bhutan because we had close trade and spiritual ties with them. This came to an end after the invasion by China" (Singh, 2016). Given Bhutan's close historical ties with India, the latter remains its most trusted partner. This was witnessed during the Doklam (China's boundary issue) crisis in 2017, which lasted for 73 days. India has a tremendous strategic interest in maintaining the status quo on Bhutan's border with China. However, given China's rise, the Bhutanese private sector and the youth are keen to woo Chinese investments and expand trade. Despite the lack of formal relations, China has emerged as the third-largest source of imports (Mishra, 2019). This is one country in which China will be viewed by its people with suspicion, especially after the 2017 and 2020 border incursions.

In 2020, China's increasing aggressiveness to change the India–China boundary status quo has brought within its ambit the Himalayan nations of Nepal and Bhutan. China has built a village two kilometers inside Bhutan's territory in mid-2020. In 2021, after 7 years, it has completed a strategic passageway to Medog county that borders India's Arunachal Pradesh. This is part of a wider infrastructure push in border areas of Tibet. These countries understand that they could become absorbed as little fingers in China's advancing palm.

3.5.4 *India*

"Political power grows out of the barrel of the gun…"

— Mao Tse-tung[13]

---

[12] https://asiatimes.com/2020/07/why-china-wants-a-himalayan-dispute-with-bhutan/. Bertil Lintner, *Asia Times*, July 13, 2020.
[13] https://www.goodreads.com/author/quotes/4797485.Mao_Zedong.

China and India share civilizational and cultural linkages over several centuries. Sino-Indian trading relations between the seventh and twentieth centuries transformed from Buddhist-dominated exchanges to market-centered commercial transactions, resulting in interactions among communities on both sides, development of urban settlements of migrants as well as a shared resistance to British imperialist designs and hostilities (Marwah, 2018, pp. 3–23).

However, the 1962 Sino-India war altered the discourse, and up to the present times, the 3488 km long undefined border across the Himalayas often results in skirmishes. The border dispute had resulted in an increasing number of incursions by the Chinese, the most recent being the escalation of June 15, 2020, when the Chinese troops killed 20 Indian soldiers. Despite several rounds of high-level talks, the stalemate at the border continued till the end of 2020. Post-June 2020, the Indian Government has taken several measures to reduce its economic dependence on China, with more than 200 apps being banned, as well as imposing restrictions on inward investment from China.

Given the large quantum of Chinese investment in Indian businesses and India's increasing trade dependency on China, experts question the viability of immediate decoupling from China. China accounted for over 5% of India's total exports in 2019–2020 and more than 14% of imports. India runs a huge trade deficit with China. Chinese exports to India comprise smartphones, electrical appliances, power plant inputs, fertilizers, auto components, finished steel products, capital goods like power plants, telecom equipment, metro rail coaches, iron and steel products, pharmaceutical ingredients, chemicals and plastics, and engineering goods, among other things, Over 14% of India's imports in FY19-20 were from China. According to Invest in India, India's imports from China jumped 45 times since 2000 to reach over US$70 billion in 2018–2019.

Foreign direct investments from China have been received in several sectors, including, among others, renewable energy (solar panels), electrical equipment, automotive, and chemicals. Data compiled by Bloomberg Quint from China Global Investment Tracker showed Chinese FDI into India at US$4.14 billion in 2019. China's commerce ministry, however, pegs the figure at US$8 billion for 2018–2019.

There are almost 75 manufacturing facilities for smartphones, consumer appliances, construction equipment, power gear, automobiles, optical fiber, and chemicals. Oppo, Vivo, Fosun International, Haier, SAIC, and Midea are some of India's largest Chinese brands and manufacturers. Chinese funds and companies often route their India investments through offices located in Singapore, Hong Kong, and Mauritius. For example, Alibaba Group's investment in Paytm came via Alibaba Singapore Holdings. Often these are not recorded as Chinese. As of March 2020, 18 of India's 30 unicorns are Chinese-funded. India's pharmaceutical industry is the third-largest in the world in volume and ranks 14 by value; however, it imports two-thirds of its active pharmaceutical ingredients, or critical ingredients of drugs, from China.[14] Despite intense economic engagement, India for several reasons, has refrained from joining the BRI.

Sino-India relations are marked by distrust, given China's assertiveness through its strategies of "string of pearls" and salami slicing of Indian territories. The relations have further nose-dived since the mid-2020 border standoff.

3.5.5 *Maldives*

Although it is believed that China's historical relations date back to the 7th century, it is records of the 15th century, during which the renowned Chinese explorer, Zheng He, visited the Maldives, that are more tenable. He visited the Maldives twice, the first time in 1412 and the second time in 1430.[15] China's increasing penchant for enhancing maritime capabilities has ensured that Maldives' geostrategic positioning makes it an essential partner for China's ambitions. The Maldives is a small country with less than 5,00,000 people spread over 26 atolls covering a substantial maritime area stretching 750 kilometers from north to south. Its atolls/islands ensure that it is within the purview of China's Belt and Road Initiative. China and the Maldives entered into diplomatic relations in 1972, and post-1984, the bilateral relations have been further cemented. China has also been engaging with the political parties and individual leaders to continue its sway over this country (Lintner, 2019, p. 170).

In its effort to strengthen its presence in the Maldives, China opened an embassy in 2013, as part of its larger BRI and Indian Ocean strategy. In July 2015, the Maldivian Government allowed foreigners who could invest more than US$1 billion to purchase land in the project site provided

---

[14]Read more at https://www.bloombergquint.com/economy-finance/six-things-to-know-about-india-china-economic-relations.

[15]http://maldivesembassy.cn/china-and-maldives-friendship-history/, accessed on July 12, 2020.

70% of the land was reclaimed from the sea. This was a tactical move move, especially undertaken, to accommodate China. In August 2017, three Chinese warships docked in the Maldives. In December 2017, the Maldives–China Free Trade Agreement was signed. A total of 70% of the country's debt is incurred through projects funded by China. China's plans in the Maldives include an US$800-million expansion of the country's main airport by a Chinese company, China–Maldives Friendship Bridge, US$224.2 million, 7,000 apartment housing project of Hulhumalé Phase II. According to Lintner, Maldives represents an essential pearl in the Indian Ocean, sought by China.

3.5.6 *Nepal and China: Handshake across the Himalayas*

Nepal and China relations have progressed gradually since the early visits of Chinese monks and scholars like Monk Fa Xian (Jin Dynasty) and Monk Xuan Zang (Tang Dynasty). The two countries established diplomatic relations on August 1, 1955. Both countries, as stated, have relentless faith in the ideals of the Five Principles of Peaceful Co-existence. Nepal is firmly committed to the One China policy and is also determined not to allow its soil to be used for any adverse activities, especially by Tibetans, against China.[16]

In 2008, after the ending of the monarchy's reign and the ascendance of the Maoists in power, there was a significant shift in China's foreign policy toward Nepal. What creates anxiety for China is the settlements of Tibetans in Nepal and their frequent protests. This aided China's interference in the internal affairs of Nepal. Given that Tibet (China) has a 1,236 km long border with Nepal, the Chinese are over-cautious. Moreover, protests by Tibetans in 2008 during the Beijing Olympics alerted the Chinese to the possibility of the China–Tibet border becoming a fertile ground for subversive activities.[17] Since 2001, Nepalese leaders have participated in the Boao Forum for Asia, deepening understanding among politicians, bureaucrats, and intellectuals (Lohani, 2014, pp. 256–268).[18]

---

[16] https://mofa.gov.np/nepal-china-relations/, accessed on July 12, 2020.

[17] https://idsa.in/idsastrategiccomments/NepalNewStrategicPartnerofChina_NNayak_300309, accessed on July 12, 2020.

[18] Inauguration Ceremony of BFA was held Feb. 26–27 2001 in Boao; this Boao Forum for Asia is a non-governmental forum committed to promoting regional economic integration.

Given that Nepal has become a close ally of China in its Belt and Road Initiative, formally since 2017, China has sought to engage Nepalese political actors at all levels, primarily to secure Nepal's border. When the Maoists came to power in 2008, China hoped to use its ideological commonalities to suppress Nepal's Tibetan movement. China has both strategic and economic interests in Nepal, in terms of energy from hydro projects and as a transit country between China and India.

According to Mr. Pandey, a former Nepalese diplomat, in an interview.

"There is a consistency in the way Chinese think and move ahead as an economic power. There has also been a consistency under the Chinese leadership of their policies toward Nepal. There is consistency from the time of Mao to President Hu Jintao. The visit of Wen Jiabao to Nepal in 2011 was possible only because of the Chinese's interest in Nepal and to tell the Nepalese people that we are still in their strategic radar. The Government was not able to conduct this visit properly. For the first time in Nepal's history, 4,470 persons, including the military, were used for the security of this visit. The Chinese Premier came only for four hours. Due to the political uncertainty, the Government had to be very careful and extra cautious during his visit. China has been firm with the Nepal Government in its dealing with Tibetan unrest. China is also making infrastructure projects in Nepal. Apartments in Nepal are being built with Chinese contractors. Bureaucrats prefer to get aid from China as there are no riders of the assistance. The Chinese built the international convention hall, which for four years was used by our constituent assembly. Moreover, they are helping to build hospitals and other infrastructure projects" (Pandey, 2012).[19]

3.5.6.1 *China's Major projects in Nepal*

US$130 million cement factory in Dhading, 164 MW Nepal Kali Gandaki Gorge
Hydropower Project, 40.27 MW Siuri Nyadi
Hydropower Plant, 600 MW Marsyangdi
Cascade Hydropower, 75 MW Trishuli
Galchhi Hydropower Project

---

[19]Interview on January 27, 2012 Interviewer: Dr. Reena Marwah Interview of Mr. Ramesh Nath Pandey, http://www.china-studies.taipei/act02.php.

In November 2014, Beijing and Kathmandu signed a new MOU committing 10 million RMB (US$1.63 million) annually from 2014 to 2018 for the development of Nepal's northern districts (Sharma, 2019). In March 2015, marking the 60th year of bilateral relations, Beijing committed a five-fold increase to its annual grant assistance to Kathmandu, with a pledge of 800 million RMB (US$130 million) earmarked mainly for infrastructure development.

When a 7.8 magnitude earthquake struck Nepal in April 2015, China responded with its largest-ever humanitarian effort to date. This helped to provide a positive spin to its geopolitical and financial relationships with Nepal. These development projects and concomitant processes of state-making are underwritten by Chinese gifts of development (Murton *et al.*, 2016; Yeh, 2013). Not only was Beijing's response to the 2015 earthquake unprecedented, but at the International Conference on Nepal's Reconstruction in June 2015, the Chinese Foreign Minister committed RMB 4.7 billion (US$480 million) for infrastructural repair and development across Nepal. In many ways, the fuel crisis, a result of the blockade of trucks from India, highlighted systemic vulnerabilities and brought forth concerns about energy insecurity, which resulted in Nepal seeking assistance from China. In May 2017, after Nepal signed onto the BRI, Nepalese officials sent Beijing a list of thirty-five potential BRI projects. However, China reduced these infrastructural demands to nine projects (Giri, 2019a). Foreign Ministers of Nepal and China officially signed a series of agreements on April 29, 2019, at the 2nd Belt and Road Forum (BRF), making Nepal a partner of BRI in South Asia. While land highways and transborder railroads were prioritized, the Agreement also establishes shipping possibilities that allow the landlocked nation of Nepal access to six Chinese ports, all of the so-called "Nepal–China trans-Himalayan Multi-Dimensional Connectivity Network". The *power* corridors are strategic for several reasons: First, the Government of Nepal has explicitly and repeatedly stated its desire to build strategic Nepal–China road corridors throughout the country as part of its official development master plan (MoPIT, 2016). Second, intensive hydropower development occurs in each of these areas: Nepal's rivers are being harnessed to achieve energy security (Lord, 2016).

During the China–Nepal meetings in October 2019, 20 cooperation agreements were signed, one of which was a pledge of US$500 million in financial aid over the next two years. They also agreed to a 70 km extension of the existing Qinghai–Tibet railway to Rasuwagadhi, then onto

Kathmandu and Lumbini (birthplace of The Buddha). The cost has been a significant concern, with the entire project already surpassing the estimated cost of US$300 million, as it requires several tunnels and bridges. Sources said China wanted Nepal to share the costs, but that has delayed matters. Before the railways, China will come up with road projects in Nepal because of the feasibility and cost concerns.

As Nepal's nine proposed BRI projects and transboundary infrastructural assemblages begin to materialize in the imagined power corridors, ongoing grounded research is essential. This would help to interpret the multi-scalar processes through which politics articulate infrastructures and infrastructures articulate politics (Murton and Lord, *Political Geography* (2020)).

Nepal takes China's Belt and Road Initiative as a significant opportunity to deepen mutually-beneficial cooperation in all fields in a comprehensive manner. However, China's increasing interference in Nepal's domestic policies, despite its stated abstinence from meddling in the internal affairs of partner countries, has resulted in an erosion of trust among Nepal's people. It has also resulted in Nepal's political instability in 2020, with the K.P. Oli government having been charged with conceding too many concessions, including territory, to the Chinese.

According to Kumar, China intends to extend the Qinghai–Tibet railway line to Kyirong in Nepal. Interestingly, the railway line was extended from Lhasa to Shigatse in August 2014, and Kyirong land port between Tibet and Nepal was opened in October 2014. This extension will bring Chinese troops closer to the Indian border and is a severe security concern to India. In 2019–2020, the power play between China and India for influence in Nepal had turned more intense, as China has signed a US$1.8 billion agreement to develop the 760-megawatt (M.W.) West Seti Project hydropower plant in Nepal. The deal marks the Asian giant's entry into a lucrative sector in the Himalayan nation — water and power — dominated by India for years. It comes at a time when several other major hydropower projects, mainly developed with Indian investment, have stalled for various reasons, including protests by Maoists against the awarding of deals to foreign companies labeling it as an "unfair share" of hydropower projects in Nepal (Kumar, 2018). According to Henry Tillman, (in response to a query by Marwah), hydro and wind energy projects are the ones which give good returns.[20]

---

[20] Henry Tillman, at an international webinar on December 9, 2020.

Due to the coronavirus, Nepal's economy has been hit, so it is unlikely to rush to take loans from China to implement projects under the BRI for fear of defaulting. China itself will not be able to offer grants for development projects as its economy has also suffered a setback. Nepal and China are discussing several connectivity projects, but the investment modality remains to be settled. However, with its share of investment in projects being the highest, China's influence in Nepal is only expected to rise further. During the pandemic, Nepal has been overly dependent on China to arrange necessary medical logistics. Nepal is also purchasing a large number of medical supplies.[21]

3.5.6.2 *The Tibet factor in China–Nepal relations*

According to Pattanaik (2019), after Tibet became an integral part of China, the two countries signed an agreement to conduct trade and pilgrimage. Since then, China has tried to demolish Nehru's theory of the Himalayas being a natural "effective barrier" that should not be allowed to be breached. The Kathmandu–Kodari road built by China in the 1960s connected Kathmandu to China's border and the Himalayas ceased to exist as a natural barrier. China's aggression in the Himalayas proves that it is planning to accomplish its "Five Finger" plan for Tibet. The President of the Tibetan Government in exile, Lobsang Sangay, said that after the occupation of Tibet, in the 1960s, Chinese leadership made it clear that Tibet is the palm and that they have to go for its five fingers — Ladakh, Nepal, Bhutan, Sikkim, and Arunachal Pradesh. Linking the 2017 Doklam stand-off between India and China with this action plan, Sangay said China's aggressive posturing in Ladakh is part of its long-term expansionist strategy. China encroached more than 64 hectares of land of various districts in Nepal including Dolakha, Humla, Sindhupalchowk, Gorkha, and Rasuwa.[22]

Some sections of the Indian media believe that PM Oli has been honey-trapped by the Chinese ambassador Hou Yanqi and assert that Nepal is going the Tibet way.

---

[21] Kamal Dev Bhattarai, https://thediplomat.com/2020/05/will-covid-19-reshape-nepals-diplomacy/, by May 8, 2020.

[22] Sidharth Shekhar, June 25, 2020, https://www.timesnownews.com/international/article/nepals-opposition-tables-resolution-on-chinese-encroachment-urges-oli-govt-to-bring-back-territory/611547, accessed on July 25, 2020.

3.5.7 *Pakistan*

Pakistan was the third non-communist country, and the first Muslim one, to recognize the People's Republic of China and establish formal diplomatic relations on May 21, 1951. From the time when Chinese traders traveled through Pakistan through the ancient Silk Route, China and Pakistan share age-old ties. It is well known that the Indian sub-continent (before India and Pakistan were partitioned by the British) hosted famous travelers and monks, including Fa Xian and Xuan Zang. The two countries share a border in Pakistan's North East of about 523 km. The border issue was settled in an agreement of 1963, in which more than 2,500 square miles of Hunza territory was ceded to China (Kartha, 2020).

China arrived early in Pakistan's orbit of bilateral relations; the two countries have enjoyed close and friendly relations since the establishment of diplomatic relations on May 21, 1951. In the 1950s, there were visits of significance among both countries. In 1955, Vice President Song Ching Ling's visit to Pakistan marked the first high-level visit from the Chinese side. In the 1960s, the two countries settled their border issue, and Pakistan International Airlines (PIA) started its flights to Beijing, becoming the first non-communist country airline to fly from Beijing. In 1978, the Karakoram Highway project, a part of the ancient Silk Road and a construction miracle that linked mountainous Northern Pakistan with Kashgar in Western China, was initiated. It was opened for the public in 1985 and has remained an essential conduit for goods and people's movement.

Although historically an American ally, Pakistan in present times views China as a guarantor of its security. Over time, the Sino-Pak relationship has blossomed into an "All-Weather Strategic Cooperative Partnership", with the CPEC at its core. Pakistan considers China one of its closest friends, and China considers Pakistan its "Iron Brother". The relationship has forged ahead through economic, cultural, political, and strategic engagement, with this being further fortified through educational exchanges. Bandwagoning with an economic juggernaut transforms nations' fortunes, and Pakistan's handholding by China is a perfect manifestation. In trade and commerce, nations do not take sides but play all sides, as is evident from China's Belt and Road Initiative, that has been building economic partnerships. For conflict-torn countries with autocratic regimes, like Pakistan, which cannot get funding from global financial institutions, China's aid and investment are of great significance. Being part of the Chinese sphere of influence may well be, or seem, a small price to pay for economic success.

China–Pakistan became close friends mainly due to Pakistan's role in the China–US rapprochement in 1972, which is also known as PingPong diplomacy. This altered China's ideological position in the world. The Pakistan–China economic relationship is discussed in detail in Chapter 4.

3.5.8 *Sri Lanka*

Ever since the first Rubber–Rice pact was signed in 1952, China–Sri Lankan relations have continued on an upward trajectory. Religious links between China and Sri Lanka continue to the present day, including the Abhayagiri Temple's renovation.

Here, it is crucial to include an excerpt from an interview of Dr. Delgoda in Colombo in 2012.

"We have been a West leaning country for a long time, but we have a long friendship with China ever since the Rubber–Rice pact concluded in 1952. However, in 1987, 1989, and the 1980s, there was a loosening of relations, but the Eelam War and the West's reaction completely changed our orientation. And as the President said, India is a relative, but China is a friend. Now just paraphrase putting that into realpolitik, and you will find relatives sometimes you cannot get away from, a friend you can stand as far away from as you like" SinhaRaja (2012).[23]

Chinese influence in Sri Lanka is growing, but the possibility that Colombo is driving this relationship cannot be overlooked. Mahinda Rajapakse's Government (before the Presidency of Maithripala Sirisena) was entirely in control of what is officially known as a "Strategic Cooperative Partnership". At the center of this has been Sri Lanka's desire to fulfill its commercial potential as the geographic center of the Indian Ocean.

Former Sri Lankan Ambassador to China Nihal Rodrigo, speaking at a SAARC event in 2013, did not express concern over China's naval expansion and development of South Asian ports. He, instead, claimed

---

[23] Interviewee: Dr. SinhaRaja Tammita-Delgoda; Interviewer: Dr. Shard Soni Date, March 22, 2012, http://www.china-studies.taipei/act02.php.

that Sri Lanka "provides it (China) easier connectivity across the Indian Ocean which benefits South Asia". Therefore, both governments have something to gain from Hambantota Port, described as one aspect of Sri Lanka's five-hub growth strategy, which aims to position and build the island as a global naval, aviation, commercial, energy, and knowledge centre (Goodman, 2014).

Sri Lanka also joined China's Maritime Silk Road (MSR) indicating the proximity of the two states' strategic aspirations and reflects the assimilation of national interests. The MSR, a strategic project for China in the Indian Ocean, has increased China's presence in South Asian shipping routes.

The Chinese invested in the *infamous* Hambantota port to please the Rajapakse regime (2005–2015) as the regime wanted to develop its home constituency The economically unviable Hambantota Port has now become a debt trap. According to Smruti S. Pattanaik, China gained a controlling stake of the strategic port and 15,000 acres of land for building an export processing zone for a lease of 99 years, when the Sri Lankan government was unable to repay the debt. The port's viability was questioned on several counts, as merely ten ships berthed in one entire year, and the business from Colombo port was diverted to Hambantota. China has defended the takeover of the port as being in the interest of Sri Lanka. The Mattala airport built by China is described as the world's emptiest airport, which the succeeding Government used to store grains. All these assets have not generated revenues; instead, they are a burden on the government. Another mega project built by China is the Colombo City Project, which includes land reclamation from the sea. The new controversial bill will convert the Colombo City project to a Chinese province. With an agreement to build a port and airport in Hambantota as part of its ambitious maritime silk route strategy and later acquiring the port on a 99-year lease on a debt–equity swap, China has consolidated its presence in Sri Lanka. The berthing of two nuclear submarines at Colombo Port is seen as part of its strategy and signals China's new naval power.

The 2020 elections have resulted in a comeback of the Rajapakshas. They now seem to underline the significance of balancing China's influence on the island country, even as they cultivate relations with other powers. The Sri Lanka–China economic relationship and the above projects are discussed in detail in Chapter 5.

3.6 China in South Asia: A Tighter Embrace in 2020

Continuing with its outreach toward South Asia, Chinese Foreign Minister Wang Yi organized the first joint virtual conference with foreign ministers from Pakistan, Afghanistan, and Nepal on July 27, 2020. The objective was to assure these neighboring countries that Chinese support would be provided through a four-point plan to contain the COVID-19 pandemic and provide them with a vaccine at the earliest, boost economic recovery and resumption of the BRI infrastructure projects.

Given that China is faced with the apprehensions of local support for the BRI projects, Wang Yi stressed the importance of continuing the work on BRI projects as well as digital connectivity. China's economic diplomacy is all geared to encompass health and digital diplomacy. In his words, "We will actively promote the building of the CPEC and the Trans-Himalayan Connectivity network (THCN), support the extension of the corridor to Afghanistan, and further unleash the dividends of regional connectivity". The strategic dimension is not lost to the Indian army, which is battling the Chinese in the Himalayas since early May 2020, with bilateral relations having come under severe stress after 45 years.[24]

3.7 Conclusion

As Marcel Mauss, the French Sociologist argued in his famous book, *The Gift*, each gift has a purpose, and therefore there is nothing which can be genuinely termed a gift. A gift is sometimes given for services rendered or as a part of future payments; the bottom line is that there is always an expectation attached. This is most evident in South Asia, a region where the small, vulnerable countries, starved of funds for infrastructural development, have become mere pawns in China's great game Mauss (1966).

---

[24] Sidharth Shekhar, June 25, 2020, https://www.timesnownews.com/international/article/nepals-opposition-tables-resolution-on-chinese-encroachment-urges-oli-govt-to-bring-back-territory/611547, accessed on July 26, 2020.

According to (Lama, 2020), Beijing has expanded its influence in the region through local, national, and regional instruments. India has sought to promote counterbalancing regional institutions such as BIMSTEC.[25]

For a country with 14 neighbors, China remained a regional power without a regional policy for a long time. In recent years, a new China has adopted a sophisticated trident approach. It must be highlighted here that China's physical inroads into the region are not new.

At the local level, the Khunjerab Pass on the Karakoram highway in Pakistan; Tatopani and Kerung-Rasuwagadhi in Nepal; the Wakhan Corridor northeast of Afghanistan; and Nathu la, Shipki la, and Lipulekh in India are meant to integrate the borderland communities. These instruments are likely to be transformed into national and cross-regional grids. For instance, the Khunjerab Pass recorded a trading volume of nearly USD One billion in 2019, and is already connected with the CPEC through the Karakoram highway. The Shigatse–Lhasa–Shanghai railway line is proposed to be extended to Nathu la in Sikkim and Kerung-Rasuwagadhi in Nepal. Additionally, the use of the Chinese renminbi (RMB) in trade — such as the US$6 billion border trade between Muse (Myanmar) and Ruili (Kunming-China) — foreign exchange reserves in RMB are being promoted.

In addition to achieving physical connectivity in India's borderlands, China's trade with South Asia has been rapidly rising. China–South Asia trade recorded an over five-times increase from a mere US$1.18 billion in 1990 to US$5.57 billion in 2000 and another 23-fold jump to US$127.36 billion in 2018. Over 23% of the total global imports of Bangladesh, 15% of India, 24% of Pakistan, and 19% of Sri Lanka are from China. All South Asian countries, except Bhutan, have a trade deficit with China.

From Hambantota and Colombo Ports in Sri Lanka to US$3 billion investments, each in the Payra Power project and the Dhaka–Chittagong railway in Bangladesh, from investing US$8.62 billion to complete eight energy projects under the CPEC to planning railway lines to Indian and the Nepalese borderlands, China has upset India's official position both as a traditionally core neighboring country and influential economic–democratic–military power.

---

[25]Lama, Mahendra, July 12, 2020. The Chinese Trishul in South Asia, https://www. hindustantimes.com/analysis/the-chinese-trishul-in-south-asia/story-qUKiiJBi66Dx6 QtD6aQtTJ.html, accessed on October 10, 2020.

At the regional level, China has adopted strategies for domination and control.

First, it has entered the SAARC process; the earliest overtures to establish some form of mutual interaction with SAARC were made in 2000 when the then Assistant Minister of Foreign Affairs Wang Yi had discussions with the SAARC Secretary-General at the Secretariat in Kathmandu. China also promoted the Bangladesh, China, India, and Myanmar Economic Corridor (BCIM) cooperation initiative. Second, it exploits forums it leads, such as the BRI, the Shanghai Cooperation Organization, and the Boao Forum, to bring mainstream South Asian countries into its fold. Third, it has effectively begun to use the newly-created development funding agencies as the AIIB and the Silk Road Fund to finance South Asian projects.

India's neighborhood is now entangled in an unparalleled balancing dilemma. Nepal's tilt toward China, even without major formal agreements and projects, is crystal clear. Small countries fear that the competitive and conflictual existence of two giant neighbors, however beneficial, can result in continuous interference in their domestic affairs and even jeopardize their sovereignty. South Asia's entire geography is fast transforming with a China that is determined to wholly or at least partially obliterate India's influence in the region (Lama, 2020).

Interestingly, in all the joint statements by China with Nepal, Bangladesh, Sri Lanka, Pakistan, and the Maldives, the words non-interference, sovereignty, and independence are a repeated theme. It is evident that the words "autonomy and independence" relate to China's tacit support of the friendly regimes (Smruti and Pattanaik, 2019).

With the pandemic continuing, and countries in South Asia experiencing the worst economic crises in four decades, it is evident that their capacity for taking on new loans, required for infrastructure projects being signed with China, would be severely limited. China in 2020 has been faced with requests for debt relief and debt restructuring by Bangladesh, Pakistan, and the Maldives.

To what extent China continues to stay the ever-generous noble ally as presently perceived by these countries is a question that only time will answer! Even as States look the other way, the fissures are visible in protests against the predator!

Chapter 4

China and Pakistan: "Iron Brothers"

It is essential to understand that the seeds of the relationship germinated as a result of the Kautilyan dictum — "Your enemy's enemy is your friend" — which was well put to practice by China and Pakistan.

As elucidated in the previous chapter, Sino-Pak axis is the core issue for India's reticence in joining the BRI. However, for China's exuberant expansiveness, it is India's non-compliance to its overtures which provide the raison d'etre for deepening engagement with this ally.

4.1 A Brief History of Pakistan

The Indian subcontinent was one of the cradles of civilization. In 327 BCE, Alexander the Great, with his Macedonian army, attacked the region. Later, Mauryans from India ruled the northern Punjab area, only to be replaced by Bactrian Greeks from Afghanistan and Central Asian tribes. Hence, different religions left their mark, including Buddhism (under the Mauryans), Hinduism, and Islam as a result of the Arab conquest in the eighth century. However, present-day Pakistan is predominantly a Muslim country.

In the early 17th century, European traders arrived in the subcontinent. The British became the dominant force through the East India Company. After the unsuccessful uprising against Britain in 1857, the British took direct control. Slowly a national Muslim identity emerged, championed by Sir Syed Ahmed Khan (1817–1889). The All India

Muslim League was established in 1907, and in 1956, Pakistan became a federal republic.

The campaign to establish an independent Muslim state came to prominence in the 1920s and 1930s. It was led by the philosopher and poet Mohammad Iqbal along with Mohammad Ali Jinnah. As an Islamic state, Pakistan was created out of the partition of UK's Indian Empire in August 1947. It originally consisted of two parts, West Pakistan (now Pakistan) and East Pakistan (now Bangladesh), separated by 1,600 km of Indian territory. However, the border areas of Pakistan and India still face political tragedies, especially in Jammu and Kashmir.

4.2 Pakistan's Economy: A Brief Overview

Pakistan's economy is the 23rd largest in terms of purchasing power parity and 42nd largest in terms of nominal GDP, with a nominal GDP per capita of US$1,357 in 2019 (according to Economic indicators data in 2019). Since the country's independence in 1947, its economy has emerged as a semi-industrialized one, based heavily on textiles, agriculture, and food production. Primary export commodities include textiles, leather goods, sports goods, chemicals, and carpets/rugs. Pakistan has been ranked 108th in Ease of doing business in 2020. In recent times, however, there has been a push toward technological diversification. Table 4.1 presents selected economic indicators for 2019.[1,2] It has one of the lowest income levels in South Asia, with a high percentage of debt to GDP.

Table 4.1:   Pakistan: GDP, GDP per capita, debt, & HDI in 2019.

Countries	Population	Annual GDP USD (Mn)	GDP per capita US$	HDI	Debt	Government Debt (% GDP)
Pakistan	200,960,000	314,588	1,565	0.562	225,435	71.69
Total SAARC	1,803,133,714	3,467,225	1,923	—	2,256,755	63.94

Sources: Country Reports, https://countryeconomy.com/countries/groups/south-asian-association-regional-cooperation, accessed on August 4, 2020.

---

[1]*Design, Websynergi*. "Pakistan Trade, Pakistan Industries, India Pakistan Trade Unit". *iptu.co.uk*.

[2]Pakistan's Top 10 Exports. Daniel Workman. World's Top Exports.

Given the pandemic situation, economic activity has been brought to a near halt in Pakistan, especially since March 2020. Most of the country has been placed under a partial lockdown. The COVID-19 crisis directly affected the largest sector in Pakistan — the service sector. Simultaneously, the drop in domestic and global demand is also compounding the strains in the industrial sector, which is hit by both supply and demand shocks. Besides, the country's leading industrial sector — textiles and apparel — is highly exposed to COVID-19-related disruptions due to its labor intensity.

4.3 China — Pakistan Relations: All Weather Friendship

China nurtured very cordial yet complex political, economic, and military relations with Pakistan for decades. The two governments habitually describe their ties in glowing terms as an "all-weather friendship" that is "higher than the mountains and deeper than the oceans" (Dumbaugh, 2010:7). Pakistan has played a vital role as a cornerstone to China's Central Asia and South Asia strategy for decades. Its geostrategic position is crucial since it serves as a doorway to the Middle East, where China seeks to access the energy-rich Persian Gulf region (Chaziza, 2016). Kumar (2007) indicates that the traditional Sino-Pakistan friendship of over five decades has a new objective: to improve the economic content of their relationship, which comprises trade, investment, and energy cooperation within a bilateral framework.

Additionally, Kumar indicates that this determination to implement the new economic agenda is visible in the quantum of Chinese investment in Pakistan. Dumbaugh gives a similar argument (2010). This historical context for Sino-Pakistan relations dates back to 1950 when Pakistan became one of the first countries to establish diplomatic relations with the People's Republic of China, even when the USA–Pakistan relationship was strong. From the onset, the two countries were brought closer by mutual tensions and border conflicts with India. Andrew Small has pieced together the story of China and Pakistan's growing, and in parts troubled, friendship. In his book the *China Pakistan Axis*, he underlines that the bilateral relationship has been shaped by Pakistan's internal strife, and the dilemmas China faces between the need for regional stability and the imperative for strategic competition with India and the USA (Small, 2019).

Given that Pakistan had a very closely aligned relationship with the United States, several cracks appeared in the relationship even before President Trump was sworn in as the US president in January 2017. The relations after 2017 have only soured between two economically and militarily close allies.

"Pakistan is now likely to align itself more closely with China. With the recent cutting of military aid by Trump, Islamabad is bound to believe that its national interests are served better by Beijing than Washington".[3]

Throughout the different historical periods and despite changes with time, Chinese and Pakistani governments and people have enriched their friendship and have established a model for friendly ties between different cultures, social systems, and ideologies (CPEC, 2017–2030:2). China has also provided Pakistan with nuclear assistance; made vital investments in Pakistan's ports, transportation, and resource development infrastructure; and contributed to Pakistan's national security by making military sales while also cooperating on weapons platform production (Dumbaugh, 2010).

Xi, in a verbal message to Pakistan President Arif Alvi in August 2020, said that China and Pakistan are good brothers and partners who share a special friendship. According to Xi Jinping, "China is also ready to work with Pakistan toward building a closer China–Pakistan community with a shared future, to jointly promote regional solidarity and cooperation, and safeguard the momentum of peace and development".[4]

Pakistan has been a willing recipient of BRI projects from China. Hence, to ensure the implementation of relevant agreements, China has also established various intergovernmental working mechanisms for Pakistan and other BRI partners. For instance, to promote the development of the CPEC, dozens of government departments from both countries and relevant local governments hold ad hoc consultations to resolve various problems.[5]

---

[3] Dr. Furrukh Khan, LUMS, Pak; Interview to Reena Marwah on August 28, 2020.
[4] CPEC is of great importance to China–Pakistan ties: Xi tells Pak president Arif Alvi, https://www.timesnownews.com/international/article/cpec-is-of-great-importance-to-china-pakistan-ties-xi-tells-pak-president-arif-alvi/640868, accessed September 9, 2020.
[5] https://news.cgtn.com/news/3d3d514f786b544f79457a6333566d54/index.html, accessed on September 17, 2020.

Jacob (2010) states that the China–Pakistan relationship has seen several ups and downs, especially since the 9/11 incident. In his opinion, this is because Beijing was concerned about political instability, including terrorism, in Pakistan, and the possibility of the spread of Islamic radicalism into China.

4.4 China — Pakistan Economic Engagement

This section analyzes China's economic engagement with Pakistan through trade, investment in BRI projects, and other economic indicators over 2000–2019.

4.4.1 *Pakistan and China: Trade*

Kumar (2007) has written about how the Chinese investments benefit Pakistan, and trade provides China access to a new market for its goods. An analysis of Pakistan's top five trading partners over the past ten years shows a significant change. In 2011, 16% (US$3.8 billion) of Pakistan's exports went to USA and 7.7% (US$1.7 billion) went to China.

In 2018, over two-thirds (70.1%) of Pakistani exports went to the 15 trade partners, namely, United States (US$3.8 Billion), China (US$1.8 billion), United Kingdom ($1.7 billion), Afghanistan (US$1.4 billion), Germany (US$1.3 billion), United Arab Emirates (US$996 million), Netherlands (US$941.6 million), Spain (US$922.8 million), Bangladesh (US$787.6 million), Italy (US$776.5 million), Belgium (US$668 million), France (US$447.1 million), India (US$382.2 million), Sri Lanka (US$357.3 million), and Saudi Arabia (US$316.9 million).[6] Figure 4.1 provides details.

The above data indicates that China has increased imports from Pakistan, but only marginally. Table 4.2 indicates the top 10 export commodities in Pakistan in 2019. The textiles and clothing industry is the largest exporting sector in Pakistan. Copper was the fastest growing mineral among the top 10 export categories in Pakistan — up by 182.6% from 2018 to 2019. However, compared to 2018, cotton export has declined by 50.2% from 2018 to 2019.

---

[6] Pakistan's Top Trading Partners, http://www.worldstopexports.com/pakistans-top-import-partners/, accessed on September 22, 2020.

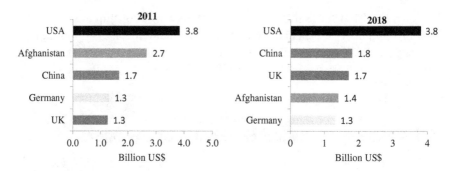

Figure 4.1:   Pakistan's top 5 export partners (US$ Billion).

Source: Using UNCOMTRADE and WITS online data created by the authors.

Table 4.2:   Pakistan's leading export industries (2019).

Rank	Export commodity	Value	Percentage
1	Miscellaneous textiles, worn clothing	US$4.2 billion	20
2	Clothing, accessories (not knit or crochet)	$3.5 billion	16.7
3	Knit or crochet clothing, accessories	$3.3 billion	16.1
4	Cotton	$1.8 billion	8.4
5	Cereals	$1.2 billion	5.9
6	Leather/animal gut articles	$716.7 million	3.5
7	Copper: $596.7 million	$596.7 million	2.9
8	Optical, technical, medical apparatus	$421 million	2
9	Mineral fuels, including oil	$393.8 million	1.9
10	Fish	$372.5 million	1.8

Source: UNCOMTRADE online data.

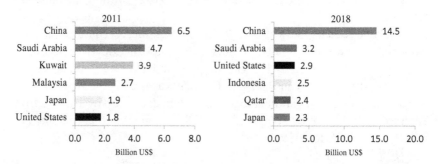

Figure 4.2:   Pakistan's top 6 import partners (US$).

Source: Using UNCOMTRADE and WITS online data created by the authors.

Table 4.3: Pakistan's imports from China and growth rate of imports (2010–2018).

Year	Imports from China (US$ Thousand)	Import growth rate
2010	5247712.59	—
2011	6470653.43	23
2012	6687565.99	3
2013	6626322.95	−1
2014	9588418.04	**45**
2015	11019005.36	15
2016	13680153.11	24
2017	15383397.8	12
2018	14544686.75	—

Source: Using WITS online data calculated by the Authors, accessed on September 10, 2020.

In 2019, Pakistan imported an estimated US$37.3 billion worth of goods from all countries. Since 2011, China has been Pakistan's main import partner (refer Figure 4.2). In fact, in 2018 the import amount was US$14.5 billion (an increase of more than double within seven years) compared to US$6.5 billion in 2011. However, in 2019, despite overall imports having declined by 14% since 2015, there was a significant rise in Chinese goods imports. This appears to coincide with the commencement of BRI projects in Pakistan in 2013–2014 (see Table 4.3). This indicates that with BRI projects, China has dominated Pakistan's import market with benefits accruing to China indirectly (imported raw materials for BRI construction and other projects). This scenario is similar to the Sri Lankan situation, explained in the next chapter.

4.5 Chinese Investments in Pakistan

Both China and Pakistan have underlined the importance of developing the CPEC. In May 2013, Chinese Premier Li Keqiang proposed the initiative of CPEC during his visit to Pakistan, which received an immediate and positive response from the Pakistani Government. In July 2013, during Prime Minister Sharif's visit to China, an MOU was signed to start work on CPEC. CPEC, with a range of projects, has gradually entered into the stage of full implementation and is catalyzing the substantive bilateral cooperation. On August 2, 2020, President Xi Jinping defined the CPEC as a landmark project under the BRI, defining this as the distinctive manifestation of the all-weather strategic cooperative partnership between the two countries.[7]

The focus is on connecting China with the Chinese-invested Pakistani port of Gwadar through highways, and rail and pipeline infrastructure. Project plans had a five-year horizon for implementation, and the sums involved — ranging between ten and twenty billion USD — were moderate compared to China's current ambitions in Pakistan.

It is the economic corridor that leads China's Belt and Road Initiative (Malik, 2020). This plan is effective until 2030. The short-term projects include those to be completed by 2020, medium-term projects by 2025, and long-term projects by 2030.[8]

4.5.1 *CPEC (2017–2030)*

A report published by the Pakistan Government notes that, "The CPEC is a development belt featuring complementary advantages, collaboration, mutual benefits and common prosperity. With the comprehensive transportation corridor and industrial cooperation between China and Pakistan, and with concrete economic and trade cooperation, and people to people exchange and cultural communications as the engine, CPEC is based on major collaborative projects for infrastructure construction, industrial development, and livelihood improvement, aimed at socio-economic development, prosperity and security in regions along with it" (CPEC, 2017–2030, p. 4). The CPEC covers China's Xinjiang Uygur Autonomous Region and the entire territory of Pakistan. The corridor passes through the nodal cities, including Kashgar, Atushi, Tumshuq, Shule, Shufu, Akto, Tashkurgan Tajik, Gilgit, Peshawar, Dera Ismail Khan, Islamabad, Lahore, Multan, Quetta, Sukkur, Hyderabad, Karachi, and Gwadar.

---

[7]CPEC is of great importance to China–Pakistan ties: Xi tells Pak President Arif Alvi, https://www.timesnownews.com/international/article/cpec-is-of-great-importance-to-china-pakistan-ties-xi-tells-pak-president-arif-alvi/640868, accessed September 9, 2020.

[8]CPEC, www.cpec.gov.pk, accessed by September 10, 2020.

The government of Pakistan underlines the importance of the CPEC as a framework of regional connectivity. CPEC, as advocated, will benefit China and Pakistan and have a positive impact on Iran, Afghanistan, India, the Central Asian Republic, and the region. Improved road, rail, and air transportation systems with free exchanges of growth and people-to-people contact would enhance geographical linkages. Enhancing understanding through academic, cultural, and regional knowledge and culture, a higher volume of flow of trade and businesses, producing and moving energy to have more optimal businesses and enhancement of cooperation by the win–win model will result in a well-connected, integrated region of shared destiny, harmony, and development. Therefore, the CPEC has been pitched as the hope of a better future for the region with peace, development, and economic growth.[9]

During President Xi Jinping's visit to Pakistan in April 2015, the all-weather strategic cooperation partnership was enriched with new connotations. The two sides have set up the "1+4" cooperation model. They take CPEC as the core while prioritizing Gwadar, Energy, Transport Infrastructure, and Industrial Cooperation, opening a new chapter for CPEC construction.[10]

The CPEC is divided into five functional zones from north to south: Xinjiang foreign economic zone, northern border trade logistics and business corridor & ecological reserve, eastern and central plain economic zone, western logistics corridor business zone, as well as the southern coastal logistics business zone. Transportation corridors and industrial clusters are concentrated in the node cities.

The Pakistan Government's intentions through CPEC was to leverage Chinese capital, production capacity, and know-how to upgrade Pakistan's infrastructure and build a "mechanism for sustainable economic growth". In return, Beijing gains access to the Arabian sea, providing a contingency trade route to the risk-prone Straits of Malacca in Southeast Asia. However, as with the broader BRI, there are multiple drivers; and the importance of grand geostrategic designs should not be overstated. Creating trade routes and demand in Pakistan also furthers the stability-driven development of China's western interior.

---

[9] China–Pakistan Economic Corridor, http://cpec.gov.pk/introduction/1, accessed on September 10, 2020.
[10] CPEC, www.cpec.gov.pk, accessed on September 10, 2020.

The estimated CPEC cost is US$46 billion. Therefore, the two governments drew up a Long-Term Plan, starting in 2017 and drastically expanding the projected timeline for implementation up to 2030. Hence, projected costs increased to US$62 billion, and Pakistani officials have since mentioned even higher numbers.[11]

22 "early harvest" projects were launched in 2014–2015 under the CPEC. These projects included building new roads and power plants, and operationalizing the deep-water strategic Arabian Sea commercial port of Gwadar, which overlooks some of the world's busiest oil and gas shipping lanes (Gul, 2019). He also shows how Pakistan is suffering from an increased debt burden due to the BRI projects rather than the expected boost to economic growth. Figure 4.3 indicates the location of the BRI projects in Pakistan.

4.6 BRI Projects

A few key projects are discussed here.

4.6.1 *Port city of Gwadar*

Gwadar's port city is a hub of connectivity for the corridor and an essential transaction point for the Silk Route. Its strategic location and vast potential as a deep-sea port are emphasized because it is just 600 kilometers from the Strait of Hormuz. That is one of the key reasons that Gwadar is now leased to China, and the Chinese Government is set to reap the benefits from the region's development.[12] This project has seen a significant investment from the corridor budget.

China's resource-rich Xinjiang province and Pakistan's Gwadar port in Balochistan connect through a CPEC project, the cost of which was US$60 billion. The Gwadar project includes future operations, including constructing a crude oil pipeline that will start from there and span the entire CPEC. At the same time, China also proposes setting up an

---

[11] The BRI in Pakistan: China's flagship economic corridor, https://merics.org/en/analysis/bri-pakistan-chinas-flagship-economic-corridor, assessed on September 10, 2020.

[12] what-are-the-major-chinese-investment-projects-in-pakistan, https://www.cpicglobal.com/what-are-the-major-chinese-investment-projects-in-pakistan/, accessed on September 10, 2020.

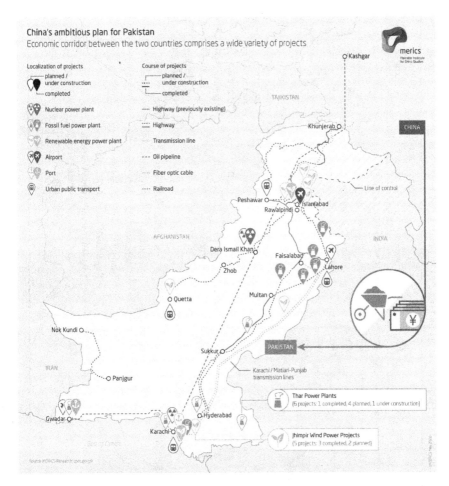

Figure 4.3: China's ambitious plan for Pakistan.

Sources: The BRI in Pakistan: China's flagship economic corridor, https://merics.org/en/analysis/bri-pakistan-chinas-flagship-economic-corridor, assessed on September 10, 2020.

industrial park with many commercial establishments. This also includes the installation of Breakwaters at Gwadar port which will cost almost US$130 million to construct. China had also committed to dredging the berths in Gwadar harbor. That, alone, will cost US$27 million.[13] (See Table 4.4 for all the projects related to Gwadar Port under CPEC).

---

[13] *Ibid.*

Table 4.4:   Financial terms and expected economic benefits of major Chinese projects.

Project Name	Type	Project cost	Location	Financing	Implementing agency	Duration/ Completion
Port city of Gwadar Including • Coal power plant • Desalination plant • New city airport. • Iran–Pakistan pipeline **More details of the Gwadar project are in Table 4.5**	Sea Transport, Air Transport and Energy	Over $1 billion (Port $130 million, Pipeline $1724 million, etc.)	Resource-rich Xinjiang province with Pakistan's strategic Gwadar port in Balochistan	See Table 4.5	See Table 4.5	See Table 4.5
Karakoram Highway	Transport (Road Infrastructure)	USD 1.3 billion for the Thakot– Havelian section USD 930 million for Karakoram Highway Phase II	Kashgar, Xinjiang China/Hasan Abdal, Punjab Pakistan	China's Export Import Bank concessional loan (1.6% low-interest rate	China–Pakistan Economic Corridor (CPEC)	2013–2017 Section Havelian- Abbottabad- Mansehra May, 2018 Phase II March, 2020 Thakot-Havelian: December, 2019
Railway Projects • Main Line-1 (ML-1)	Transport (Road Infrastructure)	$8.2 billion	Karachi to Peshawar	People's Republic of China & Government of Islamic Republic of Pakistan	Still under the bidding process 10% from Pakistan Government and 90% from China under CPEC	2021
Energy Projects	—	$33 billion	—	—	—	—

Source: Using diverse sources; created by the authors.

Other projects involve a coal power plant and a desalination plant, but the most significant investment to date surrounds the new city airport. An airport at Gwadar will become the biggest airport in Pakistan with a Chinese investment of US$230 million.[14] Gwadar's most important project is the Iran–Pakistan pipeline project which is 2775 km long and worth US$1724 million. Thus, the southern end of the CPEC is the deep-water port at Gwadar.

Like the Karakoram Highway (KKH), the Gwadar project is not a convincing commercial proposition and, consequently, much of the promised Chinese development has not transpired. By 2008, "Gwadar stood virtually isolated" (Small, 2015, p. 101). Part of the problem is that the entire project is targeted by Baloch nationalist groups who fear that the massive project will render them a "minority in their land". In fact, it has been calculated that the cost of sending [one barrel of oil] overland via Gwadar and Xinjiang would run at between four and five times that of the sea route through Shanghai" (Small, 2015, p. 102).

Through its deep-sea port, Gwadar has helped realize the goal of a 21st Century Maritime Silk Route, which will benefit China, Pakistan and Central Asia by becoming the region's key entrepot.

However, during the interview with Dr. Reena Marwah on September 20, 2020, Dr. Pervaiz Ali Mahesar said it would not be wrong to assume that Gwadar port is more beneficial to China than Pakistan. This is because Pakistan holds a pivotal position in the exchanges through trade, investment, and goods in the region. This is critically linked to Pakistan enhancing its competitiveness to take advantage by increasing exports".

Table 4.4 summarizes all the CPEC projects in Pakistan under different categories such as Seaport and Construction, Highways and Railways, and Energy projects, with their estimated costs.

It is evident from Tables 4.4 and 4.5 that the terms of financing the projects appear favorable for Pakistan. While the energy and highway related projects may fuel Pakistan's growth, the returns generated from the port project are more strategic than commercial for China. A Chinese SOE has signed a 40-year lease with the Pakistani Government in 2017 to become the Gwadar port's sole operator (Russel and Berger, 2020).

---

[14] *Ibid.*

Table 4.5: Details of Gwadar project.

Project Name	Company Name	Status	Progress (%)	Estimated cost	Financing	Completion date
Gwadar Eastbay Expressway (19 km, connecting Gwadar Port to Makran Coastal Highway)	TBD	Government Framework Agreement Signed	60	168 (US$ML)	Government Interest-Free Loan	October 2020
Gwadar New International Airport	Civil Aviation Authority	Government Framework Agreement Signed	40	230 (US$ML)[a]	Chinese Government Grant	Construction work started on October 31, 2019
Gwadar Free Zone	China Overseas Ports Holding Company Ltd. (COPHC)	1st phase completed	60	32 (US$ML)[b]	GPA, GIEDA, and EPZA Or any Financial Framework Agreement under CPEC	1st phase completed and inaugurated in January 2018
Gwadar Smart Port City Master Plan	TBD	Contract negotiations underway	20	4 (US$ML)[c]	n.a	n.a
Expansion of Multi-purpose Terminal including Breakwater and Dredging	TBD	Feasibility stage	15	123 (US$ML)[d]	Mix of Chinese Government Concessional Loan & Grant	n.a

Project	Company	Status		Cost	Government Interest	Date of Completion
Gwadar Eastbay Expressway II (19 km, connecting Eastbay Expressway 1 to New Gwadar International Airport)	TBD	Feasibility stage	15	168 (US$ML)[e]	Free Loan	October, 2020
Fresh Water Supply, Wastewater Treatment Plants for Gwadar City	TBD	Feasibility stage	15	130 (US$ML)[f]	Chinese Government Grant	
China-Pakistan Faqeer Primary School Project	China Communications Construction Company Ltd. & CCCC-FHDI Engineering Co., Ltd	Completed	100	0.4 (US$ML)[g]	n.a	Opened On August 26, 2016
Gwadar Pak–China Friendship Hospital Upgradation	TBD	Feasibility study underway	10	100 (US$ML)[h]	Chinese Government Grant	n.a
Gwadar Pak–China Friendship Technical and Vocational College	TBD	Feasibility study underway	10	10 (US$ML)[i]	Chinese Government Grant	n.a

Notes: * n.a. = Not available.

[a] http://cpec.gov.pk/project-details/33, accessed by December 12, 2020.
[b] http://cpec.gov.pk/project-details/36, accessed by December 12, 2020.
[c] http://cpec.gov.pk/project-details/63, accessed by December 12, 2020.
[d] http://cpec.gov.pk/project-details/34, accessed by December 12, 2020.
[e] http://cpec.gov.pk/project-details/32, accessed by December 12, 2020.
[f] http://www.cpec.gov.pk/project-details/37, accessed by December 12, 2020.
[g] http://pk.chineseembassy.org/eng/zbgx/CPEC/t1627110.htm, accessed by December 12, 2020.
[h] http://cpec.gov.pk/project-details/38, accessed by December 12, 2020.
[i] http://cpec.gov.pk/project-details/39, accessed by December 12, 2020.
Sources: Gwadar Port City, http://cpecinfo.com/gwadar-port-city-1/, accessed on September 22, 2020

4.6.2　*Karakoram Highway (Upgraded)*

The Karakoram Highway, being the only overland link, has a total length of 1,300 km. It connects the Pakistani provinces of Punjab, Khyber Pakhtunkhwa, and Gilgit-Baltistan with China's western Xinjiang Uyghur Autonomous Region. On the Chinese side, it becomes the China National Highway 314. The highway passes through the Karakoram mountain range at an elevation of 4,714 meters making it a popular tourist attraction. It was built by the governments of Pakistan and China in the late 1970s.[15]

The current CPEC project is an upgraded project to extend the Karakoram Highway to several arterial roads. China's Export–Import Bank provided a low interest rate (1.6%) concessional loan, which covers part of the upgrading and reconstruction costs of certain highway sections. The Thakot–Havelian section is 90% financed through a loan by China's Export–Import Bank. The China Development Bank will also finance part of the reconstruction of the Hasan Abdal–Raikot section. In December 2017, China stopped funding for the construction of the Raikot–Thakot section due to high-level of corruption.[16]

The highway cuts through the collision zone between the Eurasian and Indian plates, where China, Tajikistan, Afghanistan, and Pakistan come within 250 kilometers (160 miles) of each other. Owing largely to the extremely sensitive state of the Kashmir conflict between India and Pakistan, the Karakoram Highway has strategic and military importance for Pakistan and China. The border crossing in-between is only open during the summer months. Due to the high altitude of parts of the highway as well as its narrow and curvy roads, fatal accidents are frequent. At least 810 Pakistanis and about 200 Chinese workers lost their lives during the construction work itself. In order for the Highway to deal with more frequent CPEC traffic, the extension and upgrading of the Karakoram Highway are considered essential (see Table 4.4 for more details of KKH Project).

4.6.3　*Railway projects*

The country's first and biggest railway transport project, i.e. Main Line-1 (ML-1), will connect Karachi to Peshawar, and is expected to be entirely

---

[15] https://www.beltroad-initiative.com/karakoram-highway/, accessed on September 18, 2020.
[16] BRI, https://www.beltroad-initiative.com/karakoram-highway/, accessed on September 18, 2020.

rebuilt by 2021. The Original cost of this project was US$8.2 billion. The project involves laying down of new tracks to allow 160 km/per hour speeds for railways, rehabilitation and construction of bridges, provision of modern signaling and telecom systems, replacing of level crossings with underpasses/flyovers, fencing of the track, the establishment of a dry port near Havelian and up-gradation of Walton Training Academy (Lahore).[17]

Under the framework agreement signed between the People's Republic of China and the Government of the Islamic Republic of Pakistan, only Chinese companies/consortia are eligible to participate in the bidding process. The PRC had also set a deadline of October 22, 2020 for the submission of bids for the project. The Executive Committee approved the ML-I project of the National Economic Council (ECNEC). Under a proposal, the federal government plans to contribute 10% of the project's total cost as its equity while China will meet 90% cost under the CPEC.[18] To what extent this railway line and its velocity will help the people of Pakistan is anyone's guess. In several countries in Southeast Asia including Laos, Thailand, Malaysia, and Myanmar, these rail projects costing over US$2 billion have been termed as "troubled transactions".[19]

4.6.4 *Energy projects*

An estimated US$33 billion has been allocated for investment in energy projects in Pakistan under CPEC projects. There will be construction of significant projects of thermal power, hydropower, coal gasification, and renewable power generation supporting power transmission networks to enhance power transmission and supply reliability.

According to Mardell (2020), the MERICS database marks US$25.5 billion worth of projects as completed, with 75% of that figure being energy projects. This includes solar, hydro, and wind-powered generation, but fossil-fuel-fired capacity constitutes roughly 60% of the added mega

---

[17] https://www.youtube.com/watch?v=wSlPcOcL138, accessed on September 18, 2020.

[18] Railways to invite bids for $6.8 bn ML-1 CPEC project, https://www.dawn.com/news/1578880, accessed on September 18, 2020.

[19] China Power Team. "How Are Foreign Rail Construction Projects Advancing China's Interests?" China Power. November 12, 2020. Updated December 8, 2020, https://chinapower.csis.org/rail-construction/, accessed on December 15, 2020.

Table 4.6:   CPEC–Energy priority projects.

#	Project Name	MW	Estimated Cost (US$ M)
1	Sahiwal 2×660 MW Coal-fired Power Plant, Punjab	1320	1912.2
2	2×660 MW Coal-fired Power Plants at Port Qasim Karachi	1320	1912.2
3	HUBCO Coal Power Project, Hub Balochistan	1320	1912.2
4	Engro 2×330 MW Thar Coal Power Project	660	995.4
	Surface mine in block II of Thar Coalfield, 3.8 million tons/year	—	630
5	Quaid-e-Azam 1000 MW Solar Park (Bahawalpur) Quaid-e-Azam	400 600	520 781
6	Hydro China Dawood Wind Farm (Gharo, Thatta)	49.5	112.65
7	UEP Wind Farm (Jhimpir, Thatta)	99	250
8	Sachal Wind Farm (Jhimpir, Thatta)	49.5	134
9	Three Gorges Second and Third Wind Power Project	100	150
10	SSRL Thar Coal Block-I 6.8 mtpa & Power Plant (2×660 MW) (Shanghai Electric)	1320	1912.12
11	HUBCO Thar Coal Power Project (Thar Energy)	330	497.7
12	ThalNova Thar Coal Power Project	330	497.7
13	Karot Hydropower Station	720	1698.26
14	Suki Kinari Hydropower Station, Naran, Khyber Pakhtunkhwa	870	1707
15	Matiari to Lahore ±660 kV HVDC Transmission Line Project	—	1658.34
16	300 MW Imported Coal Based Power Project at Gwadar, Pakistan	300	542.32
17	Thar Mine Mouth Oracle Power Plant (1320 MW) & surface mine	1320	Yet to be determined

Source: http://cpec.gov.pk/energy.

wattage if we exclude nuclear. Hence, there exists a need to optimize the sourcing and use of coal, to minimize carbon emissions.

Tables 4.6, 4.7, and 4.8 provide more details of the CPEC energy projects in Pakistan with CPEC–Energy Priority Projects, CPEC–Energy Actively Promoted Projects, and CPEC–Potential Energy Projects.

Table 4.7:   CPEC–Energy actively promoted projects.

#	Project Name	MW	Estimated Cost (US$ M)
18	Kohala Hydel Project, AJK	1100	2364.05
19	Cacho 50 MW Wind Power Project	50	n.a
20	Western Energy (Pvt.) Ltd. 50 MW Wind Power Project	50	n.a
21	Azad Pattan Hydel Project, AJK	701	1,650

Note: n.a = Not available.
Source: http://cpec.gov.pk/energy.

Table 4.8:   CPEC–Potential energy projects.

#	Project Name	MW	Estimated Cost (US$ M)
22	Phandar Hydropower Station	80	n.a
23	Gilgit KIU Hydropower	100	n.a

Note: n.a = Not available.
Source: http://cpec.gov.pk/energy.

- ***Suki Kinari Hydropower Station*** — Worth US$1.9 billion and currently under construction, this is the largest private-sector project in Pakistan. However, there are doubts whether this is a project under CPEC or not.
- ***Diamer Bhasha Dam*** — This is the largest project under CPEC worth US$14 billion.
- ***Azad Pattan Hydel Power project*** — This project involves generating 700.7 megawatts of electricity and is part of the controversial CPEC. The project has been sponsored by the Chinese China Gezhouba Group Company (CGGC), at a whopping US$1.54 billion as well as by China's Three Gorges Corporation.[20]
- ***Kohala Hydropower Projects*** (2016–2021) — This project is located 90 km from Pakistan's capital Islamabad. It is expected to be completed by 2026 and sponsored by International Finance Corporation (IFC) and Silk Road Fund.[21]

---

[20] https://www.timesnownews.com/international/article/massive-protests-erupt-in-pok-against-china-pakistan-over-construction-of-dams/649336, accessed on September 9, 2020.
[21] *Ibid.*

Dams continue to be constructed by Chinese companies, even as locals fear that they pose an existential threat to the population. It was on August 8, 2020, when massive protests erupted in Pakistan occupied Kashmir (PoK) over two mega-dams. People protested in large numbers and condemned the proposed construction of dams on the Neelum and Jhelum rivers.[22] Table 4.6 presents some details of the CPEC Energy Priority Projects. Out of the 17 projects, more than half are coal-fired and will increase carbon emissions, while adding to the pollution levels. In fact, the building of coal-fired power plants by Chinese companies, while providing desperately needed energy, is a dirty and expensive way to overcome Pakistan's chronic shortages.[23]

4.7 Costs & Benefits of BRI Initiatives in Pakistan

Pakistani Prime Minister Imran Khan asserted on July 4, 2020, that the CPEC will be completed, as per schedule. He said that "The corridor is a manifestation of Pakistan–China friendship and the government will complete it at any cost and bring its fruit to every Pakistani".[24]

In an interview with *The Kootneeti*, Prof. Swaran Singh, speaking on the implications of CPEC said, "China's fast-paced investments will continue setting in path dependencies for host nations and push forward China's 'extraction economy' model where China's sole motive remains accessing and exploiting resources of host nations".[25] In his lecture organized by the Association of Asia Scholars, Dr. Siegfried Wolf mentioned how the CPEC serves as a laboratory prototype of issues that one might face on the BRI projects — ranging from project non-negotiations to connectivity issues (Wolf, 2020).

However, it is essential to present an objective assessment of the project's benefits and costs in Pakistan.

---

[22] *Ibid.*

[23] https://science.thewire.in/environment/cpec-china-pakistan-military-environment-coal/.

[24] https://thekootneeti.in/2020/07/15/china-pakistan-economic-corridor-implications-and-challenges/, accessed on September 23, 2020.

[25] *Ibid.*

4.7.1 *Benefits of BRI*

- These projects will help **boost employment** and tax collection, strengthen the provincial road connectivity, promote economic development as well as improve people's living standard. According to Chinese officials, the CPEC will create around 2.3 million jobs in Pakistan by 2030. Till mid July 2020, only 75,000 jobs had been created according to an estimate by a Pakistan senator. Possibly, many of these are contractual short-term jobs for construction workers.

- **China–Pakistan cooperation on economic and social development has made remarkable progress.** In the past five years, China–Pakistan trade has continued to grow rapidly, with an annual growth rate of 18.8% on average; bilateral investment has also been soaring, and China has become the most significant source of foreign capital for Pakistan. International economic and technological cooperation has shown strong momentum, expanding into more areas and reaching a higher level. The social and people-to-people exchanges have increased and bilateral ties have improved. Evidently, China is the largest source of funding for Pakistan's fragile economy.

- Pakistan owns rich human and natural resources, and has enormous **potential for economic growth** and broad market prospects besides a beneficial geo-strategic location. In contrast, China has advantages in infrastructure construction, high-quality production capacity in equipment manufacturing, iron & steel and cement industries, and financing for investment. The orderly and timely flow of economic factors in both countries along the CPEC will significantly improve the resource allocation efficiency and bring into full play the **comparative advantage** of each country.

- The CPEC will greatly **speed up the industrialization and urbanization process** in Pakistan and help it grow into a highly inclusive, globally competitive and prosperous country capable of providing high-quality life to its citizens. However, local businessmen in Pakistan have largely been left out of the investment opportunities. The President of the Federation of Pakistan Chambers of Commerce and Industry, an important organization in Pakistan, has stated, "Pakistan may enter into the second phase of the China–Pakistan Free Trade Agreement with China, but not at the cost of closing our local industries and adversely affecting the economy at large". This is also in sync with comments from Ehsan Malik, the Pakistan Business

Council President, who suggested that "incentives under CPEC need to result in a net increase…simply getting Chinese industry to move and giving them incentives at the expense of present businesses will not benefit the country". Apparently, local businesses are not operating in a level playing field.[26]

- **Improvement of the macroeconomic environment** has benefitted after the initiation of CPEC. According to Prof. Furrukh Khan, in an interview on August 28, 2020, with the authors, "Prime Minister Imran Khan has made efforts to reduce corruption and improve transparency in projects. His policies have also helped the country improve its macroeconomic indicators".
- While increasing the connectivity between China and Pakistan and Pakistani rural and urban areas, the CPEC also increases external intra-Asian connectivity and manifests as **a transnational network**. This facilitates the role of CPEC as an optimal benefit maximizing economic corridor over only a transportation one.

4.7.2 Costs of BRI

- *Balance of payments & Trade deficits*

The CPEC jumbo project worth US$62 billion was expected to be a game-changer for Pakistan. However, the progress of CPEC has been affected in the wake of the economic crisis since 2018.

Figure 4.4 shows the bilateral trade. It indicates clearly that after the CPEC projects in Pakistan, Chinese imports into Pakistan have risen significantly. These imports mainly increased for raw materials and capital goods, which were imported from China directly. This has resulted in an increased trade deficit in Pakistan in the post-CPEC era.

- *Budget deficits and Debt Trap*

Chinese foreign loans and domestic borrowing increased the fiscal deficit to an unsustainable level and worsened the country's debt profile. As a result, Pakistan's debt-to-GDP ratio increased significantly by six percentage points from 67% of GDP in 2016–2017 to 73% of GDP in

---

[26]https://www.cipe.org/blog/2019/07/11/pakistani-businesses-consider-cpec-projects-non-participatory/, accessed on December 15, 2020.

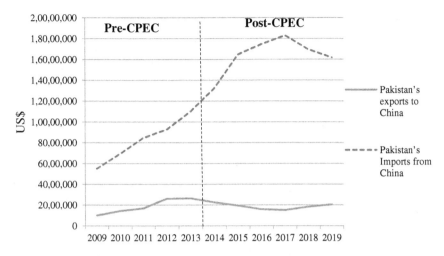

Figure 4.4:   Bilateral trade between China and Pakistan (2009–2019).

Source: Calculations based on data from the International Trade Centre (2019), "Trade Map Database".

2017–2018 — well beyond the debt sustainability limit of 60% of GDP defined under FRDL Act 2005.[27]

Pakistan relies more on China, both in terms of CPEC-related as well as short-term commercial loans. However, the increased borrowing from China, both CPEC-related and commercial, at US$3.9 billion and US$4 billion, respectively, in 2016–2017 and 2017–2018 has important debt sustainability implications. With increasing debt, Pakistan's current account deficit in 2017 and 2018 increased to US$19 billion (5.9% of GDP), leading to reduced foreign exchange reserves and a financial crisis in 2018. This imbalance increased the country's gross financing needs and the vulnerability of the balance of payment account during 2018 and 2019.

In his book *The China–Pakistan Economic Corridor of the Belt and Road Initiative: Concept, Context and Assessment*, Siegfried Wolf analyzed the role of Sinosure, a Chinese state-owned company, in CPEC energy and infrastructure investments. His research revealed that Pakistanis are charged an insurance fee for "debt servicing" (Wolf, 2020,

---

[27]CPEC and Pakistan's debt burden, https://www.thenews.com.pk/print/569919-cpec-and-pakistan-s-debt-burden, accessed on September 22, 2020.

Table 4.9:   Pakistan's external public debt.

Year	2014	2015	2016	2017
Total external public debt (US$)	66,712,407,469	73,093,237,631	86,070,445,355	90,957,392,314
Debt growth rate (Compared to the Previous year)	7.2%	9.56%	17.75%	5.68%

Source: State Bank of Pakistan.

p. 188, note 99) of 7% on energy and infrastructure projects as a condition for receiving loans from Chinese state banks. Thus, a concealed tax is added to what is frequently called "concessionary", low-interest loans, adding to the Pakistani state's debt burden; refer Table 4.9. The costs are also passed on to Pakistani consumers in high energy charges.[28]

There have been reservations among international donors that CPEC loans have resulted in enormous imports of Chinese equipment and materials, leading to a higher debt burden for Pakistan in 2018. In this context, it is crucial to examine Pakistan's debt sustainability and dependence on Chinese loans. Pakistan's total external debt and liabilities increased by US$31.6 billion between 2015 and 2018, to reach US$96.7 billion by September 2018. The increase in the public external debt was primarily due to disbursements from IFIs, China, foreign commercial banks and the Sukuk bond proceeds, and on account of revaluation losses during this period.[29]

State Bank of Pakistan data indicates that the external debt increased to US$112,858 million in the second quarter of 2020 from US$109,949 million in the first quarter of 2020. The lowest debt rate recorded in Pakistan is US$33,172 million in 2014 (third quarter). Figure 4.5 indicates the flow of debt rate in Pakistan from 2009 to 2018. It shows very clearly that the debt rate has been rapidly increasing after 2015 post-BRI investments.

---

[28] *The China–Pakistan Economic Corridor of the Belt and Road Initiative*, by Dr. Wolf, https://www.oboreurope.com/en/china-pakistan-wolf-sadf/, accessed on September 20, 2020.

[29] CPEC and Pakistan's debt burden, https://www.thenews.com.pk/print/569919-cpec-and-pakistan-s-debt-burden, accessed on September 22, 2020.

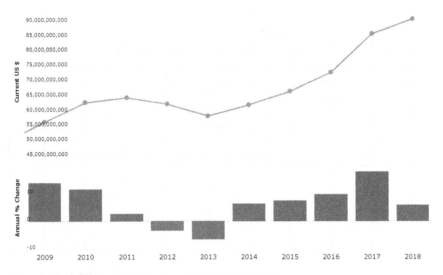

Figure 4.5: Pakistan's total external debt (2009–2018).

Source: macrotrends.net, https://www.macrotrends.net/countries/PAK/pakistan/external-debt-stock, accessed on September 23, 2020.

During the interview with Dr. Reena Marwah on September 20, 2020, Dr. Pervaiz Ali Mahesar, talking about Pakistan debt, said, "there are also concessional loans. These loans will be repaid with 2% interest. The time frame is from 20 to 25 years. But at the same time, there would be a sharp increase in the debt servicing up to US$910 million annually given the nature of CPEC projects". This does not augur well for a cash-trapped economy.

He added, "Undue delays in the disbursement of funds, corruption, increasing power tariffs, and increasing imports may not serve the purpose with which CPEC projects were visualized. Pakistan is expected to start its repayment to China in the year 2021. It will have to repay US$6.017 billion as concessional as well as interest-free loans. The concessional loans (US$5.874 billion) provided by China in the transport sector are based on the 2% interest rate. Pakistan's total external debt is about US$106 billion, of which approx. 11% is comprised of debt from China. China is offering Pakistan not only interest free loans but concessional/soft loans, too. There is no denying that Pakistan will have to repay Chinese debt, but it is unlikely that it could coerce Pakistan to repay its debt as soon as possible. The dates for debt repayment could be extended to help Pakistan come out of the economic crisis". The pandemic has only accentuated Pakistan's debt-related distress.

- ***Internal security risks***

On July 18, 2018, China launched two remote sensing satellites to monitor the CPEC and investigate the progress of the projects in Pakistan. This can create a huge security problem for Pakistan in the future.[30] Earlier, in 2017, 44 Pakistani workers were killed by militancy while working on the projects under CPEC. Other minor incidents of backlash also continue, even as Pakistan spends large sums for securing the Chinese funded projects.

With conditions attached to Chinese loans and funding for infrastructure development constructed by state-owned enterprises, the financing of CPEC seems like a coordinated attempt by the Chinese state to maximize its chances of recovering investment capital and increase its interference over Pakistan's internal affairs.

- ***Corruption and Cronyism***

Often, discreet amounts for project funding are channelized through the officials from the government and army who act as intermediaries for inward investment. The project primarily benefits the core of the country — in Punjab — over its dispossessed periphery. Wani (2020) indicates that CPEC's real objective is to exploit Pakistan's shrinking economy by creating a corrupt elite and a friendly army establishment. He also mentions that an internal report of a committee formed by the Pakistani Government in August 2019 has shed light on corruption and lack of transparency in the projects related to the CPEC.

According to Siddiqa-Agha (2001), Pakistan's hybrid "civilian–military" government has weakened the already weak democratic forces, much needed to ensure project accountability and ascertain their viability. The military in Pakistan exerts influence on both the government and businesses, stretching the concept of a military–industrial complex to an extreme (Wolf, 2019).

For example, in 2017, the CPEC infrastructural projects faced heavy criticism of corruption, forcing Beijing to stop funding three major road projects. According to Mardell (2020), 32 so-called "early harvest" projects have been completed as of 2020, but many projects have been delayed and exceeded budget estimates.

---

[30]The China–Pakistan Economic Corridor: How China is Reconstructing Pakistan, https://www.youtube.com/watch?v=wSlPcOcL138, accessed on September 18, 2020.

4.7.2.1 *Project constitutional issues*

The bulk of BRI-related activities in Pakistan and their stated goals align with China's main BRI policy documents. CPEC does not cover all joint Sino-Pakistani infrastructure efforts that can be seen as furthering BRI goals. CPEC projects, moreover, do not always involve China directly. In line with the methodology behind the MERICS[31] Belt and Road Tracker, non-CPEC projects have been included when they fall within the range of BRI goals.[32]

- At times, the commercial logic of CPEC appears at odds with the overarching goal of bringing prosperity to Pakistan. Chinese companies have often obtained long-term contractual rights to operate road and energy infrastructure and collect electricity or toll fees at guaranteed high prices. These high prices threaten to put Pakistan at a disadvantage compared to regional competitors like Bangladesh.

- ***The restraints of natural and geographical factors***
Southern Xinjiang of China, bordering Pakistan, suffers from a weak industrial base and limited economies of scale. Because of the unique natural and geographical conditions in this area, the construction, operation, and management of major infrastructure projects are costly. In Pakistan, the Indus River valley is comparatively economically advanced, but the scope for further development is limited due to high population density and limited resource carrying capacity. At the same time, the western area is poorly developed and troubled with harsh natural conditions.

4.7.3 *Other economic aspects*

There are several economic aspects within the CPEC projects, which continue to be questioned on their viability. The environmental costs of the traditional coal-fired energy projects will be high. Additionally, the public debt-to-GDP ratio is expected to increase and remain elevated over the medium term, with Pakistan's exposure to debt-related shocks remaining high. Dr. Wolf also notes a distortion between various entrepreneurs: local,

---

[31] Mercator Institute for China Studies.

[32] The BRI in Pakistan: China's flagship economic corridor, https://merics.org/en/analysis/bri-pakistan-chinas-flagship-economic-corridor, assessed on September 10, 2020.

Chinese, military, and military companies and public entrepreneurs (Wolf, 2020). This is visible in the insufficient investment in Pakistani railways despite their indispensable character.

4.7.3.1 *Post-COVID-19 economic impacts*

The World Bank has indicated that the exchange rate, which had remained relatively stable throughout June 2019-February 2020, depreciated by 7.3% in March, 2020. As a result, Pakistan's public debt, which stood at 87.5% of GDP at the end of 2019, may have risen. Imports contracted more than exports, so export growth may remain negative at the end of 2020, given that imports of intermediate goods are required for export growth. Moreover, due to showdown in the Gulf Cooperation Council economies, remittances by Pakistani citizens are expected to contract in 2020 and 2021. Increased multilateral and bilateral flows are expected to be the primary financing sources over the medium term.[33]

4.7.3.2 *Financial cooperation*

China also supports Pakistan within the framework of the AIIB. Both countries promote the mutual opening of their respective financial sectors. This is meant to improve the cross-border credit system and promote financial services such as export credit, project financing, syndicated loans, trade finance, investment bank lending, cross-border RMB business, assets management, e-bank, and financial lease. It also supports project financing by RMB loans, and establishes the evaluation model of power bill in RMB.

China's footprint in terms of internationalization of its currency in Pakistan is expected to rise in the coming years. Hence, CPEC will be an important testing ground for the internationalization of China's currency. The BRI, including the proposed CPEC project financing, will brighten prospects for RMB internationalization, but market realities and China's own economic rules ensure that progress will be slow.[34]

---

[33] The World Bank in Pakistan, https://www.worldbank.org/en/country/pakistan/overview, accessed on September 18, 2020.

[34] Pakistan and the Belt and Road: New Horizons for a Globalized RMB By Muhammad Tayyab Safdar and Joshua Zabin https://thediplomat.com/2020/09/pakistan-and-the-belt-and-road-new-horizons-for-a-globalized-rmb/, accessed on September 27, 2020.

4.8 Conclusion

Given the nature of the China–Pakistan relationship, it is evident that the latter's dependence on China will only continue to grow. While the China–Pakistan Economic Corridor will fundamentally change the country's physical infrastructure from the road to rail connections, to power and water supply, it is also evident that China's influence will be far more pervasive. On the flip side, the pandemic -led disruptions have also placed several projects on the backburner.

In its defense, according to the Pakistan Government, the CPEC long-term plan is a live document and is recommended for reviewing every two years by both sides. CPEC appears to be an attractive gamble for the leaders of China and Pakistan, with objective economic and financial feasibilities of projects being largely disregarded. Nevertheless, the clock is ticking, and CPEC now only has ten years to achieve its stated goal of transforming Pakistan into a prosperous regional trade hub. Credit lines for CPEC have been justified by reference to future growth and revenue (Mardell, 2020).

Priscilla Moriuchi[35] has cautioned that "The focus of Belt and Road is on roads and bridges and ports, because those are the concrete construction projects that people can easily see. However, it is the technologies of the future and technologies of future security systems that could be the biggest security threat in the Belt and Road project".[36]

Given that CPEC is considered as Pakistan's only hope for economic growth and development, there is scant analysis of its costs and benefits. While China will inevitably gain in the long run, some public sector infrastructure and energy development projects, in say, Punjab, are tax-exempted. This is to appease the local consumers. However, this implies that raising money for Chinese loans is impossible and making repayments to China is difficult. Interestingly, in mid-December 2020, China has sanctioned a US$1.5 billion finance line to Pakistan to repay a US$2 billion debt owed to Saudi Arabia.[37]

---

[35] the director of strategic threat development at Recorded Future, a cyber threat intelligence monitoring company based in Massachusetts.

[36] https://www.nytimes.com/2018/12/19/world/asia/pakistan-china-belt-road-military.html, assessed on September 10, 2020.

[37] https://www.moneycontrol.com/news/business/china-bails-out-pakistan-sanctions-1-5-billion-loan-for-saudi-arabia-debt-report-6221461.html, accessed on December 14, 2020.

Pakistan has been able to avoid being in the black list, of the Financial Action Task Force (FATF), as a result of support from China, Turkey, and Malaysia. However, it continues to be on the gray list of the FATF, a watch dog institution for terror financing. Hence, it has become increasingly difficult for it to get financial aid from the International Monetary Fund (IMF), World Bank, ADB, and the European Union, exacerbating problems for the cash-strapped country. Evidently, Pakistan is now in a debt-trap embrace with China.[38]

However, several experts have cautioned Pakistan about how Chinese terms and investments turned sour in Sri Lanka, Tajikistan, and several parts of Africa. In Sri Lanka and Tajikistan, with rising costs and debts incurred by the host countries, large chunks of land were handed over to the Chinese instead of unpaid funds. There are fears that Pakistan could become a "vassal state". Moreover, while China has consistently down-played its port projects' military or defense-related characteristics, two reports released by the Pentagon stated that China's overseas military base is justified by its perceived need to provide security for projects abroad (APSI report, 2020). Given the challenges in leveraging the Gwadar project for economic reasons, and with Chinese warships visiting and being stationed at the Karachi port, there remains hardly any doubt that the only purpose it will fulfil is military and strategic. The economic raison d'etre is only the garb.

---

[38] https://www.livemint.com/news/world/pakistan-to-stay-on-global-watchdog-fatf-s-grey-list-till-feb-2021-11603463593110.html, accessed on December 15, 2020.

Chapter 5

China in Sri Lanka: A Small Island Syndrome

5.1 The Context: *When the West Chides, China Commends*

The depth of the present political dispensation's relations with China are well-known. It was in May 2009, when European efforts to launch a war crimes probe in Sri Lanka were thwarted at the 47-member United Nations Human Rights Council. Colombo could not have wished for more when it received the unflinching support of Beijing in passing a Sri Lankan authored resolution that applauded the Government's actions, congratulated it for liberating the North from the LTTE and reaffirmed "the principle of non-interference in matters which are essentially within the domestic jurisdiction of states" (Wheeler, 2012, p. 22). This friendship between a small island nation in the Indian Ocean with China matured faster in the past decade, because when the West chides, China commends.

A former Foreign Minister once said, "China has never tried to … dominate, undermine or destabilize Sri Lanka. She has come to our rescue with timely assistance on several occasions when there were threats to Sri Lanka's security and territorial integrity" (Wheeler, 2012).

What are the motivations for this friendship between a small island nation of about 21 million and a country of 1.44 billion people? Evidently, it is more than securing a nation battered by a conflict that lasted three decades. This chapter discusses China–Sri Lanka relations, with an emphasis on Chinese interests and investments through BRI projects.

5.2 A Brief History of Sri Lanka

In ancient times, Sri Lanka was known by various names: ancient Greek geographers called it *Taprobane*, while the Arabs referred to it as *Serendib* (the origin of the word "serendipity"). *Ceilão* was the name given to Sri Lanka by the Portuguese when they arrived on the island in 1505 — Ceylon. In 1972, the country's name was changed to *Free, Sovereign and Independent Republic of Sri Lanka*, or the Democratic Socialist Republic of Sri Lanka.

Sri Lanka, the resplendent island at the southeast tip of India, has a population of about 21 million. The vast majority, 74%, are Sinhalese, the descendants of 4th century BCE Buddhist immigrants from India. About 18% of the population is Tamil, descendants of either the ancient migrants from south India who came around 100 BCE or the more recent importation of laborers for the British tea plantations in the 19th century. Another 7% of the population is Muslim; they are called the Moors. There are other ethnic groups in Sri Lanka: some are the descendants of the aboriginal tribes, the "Veddhas", and some trace their ancestry to the Portuguese or the Dutch, who colonized the country in the 16th and 17th centuries, respectively. The British seized the Southwestern Sinhalese coastal area and northern Tamil territory from the Dutch in the 19th century and subsequently repressed the interior Sinhalese Kingdom of Kandy.

5.3 The Sri Lankan Economy: In Brief

In the 19th and 20th centuries, Sri Lanka became a plantation-based economy. Coffee-growing helped to revolutionize the Sri Lankan economy. However, the coffee economy was destroyed by a leaf disease toward the end of the 19th century. It was also adversely impacted by falling coffee prices due to the economic recession in Europe. Hence, plantation owners turned to grow tea as a substitute crop for the erstwhile coffee plantations.

Given that tea plantations required a permanent workforce and the local Sinhalese were unwilling to work, the British colonial rulers

Table 5.1: Trends in human development and income.

	1975	1985	1995	2000	2010	2014	2019
GDP Per Capita (Current US$)	281	377	718	855	2747	3795	3,853
HDI Score	0.614	0.674	0.717	0.679	0.738	0.757	0.78
Life expectancy at birth	66	69	69	71	74	75	77

Note: *HDI score until 1995 from (Siddique *et al.*, 2012) from 2000 by UNDP Human Development Report online data.
Source: World Bank — WDI, GDP per capita in (current US$).

imported workers from India's Tamil region. Tamils on the island had ancestors who had settled in north Sri Lanka nearly a thousand years ago. These are called the Sri Lankan Tamils. Toward the end of the 19th century, rubber plantations were developed as an additional source of export earnings. The cultivation of three cash crops, (cinnamon, rubber, and Ceylon tea) became the country's primary revenue source. The other two major Sri Lanka crops, rice and coconuts, were produced primarily for the domestic market. After independence from the British in 1948, socialism strongly influenced the government's economic policies until the 1970s. Although a welfare state was established, and the standard of living and literacy improved significantly, its economy suffered from inefficiency. Sri Lanka's industries were mostly labor-intensive. The country's mineral resources included clay, gems, graphite, limestone, mineral sands, and phosphate rock. Its primary export earners were agricultural products, coconut, minerals and gems, rubber, tea, textiles, and clothing and the principal export markets were Australasia, Germany, Japan, the Middle East, the United Kingdom, and the United States.

With one of the highest Human Development Index (HDI) ranking in South Asia, Sri Lanka further improved its ranking in HDI 2019 by five places compared to the previous year.[1] According to the HDI 2019 report, Sri Lanka's average life expectancy at birth is 80.1 years for females and 73.4 years for males. Table 5.1 presents the data of GDP per capita, HDI score, and life expectancy since 1975–2019.

[1] 71 out of 189 countries according to "the UNDP HDI 2019".

GDP per capita of Sri Lanka in 1960 was US$144; this increased to US$3,853 by 2019. In 2012, Sri Lanka achieved a 12% growth rate, the highest in its economic history. This resulted from the end of the 30-year long civil war. Post the end of the conflict, i.e. since 2009, Sri Lanka emerged as a tourist destination. The China–Sri Lanka relationship also received a fillip under the Rajapaksha regime which was in power from 2005 to 2015. Mahinda Rajapaksha lost the mandate of the people in 2015, and Maithripala Sirisena was elected. Sirisena's government decided to partially stall or review the much-criticized Chinese funded projects, which were the legacy of his predecessor.

The April 2019 terrorist attacks impacted the tourist sector adversely, and Sri Lanka's GDP growth rate declined to 2.28%. With the COVID-19 pandemic gripping the tourism industry, the GDP growth rate is expected to decline further. However, with the new President-elect in late 2019 (President Gotabaya Rajapaksha), people hope past mistakes would not be repeated. They look forward to infrastructure development and support for the small and medium enterprises to boost the flailing export sector.

5.4   China–Sri Lanka Relationship

There exists a long history between China and Sri Lanka, commencing with their Buddhist linkages. According to Elman and Liu (2017), it was in 410 BC when Fa Xian travelled to Sri Lanka and stayed for two years before returning to China. Amoghavajra, a powerful Buddhist monk in Chinese history is also well known for translating the *Karandamudra Sutra* into Chinese and taking it back to China in the 8th century. Buddhist nuns from Sri Lanka also travelled to China in 429 and 433 BC. Additionally, Porter and Low (1999) write of the influence of Chinese/ East Asian architecture, alongside Indian architecture on Sri Lanka.

Furthermore, during the Ming dynasty, Admiral Zheng He's fleet visited Sri Lanka and fought in the Ming–Kotte War. The Galle Trilingual inscription, dated 1409, was erected in Galle, to commemorate Zheng He's second visit to the country and recognize the Ming emperor's legitimacy among foreign rulers.[2] Chinese immigrants migrated to Sri Lanka during the 18th and 19th centuries, though they were miniscule compared

---

[2] https://web.archive.org/web/20060527043643/http://www.china.org.cn/english/features/zhenhe/134661.htm, accessed on August 2, 2020, "The BRI and the Buddhist Kingdom of Lanka". *Sunday Observer*. November 11, 2017.

to those from neighboring countries like India, Myanmar, or other parts of Southeast Asia.

Historical and cultural ties between the two countries date back to hundreds of years. It was the Ceylon–China Rubber–Rice Pact, signed in 1952, which proved to be the cornerstone of the early years of diplomatic relations. Diplomatic ties between Sri Lanka and China have been strong since; especially during the Sri Lanka Freedom Party governments since the 1950s. It was on February 7, 1957, that China and Sri Lanka established diplomatic relations. Since then, the two countries have regularly exchanged high-level visits resulting in several agreements. These have led to the construction of the Bandaranaike Memorial International Conference Hall by China to honour former Prime Minister SWRD Bandaranaike in 1973. In 1996, then Sri Lankan President Chandrika Bandaranaike Kumaratunga (second daughter of Mr. Bandaranaike) paid a state visit to China at the invitation of the Chinese President Jiang Zemin, during which two agreements were signed to enhance economic cooperation.

The tenure of Sri Lankan President Mahinda Rajapaksa (2005–2015) resulted in many agreements and closer relations between the two countries due to Rajapaksa's pro-China stance.[3] The Sri Lankan president, Maithripala Sirisena, who served the country from January 2015 to November 2019, tried to balance both Chinese and Indian influence in the country.[4] In 2020, Mahinda Rajapaksha was re-elected as Prime Minister for the fourth time, since first having been elected in 2004.

The relationship between China and Sri Lanka has, over the past few decades, developed into an all-round partnership, from the economic to the technical and the strategic aspects.

5.5 China–Sri Lanka Economic Engagement

This section analyzes China's economic engagement with Sri Lanka, through trade, investment in BRI projects, and tourism in the two decades of this century. Kelegama (2014) and Fernando (2010) have written extensively on China–Sri Lanka Economic Relations.

---

[3] Goh, Evelyn (April 22, 2016). *Rising China's Influence in Developing Asia*. Oxford University Press. ISBN 9780191076145 — via Google Books.

[4] President Sirisena's second visit to Beijing to boost China–Sri Lanka ties. Archived October 7, 2016, at the Wayback Machine.

5.5.1 *Contemporary trade data*

In 2000, Chinese imports comprised only 3.5% of Sri Lanka's total imports. However, this share had risen to 20% by 2017 and to 23% by 2018, when China became Sri Lanka's largest import source in less than two decades, surpassing India. The rise of Chinese imports in Sri Lanka is a relatively recent phenomenon; Chinese imports increased by almost four times from 2011 to 2018. Figures 5.1 and 5.2 compare the top six trading partners in Sri Lanka in 2011 and 2017.

In 2018, Sri Lanka imported US$18.7B worth of commodities, making it the world's 80th largest importer. The most recent imports include refined petroleum (US$2.3B), cars (US$2.2B), light rubberized knitted

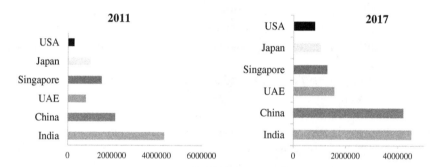

Figure 5.1:   Sri Lanka's top six import partners (US$).
Source: UN COMTRADE online data.

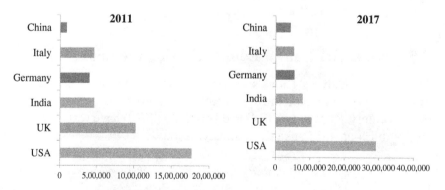

Figure 5.2:   Sri Lanka's top six export partners (US$).
Source: UN COMTRADE online data.

fabric (US$760M), broadcasting equipment (US$367M), and packaged medicaments (US$307M).

Sri Lanka's top 6 export partners in 2018 were the USA (24%), India (8%), UK (7%), Germany (7%), Italy (4%), and China (3%). In 2018, Sri Lanka exported US$11.1B, making it the 84th largest exporter in the world. The most recent exports include tea (US$858M), knit women's undergarments (US$556M), other women's undergarments (US$635M), knit women's suits (US$493M), and non-knit women's suits (US$476M).[5] The most important import partners for Sri Lanka in 2020 were India (US$4.25B), China (US$4.23B), Singapore (US$1.73B), Japan (US$1.17B), and Malaysia (US$708M). The top six import partners were India (23%), China (23%), Singapore (9%), Japan (6%), and Malaysia (4%), respectively.

China has come to dominate the Sri Lankan import market within a short period. In contrast, Sri Lankan exports to China increased marginally. There is a bilateral FTA that is being negotiated, post which trade is expected to increase further. With lower tariffs, there is every possibility that Chinese products will penetrate deeper into Sri Lanka's consumer market, increasing China's already huge US$3.4 billion trade surplus. Colombo is already indebted to Beijing to the tune of US$9.6 billion, given at interest rates of between 2% and 5%, and falling behind repayments.[6,7]

5.6 Chinese Investments & BRI Projects in Sri Lanka

China had investment projects even before the BRI. China's initial infrastructure investments in Sri Lanka took place in the 1970s in the form of outright grants, including constructing a convention centre. However, the decades of 2000s and 2010s saw a substantial inflow of foreign investment into Sri Lanka from China.

China's investment has recently come under examination due to the growing geopolitical rivalries in the Indian Ocean as well as Sri Lanka's

[5] OEC. World https://oec.world/en/profile/country/lka/, accessed on August 7, 2020.

[6] Chinese investments in Sri Lanka, https://www.gatewayhouse.in/chinese-investments-sri-lanka-2/, accessed on August 7, 2020.

[7] Department of External Resources, Government of Sri Lanka, *Foreign Aid Review Report 2005 and Performance Reports 2006–2015.* < http://www.erd.gov.lk/publication.html>.

location and ports in this region. Several experts have written about the strategic geopolitical significance of the island nation. Bruno Macaes in his 2019 book describes how the changing world symbolizes a new phase in China's ambitions as a superpower: to restructure the world economy and crown Beijing as the new center of capitalism and globalization (Maçães, 2019). Additionally, in his new book *The Costliest Pearl*, Swedish journalist Bertil Lintner describes the new "great game" being played in the Indian Ocean. China, on the one hand, and the US and India, along with extra-regional powers such as France, Australia, and Japan, on the other, are moving their chess pieces one by one to gain and sustain control over the vast ocean and its strategic sea lanes.[8] However, these moves along with China's construction of a string of ports in Myanmar, Bangladesh, Sri Lanka, Pakistan, Djibouti, Mauritius, and Comoros, among other places, have naturally alarmed the two leading powers who have held control over the Indian Ocean — India and the US (Lintner, 2019). Abeyagoonasekera (2019) further delineates aspects of China's expanding influence in South Asia and the growing conversation about the Indo-Pacific region. The pull between developmental imperatives and rising external debts has placed the Sri Lankan economy in a precarious situation. Singh (2019) explains that BRI was launched by China to gain access to world markets that resulted in the Chinese acquisition of high-tech capabilities in terms of political, financial, and military power.

5.6.1 *BRI projects*

Under the BRI projects, Sri Lanka has currently secured up to $8 billion of financing from China. Some of these projects were linked to China's Belt and Road Initiative. Figure 5.3 shows the rise in development assistance to Sri Lanka in the post-2013 phase, with the completion of some ongoing projects and the negotiation of new ones.

The key projects are:

1. Southern Expressway (ongoing, construction started in 2011)
2. Outer Circular Highway Project (ongoing, construction started in 2014)

---

[8] Book review: The Costliest Pearl describes the new "Great Game", https://www.new indianexpress.com/lifestyle/books/2019/aug/04/book-review-the-costliest-pearl-describes-the-new-great-game-2012988.html, accessed on August 27, 2020.

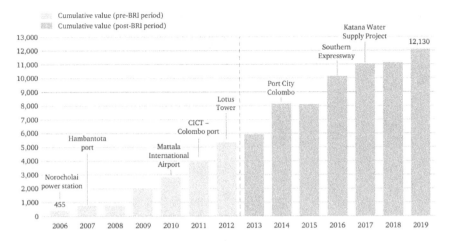

Figure 5.3: Chinese Development Finance to Sri Lanka (US$ million).

Note: The chart shows committed funds only up to July 2019.

Source: Wignaraja *et al.* (2020). calculations based on data provided by the Central Bank of Sri Lanka, Department of External Resources, Ministry of Finance, Sri Lanka; Board of Investments, Sri Lanka, and various interviews with key persons.

3. Colombo Katunayake Expressway (completed in 2013, construction started in 2009)
4. Hambantota International Airport project (completed in 2013, construction started in 2010)
5. Hambantota Port Development Project (completed, construction started in 2007)
6. CICT Colombo Terminal (completed in 2014, construction started in 2011)
7. Norocholai power station (completed in March 2011, construction started in 2006)
8. Colombo Port City (CIFE) (ongoing, to be completed in 2042, construction started in 2014)
9. Lotus Tower (completed in September 2019, construction started in 2012)

There are nine major projects under the BRI and Chinese investments in Sri Lanka; each one employs Chinese contractors. Table 5.2 provides detailed information about all projects with project title, loan-based or investment-based nature of the project, investment amount, foreign lender or investor's details, implementing agency, contractor, and economic benefits.

Table 5.2: Financial terms and expected economic benefits of major Chinese projects.

Project Name	Loan/ Investment	Amount (US$ million)	Loan terms	Foreign lender/ Investor	Implementing agency	Contractor	Economic benefits
Southern Expressway (ongoing, started construction in 2011)	Loan	1,545	Fixed-rate – 2%	EXIM	Road Development Authority	CCC	• 48% of total expressways. • Commute to Galle from Colombo has halved from 3 hours to 1.5 hours. • Better infrastructure has allowed the southern coast to develop as a tourist hotspot.
Outer Circular Highway Project (ongoing, started construction in 2014)	Loan	494	Fixed rate – 2%	EXIM	Road Development Authority	Metallurgical Corporation of China Ltd	• 5% of total expressways. • Easier commute to Colombo from suburbs.
Colombo Katunayake Expressway (completed in 2013, started construction in 2009)	Loan	248	Fixed-rate – 6.3%	EXIM	Road Development Authority	China Metallurgical Group Corporation	• 15% of total expressways. • Reduced commuting time to the airport from 2 to 1.5 hours from Central Colombo.
Hambantota International Airport project (completed in 2013, started construction in 2010)	Loan	190	Fixed rate – 2%	EXIM	Airport & Aviation Lanka Limited	CHEC	• Emergency landings are possible with a second airport. • Saved Sri Lanka $1.5 M per flight if diverted to Southern India during an emergency. • Increased national passenger capacity, reducing congestion at Colombo Airport.
Hambantota Port Development Project (completed, started construction in 2007)	Loan	1,335.7	Fixed (2–6.5%) and Variable Rates	EXIM	Sri Lanka Ports Authority	CHEC	• Industrial zone will bring in more primary industries. • Diversified port operations through the addition of value added services.

Project	Type	Amount	Interest	Financier	Implementing agency	Contractor	Remarks
CICT Colombo Terminal (completed in 2014, started construction in 2011)	Investment	500	N/A	CMPH	Sri Lanka Ports Authority	CHEC	• Currently the only deep-water terminal in South Asia equipped with facilities to handle the largest vessels afloat. • CICT has helped the Port of Colombo to move up the Drewry's Port Connectivity Index to be ranked the 11th best-connected port in the world in 2018.
Norocholai power station (completed in March 2011, started construction in 2006)	Loan	1,346	Fixed rate − 2%	EXIM	Ceylon Electricity Board	China Machinery Engineering Corporation	• Accounts for 31% of the total installed capacity of CEB-owned power plants. • Accounts for 33% of Sri Lanka's total power generated in 2018.
Colombo Port City (ongoing, to be completed in 2042, started construction in 2014)	Investment	1,300	N/A	CHEC	N/A	CHEC	• Adding 1.5 million units of A-Grade office space (tripling total office space in Colombo). • Would improve Sri Lanka's ease of doing business rankings. • Likely to attract high-tier financial services.
Lotus Tower (completed in September 2019, started construction in 2012)	Loan	88.6	N/A	EXIM	Telecommunications Regulatory Commission of Sri Lanka	China National Electronics Import & Export Corporation	• Improve telecommunications infrastructure. • Reduce the number of downtime incidences. • Organize leisure activities for the public.

Notes: EXIM: Export–Import Bank of China; CMPH: China Merchant Port Holdings; CHEC: China Harbour Engineering Company; CCC: China Communications Construction Company Limited.

Source: This table was taken from Wignaraja *et al.* (2020). Calculations based on data provided by the Central Bank of Sri Lanka, Department of External Resources, Ministry of Finance, Sri Lanka; Board of Investments, Sri Lanka, and various interviews with key persons.

5.6.1.1 *Expressways*

Given the imperative for increasing connectivity in the island state, roads and **expressways are the largest subsectors for Chinese investment** in Sri Lanka. Since 2009, China's investment has helped to build an estimated 116.1 km or 68% of the length of all expressways. Three major expressway projects are the Southern Expressway, the Colombo–Katunayake Expressway, and the Colombo Outer Circular Highway. These infrastructure projects have significantly contributed to improving national road connectivity, enhancing road safety, and reducing journey times. This could not have been possible without funding from the Export–Import Bank of China (EXIM Bank China) totaling US$1.6 billion between 2014 and 2017 (Wignaraja *et al.*, 2020, p. 8).[9]

5.6.1.2 *Ports*

Ports are the second-largest sector for Chinese investment in Sri Lanka. The fourth terminal construction at Colombo port and the new Hambantota port in Southern Sri Lanka were among the port development projects. A significant reason for the Colombo port's success is an initial Chinese investment of $500 million in 2011 by China Merchant Port Holdings Company in the CICT. This is the only state of the deep-water terminal in South Asia which can handle ultra-large container carriers (ULCC) or more than 20,000 twenty-foot-equivalent-unit (TEU) vessels. CICT has helped the Colombo port become the 11th best-connected port globally due to the geographical coverage of these services and the high

---

[9] Wignaraja *et al.*, 2020, p. 8, to show these data Wignaraja *et al.* (2020) referred Calculations based on data from Department of External Resources, Ministry of Finance (2019), "Official Development Assistance Database", http://www.erd.gov.lk/index.php?option=com_content&view=article&id=89&Itemid=312&lang=en, Road Development Authority, Sri Lanka (2020), "National Highways", http://www.rda.gov.lk/source/rda_roads.htm (accessed February 3, 2020), ADB (2014), Sri Lanka: Southern Transport Development Project, https://www.adb.org/sites/default/files/project-document/81845/26522-023-pcr.pdf#page=16 (accessed February 25, 2020), Calculations based on data from Department of External Resources, Ministry of Finance (2019), Official Development Assistance Database.

frequency of mainline liner service connections (Wignaraja *et al.*, 2020, p. 9).[10]

Port of Hambantota: A case of debt-trap diplomacy: The Port of Hambantota is indispensable to China's energy security given that the country imports two-thirds of its oil through shipping lanes south of the port. Hambantota Port was financed by three fixed interest rate loans; one from EXIM Bank China amounting to US$1.4 billion, and two from Chinese SOEs China Harbour Engineering and Sinohydro Corporation. However, the project took longer than expected to complete and incurred financial losses putting a strain on Sri Lanka's public finances. Some have claimed that this is an example of unprofitable infrastructure investment and China's so-called "debt-trap diplomacy" (Wignaraja *et al.*, 2020, p. 9).

Speaking about Chinese investment in an interview with Dr. Reena Marwah on March 26, 2019, Dr. Dushni Weerakoon said, "I think we have not done our homework, we are taking short-term decisions without thinking through what 99 years means. Not just the Hambantota, the Colombo Port City, that is another 99 years".

With a view to stem financial losses, in 2017, the government of President Sirisena agreed to give Chinese SOEs a controlling interest in managing the port under a 99-year lease. Following a risk-sharing agreement, Sri Lanka received US$1.12 billion, which was used to bolster its foreign exchange reserves. After that, the Hambantota port management moved to a Chinese SOE, China Merchant Port Holdings Company Limited.

China also took control over 15,000 acres of land adjacent to the port to develop an **industrial zone in Hambantota**. The feasibility study for the industrial park identified the development of shipping services, processing of seafood, agricultural products, and other processing/manufactured industries as potential ventures. Another BRI project in Sri Lanka is the expansion and modernization of the Colombo Port — the Colombo International Container Terminal — a Sino-Sri Lanka joint venture. The neighboring industrial zone is expected to attract new foreign investment and create jobs.

---

[10] Sundy Observer, Sri Lanka (2019), "Colombo Port, 11th best connected in the World", January 6, 2019, http://www.sundayobserver.lk/2019/01/06/business, accessed on August 3, 2020.

5.6.1.3 *Energy generation*

Non-renewable energy generation is the third-largest sector for Chinese investment in Sri Lanka. In the early 2000s, Sri Lanka suffered from an unreliable electricity supply and periodic power cuts that hampered the economy.[11] The **Norocholai power station** in northwest Sri Lanka, also known as the Puttlam power plant, was developed as a longer-term solution to its electricity supply problems. It was co-financed by the EXIM Bank. Loans amounted to US$1.4 billion. The China Machinery Engineering Corporation began construction of the power station in 2007. This was built in three phases, each with a 300-megawatt capacity, over seven years. The Norocholai power station is the largest in the country, becoming a significant contributor to the country's electricity supply. This power plant comprises 31.1% of the total installed capacity of Ceylon Electricity Board-owned power plants and accounted for 33% of the total Sri Lankan power generation in 2018 (Wignaraja *et al.*, 2020, p. 10).[12]

5.6.1.4 *Colombo port city (CIFC)*

The CIFC, formerly known as the **Colombo Port City**, is being built with the aim to build a new city and financial center in Colombo by 2030.[13] Urban development in the form of the Port City Colombo project is the fourth sector for Chinese investment (Wignaraja *et al.*, 2020, p. 10). This is a city built on 269 hectares of reclaimed land and is an extension of Colombo's central business district. CHEC Port City Colombo (Pvt) Ltd, a wholly owned subsidiary of China Harbour Engineering Company (CHEC), is the primary developer and had initially invested US$1.4 billion. The Port City, the largest investment by a private company is being developed as a game-changer in financial, ICT, and professional services. These projects are to be completed in 2042. Assuming that the Port City is 60% operational, it could generate 122,000 jobs and bring in FDI close

---

[11] The Island (2018). "Power Sector in Shambles", April 2, 2018, http://www.island.lk/, accessed on August 2, 2020.

[12] 8 Ceylon Electricity Board (2019). Statistical Digest 2018, Colombo: Ceylon Electricity Board, https://www.ceb.lk/front_img/img_reports/1567487133Statistical_Digest_2018.pdf, accessed on August 3, 2020.

[13] China's Belt and Road Initiative (BRI): A sustainable partnership for Sri Lanka?, http://www.ft.lk/opinion/China-s-Belt-and-Road-Initiative--BRI---A-sustainable-partnership-for-Sri-Lanka-/, accessed July 24, 2020.

to half a billion dollars.[14] However, the danger of the Port city being turned into a Chinese colony is on the anvil, if the controversial Colombo Port City Economic Commission Bill is passed in its present form by Parliament. (This Bill aims to provide for a special economic zone to establish a commission to grant registrations, licenses, authorisations and other approvals to operate business in such economic zones).

5.6.1.5 *Airports*

In addition to seaports, China has also funded the construction of airports. The Mattala Rajapaksa International Airport (MRIA) is located in Hambantota, 241 km southeast of Colombo. The MRIA is the second international airport in Sri Lanka and was built at a cost of US$209 million, US$190 of which was received in the form of loans from China. Mattalla was selected as the site for the country's number two air transport hub, to be complemented with the Hambantota port in its vicinity. Given that the airport was built in the home state of the then President, there have been criticisms about the lack of capacity utilization of the airport. It has also been referred to as a "ghost airport".

Dr. Dushni Weerakoon, in an interview with Dr. Reena Marwah in March 2019, said "Of course there is the Mattala International Airport. They are trying to give India 30% share on a long-term lease. Japan has expressed some interest in the Eastern province. So, there is this question about the government's strategy of giving the strategic assets/infrastructures to countries that are going to be regional rivals in the years to come; they already are, but they are going to intensify".

Tourism Minister Prasanna Ranatunga, appointed on August 17, 2020, stated, "We have a responsibility to develop the Mattala Airport as the second largest airport in Sri Lanka and not second to the Katunayake Airport. The groundwork is being prepared for this. The people of the previous government did not have any sense to repair this and take advantage of it. If Mattala has suffered any setback today, the previous Rajapaksa government is responsible for it".[15]

---

[14] 1 PwC (2020). Economic Impact Assessment of Port City Colombo, https://www.pwc.com/lk/en/assets/document/2020/Port-City-Report.pdf, accessed on March 16, 2020.

[15] Mattala to be restored as a tourist, export-oriented airport, http://www.dailynews.lk/2020/08/31/local/227426/mattala-be-restored-tourist-export-oriented-airport, accessed on September 4, 2020.

Furthermore, Youth Affairs and Sports Minister Namal Rajapaksa said that with the opening of the Mattala Airport and the Hambantota Port, the ultimate goal was to transform Hambantota into an aviation and shipping hub of South Asia.[16] The future development activities of the Mattala Airport are being discussed within the elected government. The focus is on developing the tourism industry and exporting local goods to foreign countries through this airport. Meanwhile, the Indian Government has confirmed that it will not establish a joint venture company with Sri Lanka for operating the Mattala Rajapaksa International Airport.[17]

5.7 BRI Projects: Authors 2020 Survey and Analysis

A small open survey related to Chinese BRI projects in Sri Lanka was conducted in August–September 2020, wherein a questionnaire was given to over 100 respondents via the simple random sampling method. 49% of the respondents represented the age group of 20–30 years, 20% were in the age group 31–40 years, 24% were between 41–50 years, and 5% represented the over-50 years age group. In terms of their occupation, 36% were students, 42% were employed in the government sector, 8% in the private sector, 6% were unemployed, and 8% were in other categories. The sample included respondents from diverse fields: majority of them belonged to the educational field (48%), and 28% among them were university professors, senior lecturers, and lecturers (see Figure 5.4 for more details).

Questions to respondents ranged from their perception of China, projects considered successful, and future engagement of the two countries. Results showed that most Sri Lankans view China as an economic powerhouse (38%), some view it as a development partner (25%). In comparison, others (12%) think of China as a political and military powerhouse (see Figure 5.5 for more details).

98% of respondents are aware of Chinese investments in the country. Upon inquiry, 38% said that the Southern expressway is the most successful and valuable Chinese project in Sri Lanka (see Figure 5.6). Colombo port was the second most important project (31%) and Hambantota port ranked third (16%). The Colombo port city project is being projected by

[16] *Ibid.*

[17] https://currentaffairs.gktoday.in/india-will-not-run-the-worlds-emptiest-airport-mattala-rajapaksa-international-airport-072020331211.html, accessed on September 4, 2020.

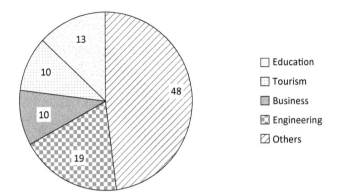

Figure 5.4:   Occupation of respondents.

Source: Sample survey August–September 2020 by the authors.

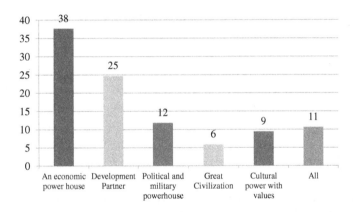

Figure 5.5:   Respondents view of China.

Source: Sample survey by the authors.

the Rajapaksha Government as a win–win for both countries, while the Opposition warns of China's ambitions to become a resident power in the region through its neo-colonialism strategy.

Likert scale was employed to rate the top five BRI projects in Sri Lanka. The results are as follows:

According to the survey, the Southern Expressway Project was the most successful project with 70% claiming that it has high benefits for Sri Lankans such as save time in commuting. The second ranked project was Colombo port city (50%) and the third rank was for the Norocholai Power Plant (46%). Hambantota Port and CICT terminal projects were identified as low benefit projects refer Table 5.3.

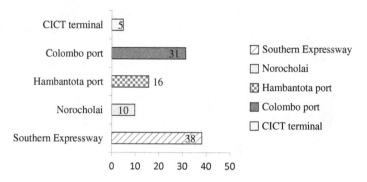

Figure 5.6:   Chinese Projects considered successful in Sri Lanka.
Source: Sample survey by the authors.

Table 5.3:   Top five BRI projects in Sri Lanka: Respondents' Assessment.

Scale	Southern Expressway (%)	Norocholai Power Plant (%)	Hambantota Port (%)	Colombo Port City (%)	CICT Terminal (%)
Highest benefits	31	9	2	11	0
High benefits	39	37	17	39	15
Medium benefits	20	26	37	31	22
Low benefits	4	13	22	7	22
Lowest benefits	6	15	13	4	20

Source: Sample survey 2020 by the authors.
Note: A few columns do not add to 100, as some respondents were unsure of any benefits accruing to people of Sri Lanka.

Upon being asked if the Chinese Government favored the Rajapaksa family while investing in Sri Lanka and vice versa, 58% of the sample population were in disagreement, while 42% agreed. Those who concur reasoned that: (1) the Chinese leadership has shared a close relationship with the Rajapaksas since 2005, (2) socialist affinities of both the parties also act as a factor here, (3) Mahinda Rajapaksa invited Chinese investment in large projects. Those projects were implemented through contracts that were never transparent, generated high profits, and enabled China to develop political power in the Asian region, (4) family connections are essential in governmental relations, (5) the Chinese Government wants to befriend Sri Lanka because of its strategic geographical location

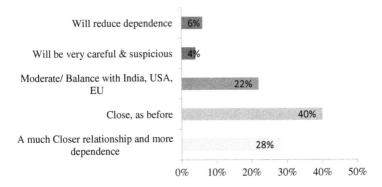

Figure 5.7:   Rajapaksha Government's relations with China in the future.
Source: Sample survey 2020 by the authors.

in the Indian Ocean, and (6) the Rajapaksha Government makes for a more congenial partner for China.

While 40% said that relations between the new government under Gotabaya Rajapaksha and China would remain close, 28% said that the two would become even closer with increased Sri Lankan dependence on China. About 22% said that the new government would continue a moderate/balanced relationship with India, the USA, and the EU (see Figure 5.7).

However, a shift in relations can be expected with the incoming of the new Sri Lankan president given his excellent relationship with the USA, due to his dual citizenship and erstwhile family life. At the same time, the Indian Prime Minister Narendra Modi wished him right after he was elected as Sri Lankan President, resonating the good relations between India and Sri Lanka. Academics have mentioned how India is like a brother to Sri Lanka, while China is a cousin. Respondents are of the view that the government should balance its relations with both India and China in the future.

5.8   Costs & Benefits of BRI Initiatives in Sri Lanka

As explained above, China made significant inroads into Sri Lanka during the Rajapaksa regime, especially over the period 2005–2015. That was when the islanders got the taste of driving on expressways, thanks to China's expertise in road construction. The Chinese constructed the Nelum Pokuna as a gift to Sri Lanka. With China's increasing assertiveness in its bilateral engagement with BRI partners, Sri Lanka would do well to take a leaf out of other countries' experiences.

This highlights how Sri Lanka is viewed as a potential stopover point in the Indian Ocean, justifying Chinese interests in developing one of Sri Lanka's ports. However, there is a pushback as people believe that the Sri Lankan authorities should not permit the Chinese workforce to do as they wish and threaten cultures and practices or disturb the peaceful way of living on the island.[18] There are identifiable costs and benefits from the BRI projects in Sri Lanka.

5.8.1 *Benefits of BRI*

- **Higher Trade Flows**

While Sri Lanka is not an important trading partner of China, the latter has emerged as Sri Lanka's second-largest trading partner after India. Initiatives, such as the BRI have the potential to enhance trade routes between countries and facilitate trade bilaterally and beyond. However, with the pandemic impacting tourism severely, the country's growth in the near term will be compromised.

- **Attracting more FDI**

This remains a priority for Sri Lanka. As part of the BRI, there have been significant Chinese investments in Sri Lanka. Existing investments in Sri Lanka as part of the BRI amount to approximately US$8 billion and China has offered an additional US$24 billion in financing. In addition to that, the exchange of technology and foreign knowledge could benefit the host country. China's FDI has clearly overshadowed that of the other countries in the island nation. In 2005, China's FDI into Sri Lanka was US$16.4 million, or just under 1% of total Sri Lankan FDI. By 2015, Chinese private investments reached US$338 million, constituting 35% of Sri Lanka's total FDI.[19]

- **Development of New Infrastructure**

The BRI holds the promise of investment in new railways, roads, ports, and other projects and improves connectivity between countries.

---

[18] http://www.dailymirror.lk/article/Will-the-Chinese-build-a-colony-in-Sri-Lanka--136470.html, accessed on July 24, 2020.
[19] Chinese investments in Sri Lanka, https://www.gatewayhouse.in/chinese-investments-sri-lanka-2/, accessed on August 7, 2020.

However, the success of the BRI will require more than just building physical infrastructure. Soft infrastructure, which means facilitating people's movement, goods and services across borders, is critical. Significant gains have not accrued in terms of employment.

5.8.2 Costs of BRI

- **Balance of payments, Budget deficits, & International Trade**

Chinese infrastructure projects in Sri Lanka have relied heavily upon imported capital goods and intermediate goods from China. For instance, the Southern Expressway was built with Chinese road construction equipment and road construction materials. Chinese imports of road construction equipment include motor graders, road roller machines, asphalt mixing plants, forklift trucks, etc. Chinese imports of road construction materials include bituminous materials, soil, cement, structural steel, etc. (Wignaraja *et al.*, 2020).

Prior to the BRI, Sri Lanka's capital imports from China accounted for around 17% of Sri Lanka's total capital goods imports in 2006–2012, which rose to 27% in 2013–2017. Sri Lanka's intermediate goods imports from China rose from 58% of the country's total intermediate goods imports to 62% from 2013 to 2017. This is clear evidence of the fact that the host country is expected to import its requirements of machines and materials from the home country.

Figure 5.8 clearly indicates the bilateral trade between China and Sri Lanka, in the post and pre-BRI periods. The data indicate that the trade gap became wider after the BRI initiatives. Table 5.6 appended to this chapter shows the overall statistics of the trade balance between China and Sri Lanka. Sri Lanka's overall trade deficit with China (as a share of Sri Lanka's GDP) rose from 2.6% in 2006 to 4.8% in 2019 (Wignaraja *et al.*, 2020, p. 13).

- **Debt Trap**

Based on some reports, between 2004 and 2014, during the reign of Rajapaksha, China provided US$7 Billion in loans and investment,[20] including loans for the construction of the port in Hambantota. However, both local and international experts believe that Sri Lanka cannot afford

---

[20] Sri Lanka snubs India, opens port to Chinese submarine again". *The Times of India.* Retrieved 2017-08-04.

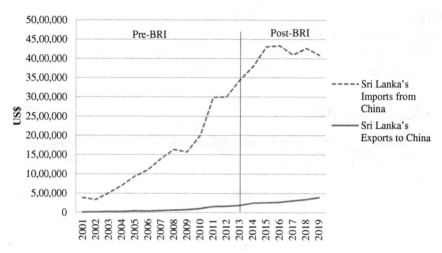

Figure 5.8:   Bilateral trade between China and Sri Lanka (US$).

Source: Calculations based on data from the International Trade Centre (2019), "Trade Map Database".

these loans since the nation already has incurred a total external public debt of US$64 billion. About 95% of the government's revenue is used to pay back loans.[21] Debt to China amounts to about 6% of Sri Lanka's GDP (see Table 5.4).

Sri Lanka's external public debt to China doubled from US$2.2 billion to US$5 billion over the period 2012 to 2018. As a percentage of GDP, in the same period this rose from 3.2% to 5.6%. In 2019, it increased to about US$6 billion (Weerkoon and Jayasooriya, 2019). However, Sri Lanka recorded a total government debt equivalent to 77.60% of its GDP in 2017 and 86.80% of the country's GDP in 2019.[22] Accordingly, while in 2006, only 6% of external debt was commercial debt, by 2012, this rose to 50%, resulting in a surge in interest payments.[23]

---

[21] Limaye, Yogita (2017-05-26). "Sri Lanka: A country trapped in debt". BBC News. Retrieved 2017-08-04.

[22] Trading economics, https://tradingeconomics.com/sri-lanka/government-debt-to-gdp, accessed on August 7, 2020.

[23] Moramudali, U. (2017). Sri Lanka's Debt and China's Money, https://thediplomat.com/2017/08/sri-lankas-debt-and-chinas-money/, accessed on August 5, 2020.

Table 5.4:   Sri Lanka's external public debt.

	2012	2015	2018	2019
Total external public debt* (US$ billion)	23.7	28.6	34.7	55.9
China **(US$ billion)	2.2	4.8	5.0	6

*Notes:** Total external public debt is calculated as the central government's external debt plus SOEs and public corporations' external debt.** Includes central government debt held by the Chinese government, China Development Bank, and the EXIM Bank China, as well as Chinese loans to SOEs. *Source*: Wignaraja *et al.* (2020).

- *Autonomy, sovereignty, & security risks for Sri Lanka and the neighborhood*

With a significant portion of investment and funding in BRI coming from Chinese public entities, a growing debt burden has resulted in weaker negotiating strength and loss of sovereignty. According to Asia Maritime Transparency Initiative (2018), a common critique of Chinese investment projects is that they are "dual-use" (for both commercial and military use). The Hambantota Port is often cited as an example of such a potential dual-use facility due to its 99-year lease by China Merchants Port Holdings Company. Jabbar (2015) cautions of the Lotus Tower's potential surveillance and cyber risks.

With a view to maintaining the country's sovereignty, the Government of Sri Lanka (2017) (in the Hambantota Port agreement) completely restrains port operating companies from indulging in military activities, within the port or on any other Sri Lankan territory, whether on land, in the air, or at sea. Panditaratne (2020) refutes this as he stated that the Hambantota Port authority had permitted several naval ships to visit the island since 2016.

Gotabaya Rajapaksa won the presidential elections in 2019, assuring his country's people that he would renegotiate the terms of the Hambantota Port. However, as expected the Chinese are keen to fast track the project. As stated by Amitendu Palit, an economist at the National University of Singapore, "The ability of a country to renegotiate deals would depend on its economic size, performance, and strategic outlook".[24] Sri Lanka has barely any leverage to renegotiate deals.

Rutnam (2018) indicates that several hundred Chinese personnel are stationed at the Sri Lankan Navy (SLN) base in Hambantota, and three

---

[24] https://www.scmp.com/news/china/diplomacy/article/3040982/sri-lanka-wants-its-debt-trap-hambantota-port-back-will-china, accessed on August 10, 2020.

units of four officers each patrol the port premises. It is evident that China has won, and for any government to retrace commitments is impossible. The Chinese are continually expanding their strategic footprint on this island country, buttressed with economic influence.

- **Environmental damage**

Chinese investment projects in Sri Lanka have encountered several environmental challenges in their design, implementation, and operation. Sri Lanka's ecological landscape and biodiversity have been adversely affected by earlier projects. The Norocholai power station is one project that has been criticized for its disregard of domestic environmental norms, while other projects like the Hambantota Port have experienced environmental challenges during the construction phase.[25]

The construction and ongoing operations of the Norocholai power station have led to significant carbon emissions.[26] Additionally, fine ash particles emitted from the Norocholai power station, linked to chronic illness in humans and animals, have been found in Colombo, 145 km away.[27] Moreover, the power station located in the Kalpitiya peninsula is home to dolphins, whales, and other marine life. As it is located only 50 km from Wilpattu National Park, the country's largest national park, home to Sri Lankan elephants and leopards, and other diverse fauna and flora, the vulnerability for the ecosystem is high. However, the project began in 2006 despite strong protests from civil society and environmental organizations.[28]

Given the local level pushback, recent projects such as the CICT and Port City in Colombo have adapted to stricter environmental standards. The CICT terminal of the Colombo port, for example, explicitly

---

[25] BBC News (2011). "Rock on seabed delays Sri Lanka's Hambantota port", August 5, 2011, https://www.bbc.com/news/world-southasia-14418114, accessed on August 4, 2020.

[26] *The Sunday Times*, Sri Lanka (2019). "Tests show Lakvijaya plant spews out dust 16 times over the limit", June 2, 2019, http://www.sundaytimes.lk/190602/news/tests-show-lakvijaya-plant-spews-out-dust-16-times-over-the-limit-352005.html, accessed on August 4, 2020.

[27] 8 *The Sunday Times*, Sri Lanka (2019). "Norochcholai ash contaminates Lanka's western atmosphere", March 10, 2019, http://www.sundaytimes.lk/190310/sunday-times-2/norochcholai-ash-contaminates-lankas-western-atmosphere-339797.html, accessed on August 4, 2020.

[28] 5 BBC Sinhala (2005). "Residents oppose HSZ in Norochcholai", 24 April 2005, https://www.bbc.com/sinhala/news/story/2005/04/050424_norochcholai.HTML, accessed on August 5, 2020.

prioritizes green technology.[29] Over 80% of the electricity used in the CICT terminal operations is generated using solar technology (Wignaraja *et al.*, 2020). International Institute for Sustainable Development (2001) indicates that a sustainability master plan guides the Colombo Port City.[30]

However, even though the Port City received all the environment-friendly recognitions and certificates, there is still some concern regarding the disruptions to marine habitats and the local fishing industry's economic challenges. The Port City is also expected to have a "severe and highly detrimental" effect on the surrounding coastline, fish stocks, and marine biodiversity Wignaraja *et al.* (2020).

In 2015, construction of the Port City had halted due to concerns of the impact on fishing and tourism. However, the work was resumed the very next year, most evidently due to Chinese insistence. "The new Environmental Impact Assessment (EIA) simply green-washed the project without adding substantial changes", explains Withanage, head of the environmental organization that in 2015 filed a lawsuit against the Port City.[31]

- *Knowledge transfer & Spillover effects*

Rand (2015) has shown that FDI results in a diffusion of technology and management practices to home-country firms, which improves their productivity and competitiveness. Studies often distinguish between direct spillover effects of FDI (specific firm-to-firm knowledge transfers) and more indirect spillover effects from FDI (increased FDI presence, productivity improvements, and industrialization).

The available data suggest limited indirect domestic spillovers in terms of sectoral shifts, exports, and employment from Chinese infrastructure investment since 2009. Information on sectoral shifts shows that Chinese infrastructure investment has been the dominant FDI into Sri Lanka since 2009, accounting for 88.7% from 2009 to 2012 and rising to 99.4% from 2017 to 2018 (Wignaraja *et al.*, 2020, p. 14). However, Chinese firms in manufacturing and services have contributed

---

[29] Colombo International Container Terminals (2018). "CICT invests over $10 m towards green infrastructure at Colombo Port", http://www.cict.lk/read/news/3, accessed on August 4, 2020.

[30] CHEC Port City Colombo (Pvt) Ltd (2017). "Sustainability", http://www.portcitycolombo.lk/sustainability/, accessed on August 4, 2020.

[31] https://www.trtworld.com/magazine/chinese-debt-diplomacy-is-drowning-sri-lanka-s-economy-and-environment-25523, accessed on August 10, 2020.

insignificantly to either exports or employment during their operations in Sri Lanka from 2009 to 2018. These firms accounted for less than 1% of the exports of all firms that work with the Board of Investment, (Sri Lanka's investment promotion agency), and about 1% of employment of those firms.[32]

- ### *Labor & Employment*

The number of Chinese workers in Sri Lanka is rising, posing challenges for unemployed locals. BRI projects could provide new job opportunities to local workers, only if they possessed the necessary skills. There were roughly 7,500 Chinese migrant workers in Sri Lanka in mid-2020 (Wignaraja *et al.*, 2020, p. 15). According to Sri Lanka's Department of Immigration and Emigration, the number of residence visas issued to Chinese nationals rose from 4,134 in 2013 to 6,504 in 2018, which is an increase of almost 50%; however,[33] Chinese workers accounted for only 0.1% of Sri Lanka's labor force in 2019. Abi-Habib (2018) has stated that unskilled and semi-skilled local workers are recruited in Chinese con-struction firms. Additionally, private firms bring skilled Chinese person-nel to work on infrastructure projects in Sri Lanka. However, the presence of illegal workers should not be overlooked.

Most BRI projects in Sri Lanka are large-scale infrastructure develop-ments that require both a skilled and sizeable labor force. For example, the Colombo Port City had 1,637 workers, out of which 22.4% are Chinese migrant workers. CICT, which operates a terminal of the Colombo port, has 1,350 employees, of which less than 2% are Chinese. Similarly, Hambantota Port now employs about 900 workers, of which only 3.3% are Chinese.

5.8.3 *Other external impacts of BRI on Sri Lanka*

- ### *Tourism*

Sri Lanka has become a top-rated destination for Chinese tourists and now constitutes the largest nationality of tourists coming to the country.[34] In the first seven months of 2016, 1,173,618 Chinese tourists visited

---

[32] *Ibid.*

[33] Department of Immigration (2019). "Database on Chinese Resident Visa Holders".

[34] "Info" (PDF). ar.unesco.org. Retrieved 2019-12-26.

Table 5.5: Top three nations for tourist arrivals in Sri Lanka (2018 and 2019).

	2018				2019		
Rank	Country of Residence	Tourists Arrivals	Percentage Share	Rank	Country of Residence	Tourists Arrivals	Percentage Share
1	India	424,887	18.2	1	India	355,002	18.6
2	China	265,965	11.4	2	United Kingdom	198,776	10.4
3	United Kingdom	254,176	10.9	3	China	167,863	8.8

Source: Annual Statistic report 2019 — Sri Lanka Tourism Development Authority.

the country.[42] Almost 1.8 million visited in 2015.[35] In 2019, tourists from India represented the largest number of international arrivals. China was the third primary source of tourists to Sri Lanka (8.8%). However, in 2018, China ranked number 2 with 265,965 tourist arrivals. Thus, when we compare the years of 2018 and 2019, there is some decline of Chinese tourists in 2019 due to Easter terrorist attacks in Sri Lanka (which is true not just for China but also for other arrivals which have declined as seen in Table 5.5).

The pertinent question is: To what extent do Chinese tourists benefit Colombo and other cities' local economies? Given that there is a trend of using cashless payment modes like *"Alipay"*.[36] the benefit accrues to the Chinese company. Alipay has been slowly expanding its payment gateway. The first Alipay partnership with Sampath Bank started in February 2018; Interlocks facilitated it, and this partnership allowed merchants to accept payments via Alipay. This could be done using the application or by integrating it into existing POS machines.[37] A second partnership was signed with Flamingo Duty Free, Cargills Bank, and Supreme Paysez, which introduced Alipay as a payment option at the Flamingo duty-free shops inside Bandaranaike Internatio nal Airport. Additionally, this partnership allowed Flamingo to offer

[35] "Chinese tourists to Sri Lanka increase by 28.8 per cent in June — Lifestyle — Chinadaily.com.cn". *www.chinadaily.com.cn*.

[36] Alipay is China's leading mobile payment platform.

[37] Alipay is expanding its presence in Sri Lanka. But why? https://www.readme.lk/alipay-expanding-presence-sri-lanka/#, accessed on August 7, 2020.

targeted shopping offers to Chinese tourists using the mobile payment platform.[38] Another critical partnership with Dialog Axiata will make the Alipay mobile wallet service available to eZ Cash merchants. Chinese shops, businesses, and restaurants will further aid the spread of digital wallets and payment portals which directly benefit the Chinese companies.

Shangri-La Hotels and Resorts has also allowed the online payment service with Alipay at all its hotels and resorts globally. With this pioneering payment option, guests can choose to pre-pay for room reservations at any one of the Shangri-La Hotels.[39]

According to Mr. Prasanna Liyanage, in an interview with Dr. Ramanayake on August 20, 2020, there is a significant increase in the number of restaurants and hotels owned by the Chinese in Sri Lanka. He explained that Chinese customers who booked the hotels online are entitled to special discounts.

5.8.3.1 *Economic, Industrial, and Commercial footprint of China*

Another exciting trend is the increasing flows of Chinese private money, mainly from Hong Kong, that capitalizes on Sri Lanka's cheap and productive labor and the island nation's coveted access to the South Asian, EU, and American markets. The prominent investors are Hong Kong billionaires, including Lai Weixuan's AVIC International Hotels, Lanka, which are investing US$250 million in luxury housing in Colombo. Others include Robert Kuok's Shangri-La Hotels, Lanka, with an investment of US$16 million in a five-star hotel in Colombo, and Li Ka-Shing's Hutchison Telecommunication's US$20 million investment on improving its mobile network in Sri Lanka.

These large private investments have enabled Chinese companies to gain local market dominance. For instance, Huawei, the world's largest telecom equipment manufacturer, is the second-largest player

---

[38] *Ibid.*

[39] https://en.prnasia.com/releases/apac/Shangri_La_Welcomes_Online_Payment_with_Alipay_Globally-143631.shtml, accessed on August 7, 2020.

with an estimated 24% share of the smartphone market in Sri Lanka.[40,41]

Additionally, China has strategic plans in the cultural and socio-political arenas. For example, Beijing's US$100 million grant in 2009 to develop the international Buddhist Institute near one of Sri Lanka's holiest shrines in Kandy attracts Buddhist pilgrims and students to Sri Lanka.[42]

5.8.3.2 *Sri Lanka's Forex reserves*

The country's Gross External Reserves in 2020 amounted to US$9.1 billion. Gold Reserves remained unchanged at 6.70 tonnes in the first and second quarter of 2020. Hence, this shows a drastic decline, compared to July 2018, when it was 22.3.[43]

5.8.3.3 *Justification for reliance on Chinese loans*

Sri Lanka has been in the throes of a perennial (Balance of Payments) BOP crisis due to inadequate export earnings and poor tax collection. Hence, with project loans being tied, the country issued International Sovereign Bonds (ISB) through which dollar-denominated loans were obtained from international capital markets. Factors such as financial autonomy, and the reduction of concessionary loans provided to Sri Lanka after its upgrade to middle-income status, made ISBs a widely adopted method by successive Lankan governments to obtain foreign loans. Sri Lanka issued its first ISB in 2007 and, as of the end of 2019, approximately 47% of its total foreign loans had been ISBs. However, the

---

[40] Chinese investments in Sri Lanka, https://www.gatewayhouse.in/chinese-investments-sri-lanka-2/, accessed on August 7, 2020.

[41] "We will further invest in Sri Lanka: Huawei Country Head Henry Liu", *DailyFT*, September 28, 2016, http://www.ft.lk/article/570172/-We-will-further-invest-in-Sri-Lanka—Huawei-Country-Head-Henry-Liu.

[42] Chinese investments in Sri Lanka, https://www.gatewayhouse.in/chinese-investments-sri-lanka-2/, accessed on August 7, 2020.

[43] Sri Lanka Gold Reserves, https://tradingeconomics.com/sri-lanka/gold-reserves, accessed on September 4, 2020.

short-term maturity structure of ISBs and high interest rates exerted an adverse outcome on the BOP situation.

To surmount this issue, Sri Lanka started to consider alternative methods of foreign financing. One option was to seek a Foreign Currency Term Facility (also known as a "syndicated loan"). In 2018, a US$1 billion syndicated loan from the China Development Bank (CDB) was obtained, with a payback period of 8 years, extendable to 11 years. This loan was increased in March 2020, and another US$500 million syndicated loan was obtained from the CDB, including an extension of the payback period to 10 years. The interest rate was based on the global benchmark rate to which a margin was added.

According to Sri Lankan economist, Moramudali, "In the next three years, sovereign bond repayments would amount to US$6.3 billion. Within the next five years the Sri Lankan Government is likely to use Chinese syndicated loans or such loans obtained from other lenders to finance a portion of large debt repayments instead of entirely relying on sovereign bonds. With the potential high interest to be paid on sovereign bonds due to the downgraded country ratings, syndicated loans would be an attractive alternative to the government". He also views syndicated loans from China in the next five years i.e. upto 2025; as an alternative to IMF loans to tackle BOP issues. This would not require the country to seek IMF loans, which come with conditionalities.[44]

Domestically, given the adverse impact on industrial production during the 2020 pandemic, the new government is extending concessions to reduce interest on bank loans from 11.5% to 8% to potential investors. Credit card interest has been reduced from 28% to 15–17%. The government is also making renewed efforts to reduce the country's debt burden.

China has always endeavored to present itself as a benevolent aid giver to smaller nations and remains conscious of the way it is perceived. The Sri Lankan story of the 99-year lease on the port of Hambantota, negotiated on a Sunday, behind closed doors, and its debt trap diplomacy, has resonated with suspicion in all BRI partner countries. China has sought to alter the narrative, but understands that caution is the way forward.

---

[44] P.K. Balachandran, https://www.thecitizen.in/index.php/en/NewsDetail/index/6/19543/Lankan-Economist-Explains-why-Sri-Lanka-Goes-in-for-Chinese-Loans, accessed on October 27, 2020.

5.9 Conclusion

China's assistance to the Sri Lankan Government during the years of the civil war, which it helped end militarily in 2009, aided in cementing bilateral ties. This trust led to an increase in China's investments and BRI projects in Sri Lanka.

Yet, in 2020, Sri Lanka is walking on a tight rope, seeking economic and other benefits from China under the BRI while maintaining close relations with its rivals — the US, Japan, and India. The BRI has raised concerns about China's intentions in the Indian Ocean. Not surprisingly, India is not a party to the BRI.

China's growing public diplomacy in Sri Lanka is via multiple intersecting strategies. These strategies include Chinese cultural and language centres and visits of members of Parliament, journalists, academics, and business leaders to China; funding student scholarships to China; the local presence of Chinese media like China Radio International (CRI) and China Global Television Network (CGTN). The soft power diplomacy also includes promoting cross-country Buddhist links and supporting local think-tanks, universities, and forums to discuss Chinese projects. These strategies largely resemble the public diplomacy methods of Western nations.

A critical positive trend in Chinese public diplomacy in Sri Lanka is the emergence of Chinese companies' corporate social responsibility (CSR) activities. For example, CHEC Port City Colombo (CPCC), a local subsidiary of China Communications Construction Company, which is developing the Colombo Port City, spent roughly $3 million from 2016 to 2019 to support around 9,000 fishing families that were potentially affected by the project. This is to ensure the buy-in of the projects by the local communities and dissipate some of the criticism it has faced. In terms of the environmental issues, it is well known that earlier projects have had a more significant negative environmental impact; however, recently commissioned projects appear to be making progress in adapting to environmental needs and standards.

According to the Ministry of Finance in Sri Lanka (2019), President Gotabaya Rajapaksa (elected in November 2019) has set out a national policy framework with a focus on an infrastructure-led growth model of economic development for Sri Lanka to reach high-income status. However, institutional weaknesses in Sri Lanka, including a lack of policy planning and transparency, have resulted in non-performing infrastructure projects funded by Chinese investments (Wignaraja *et al.*, 2020). Therefore, it is expected that the newly elected government in August 2020, (with Gotabaya Rajapaksha as President and his brother Mahinda Rajapaksha as Prime Minister) will scrutinize new Chinese projects before signing them. The people have reposed their trust in the family, even as they hope for more transparent governance. A burgeoning external debt burden and high fiscal deficits are not in the interest of the island state (Ministry of Finance, Sri Lanka, 2019).

The Rajapaksha's allegiance to China is unquestionable. According to Dr. Patrick Mendis, "every major decision taken by the Rajapaksha Government is taken after consultation with China. When Sri Lanka was unable to get a loan from any other source, China gave a US$500 million loan to bolster the country's official reserves in March 2020".[45] The rationale as well as the opaqueness of loans and the conditionalities they embed are closed to public purview.

Hence, the small state syndrome and the obligations of past projects, that were ill-conceived and faulty in several respects, will continue to haunt the Rajapaksas in their present tenure. The Colombo Port city project is another manifestation of a Chinese buyout of the regime, in the name of catalyzing foreign investment and growth. The economy's challenges are only burgeoning as exports and tourism revenue decline, and debt mounts in 2020 and beyond. Even as Mahinda Rajapaksa apologized for the Hambantota Port, referring to it as a mistake, the writing on the wall is clear. The recipient countries have learned that China's debt diplomacy and cheque book outreach have strings. These strings will allow internal interference in the small island country's political moorings and influence how the port infrastructure is used. To control the visits of Chinese warships to Sri Lankan ports will be an insurmountable challenge. After all, the Indian Ocean is the costliest pearl for China.

---

[45] Patrick Mendis, Taiwan fellow, Ministry of Foreign Affairs, Taiwan, in a lecture delivered on September 30, 2020, at the Association of Asia Scholars).

Appendix

Table 5.6:   Bilateral trade between China and Sri Lanka.

Year	Sri Lanka's Imports from China	Sri Lanka's Exports to China	Trade Balance (Export–Imports)
2001	386,446	10,141	−376,305
2002	336,752	14,336	−322,416
2003	504,436	19,802	−484,634
2004	694,856	22,590	−672,266
2005	939,670	36,595	−903,075
2006	1,106,412	34,834	−1,071,578
2007	1,389,759	48,032	−1,341,727
2008	1,630,094	60,541	−1,569,553
2009	1,569,465	70,149	−1,499,316
2010	1,994,848	102,275	−1,892,573
2011	2,988,724	152,888	−2,835,836
2012	3,001,305	161,955	−2,839,350
2013	3,436,549	182,564	−3,253,985
2014	3,792,797	248,273	−3,544,524
2015	4,308,107	259,235	−4,048,872
2016	4,331,231	272,991	−4,058,240
2017	4,096,695	309,058	−3,787,637
2018	4,266,680	340,882	−3,925,798
2019	4,088,061	396,576	−3,691,485

Source: Calculations based on data from International Trade Centre (2019), 'Trade Map Database', https://www.trademap.org/Bilateral_TS, (accessed on August 2020).

Chapter 6

China's Visible Influence in Southeast Asia: People, Polity, and Prowess

This chapter delineates how countries in Southeast Asia (SEA) are in their large neighbor's embrace and influence due to their continental and maritime proximity. This command is even more profound and complex than China's relatively newer alliances forged in South Asia. The first section provides the historical and contemporary multidimensional overview of China's engagement in Southeast Asia.

China's historical relations with Southeast Asia are well-documented (Wang, 1995; Skinner, 1957; Reid, 1993 etc.)

6.1 The Context: Southeast Asian Historical Connections with China

A brief of the historical relations between China and Southeast Asia will help understand how the Chinese people settled in several of these countries and made these their permanent abode. China and Southeast Asia share a "kith and kin" relationship (Marwah, 2018, p. 216) dating over two thousand years. During those years, relations between successive Chinese dynasties and the various kingdoms and principalities of Southeast Asia were conducted according to Chinese-imposed rules, constituting what has been called the Chinese, or Sinocentric, world order (Stuart-Fox, 2004).

In the 19th and 20th centuries, for one hundred years, the imperialists humiliated China. China suffered defeats in the First and Second Opium

Wars with the British in 1939 and 1942, respectively, as well as wars with the French, Portuguese, and even the Japanese. These losses in battles under the Qing Government resulted in the signing of a series of "unequal treaties", conceding Hong Kong, Macau, and other major port cities to Western control. The Chinese consider this period as "a century of humiliation".

After China's independence in 1949 and the PRC's creation, despite it having lost some of its influence in parts of SEA, the Mongols, Tibetans, and Uighurs continued to be under Chinese control. Given that Southeast Asia was a collection of principalities, kingdoms, and fiefdoms, with many ethnic groups, languages, and cultures some of whom had moved from South China, the affinities continued (Stuart-Fox, 2004). With a cosmic role, the Chinese emperor presided over a hierarchical social order, which translated as the Middle Kingdom or "all under Heaven" (tian-Xia). Hence, it was the emperor's moral duty to extend Chinese civilization's benefits to all who accepted the Chinese world order.

Southeast Asia's early kings and kingdoms accepted this Chinese-imposed world order mainly for trade and commercial purposes. Their view of the world was rather different, shaped by Indian (Hindu or Buddhist) beliefs about karma workings (the belief that past actions determine present status). Over the centuries, China and the kingdoms of Southeast Asia learned to thrive with each other; Vietnam was the rare exception. As the only state in Southeast Asia that had been for over one thousand years a province of the Chinese empire, Vietnam was always conscious of China's threat. Given the Chinese emperors' penchant to add territory, their armies invaded Vietnam far more often than any other Southeast Asian kingdom. Each time, a befitting response was given by the Vietnamese. The Macartney's mission of 1793 brought significant changes in the Qing-led world order, which transformed Europe's relations with China. In 1882, King Chulalongkorn of Siam (Thailand), Rama V, the last independent Southeast Asian state, abrogated his tributary recognition of Chinese suzerainty (Marwah, 2020, p. 27). The second Sino-Japanese war from 1937–1945 resulted in a considerable decline in China's influence in Southeast Asia.

It is interesting to note that the CCP came to power just as Western imperialism was withdrawing from Southeast Asia. This provided Beijing with an opportunity to develop new bilateral relations with regimes of independent states. However, the process of decolonization (though brief in the case of Burma), was accompanied by episodes of long-drawn violence. China's support for anti-colonial revolutionary movements, particularly in Malaya and Indochina, made it challenging to establish satisfactory relations with newly independent governments, who continued to be compliant for their security with the West under the aegis of the United States.

Hence, each of the countries in Southeast Asia is a colonial creation carved by the metropole's needs. Even Siam, which retained independence, was formed in response to European colonialism. Like other colonial creations, it expanded to absorb a hinterland populated by different people than those at the core. Each of these states in the region is, in fact, multi-ethnic, with peripheral areas that extended well beyond easy colonial control (Marwah, 2020, p. 42).

China's reforms under President Deng Xiaoping's in 1979, also known as the 'four modernizations', placed China in a strong position. Given that ideology had been subsumed by growth and trade, even the collapse of communism in Europe and the Soviet Union could not halt China's rise. Beijing understood that increased national wealth provided the best basis for military modernization, a development whose implications were not lost on Southeast Asian elites.

In the 1990s, China was perceived as a threat to its Southeast Asian neighbors due to its conflicting claims over islands in the South China Sea (SCS) and the support of the communist insurgency. This perception began to change in the wake of the Asian financial crisis of 1997–1998, and after China's economic rise became more perceptible. Since the turn of this century, its relationship with Southeast Asia is undergoing a significant shift. In the present times, China's "charm offensive" and economic diplomacy and its proximity to authoritarian regimes have downplayed territorial disputes while focusing on economic relations, through both trade and investment in BRI projects. This has inevitably resulted in an expansion of political and security linkages. With a total population of 650 million inhabitants and a growing middle class, ASEAN reflects the potential to lead the next century of Asia's economic growth. With a vibrant population of over 1.44 billion (2020) and growing aspirations to solidify its status as an economic and military superpower, China has been asserting itself globally and within Asia. It has been discussed in an earlier chapter that Southeast Asia is being viewed as China's critical sphere of influence. This chapter will delineate aspects of China's footprint in its backyard.

6.2 ASEAN Countries: An Economic Profile

At this juncture, it is vital to present the economic indicators of countries in SEA to highlight the diversity in levels of income, human development indices, and the size of countries in terms of their population. Table 6.1 presents aspects of population size, GDP, and per capita incomes at current prices, and the percentage of population below the national poverty line of different countries.

GDP per capita ranges from about US$1,500 for Myanmar and Cambodia to more than US$60,000 in the case of Singapore. Such disparities breed divergent interests, and integration itself becomes a tricky proposition. In terms of population, Indonesia is the largest country, with the Philippines in second place. The growth rates for all ASEAN countries have been impressive over the last few years, with a significant increase in overall GDP for most countries in 2018 over 2017; Malaysia, Thailand, and Singapore also recorded significant increases in 2018 over 2017 (Marwah, 2020).

Indonesia, followed by the Philippines and Vietnam are the three largest countries in terms of population size. While the per capita incomes are the lowest in Cambodia, Laos, Myanmar, and Vietnam, it is also interesting to note that the highest poverty levels (rural and urban) in percentage terms are in Laos, Myanmar, and the Philippines. Additionally, through a comparison of people below poverty lines, from 2015 to 2017, it can be seen that this percentage has increased in the case of Myanmar, Thailand, and Vietnam. The data for 2020 would further show an increase in poverty levels in most countries, given the pandemic's deleterious effects on those living on the margins.

As shown in Table 6.1, the CLMV is very heterogeneous. Cambodia and Lao P.D.R. are geographically small and have populations of less than 20 million. Myanmar and Vietnam have larger populations of 50 million and 90 million, respectively, and much larger landmasses. According to Mathai *et al.* (2016), Vietnam is the most dynamic trading nation in the group — it is well diversified and is a significant participant in global supply chains for electronics. Cambodia has long been a significant garments exporter (to the United States and Europe). At the same time, Lao P.D.R. and Myanmar focus on natural resources and energy, exported mainly to ASEAN and China.

Hence, while there is disparity and diversity in the polities, ethnicities, and beliefs of these countries, a united ASEAN can resolve many of the

Table 6.1:   ASEAN: Demographic and economic indicators.

Country	Total Population (millions)[1]	Gross Domestic Product (current prices US$) 2017	Gross Domestic Product (current prices US$) 2018	Gross Domestic Per Capita Income (current prices US$[2]) 2017	Gross Domestic Per Capita Income (current prices US$2) 2018	Population Below the NPL in ASEAN Urban + Rural 2015 (%)	Population Below the NPL in ASEAN Urban + Rural-2017 (%)
Brunei Darussalam	442.4	12,212	13,567.6	28,465.6	30,668.3	n.a.	n.a.
Cambodia	15,981.8	22,340	24,608.7	1,421.3	1,539.8	13.5	13.5
Indonesia	2,65,015.3	1,013,926	1,039,864.4	3,866.7	3923.8	11.2	10.6
Lao PDR	6,887.1	17,090	18,095.7	2,530.8	2,627.5	24.0	23.4
Malaysia	32,385.0	317,042	358,411.7	9,892.2	11.067.2	0.6	0.4
Myanmar	53625.0	65,607	77,263.6	1,228.6	1,440.8	19.4	24.8
Philippines	1,06,598.6	313,875	329,061.8	2,991.5	3,086.9	22.0	21.6
Singapore	5,638.7	323,954	364,075.7	57,722.2	64,567.3	n.a.	n.a.
Thailand	67,831.6	455,704	505,107.1	6,735.9	7,446.5	7.2	7.9
Vietnam	94,666.0	223,927	241,038.8	2,390.3	2,546.2	7.0	9.8
ASEAN (Average)		2,765,679	2,971,095.2	4,305.0	4,577.5		

Note: NPL — National Poverty Line.
Sources: Asean Statistics Yearbook 2019.

bilateral differences over time. ASEAN's normative architecture since 1967 is a function of a confluence of national interests, principally in the economic field. Hence, as an ASEAN Economic Community, the countries trade and invest in one another, enabling intra-ASEAN trade of 23% of the overall trade in 2018. Intra-ASEAN market constitutes 24.1% and 21.8% of ASEAN total merchandise exports and imports, respectively.

China (17.2%), EU-28 (10.2%), and USA (9.3%) were ASEAN's top three trading partners in 2018. The largest external markets for ASEAN exports in 2018 were China (13.9%), EU-28 (11.2%), USA (11.2%), and Japan (7.9%). As for imports, China is the region's largest external source of imports with a share of 20.5%, followed by EU-28 (9.2%), Japan (8.4%), and the USA (7.4%). The rapid rise in China's share as a trading partner of each ASEAN country and the ASEAN bloc is discussed in detail in the subsequent section.

Table 6.1 indicates the rising ASEAN–China trade, with China's share in ASEAN's overall trade having risen from less than 12% in 2010 to more than 17% in 2018. This is further explained through the country studies, showing how Thailand and Myanmar are trading much more with China than any other country. For China, too, trade with ASEAN has overtaken that of the EU. While exports and imports have risen, it is evident that ASEAN's exports to China have less than doubled, while imports have increased by almost two and a half times. Hence, the trade deficit, which rose sharply post 2010 (a rise of more than three times in 2012), has increased by more than nine times in 8 years. Clearly, in trade, it has been an advantage for China!

6.3 ASEAN–China Free Trade Area (ACFTA)

Post the 1997 Asian financial crisis, China–ASEAN relations became more robust. In November 2001, ASEAN and China agreed to establish the ASEAN–China free trade agreement. Chirathivat (2002) highlights that the demand for natural resource and intermediate-based products in China would require more imports from ASEAN countries. According to Wattanapruttipaisan (2003), China's accession to the World Trade Organization would provide greater market access in resource- and agro-based products and some manufactured goods, especially for the ASEAN-4 countries, namely, Cambodia, Laos, Myanmar, and Vietnam. He further stated that there would be greater competition from China in both

ASEAN-4's home and third-country markets, especially in a wide range of labor- and technology-intensive manufactures. At the same time, Tongzon (2005), Tambunan (2006), Lakatos and Walmsley (2012), and Cai (2003) and other studies have discussed China–ASEAN FTA in detail. According to Aslam (2011), China's relatively low production cost compared to ASEAN members has decreased ASEAN's export competitiveness. The intense competition between the international commodity market regions and productive foreign capital also created stress on ASEAN economies, especially in trade.

Over the decade 2005–2015, trade and investment between ASEAN member states and China have expanded significantly under the ambit of the ACFTA. The Agreement on Trade in Goods was signed in 2004 and implemented in July 2005 by all the member countries. Under the agreement, the six original ASEAN members and China decided to eliminate tariffs on 90% of their products by 2010, while Cambodia, Lao PDR, Myanmar, and Vietnam — commonly known as CLMV countries, had until 2015 to do so. Since the agreement's signing, China has consistently maintained its position as ASEAN's largest trading partner. In 2015, ASEAN's total merchandise trade with China reached US$346.5 billion, accounting for 15.2% of ASEAN's total trade.

Table 6.2 points to the rising levels of deficits in trade with ASEAN. In less than ten years, the overall deficit has risen by more than nine times, an indicator of China's rapidly rising share in overall trade and the rising pace of imports from China. The increase in interdependence is also evident. According to Rastogi (2017), were it not for the pandemic, by 2020, ASEAN and China were committed to doubling the current trade level to achieving a joint target of US$1 trillion in trade and US$150 billion in investment through the ACFTA. With ASEAN in RCEP, this may yet be possible by 2025.

Given the rising pace of imports into SEA, ASEAN became China's largest trading partner in the first six months of 2020, surpassing both the EU and the United States, given that the latter reduced imports even as they were enmeshed by the pandemic. During the first three months of 2020, ASEAN–China trade increased by 6% year-on-year to US$140 billion, accounting for 15% of China's total trade volume. China's imports from Vietnam and Indonesia rose by 24 and 13% year-on-year, respectively, highlighting the increasingly integrated supply chains between the two regions. ASEAN had already become China's second-largest trading partner in 2019 with trade valued at US$644 billion, overtaking the US amid

Table 6.2:   China's trade in goods with ASEAN (US$ Million).

	2010	2012	2014	2016	2018	2020+
ASEAN Trade in Goods with China	2,34,295.60	3,16,983.90	3,62,644.60	3,68,693.90	4,83,764.70	New Data awaited
% of total	11.75	12.83	14.38	16.47	17.12	
Total	19,94,831.30	24,71,077.30	25,22,078.30	22,38,600.60	28,25,263.30	
ASEAN Exports to China	1,12,512	1,42,362	1,53,656	1,44,175	1,98,955	
ASEAN Imports from China	1,21,783	1,74,621	2,08,988	2,24,518	2,84,809	
Trade Deficit/Surplus	−9271	−32,261	−55,332	−80343	−85,854	

Source: https://asean.org/?static_post=external-trade-statistics-3.

friction between the world's largest economies. To offset the trade war's impact, China looked to other regions to fill the gap, most notably ASEAN nations (Medina, 2020). China's State Council decided in 2019 to establish six new economic zones, to encourage companies from regional ASEAN and other border countries to supply China with more products. The ASEAN-influenced economic zones will be built near the borders of Vietnam, Laos, and Myanmar. There are additional reasons for China to do this — it has a comprehensive free trade agreement with ASEAN (Devonshire-Ellis, 2019).

Even as China seeks to write the rules of the global order, and given the fact that Trump walked out of the TPP, in 2017, (citing this as the worst trade deal), the time was opportune for China to push forward the signing of the Regional Comprehensive Economic Partnership in 2020.

6.4 RCEP and ASEAN

RCEP negotiations commenced in 2013 to create a mega trade grouping of sixteen countries including ASEAN and India, Australia, China, Japan, Korea, and New Zealand. The RCEP has been signed by fifteen countries in November 2020 in Hanoi, Vietnam, even though India walked out of this trade grouping in November 2019, citing several concerns that had been left unaddressed during the negotiations.

The ASEAN countries, Japan, and Australia had expressed the importance of India joining the deal. Japan was initially reluctant to sign the deal without India in the grouping, as it understands that without Indian participation, Chinese influence will be all the more significant. Moreover, according to Shin Kawashima, "If Japan opted out because of India's exit, then China's trade and economic influence in Southeast and Northeast Asia would grow further. Hence, Japan would continue to be a member of the grouping" (Kawashima, 2020). RCEP will ensure that China continues to benefit from the reduced tariffs, even as it already has free trade agreements with most countries. With ASEAN, China's bilateral trade issues are further eased.

It is well known that China's agreements are initially limited and then expanded substantially over time. Hence, China's gradualist approach, according to Sampson (2019), negotiating regional trade agreements, surmounting its economic weight vis-à-vis its counterparts, which are smaller and weaker, increases opportunities to maximize its growing bargaining leverage and influence over time. The investment negotiations are also critically linked to China's growing economic clout.

6.4.1 *Inward FDI flows from China to ASEAN (2010–2018)*

It is not surprising that China's share in inward FDI to ASEAN countries has increased significantly over 2010–2018. ASEAN received US$8.2 billion in foreign direct investment (FDI) from China in 2015, placing China as ASEAN's fourth largest source of FDI refer Table 6.3.

In 2018, 15.9% of total ASEAN FDI inflows or US$24.5 billion originated from within the region; this was an increase of almost 150% from the level in 2005. The EU remains the largest extra-ASEAN source of FDI inflows, although its share had decreased from 28.3% in 2005 to 14.2% in 2018. This is followed by Japan (13.7%), China (6.6%), and Hongkong, China (6.6%). In particular, China has emerged as a significant investment partner, mirroring its contribution to trade in the region. What is even more interesting is that while the overall inward FDI increased by about 40%, the quantum increase from China is almost 250%. This is a result of the increased funding for BRI projects. The doubling of inward FDI to ASEAN from 2010 to 2012 is explained by the implementation of the China–ASEAN FTA in 2010.

Concerning the BRI, infrastructure projects are being pursued across ASEAN (Yan, 2018, p. 8). Countries, such as Singapore, with specific expertise in dispute resolution, finance, insurance, and infrastructure, have also signed MoUs with China to advance BRI projects in third-party countries. These are intended to promote the adoption of best practices and the bankability and viability of such undertakings. In broad terms, ASEAN's posture toward the BRI can thus be best described as supportive.

Table 6.3:   Inward FDI to ASEAN from China (2010–2018).

	2010	2012	2014	2016	2018
From China	3488	7975	6811	9609	9940
% of the total	3.22	6.83	5.23	8.08	6.51
Total Inward FDI	1,08,174	1,16,774	1,30,114	1,18,959	1,52,755

Source: https://asean.org/?static_post=external-trade-statistics-3.

ASEAN's view of China's BRI and expanding economic influence, according to the 2020 ISEAS Survey, interestingly points to the fact that BRI projects exude little or no confidence in 57% of the respondents of the ISEAS survey 2020. Additionally, 62.7% of people believe that their sovereignty could be at risk from China if they grow politically and militarily.

6.4.2 *Tourism*

ASEAN countries, especially Thailand, receive a large number of tourists from within the region and across the globe. Figure 6.1 shows that Thailand welcomed more than 38 million tourists in 2018. Malaysia, another popular tourist destination, received over 25 million tourists. Chinese tourists to SEA have also been increasing with their rising per capita incomes. China's growing footprint is also evident from the number of Chinese tourists visiting SEA countries, especially Thailand, Malaysia, Singapore, and Indonesia. According to Prof. Chayan Vaddhanaputhi from Chiang Mai University, in an interview to Reena Marwah in May 2019, an increasing number of Chinese-owned hotels and travel

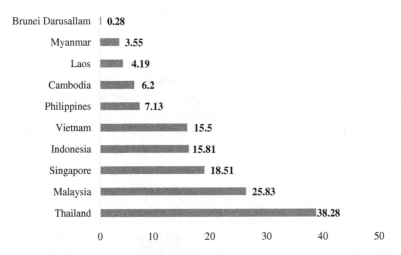

Figure 6.1: Tourist arrivals in ASEAN by country (Year 2018 — in millions).

Sources: statista.com, https://www.statista.com/statistics/645730/tourist-arrivals-in-asean-region-by-country-of-arrival/, accessed on December 10, 2020.

businesses were being established in different parts of Thailand. Chinese tourists also use Alipay and other Chinese digital payment platforms, hence adding little to the local economy.

In 2019, almost 11 million tourists to Thailand were Chinese. In other countries of SEA too, there has been an increase of Chinese tourists. About 3.63 million Chinese tourists visited Singapore. According to Tourism Malaysia's data, China contributes the third-highest number of tourists to Malaysia with 2,944,133 visitors in 2018. As for spending by Chinese tourists in Malaysia, the amount spent was the second-highest among tourists from all other countries, this being RM12.3 billion in 2018 (Lim, 2019).

In 2019, while tourists from ASEAN to Thailand numbered 10,626,511, Chinese tourists were even higher at 10,995,000.

6.5 Economic and Political Indicators of ASEAN Countries and China

As stated earlier, the ten countries in ASEAN vary significantly in size and economic indicators. Table 6.4 also points to other indicators that explain the reasons for China's increasing influence.

The country indicators, in Table 6.4, show a stark comparison, particularly between Singapore and some other members of ASEAN. In terms of fragile state rank, the Philippines, Laos, and Cambodia are in the top 60 countries. Cambodia, Laos, and Myanmar also score poorly in terms of corruption; in this indicator Vietnam and Thailand are also ranked low compared to Singapore, which is ranked as 3rd among 180 countries. Similarly, the global competitiveness index shows clearly that Laos and Cambodia lag way behind the other States. Myanmar's data is unavailable. According to the EIU Report, 2019, Singapore, Indonesia, Malaysia, Philippines, and Thailand are flawed democracies. Myanmar, Vietnam, Cambodia, and Laos are listed as authoritarian regimes (EIU Democracy Report, 2019).

Table 6.4 highlights many factors that substantiate the argument that weak economies with high levels of corruption can fall easy prey to Chinese aid and influence in multiple sectors. It is hence significant to bring here the SEA sub-regional grouping for the development of the Mekong River Basin. To be fair to China, it is also true that smaller states tend to gravitate toward a country they consider a development partner.

Table 6.4: Key indicators of ASEAN countries and China.

Country	Debt (as % of GDP)	Fragile State Rank 2018	Democracy Index- Score/10	Rank/	El. Process & Pluralism/10	Civil Liberties/10	Corruption Index 2018	CPI* Rank/180 countries 2019	Global Competitiveness Index
Brunei Darussalam	2.59	124	n.a.			n.a.	63	31	56
Cambodia	28.64	53	3.53	124	0.83	3.24	20	161	101
Indonesia	30.09	91	6.48	64	7.92	5.59	38	89	50
Lao PDR	55.80	60	2.14	155	0.00	1.18	29	132	113
Malaysia	55.57	116	7.16	43	9.17	5.88	47	61	27
Myanmar	n.a.	n.a	3.55	122	3.08	2.35	29	132	n.a
Philippines	38.92	47	6.64	54	9.17	7.06	36	99	64
Singapore	113.63	161	6.02	75	3.92	7.06	85	3	1
Thailand	42.08	77	6.32	68	7.42	6.47	36	99	40
Vietnam	58.22	107	3.08	136	0.00	2.65	33	117	67
ASEAN (Average)									
CHINA	50.64	89	2.26	153	0.00	1.18	39	87	28

Note: n.a. = Not available.
Sources: Countryeconomy.com/, accessed on August 11, 2020.

6.6 China's Water Diplomacy: Lancang–Mekong Cooperation

It is important to elucidate China's water diplomacy for the Mekong River, whose waters are shared by China and the lower riparian states of SEA. The river originates high in the Tibetan plateau and passes through six countries: China, Myanmar, Thailand, Laos, Cambodia, and Vietnam. Estimated by the Mekong River Commission at about 4,909 kilometers long, it is the seventh longest river in Asia and the 10th longest in the world.[1] This River Basin supports over 70 million people in terms of food, water, transport, and many other aspects of their daily lives.

The Mekong River Commission (MRC) was formed in 1995 by a grouping of four countries, viz. Thailand, Laos, Cambodia, and Vietnam. The objective of the MRC was to cooperate on development in the basin. In 2002, Beijing joined as a "Dialogue Partner", and helped the MRC by sharing data on water levels from two monitoring stations it has on the Lancang (Mekong river is known as Lancang in China) only.

The lower Mekong has been affected in recent years by climate change and China's stocking up of water. It is important to note here that while China did not join the MRC as that would require transparency on issues of water levels, it chose to establish the Lancang–Mekong Cooperation (LMC) in 2014, an alternative initiative which it can manipulate. Given that it has expanded its trade and geopolitical power in Thailand, Laos, and Cambodia, China was expected to treat these countries as its partners and friends by sharing information about how much water it has been impounding and discharging from the Mekong. Instead, China built dams on the river, which impacted the sedimentation and water flow for the people dependent on this basin for their livelihoods (Editor, 2020).

A study by Eyes on Earth released in April 2020 has stated that the 11 Chinese dams have stored a high volume of water over the past three decades. China has never been transparent about the extent of water it withheld or released from its reservoirs since it started building dams on the Lancang in the 1990s. The prevailing view of the LCM is that it is intended to exploit MRC weaknesses and entrench China's regional standing as Beijing disperses aid and gains influence over development projects along the waterway (*Japan Times*, Mekong, 2020).

---

[1] https://opendevelopmentmekong.net/topics/the-mekong/, accessed on August 16, 2020.

According to Brahma Chellaney, farmers in this area, known as Asia's Rice Bowl, can produce enough rice to feed 300 million people per year. The basin also boasts the world's largest inland fishery. This is almost 25% of the entire world's freshwater catch. This vital waterway is now under threat, mainly due to the Chinese-built mega-dams near the Tibetan Plateau border, just before the river crosses into Southeast Asia. The 11 dams currently in operation in 2019 had a total electricity-generating capacity of 21,300 megawatts — more than the installed hydropower capacity of all the downriver countries, resulting in environmental, economic, and geopolitical havoc.[2]

Although as a downstream country, Thailand is adversely affected, too, its requirements of energy are also at fault. Thai companies and state-owned enterprises collaborate with the Lao PDR government to build more hydropower dams in Laos and import the electricity into Thailand. Much of this electricity is used in Bangkok. Middle and upper-class residents of Bangkok enjoy inexpensive power while major shareholders of Thai companies in the energy, real estate, construction, and finance sectors reap large profits — as do Lao government leaders. Simultaneously, local rural communities and wildlife in Laos bear the brunt of the environmental and social damage caused by these dams. Some communities are forced to resettle and later are often worse off (Marks and Zhang, 2019).

The environmental consequences are to be borne by Thailand, too. At one gauge in Chiang Saen, such low water levels had never been recorded before in northern Thailand. Overall, during the 28 years they studied this gauge, Mr. Basist and his team calculated that China's dams had held back more than 410 feet of river height. In the words of Mr. Basist. "The Chinese are building safe deposit boxes on the upper Mekong because they know the bank account is going to be depleted eventually; they want to keep it in reserve" (Suhartono, 2020).

According to Santasombat (2015), in the Mekong region, China is perceived as the primary source of all environmental problems. China's mining activities, including copper mining in Myanmar, bauxite mining in Vietnam, gold mining in Laos, and tourist resorts in Cambodia have all

---

[2] Brahma Chellaney, https://www.project-syndicate.org/commentary/china-dams-mekong-basin-exacerbate-drought-by-brahma-chellaney-2019-08?barrier=accesspaylog, accessed on August 16, 2020.

been undertaken with no regard to their environmental impacts, especially on the local people.

It was a win for Mekong conservationist groups when Thailand's cabinet agreed on February 4, 2020, to end a twenty-year Chinese-led project to improve the navigation channel in a segment of the Mekong River. This was a result of fierce resistance by residents and conservationists, fearful of the project's severe environmental and social impact. Conservationists lauded the Thai government and stated that this move could signal a shift in how downstream Mekong states deal with their gargantuan neighbor's development ambitions. They underlined that this was the culmination of decades of continuously voicing concerns over the dangers that the project posed. Possibly, there is hope for the Mekong (Ganjanakhundee, 2020).

According to Chellaney, droughts have become more frequent and intense in the downriver countries, after China's dam-building on the Mekong. However, even as China seeks to play savior through the LMC, it has promised to release more dam water for the drought-stricken countries. This only reiterates the fact that downstream countries of SEA depend on Chinese goodwill — a dependence that is set to deepen as China builds more giant dams on the Mekong.[3]

It is important to briefly discuss China's bilateral relations with each Southeast Asian country to further understand the geostrategic motivations for economic engagement refer Figure 6.2.

6.7 China and Southeast Asian Countries: A Brief Overview of Bilateral Relations

As stated earlier, Southeast Asia is vital for China. Perhaps the most strategically significant is the mainland as opposed to the maritime states, which provides potentially the most fruitful and receptive region for the projection of Chinese influence (Marwah, 2020, p. 118). Over time, each of Southeast Asia's nation states has evolved their bilateral foreign relations with China.

---

[3] Brahma Chellaney, China is weaponizing water and worsening droughts in Asia, October 28, 2019, https://asia.nikkei.com/Opinion/China-is-weaponizing-water-and-worsening-droughts-in-Asia.

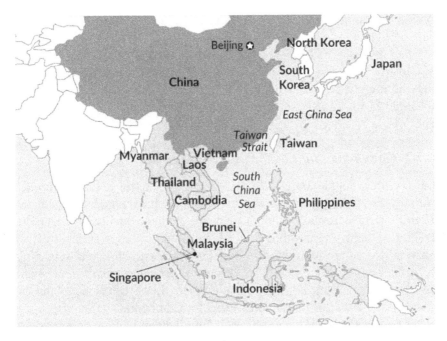

Figure 6.2:   China and Southeast Asia.

Source: https://www.gisreportsonline.com/southeast-asias-future-tied-to-great-power-competition, politics,3054.html

6.7.1 *Brunei*

Brunei is a small state in Southeast Asia on the north-west coast of the island of Borneo, in the Indonesian Archipelago, with a population of about 465,000. Its 161 km coastline faces the South China Sea. On the land side, it is enclosed by the Malaysian state of Sarawak. Also known as the "Abode of Peace", it is the only absolute *monarchy* left in Asia. The majority of its people are ethnic Malays (66%) and Chinese (10.3%). Brunei and China established diplomatic relations in 1991, making it the last ASEAN country to do so. Brunei Darussalam joined ASEAN on January 7, 1984. Since 2011, after the first ever visit of a Chinese President, the two countries' relationship progressed with several cooperation documents being signed. Xi Jinping has also deepened economic and strategic cooperation with Brunei. Diplomatically, both countries appear to have reached a consensus on how to address the areas of the South China Sea that both countries dispute about, the only

ASEAN member involved in the dispute to have done so (Druce and Julay, 2018).

For residents of Brunei, critical security challenges include the economic downturn and climate change. The ISEAS Survey 2020 also shows that the highest level of recognition for China's economic influence was recorded by almost 85% of Brunei respondents.

6.7.2 *Cambodia and Laos: Political twins*

Laos, with a population a little over 7 million, shares a 423 km border with South China's Yunnan province. Cambodia has a population of about 17 million. It shares borders with Vietnam, Thailand, and Laos. Given the loyalty of Laos and Cambodia to China, both countries also known as political twins, are intertwined with China in terms of mutually reaping benefits. Both governments are keen to get investments and grant assistance they deem key to graduating from Least Developed Country status — by 2020 for Laos and by 2025 for Cambodia.

China has undertaken a total of 785 projects in Laos, with an investment of US$12 billion. This makes it the largest investor in this country. In Cambodia too, China is the largest investor, contributing about a fourth of Cambodia's total investment. From railway lines to highways, from illegal mining to gambling cities, these countries are completely under Chinese influence.

Despite having been brought into the ASEAN grouping, these two countries would choose not to annoy China, even at the expense of projecting disagreement with other ASEAN countries. According to analyst Edgar Pang, (Yushof Ishak Institute), China's footprint will continue to grow in Laos and Cambodia, in many ways replacing what was till the late 1990s Japan's critical role as a source of assistance and investments. He also cautioned that there are differences in the polity of the two countries, resulting from which it may not be tenable to place them precisely in the same frame. "While Laos and Cambodia share similar imperatives in embracing China, there are deep dynamics and undercurrents in Lao and Khmer politics which have a strong bearing on how they navigate their asymmetry vis-à-vis China". Hun Sen, who has been Cambodia's authoritarian Prime Minister since 1985, has been supporting China in every way.

There is increasing pressure on all countries within ASEAN to view China's disputes in the South China Sea in a consensual way. As ASEAN chair in 2016, Laos successfully managed to strike a compromise between claimants like China and Vietnam so that the ASEAN foreign ministers' joint communiqué could categorically express "serious concern" over "land reclamations and escalation of activities" in the maritime space (Son, 2019).

6.7.3 *Indonesia*

Indonesia, located off the coast of mainland Southeast Asia in the Indian and Pacific oceans, is composed of some 17,500 islands, (of which more than 7,000 are uninhabited). ASEAN remains the "cornerstone" of Indonesian foreign policy, as it has the largest population.

This was the first Southeast Asian country that established official diplomatic relations with China, in July 1950. However, diplomatic ties with Beijing were suspended by the Indonesian Prime Minister Suharto from 1967 to 1990. Ever since, bilateral ties have remained complicated, even though China is viewed as an economic partner of significance. Indonesia and China both lay claims to islands in the Natuna Sea. Indonesia has been managing its diplomatic relations with China by being firm on its claims in its territorial waters (Devare *et al.*, 2014).

It is well known that Indonesia has exercised caution in proceeding with BRI projects, primarily because of the anti-Chinese sentiment among the people and the bureaucratic delays and hurdles in proceeding with projects. While many recognize that the Indonesian way is not truly the best, even though the country avoided many reckless, grandiose projects offered by China, the only real albatross, a planned high-speed railway from Jakarta to Bandung, is a cautionary tale. In 2015, China beat Japan to bid for its construction by not insisting on government guarantees for its loans. However, problems emerged: even the air force, with a base in the train's path, objected. In 2019, the land was finally acquired, after delays of several years and exceeding the budget estimate. Since no broader high-speed network offers economies of scale, the 150km line will never pay for itself. The railway, China's flagship project in Indonesia, has been brought in through the clandestine route, often employed in countries where there is a pushback from the people. It is no surprise then that almost 70% of Indonesians did not have confidence in China's BRI. Only 5.6% of respondents stated that they share the same world view and political culture as that of China (ISEAS Survey, 2020).

However, given Indonesia's large Muslim population (88% of total) of over 220 million, China's treatment of the Uighur Muslims in its territory also poses some concern. Matsumuro indicated during an interview, "Indonesia is an important country for China, especially as Indonesia has several resources — coal, rare metals, and others. China has already taken a large part of the world market" (Setiono, 2016).

Hu Zhiyong, of International Relations of the Shanghai Academy of Social Sciences, said China–Indonesia relations had shown "all-round friendly cooperation" in terms of economic partnership. Evan A. Laksmana, of the Centre for Strategic and International Studies (CSIS) think tank in Jakarta, said that from Indonesia's standpoint, issues involving China could easily become "a major domestic political problem" as even minor irritants could get inflamed into a big "China problem".[4]

China's investments in 2019 were US$4.7 billion with 2,130 projects, making it the second-largest investor in the archipelagic nation after Singapore. According to the Indonesian Investment Coordinating Board, this was 16.8% of total foreign investments in the country. It is also well known that Chinese tourists comprise at least 25% of all tourists who visit Bali, Indonesia's tourism hub.

6.7.4 *Malaysia*

Malaysia's location needs to be understood as: Peninsular Malaysia, which borders Thailand and connects with neighboring Singapore with a causeway and bridge, as well as Island Malaysia that borders Indonesia and Brunei. The Malacca Straits, which is the waterway connecting the Andaman Sea (Indian Ocean) and the South China Sea (Pacific Ocean), runs between the Indonesian island of Sumatra to the west and peninsular (West) Malaysia and extreme southern Thailand to the east and has an area of about 25,000 square miles (65,000 square km). Since antiquity, this has been the busiest waterway, with Roman, Greek, Chinese, and Indian traders all taking advantage of this natural channel. Its strategic importance has also made it a source of international friction from the 15th century to the modern day.[5] Hence, given that the Straits of Malacca are one of the most significant sea lanes of communication (SLOC), in present times,

---

[4] https://www.habibiecenter.or.id/contain-news-After-70-years-of-ties-China-and-Indonesia-have-a-fruitful-complicated-relationship, accessed on December 18, 2020.
[5] Tomas Hirst, May 21, 2014, https://www.weforum.org/agenda/2014/05/world-most-important-trade-route/, accessed on August 18, 2020.

especially for China, India, and Japan, Malaysia understands the sensitivity of maintaining a balance with regional powers for regional stability in these waters. Though Malaysians view China as the most influential economic power in Asia, they have apprehensions about China's domination in political terms. China's treatment of its Muslim population in the region of Xinjiang is another sore point with the Malaysians given that the country is home to 61% followers of Islam. Beijing has faced international condemnation, and protests from Muslim groups here, for confining an estimated one million Uighurs and other mostly Muslim ethnic minorities in internment camps in the north-western region of Xinjiang.[6]

In 2018, about 17% of Malaysia's exports went to China and 20% of its imports came from it. In the same year, China was Malaysia's largest source of foreign direct investment. Against a backdrop of international financial scandals and controversial Chinese infrastructure investments in Malaysia, the East Coast Rail Line (ECRL) project is not exceptional. The Malaysia Rail Link, an entity established for the ECRL by the Malaysian Ministry of Finance, has been expected to reconcile the terms for contracting, procurement, and management written into the Chinese ECRL investment to ensure opportunities for the involvement of local contractors. Mahathir Mohammed canceled two Chinese projects in 2018, citing the country's high debt level, which is 56% of GDP. One of the projects, i.e. the ECRL, would have connected the South China Sea with strategic shipping routes in Malaysia's west, providing an essential trade link. The other was a natural gas pipeline in Sabah, a Malaysian state on the island of Borneo.

Political opposition's calls for increased project transparency on the process and cost justification will remain a prevalent issue for the ECRL project, especially during the 1MDB money-laundering investigations that brought former Prime Minister Razak and his leadership under political scrutiny (Interestingly, Razak, who was ousted in 2018, returned to power in February 2020). Fei underscores the imperative for Malaysia to resolve issues of inefficiency, low productivity, and corruption so as to compete in the global maritime space (Fei, 2020).

According to Hugh Harsono, in the *Diplomat*, Malaysia has experienced unprecedented growth due to participation in the startup and e-commerce space, with possibilities of Malaysia's e-commerce industry being worth over US$8 billion by 2025. Moreover, three in five of all

---

[6] https://www.malaymail.com/news/malaysia/2020/01/22/in-malaysia-are-chinas-citizens-becoming-the-new-bogeyman/1830299, accessed on July 12, 2020.

e-commerce consumers place their orders via smartphones. These factors, among others, spurred the launch of the Digital Free Trade Zone Initiative (DFTZ) between China and Malaysia in March 2017. Although this points to the intersection of merging national defense, technology, politics, and economics, it is essential for Malaysia to understand the dynamics involving both private and public enterprises. These are inevitably at risk of becoming leveraged and overly dependent on Chinese banks and Chinese companies following prolonged investment from them.[7]

However, Michele Ruta, an economist, added that for some countries, "the financing required for BRI projects may expand debt to unsustainable levels". Big infrastructure projects can also carry "environmental, social, and corruption risks", he said, especially "in countries involved in the BRI, which tend to have relatively weak governance".[8]

Should Malaysians become more vocal about their concerns and transmit them through their elected leaders, Malaysia's foreign relations with China could very well veer in a different direction.[9] Malaysia's political situation continues to remain fluid despite a new prime minister.

6.7.5 *Myanmar*

Burma was separated from the rest of the Indian Empire in 1937, just ten years before India's independence from the British. Its name was changed from Burma to Myanmar in 1989 by the then ruling military government.

Myanmar, formerly known as Burma, is the northernmost country of Southeast Asia. The country shares borders with China (2,129 km in the north and northeast), Laos 238 km to the east, Thailand 2,416 km to the southeast, the Andaman Sea and Bay of Bengal to the south and southwest, Bangladesh 271 km to the west, and India 1,468 km to the northwest. This region is home to many of Asia's great rivers, including the Irrawaddy, which rises and flows wholly within Myanmar, and the Salween (Thanlwin), which rises to the north in China.

---

[7] https://thediplomat.com/tag/chinese-investment-in-malaysia/, accessed December 10, 2020.

[8] https://www.washingtonpost.com/world/asia_pacific/malaysia-cancels-two-massive-chinese-projects-fearing-they-will-bankrupt-the-country/2018/08/21/, accessed on December 12, 2020.

[9] https://www.fpri.org/article/2020/01/a-faint-breeze-of-change-malaysias-relations-with-china/, accessed on December 14, 2020.

The country with a population of almost 55 million is ethnically diverse with 135 ethnic groups recognized by the government. There are at least 108 ethnolinguistic groups in Myanmar. The Bamar comprise 68% of the population, followed by the Shan (10%), Kayin (7%), Rakhine (4%), and overseas Chinese (3%). Other ethnic groups include the Mon (2%), Overseas Indians (2%), and the Kachin, Chin, Anglo-Indians, Nepali, and Anglo-Burmese. Myanmar's main religions are spread across Buddhists with 87.9%, Christians 6.2%, Muslims 4.3%, Animists 0.8%, Hindus 0.5%, other 0.2%, and none at 0.1% of the population.

Since 1950, when the two neighboring countries established diplomatic relations, China had become a close ally of Myanmar, mostly when the Southeast Asian country was under the military regime in the late 1990s. This, as well as its proximity to China, is the raison d'etre for this country to merit a separate discussion.

In 2011, the rule of the military dictatorship that lasted from 1962 to 2011 officially ended. Despite the country's opening-up, the nation's major industries are still controlled by the military, which also commands a significant share of parliamentary seats. Since 2018, with planned special economic zones, cross-border railway links between the two countries, and other mega-development projects, Myanmar has officially been involved in Chinese President Xi Jinping's BRI, shaping future relations between the neighboring nations.

The bilateral economic relations between China and Myanmar will be discussed at length in Chapter 7.

6.7.6 *Philippines*

Philippines archipelago comprises 7,100 islands divided into three island groups. While the northern islands are occupied mainly by Tagalog speakers who moved here from Southeast Asia, the southern islands are inhabited by Muslim Moros. They are ethnically closer to the Malaysians and Indonesians than the inhabitants of Luzon. What makes the Philippines a significant country for the major world powers — the USA and China — is its geo-strategic location in the South China Sea. Simultaneously, its 22,000 miles of coastline makes it difficult for the nation to secure its Shoals and Reefs and leaves it vulnerable to external maritime aggression. The Philippines remained a treaty ally of the United States since World War II. The nation does not have a strong navy; its army is better manned and has been mainly occupied with handling insurgencies in Mindanao's southern islands. In 1992, the United States closed America's Subic Bay Naval Station and Clark Airfield station. Just three years later, in 1995, China occupied the Mischief Reef in the Spratlys. Ever since, tensions in the South China Sea have heightened.

In a bid to counter China's growing footprint in the SCS and its continuous occupation of reefs and shoals within the Philippines' territorial waters, the United States also dispatched two aircraft carriers — the Nimitz and Ronald Reagan to the SCS in 2020. Given that China continues to navigate the waters of the SCS as its lake, with the help of it's People's Liberation Army Navy (PLAN), backed by it's Second and Third Sea Forces, it is evident that in the long-term there will be a continuous play of geopolitical competition between the US and China over the Philippines. According to Grossman (2020), Beijing will only be emboldened to pursue this course with Duterte in office, who has clear pro-China proclivities. Thus, the United States and its partners should not expect China to back down anytime between now and the end of Duterte's tenure in 2022, which could make this period particularly turbulent.[10]

The two countries are linked together through trade and investment ties. In 2018, China ranked first in foreign investments to the Philippines, amounting to US$975 million. This growth was led by businesses and companies from sectors like IT & communications, manufacturing, real estate, and electricity. In 2019, China continued to show strong interest and ranked as the second top source of investments, with US$ 1.7 billion, amounting to 32% of total foreign investments. The biggest project was the development of the 3rd telecommunications provider, a joint venture with China Telecom. This investment is attracting related projects in telecom, infrastructure, and services.[11]

According to Chen Min'er, "President Xi Jinping has stressed the need to promote the synergy between the BRI and the Philippine 'Build, Build, Build' program. As a vital player and promoter of the BRI, China is building the New International Land–Sea Trade Corridor (ILSTC), which links the Belt and Road and the Yangtze River Economic Belt and is a hub of ILSTC.[12] The scope for bilateral coopera-

---

[10] Derek Grossman, The Diplomat, https://thediplomat.com/2020/07/china-refuses-to-quit-on-the-philippines/, accessed on December 12, 2020.

[11] https://boi.gov.ph/cifit-2020-philippines-china-business-relations/#, accessed on December 12, 2020.

[12] Rui Hu, https://www.ichongqing.info/2019/09/20/philippines-china-chongqing-trade-and-investment-forum/, accessed on September 20, 2019.

tion is extensive, especially to scale up investment and trade. Philippines is economically dependent on China for its exports and for financing its infrastructure projects. The country is too weak economically to resist Chinese overtures and the USA is too far to secure its economy.

6.7.7 *Singapore*

The City State of Singapore was founded by Sir Thomas Stamford Raffles of the British East India Company in 1819, although it had been discovered a few centuries earlier. Raffles's idea was to make Singapore the principal trading place between India and China. Singapore has always played a central role for Southeast Asian overseas Chinese and it is here that almost three-fourths of the population is Chinese and controls most of the local businesses. As of June 2019, the population of Singaporeans who were ethnic Chinese was around 2.99 million, out of a population of about 6 million. Singapore is home to all religions; its religious composition includes Buddhists 33.2%, Christians 18.8%, Muslims 14%, Taoists 10%, Hindus 5%, in terms of ethnicity (Margolin, 2014; Devare *et al.*, 2014, pp. 228–240).

After the Sino–US rapprochement in 1971–1972, Singaporean leaders began to develop more formal relations with China. In 1976, when Lee Kuan Yew visited China, though he firmly expressed strong ideological opposition to China, he also signaled that Singapore would not be anti-China. From the 1990s, especially when diplomatic relationships between the two countries were re-established and China initiated its second stage of reforms and privatization, bilateral relations deepened. The relationship became more political while rapidly strengthening on the economic level. Since 2013, China has been Singapore's largest trading partner, and Singapore has been China's largest foreign investor. The two countries agreed to commence negotiations to upgrade the 2009 China–Singapore Free Trade Agreement (CSFTA). The upgrade of the CSFTA was concluded in November 2018.[13] Interestingly, every wave of Chinese commercial expansion went along a corresponding wave of Chinese emigration overseas, given that China's investments in partner countries have been "labor-intensive". Singapore is no exception.

---

[13] https://www.mfa.gov.sg/SINGAPORES-FOREIGN-POLICY/Countries-and-Regions/Northeast-Asia/Peoples-Republic-of-China.

6.7.8 *Thailand*

Thailand, mainly a Buddhist country with a population of about 70 million, has the largest overseas Chinese community in the world. About 11 to 14% of Thailand's population are considered ethnic Chinese. According to one estimate, the share of those with at least partial Chinese ancestry is about 40% of the Thai population.

With Thailand, several factors, including Thailand's geo-strategic location on mainland SEA, explain why China has become its new best friend. Two factors of significance are: First, Beijing's lack of criticism of political developments in the Kingdom. Second, the incredible attention China has given to Thailand's leaders. High level visits and side meetings between the two countries exceed that Thailand has with other countries. In contrast, Western leaders have struggled in their interactions with the military government and the Pheu Thai party, and remind Thailand to uphold principles of liberal democracy. In contrast, the Thai–Chinese relationship shows the strength of China's diplomacy.[14]

In October 2003, the first trade agreement between China and an ASEAN country, i.e. the Sino-Thai free trade agreement, was signed. Since then, there have been developments in the bilateral ties, but more recently, the ties have fortified in several areas. Since 2012, China has been Thailand's largest trade partner. Previously, Japan held this position since at least 1993. Foreign Direct Investment spurs Thailand's economic growth and export-led economy. Japan always tops the list of FDI sources by a huge margin.

As ASEAN's second-largest economy, Thailand is an essential country for China — both in terms of trade (China provides a market for 14% of all exports from Thailand and its share in Thai imports constitutes 18%) as well as in terms of its growing clout both internally and externally. Indian business people (Satish Sehgal, D.K. Bakshi, Mr. Bajaj), in their interviews with Reena Marwah in 2015, shared that the Chinese own at least 44% of businesses. Chinese people take on Chinese names and integrate seamlessly into Thai society.

The Thai Government has outlined its vision for developing the Eastern Economic Corridor, to further provide an impetus to pitching Thailand as a central hub of industrial production. In the words of

---

[14] The Curious Case of Thai–Chinese Relations: Best Friends Forever? March 30, 2016, By Sasiwan Chingchit.

Thailand's Deputy Prime Minister Prawit Wongsuwan, "The Thai Government has formed the Eastern Economic Corridor as one of the major mechanisms to drive our 20-year national economic strategy through technology and innovation". He said the EEC was closely linked to China's Belt and Road Initiative. "The EEC and Belt and Road complement each other", he added. The e-commerce base is also fast growing in partnership with China's Alibaba group and more than 100 Chinese companies have opened factories on a huge Thai–Chinese industrial zone. Additionally, a large number of Chinese tourists visit Thailand each year. However, it has been learned that most of the tourists are booked through Chinese travel agents in Chinese-owned hotels, using Alipay, adding little to the local economy.

China–Thailand economic relations are discussed in Chapter 8 of this book.

6.7.9 *Vietnam*

Vietnam and China share a long history of engagement, disengagement, and conflicts. Although the Vietnamese were under the Chinese's direct rule for almost ten centuries (from 3 BC to 1000 AD), and despite some aspects of tradition and language becoming embedded, the people continued to be highly nationalistic.

The relations between Vietnam–China have been a function of geographical proximity with the countries sharing an about 1,300 km long border and intersecting interests in the South China Sea. This is in addition to the relations between the Chinese, the Soviets, and the Americans. It can be stated that when Vietnam's relations broke down with China during the period 1979 to 1991, it was primarily a result of the country's difficulty in maintaining a balance between China and the former Soviet Union. Post-Cold war, the two countries re-examined their relationship, after which the economic engagement has continued to rise (Guan, 1998).

Vietnam is significantly impacted as a result of the maritime disputes in the South China Sea. The Paracel Islands lie at the center of the dispute between China and Vietnam, which the former claims are within its nine-dash line. Given that in 2020 Vietnam was Chair of ASEAN and a non-permanent member of the UNSC for 2021 and 2022, according to Derek Grossman, Vietnam could attempt to bring greater international prominence to the South China Sea via the UNSC in the future. It may also seek to deepen partnerships with other powers including the United States, Australia, Japan, and India, to ring-fence China's assertiveness in the region (Grossman, 2020).

While Vietnam may not join the Quadrilateral Security Dialogue or Quad coalition of countries viz. USA, India, Australia, Japan, it would seek to formalize, during its chairmanship in 2020, a binding Code of Conduct on China. Almost 62% of Vietnamese respondents believed that ASEAN needed to build its resilience and not be dependent on either the United States or China. Given the possibilities of decoupling manufacturing facilities from China by the USA, over 55% of Vietnamese respondents believe that the USA and China's trade war will benefit their country.

6.8 Summary and Conclusion

China's expanding economic influence buttressed by projects streamed through the BRI is, according to Wang, not driven by legal structures, however formal or loose, but by an implicit desire to put the law at the service of commerce to achieve operational results. Hence, ASEAN's informal nature concurs with the fact that there is no Belt and Road charter. It suits the countries of Southeast Asia, especially those with authoritarian regimes and low levels of development, like Cambodia and Laos, to accept connectivity projects and commercial and cultural exchanges for integration with a powerful neighbor. This initiative is slowly being built by specific, bilateral project investment undertakings and an interconnected network of "soft-law" memoranda of understanding (Wang, 2019).

It is instructive to understand ASEAN countries' perceptions through Surveys conducted by ISEAS, as shown in Table 6.5. The 2019 and 2020 surveys have brought forth interesting insights. China continues to be the most influential power in the region, with 79.2% of respondents stating this in 2020 compared to 73.3% in 2019. China's economic stranglehold on countries in SEA has further solidified. Out of those who believe in this, over two-thirds are worried about China's rising economic influence; this is highest in the Philippines, Vietnam, and Thailand. While underscoring the fact that the influence of the United States is declining in the region, it is also important to note that 85% of the respondents are worried about China's rising political and strategic influence. When asked to choose between China and the USA, ASEAN favored the United States (53.6%) against 46.4% for China. In terms of Huawei's preference over

Table 6.5:   ISEAS survey results: 2019 and 2020.

	All % 2020	All % 2019
China will be a benign and benevolent power	1.5	8.9
China will remain a status quo power and continue to support the existing regional order	7.1	22.5
It is too early to ascertain china's strategic intent at this time	18.5	25.7
China will provide alternate regional leadership	34.7	35.3
China is a revisionist power with the intent to turn SEA into its sphere of influence	38.2	45.4

Source: ISEAS Surveys, 2019 and 2020, excerpted by the authors.

Samsung, the only countries who preferred the Chinese 5G network were Malaysia, Cambodia, and Laos. The other seven countries preferred Samsung.

Additionally, Japan, EU, and to a lesser extent Australia emerged as the preferred strategic partners of ASEAN. The Quad finds the greatest support in the Philippines, Vietnam, and Myanmar. Cambodia and Laos are entirely opposed to it. 38.2% of the respondents consider China a revisionist power; only 7% in ASEAN believe that China will maintain the status quo. At least 60% of respondents in Myanmar and Thailand have little or no confidence in the BRI. Japan and the EU are expected to be the most reliable partners in the future. In terms of language used for work, ASEAN preferred English (95.4%), with Mandarin scoring reasonably high at 39%, 73% for Singapore and 49% for Malaysia. Concerning the trust issue, it is interesting to note that Japan emerged as the most trusted, significant power in 2020 (61.2%) followed by the EU (38.7%), the US (30.3%), China (16.1%), and India (16%). Japan retains its number one position as the most preferred strategic partner and a source for regional leadership. Thailand, Singapore, and Vietnam gave Japan the highest scores (ISEAS Survey, 2020).

Only 2.5% of respondents in ASEAN had full confidence in BRI projects. 63.6% of respondents have little or no confidence in China's new clean and green BRI of Xi Jinping. The states most optimistic about the role of China are Brunei, Laos, and Cambodia.

According to David Monyae, speaking at a discussion on August 19, 2020, given the low levels of development and backwardness in several small states in Asia and Africa, it is evident that "smaller states would always gravitate toward any country which was viewed as a development partner".[15]

Hence, China appears to view Southeast Asia as "potentially the most fruitful and receptive region for the projection of Chinese influence". This drive could potentially, but not necessarily, bring American and Chinese interests into the competition and/or conflict in Southeast Asia. As stated earlier, China's relations with Southeast Asia have been described as a "tribute system" or as part of a more Western concept of a "sphere of influence".

China's increasingly active diplomacy toward Southeast Asia can be viewed as a benign outgrowth of its efforts to achieve economic development to improve peoples welfare or as part of an assertive foreign policy. China's embrace of multilateral initiatives, such as the 2003 Treaty of Amity and Cooperation with ASEAN, the East Asia Summit, and efforts to forge a China–ASEAN Free Trade Area, which was advanced in November 2004, is viewed as evidence of a non-threatening trade-focused China. China's evolving grand strategy relies on "formal and informal mechanisms (strengthened multilateral institutions and strong economic ties, respectively) of interdependence as a de facto strategy for restraining the United States" (Vaughn, 2005; Vaughn and Morrison, 2006).

According to Koga, even as China–ASEAN relations deepened, ASEAN has attempted to incorporate external powers into its rules and norms, creating multilateral political and security institutions such as the ASEAN Regional Forum (ARF), the East Asia Summit (EAS), and the ASEAN Defence Ministers Meeting Plus (ADMM-Plus). ASEAN has also formulated a web of multilateral political and security institutions in East Asia that encompass great regional powers, which implies the existence of a strategy that will enable the institution to cope with the external strategic environment. ASEAN has created and embedded the principle of ASEAN Centrality to prevent external powers from hijacking ASEAN-led institutions. So far, this principle has been applied to all ASEAN-led institutions, including ARF, ASEAN plus 3, East Asia Summit (The EAS has 18 members – the ten ASEAN countries along with Australia, China, India, Japan, New Zealand, the Republic of Korea, the United States, and Russia), and ADMM-Plus. Thus, ASEAN remains the main actor in the

---

[15] David Monyae's lecture was hosted by Dr. Reena Marwah, on behalf of the Association of Asia Scholars.

decision-making process in ASEAN-led institutions. Hence, through this process of bandwagoning and collectively aligning with great powers, ASEAN has hoped to secure benefits as well as assurances of receiving cooperation from other powers.

The functions of a "cooperative security" arrangement, which emphasizes the importance of confidence-building measures (CBMs) through diplomatic interactions and policy discussions toward potential cooperation, provide institutional co-option examples. A case in point is the ARF. While ASEAN initially considered the establishment of the ARF as an institutional hedging tool by including in it both China and the United States, its agreed primary and initial objectives were to act as CBMs, and not to impose rules on the Member States. This had been consensually decided in the second meeting that issued the concept paper.

Given that ASEAN's decision-making process is consensus-based, and each member virtually possesses a veto power, it has been difficult for the grouping to arrive at a consensus on contentious issues, such as territorial disputes, because of the number of participants with divergent interests. Hence, although ASEAN's military weakness vis-à-vis regional great powers is a challenge, it created an incentive for ASEAN Member States to manage China's behavior politically through EAS and ADMM-Plus (Koga, 2018).

In the ultimate analysis, it is reiterated that countries in South East Asia have limited bandwidth to engage with countries other than China. The truth is that China seems to have won over most countries in this region; hence, Kishore Mahbubani's book cover title — *Has China Won?* — seems to be the least interrogated in this part of the world (Mahbubani, 2020).

Chapter 7

China and Myanmar: The "Pauk-phaw" (Fraternal) Relationship

China and Myanmar (formerly Burma) reflect elements of their traditional pauk-pauw (siblings from the same mother) relationship that accorded China seniority.

This chapter discusses China–Myanmar relations, particularly Chinese investments and BRI projects, with an analysis of the impacts of the BRI projects on Myanmar.

7.1 A Brief History of Myanmar

Colonial historians of Burma claim that its earliest civilizations had been founded under Indian influence. The civilization in Myanmar's Irrawaddy valley is ancient (3,500 years ago), and its inhabitants were farming rice, raising livestock, and using bronze implements. Bolesta (2018) explains that Myanmar's political and economic interaction with China dates back to the beginning of the last millennium and the Mongol Yuan dynasty's invasion in the thirteenth century, which at that time ruled China. Burma (the official name became Myanmar in 1989) was the first non-communist country to recognize the Chinese communist regime in 1949 and the People's Republic of China. Myanmar has borders with Bangladesh and India to its northwest, China to its northeast, Laos and Thailand to its east and southeast. Myanmar is the 10th largest in Asia by area. In 2017, the population was 54 million.[1] In 2020, over 80% of the people were Buddhists.[2] Myanmar's capital city is Nay Pyi Taw.

For most of its independent years, the country has been engrossed in rampant ethnic strife, and its diverse ethnic groups have been involved in one of the world's longest-running ongoing civil wars. Than likens this to China, when he states, "networks of personal relations and reciprocal obligations" existing at various levels of the party-state and the juncture between state and society eroded state capacity as "patron–client factionalism and localist deception" became the "main ingredients in the real politics" (Than, 2006, p. 330). For several decades after independence, the United Nations and several other organizations have reported consistent and systematic human rights violations.[3] Strict Burmese neutralism reinforced Chinese security along its long and porous southwestern border, in return for Chinese non-intervention in Burma's chaotic internal affairs, with minimal material support for the Burmese Communist Party (Stuart-Fox, 2004).

Since independence from British colonial rule, Myanmar was governed by an oppressive and brutal military junta for seven decades. In 2011, the military junta government was officially dissolved following a 2010 general election, and a nominally civilian government was installed. This, along with the release of Aung San Suu Kyi and political prisoners, has improved the country's human rights record and has led to the easing of trade and other economic sanctions (Madhani, 2012; Fuller and Geitner, 2012).[4] In the landmark 2015 elections, Aung San Suu Kyi's party won a majority in both houses. The November 2020 elections had seen a comeback of Aung San Suu Kyi's party, the National League for Democracy. However, the Burmese military was and continues to remain a powerful force in politics.

---

[1] "Myanmar Population (2018) — Worldometers". worldometers.info, accessed on October 7, 2020.

[2] A short history of Burma, https://newint.org/features/2008/04/18/history, accessed on October 7, 2020.

[3] "World Report 2012: Burma". Human Rights Watch. January 22, 2012. Archived from the original on June 30, 2013. Retrieved July 6, 2013.

[4] Madhani, Aamer (November 16, 2012). "Obama administration eases Burma sanctions before visit". *USA Today*.

Fuller, Thomas; Geitner, Paul (April 23, 2012). "European Union Suspends Most Myanmar Sanctions". *The New York Times*.

7.2 Myanmar's Economy: A Brief Overview

Myanmar is a member of the East Asia Summit, Non-Aligned Movement, ASEAN and BIMSTEC, but it is not a member of the Commonwealth of Nations. It is a country rich in jade and gems, oil, natural gas, and other mineral resources. Myanmar is also endowed with renewable energy; it has the highest solar power potential than other countries of the Great Mekong Sub-region. In macroeconomic terms, Myanmar's total exported goods represent 5.3% of its overall GDP for 2019 (US$357.3 billion valued in Purchasing Power Parity US dollars); a significant increase since 2018. This indicates an increasing reliance on products sold in international markets (Workman, 2019). Table 7.1 indicates some recent economic indicators.

As shown in Table 7.1, Myanmar's GDP per capita for 2019 was $1608, making this equivalent to 13% of the world's average. According to World Bank data, in 2019, the GDP of Myanmar was 76.09 billion US dollars. Government debt is relatively high, being 38.7% (as % of GDP) in 2019. World Bank report on poverty (2019) indicates that between 2005 and 2017, the share of the population living below the poverty line declined substantially, from 48.2% in 2005 to 24.8% in 2017.

Another important indicator of a country's economic performance is its unemployment rate. According to the International Monetary Fund, Myanmar's unemployment rate was 4% in 2019 (same as in 2018). In 2016, Myanmar ranked 145 out of 188 countries in human development (Human Development Report, 2019). Given its economic vulnerability, it seeks to maintain a balance in its relations with large neighboring countries, viz. India and China. With the former, it has deep-rooted historical links; with China the linkages are both political and economic.

Table 7.1:   Myanmar: GDP, GDP per capita, debt, and HDI in 2019.

Country	Total Population (2019)	GDP (Billion US$) 2019	GDP Growth Rate (2019)	GDP per Capita in 2019 (US$)	HDI (2019)	Government Debt (% GDP) (2019)	Life Expectancy at Birth
Myanmar	54,045,422	76.09	6.8%	1608.50	0.584 (Rank 145)	38.7%.	66.9

Source: Diverse sources including UN Human development Report, Trading economics, populationperamid.net.

7.3 China–Myanmar Relationship

Myanmar and China have a long tradition of bilateral political and economic relations; its proximity has changed with altered political circumstances. Bolesta (2018) indicates the Myanmar–China relationship in recent decades has gone beyond economic and political engagement, comprising the model of development within it.

In 1949, Mao Zedong established the Peoples' Republic of China, which was formally recognized by the freshly independent Myanmar Government. China emerged as a close friend of Myanmar, mostly when the Southeast Asian country was under the military regime in the late 1990s.

According to Rajiv Bhatia, an Indian diplomat, "The China–Myanmar bilateral relationship was strong during Ne Win's regime from 1962–1988 as well as during the subsequent period. At the time, Beijing bonded well with Myanmar's military generals. The tools with which China operates are manifold. Chinese companies bring in their own country's workers. The Party tacitly supports Myanmar's northern ethnic groups. Additionally, a method of enhancing influence is the trafficking of Burmese women into China's Yunnan province and the practice of Burmese women marrying Han Chinese men".[5]

Khin Maung Soe, shared in an interview on August 8, 2020 to Reena Marwah, "During the tenure of China's President Hu Jintao and Jiang Zemin, China–Myanmar relationship nosedived, given that China exploited Myanmar in every way. China recognizes the importance of this neighbor, especially as Myanmar has significant deposits of energy and other natural resources and China needs them to fuel its growth".

Aung San Suu Kyi of the NLD, in power since March 2016, contrary to expectations, adopted a foreign policy approach, which has been somewhat similar to that of the military junta under which China became Myanmar's most trusted friend in the region. The Chinese involvement with the Kachin Independence Organisation (KIO) is one example of that. In 2011, the 17-year-old ceasefire between the KIO and the Myanmar government broke down, and Yunnan received at least 60,000 refugees

---

[5] https://www.c3sindia.org/defence-security/interview-with-ambassador-rajiv-bhatia-ifs-retd-on-myanmar-and-its-relations-with-india-and-china-by-asma-masood/, October 7, 2020, accessed on October 24, 2020.

from the Kachin State. Disturbed by the influx of refugees, China played a middleman's role and brought the rebels and the Myanmar Government together for peace talks in 2012 in Ruili, located near Yunnan–Myanmar border area (Kundu, 2018).

Since 2018, with planned special economic zones, cross-border railway links between the two countries and other mega-development projects, Myanmar has officially been involved in the Chinese BRI, shaping future relations.[6]

2020 marked 70 years of diplomatic relations between China and Myanmar, which was celebrated with a formal visit by President Xi Jinping to Naypyidaw in January, during which 33 agreements were signed; out of these, 13 related to infrastructure development. This visit signaled renewed Chinese geo-strategic interest in the country.[7]

Barua (2020) states that modern history has been marked by what is described as a *"pauk-ph*aw", meaning kinship, relationship. She also indicates that China's support for Myanmar in the context of the Rohingya issue, when the International Court of Justice accused Myanmar of "genocidal intent", indicates its mutual benefit in providing a political cushion in the international context. Bathia (2020) also underlines this "Pauk-phaw" relationship, marking President Xi's visit in January 2020, when she writes, "close reading of what the Chinese stated before and during the visit confirms that the traditional "pauk-phaw" (fraternal) ties between China and Myanmar are in full bloom now".[8]

However, the bilateral ties are fraught with fissures as well. Lintner (2019) writes that Myanmar is pushing back at Chinese investments in the China–Myanmar Economic Corridor (CMEC). China is keen to link Yunnan with the Arakanese port of Kyaukpyu. There have been incidents of skirmishes between locals and Chinese workers in the country.

---

[6] China–Myanmar Relations, https://www.irrawaddy.com/specials/timeline-china-myanmar-relations.html, accessed on October 2, 2020.

[7] The China-Myanmar Economic Corridor and China's Determination to see it through, https://www.wilsoncenter.org/blog-post/china-myanmar-economic-corridor-and-chinas-determination-see-it-through, accessed on October 8, 2020.

[8] Myanmar's growing dependence on China, https://www.thehindu.com/opinion/op-ed/myanmars-growing-dependence-on-china/article30627576.ece, accessed on October 17, 2020.

Huang (2015) asserts that Myanmar seeks to forge ties with other powers and "balance relations" vis-à-vis China.

7.3.1 President Aung San Suu Kyi & relations with major powers

Aung San Suu Kyi has been making efforts to balance the major powers.

As Rajiv Bhatia states, "The present government under Aung San Suu Kyi, like the earlier ruling faction, wants to balance India, the US, China, and the West. But this can happen only when other parties want to balance. It was a big loss in foreign policy for Suu Kyi when Hillary Clinton did not win the US presidential elections. Myanmar's problems with ASEAN are also increasing due to Suu Kyi's rapport with her country's military".[9]

Suu Kyi knows that if she annoys the Chinese leadership, she will lose power. The situation is now altered. Suu Kyi has become China's key politician for projects and schemes, while the military, though not openly critical of Beijing, endeavors to keep a distance from its advances.[10] Lintner (2019) believes that the flipped script has been driven by geopolitics. The Rohingya refugee crisis, and Suu Kyi's refusal to condemn the atrocities the military unleashed in Rakhine state in 2017, have dramatically turned her from being courted by the West into an international pariah. Suu Kyi, the recipient of several awards for human rights (many of which were conferred on her during her long non-violent struggle for democracy against abusive military rule), have been taken away. China's double-game in Myanmar, where it has been an armed conflict mediator and supplier of arms to insurgents, is now well known. China uses the long-worn out carrot and stick approach to secure assets, namely, the CMEC and access to Myanmar's rich natural resources including copper, gold, jade, amber, and rare earth metals.

Without a doubt, the Myanmar–China relationship is mainly driven by the exigencies of geopolitics.

---

[9] C3S, *op.cit*; October 7, 2020. Interview of Rajiv Bhatia by Asma Masood.
[10] https://asiatimes.com/2020/05/china-flips-the-electoral-script-in-myanmar/Bertil, accessed on October 10, 2020.

The next section analyzes China's economic engagement with Myanmar through trade, investment in BRI projects, and other economic indicators over the period 2000–2020.

7.4 China–Myanmar Economic Engagement

China and Myanmar share 2,200 kilometers of land border. The former's interests in Myanmar have primarily been driven by its desire to secure natural resources (Li and Char, 2015), given that the political relationship undergirds the economy. The junta leader Than Shwe (as Vice-chairman of the State Law and Order Restoration Council) visited Beijing in October 1989. The military delegation secured an arms deal worth about US$1.4 billion. In December 1989, both sides signed an economic and technical cooperation agreement, post which loans and grants started to flow from Beijing (Bolesta, 2018).

In an Interview, Khin Maung Soe quoting USA's former President, Barack Obama, when he visited Myanmar in 2012, said, "I came here because of the importance of your country; Myanmar's geopolitical significance attracts the attention of USA and Western powers; China's interest is for its vested economic interests".

In an interview with a Japanese professor — Dr. AmYu_said, "Chinese — timber, sand mining, rare earth minerals, small weapons; advantage in Kachin state due to its being remote; jade; China will do anything for their interest".

7.4.1 *Myanmar and China: Bilateral trade*

In the late 1980s, bilateral trade growth accelerated in Myanmar, which led to increased Chinese investment in Myanmar. Although Myanmar's economic and political liberalization has resulted in a slowing down of bilateral trade and investment dynamics due to the growing number of international economic partners, China remains one of the most important among them (Bolesta, 2018).

In 2020, China is the largest investor in Myanmar and also its biggest trading partner. Bilateral trade was US$16.8 billion in 2019. **The 70th-anniversary visit by** President Xi (in January 2020) helped to push ahead with plans for the CMEC, a basket of projects totaling more than US$20 billion.

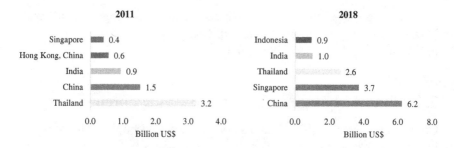

Figure 7.1:   Myanmar's top five export partners (US$ Billion).

Source: Using UN COMTRADE and WITS online data created by the authors.

Myanmar's Commerce Ministry declared the total trade between Myanmar and other countries as US$36.6 billion in the fiscal year (FY) 2019–2020. At the same time, from October 1, 2019, to September 30, 2020, Myanmar's export earnings were US$17.6 billion while its import expenditure was US$19 billion.[11]

Myanmar exports agricultural and animal products, marine products minerals, forest products, manufactured goods, and others while importing capital goods, intermediate goods, and consumer goods. The sea route is used for about 80% of the country's trade with foreign countries. Its border trade is conducted with neighboring China, Thailand, Bangladesh, and India. Figure 7.1 indicates Myanmar's top five trading partners in 2011 and 2018. According to the data, in 2011 Thailand was the biggest trading partner for Myanmar's exports (the amount was US$3.2 billion); hence, in 2018 this has changed with China being in number one position with exports at US$6.2 billion.

Table 7.2 presents the top ten export-oriented industries in Myanmar in 2019. These export product groups represent the highest dollar value of global shipments from Myanmar. Also shown is the percentage share each export category represents in terms of overall exports from Myanmar. Workman (2019) states that Myanmar's exports grew, with a 66.4% gain since 2015, and a 14.1% increase from 2018 to 2019.

Ores, slag, and ash were the fastest growing among the top 10 export categories, propelled by more robust international sales of tin, lead, and

---

[11] Myanmar's foreign trade reaches over US$36.6 billion in FY 2019–2020, http://www.china.org.cn/world/Off_the_Wire/2020-10/12/content_76798577.htm, accessed on October 14, 2020.

Table 7.2:   The top 10 export-oriented industries in Myanmar (2019).

Rank	Export Commodity	Value (US$)	Percentage of Total Exports (%)
1	Mineral fuels including oil	4.4 billion	22.9
2	Clothing, accessories (not knit or crochet)	4 billion	21.1
3	Knit or crochet clothing, accessories	2 billion	10.4
4	Ores, slag, ash	973.7 million	5.1
5	Cereals	805.4 million	4.2
6	Copper	702.1 million	3.7
7	Footwear.	581 million	3.1
8	Vegetables	535.3 million	2.8
9	Leather/animal gut articles	476.7 million	2.5
10	Fish	473.6 million	2.5

Source: UNCOMTRADE online data, accessed October 10, 2020.

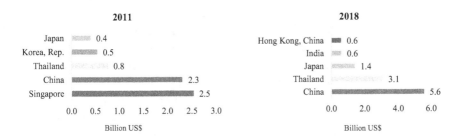

Figure 7.2:   Myanmar's top five import partners (US$ Billion).

Source: Using UN COMTRADE and WITS online data created by the authors.

manganese. 64% of Myanmar's exports of ores, slag, and ash went to China. In second place was leather or animal gut articles. Myanmar's knitted or crocheted clothing and accessories shipments posted the third-fastest gain in value, up by 131.3% (Workman, 2019).

Figure 7.2 indicates Myanmar's top five import partners in 2011 and 2018. Singapore was the leading import partner in Myanmar in 2011; the import amount being US$2.5 billion, and the second-largest importer was China (US$2.3 billion). In 2018, China became the top import partner for Myanmar, the import amount being US$5.6 billion, hence recording a significant increase in 7 years. CMEC-related projects in Myanmar have led to the import of vast amounts of raw materials from China. Thailand remained the second largest import partner in Myanmar in 2018. However, the import gap between China and Thailand is also significant (see Figure 7.2).

The latest available country-specific data from 2018 shows that 85.1% of products exported from Myanmar were bought by importers in China (33.3% of the global total), Thailand (18.3%), Japan (8.3%), India (3.4%), Hong Kong (3.4%), Germany (3%), United States (also 3%), Singapore (2.9%), South Korea (2.7%), United Kingdom (2.5%), Netherlands (2.2%), and Spain (1.9%) (Workman, 2019).

7.4.2 Chinese investments

Myanmar officially joined the BRI in 2017; while also acknowledging the China–Indochina Peninsula Economic Corridor (CIPEC) as its component. Further, China has proposed the development of the CMEC based on three pillars — the Kyaukpyu SEZ,[12] the China–Myanmar Border Economic Cooperation Zone, and the New Yangon City, all to be built with Chinese assistance. This has the potential to make China the undisputed foreign power in Myanmar (Barua, 2020).

China built several projects in Myanmar even before the recent BRI. As Bolesta (2018) stated, Chinese investment projects in Myanmar were initiated since the 2000s. Anecdotal evidence suggests that China has been involved in around 90 different energy projects in Myanmar, including the planned or ongoing construction of at least 10 dams. The dams are intended to generate jointly 20 GW of hydro-energy. The most publicized project has been the US$3.6 billion Myitsone dam, the largest (6 Gigawatts) out of seven dams to be built on Mali, the N'Mai, and the Irrawaddy rivers. The Myitsone dam construction was suspended by President Thein Sein in 2011 citing social and environmental concerns (Bolesta, 2018, p. 25).

Marwah (2020) indicates that as the land bridge between South Asia and Southeast Asia, Myanmar is significant for China, especially for its strategic pursuits in the Indian Ocean. Further, China's forays into the seas through Myanmar opens up an alternate route, as a solution, to the Malacca dilemma it finds itself in.

---

[12] SEZ — Special Economic Zones.

7.4.2.1 *What is CMEC?*

The main objective of the CMEC was to connect the Indian Ocean oil trade to China's Yunnan Province and generate dividends for China by addressing internal development priorities, the strategic vulnerabilities of China's oil supply, and its competition with India. CMEC bears a resemblance to the CPEC.[13]

China has proposed about 40 projects under CMEC; however, by 2020, only nine projects have been approved. Myanmar officials have confirmed that Myanmar will only implement the projects which guarantee mutual benefits for both sides.

President Xi, during his visit to Myanmar in January 2020, underlined that CMEC is to deepen cooperation in diverse areas like "connectivity, electricity, energy, transportation, agriculture, finance, and livelihood to deliver more benefits to both peoples".[14] This high-level visit was evidently intended to assuage Myanmar's concerns on BRI projects, several of which have been stalled.

7.4.3 *BRI projects*

Six major CMEC projects in Myanmar are discussed as follows:

- **Kyaukphyu Deep Seaport**
The deep-sea Kyaukphyu Port project was designed to include a special economic zone and other related infrastructure refer Figure 7.3. The entire area is spread over 520 hectares — 20 for a port, 100 for housing, and 400 for an industrial park. The port development was preceded by the completion of the oil pipeline project from Kunming to Kyaukpyu and also a gas pipe line between the two ports, in 2017 and 2013, respectively. These projects, meant to develop China's southwestern hinterland, encountered pushback from the local Myanmarese people, but were implemented nevertheless. In an Interview, Khin Maung Soe, speaking about the gas and

---

[13] The China–Myanmar Economic Corridor and China's Determination to See it through, https://www.wilsoncenter.org/blog-post/china-myanmar-economic-corridor-and-chinas-determination-see-it-through, accessed on October 8, 2020.

[14] Bhatia, R. (2020). Myanmar's growing dependence on China, https://www.thehindu.com/opinion/op-ed/myanmars-growing-dependence-on-china/article30627576.ece, accessed on October 17, 2020.

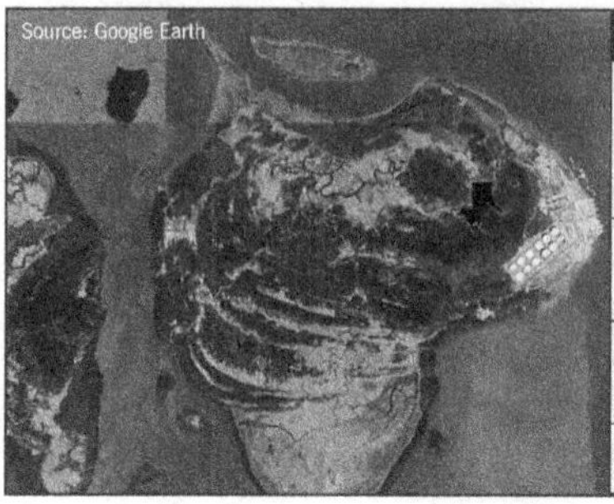

MYANMAR'S KYAUKPHYU PORT	
GEOSTRATEGIC LOCATION	• Situated in proximity to Malacca Strait Maritime Chokepoint • Access to the Indian Ocean and Bay of Bengal
OWNERSHIP	• CITIC holds a 70 percent stake and 50-year lease
DUAL-USE FACILITIES	• Port is now or will soon be able to accommodate range of PLAN vessels
DEBT TO CHINA	• 40 percent of GDP

Figure 7.3:   Myanmar's Kyaukphyu Port.

Source: Russell and Berger (2020), https://asiasociety.org/sites/default/files/2020-09/Weaponizing%20the%20Belt%20andRoad%20Initiative_0.pdf.

oil pipeline, said that it was a very controversial project. In his words, "I was invited to the head office; a consortium was set up with South Korean companies; India is also an investor; they explained that this project benefits Myanmar and other shareholders. However, many people are not happy with this project; they don't hire Myanmar's workers, there are environmental problems, and most CCP party officials are not transparent in their dealings".

The Kyaukpyu Port, despite having been downsized from US$7 billion to US$1.3 billion, is being developed as a 'model' of port development by China. Myanmar's stake in the project stands at 30%. Even this amount is too big a sum for Myanmar and there have been fears that by borrowing from Chinese Banks Myanmar may get into a debt trap as in the case of Sri Lanka (Htwe, 2018). While the deep Sea Port will only help China and not Myanmar, the deal was sweetened with a parallel project of a special economic zone for which the stakes for the two sides are yet to be finalized.[15]

Phase 1 of the port development will involve constructing two jetties with a total investment of about US$1.3 billion. The government of Myanmar was able to revise the project to postpone the SEZ until the port proved its viability in the first phase (Kapoor and Thant, 2018).

However, the development of the port has been delayed due to COVID-19. U Set Aung said to the *Myanmar Times*, "We had to postpone international tenders for the Environmental and Social Impact

[15] S. Chandrasekharan, http://www.slguardian.org/2020/06/myanmar-china-and-kyaukpyu-deep-sea-port.html, accessed on October 26, 2020.

Assessments (EIA/SIA) due to COVID-19". He further said that the EIA/ SIA was to be completed within a year according to the agreement, but the process will not be able to commence until after COVID-19. The project can begin only after the assessments are completed.

Myanmar's Kyaukphyu Port is a strategic asset for China. Alongwith Cambodia's Koh Kong Port, the two would provide the People's Liberation Army of Manipur (PLA) with greater capabilities to address its Malacca Dilemma. Bolstered by existing military platforms in the South China Sea, these two ports also better position Beijing to challenge transiting military vessels (Russell and Berger, 2020).

See Table 7.3 for financial terms and expected economic benefits of the project.

- ***Muse-Mandalay Express Railway Project***

Myanmar Rail Transportation Department officials expect that the Muse-Mandalay express railroad project would cost around US$8.9 billion. The project will be implemented with funds from organizations like the World Bank or the Asian Development Bank. Furthermore, U Set Aung, chairman of Kyaukphyu SEZ, said that, "We agreed in the Co-operation Plan that the projects would be implemented with the best and most cost-efficient sources of financing for Myanmar".[16]

The Rail Project will be 431 Kilometers long and will pass through conflict areas in Shan state. It will begin near Myitnge in Amarapura township in Mandalay and will pass through 11 townships and link up with Yunnan's high-speed railway line from Dali to Ruili. A feasibility study initiated in October 2018 completed by China Railway Eryuan Engineering has been submitted to the Myanmar Government. It is estimated to cost US$9 billion. However, the environmental and social impact assessments remain incomplete in this project.

- ***New Yangon Development Project***

This project is also referred to as the New Yangon City project. The CMEC will connect Yunnan province in China to Mandalay, Yangon New City in the south and the Kyaukphyu Special Economic Zone. The Yangon regional government-backed New Yangon Development Company

---

[16] *Myanmar Times*, https://www.mmtimes.com/news/viable-cmec-projects-be-included-myamar-project-bank.html, accessed on October 10, 2020.

(NYDC) initially signed a US$1.5 billion (2.03 trillion-kyat) framework agreement in 2018 with Beijing-based China Communications Construction Company, Ltd. (CCCC) to draw up a proposal for the infrastructure project. The 20,000 acres (nearly 8,100-hectare) New Yangon City project is slated to include five resettlement areas, two bridges, an industrial estate, as well as related infrastructure. The Yangon Government's 2019 guidebook listing the city's project — the Yangon Project Bank — estimates the New Yangon City project's total cost at US$8 billion.[17] This project has also raised questions about its viability given that it raises concerns about costs and potential floods.

The prime concerns with this project are its flood-prone location as well as CCCC's involvement. (The CCCC is blacklisted for helping militarize Chinese outposts in the South China Sea.) Since its formation, the NYDC has maintained that while CCCC was the frontrunner for the project, the selection process to identify a developer would follow the so-called "Swiss Challenge" model. Other candidate firms would be invited to beat CCCC's bid. However, the vast amount of the initial investment required has all but deterred other investors.

During Chinese President Xi Jinping's visit to Myanmar in early 2020, the two sides decided to develop the Yangon City — including the new city project — among other shareholder agreements. Chinese Ambassador to Myanmar Chen Hai also noted that construction of the New Yangon City project's pilot area would commence, as fresh progress has been made on all three pillars of the CMEC.

Even as the Chinese euphoria was rising, on September 9, 2020, a German firm was hired by the Myanmar Government to oversee a bidding process in place of the New Yangon City project. This move attempts to project transparency in the tendering procedure to "challenge" a bid from the US-sanctioned China Communications Construction Company.[18]

---

[17] Myanmar's Union Govt Splits Up Huge China-backed New Yangon City Project, https://www.irrawaddy.com/news/burma/myanmars-union-govt-splits-huge-china-backed-new-yangon-city-project.html, accessed on September 25, 2020.

[18] Interview with Ambassador Rajiv Bhatia IFS (Retd.) on "Myanmar and its Relations with India and China"; By Asma Masood, October 7, 2020; https://www.c3sindia.org/defence-security/interview-with-ambassador-rajiv-bhatia-ifs-retd-on-myanmar-and-its-relations-with-india-and-china-by-asma-masood/, accessed on October 24, 2020.

- ### *Myitsone Hydropower Project*

China Power International (CPI) and Myanmar Ministry of Electric Power signed an agreement to build the Myitsone and other smaller dams under the Irrawaddy Confluence Basin project in December 2009 during the then-Vice President Xi Jinping's visit to Myanmar. Myitsone is a Build-Operate-Transfer (BOT) project. If completed, 90% of the electricity generated would be transmitted to China, and after 50 years of operation, CPI would transfer the dam to the Myanmar Government without any cost (Sun, 2013; Kundu, 2020, p. 346). However, Kiik (2016) indicates that this project became an "actor in broader political conflicts".

The Myitsone Hydroelectric Project is the largest of seven dams (total capacity 13,360 MW) planned on the Irrawaddy headwaters (confluence of Mali Hka) N'Mai Hka rivers) in Myanmar. The US$3.6 billion project is located in an area recognized as one of the world's eight hotspots of biodiversity. They will submerge "the birthplace of Burma" in local myths, including several historical churches and temples, and the sacred banyan tree.[19]

Hilton (2013) is of the view that the suspension of the Myitsone dam project since 2011 presented a new image of Myanmar as a more confident and self-reliant country, which enthused a debate about Myanmar's desire to steer clear of China's shadow. This dam is one of the 44 Chinese-funded hydropower projects in Myanmar. Most of these 44 hydropower projects are either in Kachin State or Shan State, having borders with China (Kundu, 2020).

Post Xi Jinping's visit in 2020, the Chinese Ambassador in Myanmar has pressed the necessity of restarting the Myitsone project, citing its importance for BRI projects. However, given huge security concerns and a public backlash against it due to its potential to destroy livelihoods and displace at least 10,000 people, this US$3.6 billion project has remained suspended. Naypyidaw credited the suspension decision to the "people's will'. This is also attributed to the victory of anti-dam and anti-China movements.[20] In addition to doubts about the quality and independence of the Environmental Impact Assessment for this mega-dam project, there are concerns regarding the project's potential in exacerbating the longstanding conflict between the ethnic Kachin people and the military gov-

---

[19] Myitsone hydroelectric dam Myanmar https://www.banktrack.org/project/myitsone_hydroelectric_dam, accessed on October 14, 2020.
[20] Ruosui Zhang, *The Diplomat*, July 22, 2020; https://thediplomat.com/2020/07/chinese-investment-in-myanmar-beyond-myitsone-dam/.

ernment.[21] As experts have articulated, China would be wise to cancel this dam project itself.

- ### *Kyaukphyu-Kunming Railway*

This project includes building a high-speed railroad connecting China's southern city of Kunming and Myanmar's Kyaukphyu port on the Bay of Bengal. If this project is completed, the 1,400 kilometers railroad will be crucial in a strategic economic corridor. China's imports and exports would bypass the congested Malacca Straits and the contested South China Sea, both potential chokepoints in any conflict scenario.

This US$20 billion project had also been stalled in 2011 by President U Thein Sein due to objections from the local population and remained in limbo for several years. However, the Muse-Mandalay railway project has been initiated in late 2020 after some feasibility studies. This is a part of the Kyaukphyu-Kunming railway project refer Figures 7.4, 7.5 and 7.6.

- ### *Special Economic Zones*

Myanmar in 2018 approved three border special economic cooperation zones, as follows:

1. Kanpiketi in Kachin State's Special Region
2. Chinsh Wehw, in Shan State's Laukkai Township
3. Shan State's Muse Township (*Muse-Ruili zone*)

The creation of Special Economic Zones (SEZs) was to develop designated enclaves that facilitate imports, exports, and foreign direct investment.

Deputy Minister of Commerce U Aung Htoo said that among three China–Myanmar Border Economic Cooperation Zones, Shweli-Muse Core Zone would be implemented first; as this is what the Chinese want. He further said that, as part of the CMEC, Myanmar is expecting to develop core zones in three locations — Muse, Chin Shwe Haw, and Kan Pite Tee.[22] It was also decided that the two governments will determine the

---

[21] Myitsone hydroelectric dam Myanmar https://www.banktrack.org/project/myitsone_hydroelectric_dam, accessed on October 14, 2020.

[22] Consult Myanmar, https://consult-myanmar.com/2020/07/02/viable-cmec-projects-to-be-included-in-myamar-project-bank/#, accessed on September 30, 2020.

Figure 7.4: Muse to Mandalay railway.

Source: https://newsviews.thuraswiss.com/china-myanmar-high-speed-railway-route/

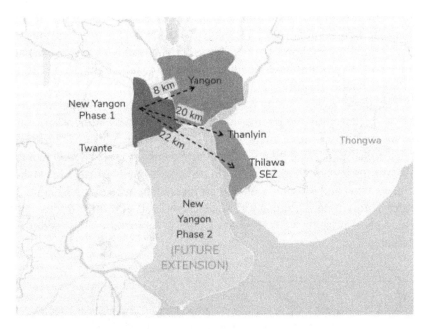

Figure 7.5: New Yangon City project.

Figure 7.6:   Kyaukphyu-Kunming Railway.

Source: https://asia.ub-speeda.com/en/chinas-one-belt-one-road-projects-asean/.

zone location and area for the Shweli-Muse Core Zone. Other factors such as financing and manpower would also be fixed in the agreement. The success of the Shweli-Muse Core Zone would decide the fate of the next two zones.[23]

Some private developers along Myanmar's borders have also used the term "SEZ", but establishing an SEZ in Myanmar requires approval from Myanmar's parliament (the Pyidaungsu Hluttaw). This approval has not been granted to any border zone. Zones in Myawaddy (Karen State) and Mong La (Shan State) have been permitted by local ethnic armed groups and questionable legality.

The three zones are in Kanpiketi town, in Kachin State's Special Region 1 (currently under the control of the New Democratic Army-Kachin militia, a border guard force allied with the Myanmar military); Chinshwehaw, in Shan State's Laukkai Township (part of the Kokang Self-Administered Zone); and in Shan State's Muse Township. Chinshwehaw and Muse are already major trading hubs along Myanmar's border with China's Yunnan Province. Kanpiketi currently trades regularly with China as well. The total cost of construction is yet to be calculated.[24]

---

[23] *Ibid.*

[24] NAN LWIN August 15, 2019; https://www.irrawaddy.com/news/myanmar-set-ink-pact-china-border-cooperation-zones.html, accessed on November 15, 2020.

7.4.3.1 *SEZs in Thilawa, Dawei, and Kyaukphyu*

In addition to the above border SEZs, China and Myanmar have three SEZs at varying development stages: Thilawa, south of Yangon, Dawei in southern Myanmar, and Kyaukphyu on the east coast in Rakhine state. These are the only zones currently covered by the 2014 Myanmar Special Economic Zone Law.

Given controversies surrounding the three border SEZs and ongoing resistance to them, it is unlikely that bona fide border SEZs will be established in Myanmar in the foreseeable future. This may be possible if laws are amended and public opinion toward SEZs changes (Thanme, 2020).

7.4.3.2 *Myitkyina economic development zone*

A Chinese company, which has secured a deal to build a 4,700-acre industrial zone in Myitkyina district, in the Kachin State, envisions this as a hub of industrial and agricultural production and processing. The only thing the Kachin state government has made public about the project is the 2018 memorandum. Yunnan's Yuntianhua International Chemical Co., Ltd. (YTHIC) is owned by the Yunnan Baoshan Hengyi Industry Group, headquartered across the border from Muse in Mangshi, Yunnan. The agreement gives YTHIC the exclusive right to form a joint venture with the government in Myitkyina for 15 years, thereby disallowing other international investment. With a complete lack of transparency, this project is similar to several others where Chinese companies' invest. Other investment companies would not operate even if the project was delayed or not implemented, said Khine Win, Sandhi Governance Institute's executive director. "These terms are concerning". The project may lead to an increase in the illegal cross-border trade of jade and timber, the Institute's report warns.[25]

Table 7.3 provides a summary of 6 main CMEC projects in Myanmar.

7.4.3.3 *Problematic project: Myitsone dam*

Myanmar's most infamous Chinese investment project is the Myitsone dam, a 6,000 megawatt hydropower project that would have displaced over 10,000 villagers in Kachin state. The mega-dam was suspended

---

[25] Thar and Aung, https://myanmar-now.org/en/news/kachin-residents-fearful-of-losing-land-to-secretive-china-backed-industrial-project, July 7, 2020.

Table 7.3: Financial terms and expected economic benefits of major Chinese projects in Myanmar.

Project Name	Loan/ Investment	Estimated cost (US$)	Implementing agency	Contractor	Economic problems
Kyaukphyu Deep Seaport	Sea Transportation	1.3 billion (cut from 7.2 billion) 2.7 billion industrial area			• debt trap • environmental and health problems • maritime security issues
Muse-Mandalay Railway Project	Railway transportation Project	8.9 billion	Using fund from the World Bank or Asian Development Bank	China Railway Erguan Engineering Corporation	• More armed conflict along the route in Shan state
New Yangon Development Project	Development Project	1.5 billion	New Yangon Development Company (NYDC)	China Communications Construction Company (CCCC)	• unnecessary project, • Raises concerns about expenses and potential floods
Three Border Economic Zones	Economic cooperation zones		Local governments		• Raises concerns about armed conflict • migrant population
Myitsone Hydropower Project Stalled	Energy	3.6 billion		China Power International (CPI) and the Myanmar Ministry of Electric Power	• Can flood an area the size of Singapore • destroying livelihoods and displacing more than 10000 people
Kyaukphyu-Kunming Railway	Railway transportation Project	20 billion	Feasibility study in progress		• Raises concerns about a potential debt trap • armed conflict

Sources: https://www.thestar.com.my/news/regional/2020/02/17/china039s-citic-to-build-myanmar039s-huge-kyaukphyu-deep-seaport-first-phase-to-cost-us13-bln, accessed on December 12, 2020 and different sources.

unilaterally in 2011 by Myanmar's then-president, Thein Sein, and attempts to revive the Myitsone dam as part of the CMEC were met with nationwide protests and rallies in early 2019.[26]

7.5 Costs & Benefits of BRI Projects in Myanmar

Chinese Foreign Minister Wang Yi announced the proposal to build the CMEC following a meeting with State Counselor Aung San Suu Kyi in November 2017. Wang said the economic corridor would enhance investment in development and trade as part of the BRI.[27] However, the CMEC projects as discussed have invited great criticism and have been referred to as being *old Wine in a New Bottle*. Here, it is important to discuss the costs and benefits of BRI/CMEC projects in Myanmar.

7.5.1 *Expected benefits of BRI projects*

- *Development*

Undoubtedly, China has been the country of great weight for Myanmar's development. It accounts for a significant share of Myanmar's international trade (22%) and a significant share of foreign investments. Due to economic, geographic, and other reasons, China's weight in Myanmar will continue to be extensive, despite the setbacks and visible pushback. Ever since the military coup in February 2021, the protests against Chinese companies have also increased, with at least 32 factories owned by Chinese businessmen having been burnt.

- *Investments from China*

Chinese companies account for much required one-third of the nearly US$44 billion of foreign investment Myanmar has approved since 1988, highlighting China's long history of dominance in this Asian neighbor. The sector where the highest investment has been approved is electricity,

---

[26] Trouble for Belt and Road in Myanmar, https://chinadialogue.net/en/business/11585-trouble-for-belt-and-road-in-myanmar-2/, accessed on October 8, 2020.

[27] In Myanmar, China's BRI Projects Are Old Wine in a New Bottle, https://www.irrawaddy.com/news/burma/in-myanmar-chinas-bri-projects-are-old-wine-in-a-new-bottle.html, accessed on October 14, 2020.

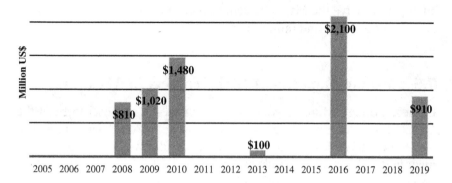

Figure 7.7:   China's investment in Myanmar (US$ Millions).

Sources: Using China Global Investment Tracker (Data compiled by The American Enterprise Institute and The Heritage Foundation) data figures created by the Authors.

at more than US$19 billion, or nearly 44% of the total. The sector received US$13.21 billion in actual investment, but despite the largesse, Myanmar continues to face an energy crisis, with more than 70% of its citizens living without regular electricity. However, oil and gas top the list of actual investment by sector with US$13.63 billion, or more than 40% of the total. Electricity follows in second position and mining occupies a distant third with just US$2.31 billion.[28] Figure 7.7 indicates China's investment in Myanmar from 2005 to 2019.

In light of these grievances, Chinese State-owned enterprises are trying to demonstrate the tangible benefits of Myanmar's participation in the BRI. As an example, in the years since the twin pipelines' construction, the Southeast Asia Gas Pipeline Corporation (majority-owned by China National Petroleum Corp.) has donated US$25 million for the construction of schools, clinics, and water supply systems for rural communities along the pipeline route.[29]

---

[28] Myanmar FDI: China accounts for one-third of foreign investment in Myanmar with US$14 billion, https://www.ibtimes.com/Myanmar-FDI-china-accounts-one-third-foreign-investment-Myanmar-14-billion, accessed on October 8, 2020.

[29] Trouble for Belt and Road in Myanmar, https://chinadialogue.net/en/business/11585-trouble-for-belt-and-road-in-myanmar-2/, accessed on October 8, 2020.

- **Agricultural development in Myanmar**

Chinese-run banana plantations in Kachin state occupied 2,500 hectares in 2007. These increased to over 40,500 hectares in 2018. The vast majority of the plantations are located in Waingmaw township, in the Kachin state, adjacent to the border with China.

7.5.2 Costs of BRI

Given the need for Xi's personal intervention in January 2020, this underscores that there are significant implementation problems for China's investments in Myanmar, leading some analysts to consider the CMEC initiatives are unlikely to ever meet Chinese expectations. As reported by the Transnational Initiative, only 9 of the 40 previously proposed projects were underway prior to Xi's January visit.[30]

- **Balance of payments and Budget deficits**

Although both Myanmar and China followed similar developmental trajectories, the two countries are at very different economic development stages (Bolesta, 2018). The Finance Commission (chaired by President U Win Myint) estimates that Myanmar anticipated a budget deficit of K 6.8 trillion during the fiscal year 2020–2021 or 5.4% of the GDP.[31]

Figure 7.8 shows that post 2015, with increasing imports from China, Myanmar's trade deficit has increased significantly.

In terms of trade, the Jade industry is one of the focal points. *In an interview, Dr. AmYu, a Japanese professor, said,* "Jade industry is worth at least US$31 billion; despite this, the Myanmar government does not get any revenue. Although the previous government sought to have a Jade center in Mandalay, the Chinese did not somehow let it open; they intentionally spoilt the plan; because if the center was set up, the control of the jade trade would become legalized". The illegality in the trading process suits the Chinese traders and smugglers.

---

[30] The China–Myanmar Economic Corridor and China's Determination to See It Through, https://www.wilsoncenter.org/blog-post/china-myanmar-economic-corridor-and-chinas-determination-see-it-through, accessed on October 8, 2020.

[31] https://www.mmtimes.com/news/budget-deficit-fiscal-2020-21-myanmar-k68-trillion.html, accessed on October 14, 2020.

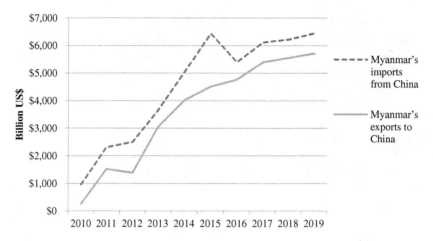

Figure 7.8:   Bilateral trade between China and Myanmar.

Sources: Using UN COMTRADE data created by the authors, https://comtrade.un.org, accessed on September 25, 2020.

- ***Debt Burden***

Figure 7.9 shows Myanmar's debt as a share of GDP. It indicates that the debt rate is increasing post-2015, with the figure being 49.4% in 2019 compared to 37.4% in 2014.

- ***Security, Defence, Borders, and Sovereignty***

The increase in armed ethnic groups' military capabilities in northern Myanmar is causing serious concern among Myanmar's military leadership. Since 2019, the military has seized several caches of Chinese-made weapons near the northern border. China is supplying sophisticated weaponry to armed groups in Myanmar and the Naypyidaw-designated terrorist group, the Arakan Army, much to the disdain of the Tatmadaw. A military source with experience in Southeast Asia confirmed that China provides approximately 95% of all Arakan Army funding. He further revealed that the Arakan Army has approximately 50 MANPADS (Man-Portable Air Defense Systems) surface-to-air missiles.[32]

---

[32] China growing anxious as Myanmar proceeds cautiously with BRI projects: Report Read more At: https://www.aninews.in/news/world/china-growing-anxious-as-myanmar-proceeds-cautiously-with-bri-projects-report20200909221059/, accessed on October 1, 2020.

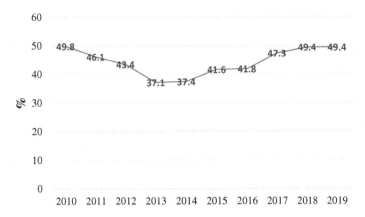

Figure 7.9:   Government debt as a share of GDP in Myanmar (%) (2010–2019).

Sources: Using TradingEconomics data, created by the authors, https://tradingeconomics.com/thailand/government-debt-to-gdp, country profiles, accessed on October 4, 2020.

Myanmar Army officials have often complained that China had been providing arms to the Kokang rebels in Yunnan Province. However, China continues to supply weapons to arm insurgent groups in addition to support-ing other illegal activities on its borders. Myanmar as well as neighboring Bangladesh have emerged as top recipients of Chinese arms supplies. Myanmar has been officially making arms purchases from China, too. In 2013, it procured roughly US$720 million worth of arms from China, including aircraft, unmanned aerial vehicles, vessels, and armored vehicles.

In 2017, the PLA sent a One Belt, One Road Navy Task Force through the South China Sea and the Indian Ocean, stopping in Cambodia, Indonesia, Myanmar, Pakistan, Sri Lanka, the Maldives, Djibouti, Saudi Arabia, and a dozen other countries for six months. Since then, PLA ships have made multiple repeat visits for port calls, joint exercises, or interna-tional exhibitions. In 2017, the PLA also held its first joint exercise with the Tatmadaw — Myanmar's military. China's port projects in Cambodia and Myanmar continue to develop as strategic strongpoints. Evidently, these nodes will over time bolster the PLA's ability to reduce or deny US access to critical waterways and challenge the ability of the US Navy to operate in the Gulf of Thailand, the Malacca Straits, and the Bay of Bengal (Russell and Berger, 2020).

Since Myanmar's constitution expressly forbids foreign troops' deployment within its territory and the country zealously guards its sovereignty, Kyaukphyu seems an unlikely candidate for an actual Chinese military base. However, the PLA already conducts port calls in Myanmar, so Kyaukphyu could efficiently serve as a direct commercial replenishment and resupply stop — a valuable logistics support point in the Indian Ocean (Russell and Berger, 2020).

- ***Environmental issues***

According to Global Climate Risk Index 2019, Myanmar is one of the three countries or territories (along with Puerto Rico and Honduras) most affected by weather-related damage in the last two decades. This is due to a combination of severe environmental vulnerability along with pre-existing social fragility and weak institutions.

Simultaneously, without more stringent regulations, the CMEC's planned road and rail upgrades threaten both rural livelihoods and ecosystems. Myanmar's rapid deforestation is a result of increased traffic through areas as the highlands of Kachin state, now made accessible by all-weather roads. Many of these roads have been built by Chinese logging corporations to transport illegally felled timber to Yunnan.[33]

The banana plantations, which disregard concerns for the environment, are just one manifestation of a political and economic system in northern Myanmar that privileges power and profit over people. Moreover, Chinese-run banana plantations in Kachin state are rapidly expanding as these plantations grow tissue culture bananas; the clonal genetic material and monoculture production require constant chemical fertilizers and pesticides. These chemicals have released poisons into the water and aquatic ecosystems, impacting the local populace adversely. As tissue culture banana cultivation depletes the soil's fertility, agri-business owners need to acquire more land for production. Some Chinese-backed plantations are now found on Kachin farmers' land.[34] Instances of land grabbing exist, but are not widely reported.

- ***Trust, Bilateral Agreements, & People's Attitudes***

*In general, Myanmar people have an aversion for China and Chinese people. So, the majority of them dislike CMEC projects from China. In an Interview, Khin Maung **Soe** said, "There is an* anti-Chinese attitude in

---

[33] Trouble for Belt and Road in Myanmar, https://chinadialogue.net/en/business/11585-trouble-for-belt-and-road-in-myanmar-2/, accessed on October 8, 2020.
[34] *Ibid.*

Myanmar. However, the country has a heavy reliance on China, due to Western embargo".

China has faced opposition at many points, especially during the Thein Sein period. It has had to downsize project capacities (Kyaukphu port) and even suspend projects (Myitsone Hydropower Project and Letpadaung Copper Mine project). The Letpadaung copper mine project experienced a two-year suspension, investigation, and renegotiation before it was resumed.[35] However, this did not dent bilateral relations, as the bilateral relationship had already been upgraded to a "strategic partnership".

- **Issues of employment**
Within Myanmar, it is believed that Chinese FDI did not benefit the average Burmese citizen. Instead, this lined the pockets of a small group of elite officials and the SOE management (Christie and Hanlon, 2014, p. 7).

It is well known that the Chinese bring their labor and resources and do not use local companies' services. Given that they prefer to keep themselves separated from the locals, they fail to provide many of the ancillary benefits the host nations expect from foreign developers' (Kulczuga, 2013, p. 37). At the same time, Moody's Analytics (2019) indicates that the decline in the unemployment rate is especially mild in Cambodia and Myanmar. These modest falls are consistent with reports that China often substitutes local labor with imported Chinese workers when building infrastructure in other countries. As a Myanmar diplomat said, "Chinese workers are preferred as one worker is equivalent to 3 Myanmar workers".

- **Misuse of Project money**
At the Second Belt and Road Forum in Beijing in April 2019, China agreed to provide a one billion yuan (US$144 million) grant to Myanmar for improving livelihoods, conducting feasibility studies for major projects, and delivering humanitarian assistance for thousands of people in northern Myanmar internally displaced by civil war. Often, such funds are siphoned off by corrupt high-ranking officials.

In an Interview, Khin Maung Soe shared, "In Myanmar, many giant businesses are owned by Chinese businesses; many business people have

---

[35] By Ruosui Zhang July 22, 2020, https://thediplomat.com/2020/07/chinese-investment-in-myanmar-beyond-myitsone-dam/.

close relations with Myanmar generals and important people in China; there is often news of corruption and nepotism — they gave bribe to Than Shwe and others". This was confirmed in another interview with the authors by a Myanmar diplomat (anonymity), who said, "The Chinese will indulge in any type of fraudulent activities including bribing officials to get what they want. They will even marry Burmese women for achieving their goals".

- ## *Floating Crypto Currencies*
According to a USIP report (2020) on Casino cities in Myanmar, Yatai New City plan calls for a digital infrastructure hosted by BCB Blockchain to manage all its public services. Therefore, technology can collaterally be used to facilitate the use of crypto or digital currencies. Hence, to ease access to these multiple functions, Yatai IHG and BCB created Fincy, a global social networking and payment application rolled out in Yatai New City in April 2020. Fancy's dynamic financial services system includes making cross-border payments, exchanging currencies, and buying cryptocurrency. Besides, it makes available social networking, automated payments, city services, e-commerce, and "games and entertainment". Its an online profile and is built on the BCB blockchain, using encryption with "no location transactions" to conceal the origin of a transfer and ensure absolute privacy for the planned half-million residents of Yatai New City.[36] Interestingly, these developments have taken place without approval from Myanmar's Central Bank or any government ministry.

   The USIP Report (2020) also states that the Chinese investors backing the project continue with their complete defiance of the country's legal institutions and banking regulations. This has implications for India's connectivity projects in Myanmar, including the Trilateral Highway and the Sittwe port operations in the state of Rakhine.

- ## *Increase of illegal business and activities in Myanmar*
Since the 1990s, Myanmar has been producing meth, which, like heroin, was initially intended for export, to support its closed, fragile economy (*The Economist*, July 18, 2020). However, it also gave rise to illegal

---

[36] Myanmar: Casino Cities Run on Blockchain Threaten Nation's Sovereignty, https://www.usip.org/publications/2020/07/myanmar-casino-cities-run-blockchain-threaten-nations-sovereignty, accessed on October 6, 2020.

smuggling and related activities. According to the UN data, in 2018 sales of illegal opiates accounted for 1–2% of Myanmar's GDP. These drugs are prevalent near the border areas, especially in Shan and Kachin states; the illegal sales to Chinese traders take place evidently in collusion with officials and soldiers posted here.

7.6 November 2020: Elections

The National League for Democracy's decisive victory in Myanmar's 2015 elections inspired hopes of a full transition from military rule and an opening of civil space. Neither has materialized, and the groups working to advance social, political, and economic change in Myanmar continue to face significant challenges.[37]

Elections of November 2020 were held as scheduled. The results were as expected. Most political observers believed that State Counsellor Aung San Suu Kyi's National League for Democracy (NLD) would win, which she did. NLD has secured the 322 seats in the bicameral legislature needed to form a government.

An entirely new paradigm had emerged in Myanmar, one where Suu Kyi was now seen as a trusted ally of Beijing and the military as a nationalistic bulwark against China's advances. Simultaneously, in November 2017, just months after hundreds of thousands of Rohingya refugees streamed across the border into Bangladesh, Suu Kyi was given red carpet treatment in Beijing (Lintner, 2020).[38] For Beijing, the Rohingya issue is internal to Myanmar's polity and does not warrant Chinese interference.

It is imminently clear that the nature of governance and constitutional politics in Myanmar will not emulate the orthodoxy suggested by liberal democratic traditions. It is ostensibly tailored for Myanmar's conditions as perceived by the military leaders. They are not prepared to leave the fate of the future of Myanmar in the hands of political parties.

---

[37] Nonviolent Action in Myanmar: Challenges and Lessons for Civil Society and Donors, https://www.usip.org/publications/2020/09/nonviolent-action-myanmar-challenges-and-lessons-civil-society-and-donors, accessed on November 16, 2020.

[38] China flips the electoral script in Myanmar, https://asiatimes.com/2020/05/china-flips-the-electoral-script-in-myanmar/, accessed on November 16, 2020.

7.7 Conclusion

2020 began with Xi Jinping's visit to Myanmar, being the first by a Chinese president in almost two decades. This is about China's geo-strategic and geo-economic influence being challenged to an extent by India and the Quad grouping of four countries comprising USA, India, Japan, and Australia in its backyard as in the Bay of Bengal and the Indian Ocean. Myanmar is considered a conduit to the Bay of Bengal. China's dependence on oil has been increasing by 6.7% each year and the demand is set to increase further; given the trade war with the US, these waters provide it an alternative route.

As has been discussed in this chapter, China is engaged through investments in several projects in Myanmar. Even as Myanmar's democratic principles ossify, there will continue to be protests against Chinese projects viewed by the people as encroaching on their territorial sovereignty and security. This has been seen in the case of the Myitsone Dam project which has been stalled since 2011. However, China always manages to find and fund alternative projects with the country, including oil pipelines. It is also evident that economic projects cannot exist in a vacuum. Whenever an economic investment is channelized to a particular country, the security interests will become a natural corollary. Hence, in CMEC, the project of greatest significance is the Kyaukpyu Port, which is the pivot for China to embed its naval and economic presence in the Indian Ocean Region. According to several experts, in the eventuality that the port is militarized, China's foothold in the Bay of Bengal waters will be assured. Hence, it is anyone's guess how long Chinese formal security arrangements do not manifest themselves in and around the port and other physical investment locations.

According to *Asia Times*, "China's double-game in Myanmar, where it serves as both an armed conflict mediator and supplier of arms to insurgents, is a long-worn carrot and a stick approach to get what it wants, namely, the CMEC and access to Myanmar's rich natural resources including copper, gold, jade, amber, and rare earth metals".

On the other hand, China is leaving no stones unturned to extend its cooperation in the times of COVID-19 with the donation of medical supplies and sending two teams of medical experts to Myanmar to help fight the pandemic. China's ambassador to Myanmar, Chen Hai, asserted in a recent interview with the *Myanmar Times* that China remains committed to investing in Myanmar. For the first time, China's increasing influence in the country became a political issue. It is seemingly favoring Suu Kyi and her party NLD than the military's aligned United Solidarity and Development Party.

Bertil Lintner writes, "An entirely new paradigm has emerged in Myanmar, one where Suu Kyi is now seen as a trusted ally of Beijing and the military a nationalistic bulwark against China's strong advances. That's a significant reversal, one that could have implications for stability in the lead-up to polls".[39]

Given that Aung San Suu Kyi has been balancing the big powers, even as China is considered the most generous benefactor, there is a push-back from among the people. The military leaders, too, do not wish to be dictated to by China. Additionally, the porous border regions with China remain as hubs of illegal activities (controlled by non-state actors), some of which are linked to the CMEC. If the CMEC is to avoid exacerbating existing problems, then China's national and provincial planners need a better understanding of how capital flows from China to Myanmar facilitate the territorial control of armed strongmen — both in the Myanmar military and non-state armed groups — who are driving the political chaos and instability of the border regions today.

It was not an ordinary moment when on September 10, 2020, the European Parliament ousted Aung San Suu Kyi from the Sakharov human rights prize community, over her inaction on the Rohingya crisis. The US is also strongly urging Myanmar's Government to comply with the ICJ ruling on the Rakhine issue. Meanwhile, Myanmar continues to receive China's political support. It remains to be seen how Suu Kyi will balance Myanmar's domestic challenges and Chinese backing, on the one hand, with Western commercial interests and political pressures, on the other. With the vast mandate received, she had another opportunity to lead her people toward national reconciliation, state-building, and democratization. Her diplomatic acumen will be tested, even as she balances relations with the big powers. The people of Myanmar will not accept being dictated to by any foreign power. The strengthening forces of democracy in Myanmar are not on China's wish list. This addition is essential as the situation in Myanmar has completely changed since February 1, 2021. The same is true for the Tatmatdaw. The forces of democracy have been

---

[39] https://www.republicworld.com/world-news/rest-of-the-world-news/china-myanmar-suu-kyi-xi-jinping-elections-army-military.html.

crushed by the coup detat on February 1, 2021, by their top military commander Senior General Min Aung Hliang. Over the period of about 100 days, more than 700 protesting civilians have been killed. Many more including Aung San Suu Kyi and other leaders have been imprisoned. The tense and fragile situation continues. A war is being waged within the country, even as fingers are pointed towards China and Russia. This is a nation on a knife's edge. Will the international community respond?

Chapter 8

China and Thailand: "Kith and Kin" Relations

8.1 Introduction

China and Thai relations go back hundreds of years in time. In his seminal work, *Chinese Society in Thailand* (1957), Skinner articulates that the Chinese in Thailand, by the time of the third generation, become a well-integrated segment of Thai society and cannot be considered an alien community.

To focus on contemporary relations, it was in 1975 when the two nations established diplomatic ties. During the Cold War, they formed a military alignment against Vietnamese communists in Indochina (Marwah, 2019). In the post-Cold War era, bilateral relations have remained amicable, thanks to the absence of territorial disputes, strong connections between the Thai royal family and the Chinese leadership, and the well-integrated Chinese community in Thailand.[1] Once the diplomatic relations were established, families of descendants of Chinese migrants actually accentuated their Chinese-ness, including acquiring good working knowledge of spoken Mandarin as well as written Chinese.

This chapter focuses on China–Thailand relations, particularly contemporary Chinese investments and the impacts of the BRI projects on Thailand.

---

[1]Thailand and China build ties of convenience, http://www.japantimes.co.jp/opinion/2015/08/13/commentary/world-commentary/thailand-china-build-ties-convenience/#.VlyEntlrLIV, accessed on December 5, 2015.

8.2 A Brief History of Thailand

Thailand, officially known as the Kingdom of Thailand, was formerly known as Siam. It is a country located in Southeast Asia at the center of the Indochinese Peninsula. It has 76 provinces and covers an area of 513,120 square kilometers (198,120 square meters). The population of Thailand is around 66 million people.[2]

LePoer (1989) indicates that there is evidence of continuous human habitation in Thailand from 20,000 years ago to the present day. Baker and Pasuk (2017) assert that the earliest evidence of rice growing is dated to 2000 BCE. Thai people have continued to migrate from southwestern China to mainland Southeast Asia since the 11th century.

Thailand is a founding member of the ASEAN and was an ally of the United States during the Cold War period. It has a high level of human development, the second-largest economy in Southeast Asia, and is the 20th-largest in the world by PPP. Thailand is classified as a newly industrialized economy; manufacturing, agriculture, and tourism are the leading sectors.[3]

8.3 Thailand's Economy: A Brief Overview

As stated earlier, Thailand, a newly industrialized country, is the 2nd largest economy in Southeast Asia after Indonesia and ranks midway in Southeast Asia's wealth spread. The country experienced the world's highest economic growth rate from 1985 to 1996 (averaging 12.4%) annually. In 1997, during the Asian financial crisis, increased pressure on the baht revealed financial sector weaknesses and forced the Chavalit Yongchaiyudh administration to float the currency. The economy recovered in early 2000s and in terms of GDP per capita, within ASEAN, it is the 4th wealthiest nation after Singapore, Brunei, and Malaysia. According to the World Bank, the GDP of Thailand was US$543.65 billion in 2019. This represents 0.45% of the world economy. At the same

---

[2]The entire kingdom's population, following the evidence from the population registration on December 31, 2019 (PDF). *Royal Thai Government Gazette*, January 30, 2020, accessed on June 12, 2020.

[3]Thailand and the World Bank Archived December 16, 2005 at the Wayback Machine, World Bank on Thailand Country overview.

time the GDP per capita in Thailand was US$18,463.10 in 2019, when adjusted by PPP.[4]

Thailand's industrial sector, comprising manufacturing as the major segment along with mining, construction, electricity, water, and gas, contributed 35.03% in 2017 to Thailand's GDP. The service sector accounted for 56.31% of GDP in 2017. Within services, transportation, wholesale and retail trade, and tourism and travel-related activities have been the prominent employment generators and contributors to the GDP.

The Thai economy depends heavily on exports, as exports account for more than two-thirds of GDP. In 2013, Thailand exported over US$105 billion worth of goods and services.[5] During 2020, as expected, exports from Thailand shrank 3.86% from year on year to US$19.62 billion, amid the prolonged impact of the COVID-19 crisis. Thailand's major exports include cars, computers, electrical appliances, rice, textiles and footwear, fishery products, rubber, and jewelry.

The Thai auto industry is well-developed and Thailand is being envisioned as an automobile hub for SEA. Thai automotive industry is the largest in Southeast Asia and the 9th largest in the world.[6] Most of the vehicles built in Thailand are developed and licensed by mainly Japanese and American producers. The Thai car industry takes advantage of the ASEAN Free Trade Area (AFTA) for exporting many of its products. Eight manufacturers, five Japanese, two US, and Tata of India, produce pick-up trucks in Thailand.[7] Other significant industries include electric appliances, components, computer components, and vehicles.

The tourism industry contributes 12% of the Thai GDP. When including the indirect effects of tourism, this accounts for 20.2% (2.4 trillion baht) of Thailand's GDP.[8] Tables 8.1 and 8.2 provide insights into GDP,

---

[4] Thailand GDP per capita PPP, https://tradingeconomics.com/thailand/gdp-per-capita-ppp, accessed on November 2, 2020.

[5] Following the population registration evidence on December 31, 2019 (PDF), the entire kingdom's population. *Royal Thai Government Gazette*. January 30, 2020, accessed on June 12, 2020.

[6] Santivimolnat, Santan (August 18, 2012). "2-million milestone edges nearer". *Bangkok Post*.

[7] Takahashi, Toru (November 27, 2014). "Thailand's love affair with the pick-up truck". *Nikkei Asian Review*, accessed on January 3, 2015.

[8] *Travel and Tourism, Economic Impact 2014: Thailand* (PDF) (2014) (ed.). London: World Travel & Tourism Council. 2014. Archived from the original (PDF) on March 19, 2015, accessed on March 10, 2015.

Table 8.1:   Thailand: GDP, GDP per capita, and debt.

Country	Total Population (millions)[a]	GDP (current US$) 2018 (in billion)	GDP Per Capita (current US$[b]) 2018	Population Below the NPL in ASEAN Urban + Rural 2015 (%)	Population Below the NPL in ASEAN Urban + Rural-2017 (%)
Thailand	67,831.6	505,107.1	7,446.5	7.2	7.9

Source: The World Bank Data.
[a] Source: ASEANstats; Refers to/based on mid-year total population based on country projections.
[b] Source: ASEANstats.

Table 8.2:   HDI in Thailand.

Year	2010	2012	2013	2014	2015	2016	2017	2018	2019
Thailand	0.72	0.73	0.73	0.74	0.75	0.75	0.76	0.77	0.77

Source: U.N. Human Development report data.

GDP per capita, and HDI over 2010 to 2019. In 2014, Credit Suisse reported that Thailand was the world's third most unequal country, behind Russia and India. Thailand had experienced a marginal increase in unemployment from about 2% in 1991 to 3% of its labor force in 2018. Despite this, the HDI value has steadily risen from being 0.72 in 2010, to 0.77 in 2019, due to improved levels of literacy and income (see Tables 8.1 and 8.2).

In terms of investments, Japan remains the largest overseas investor in Thailand and accounts for slightly more than half of FDI inflows. It committed 143 billion baht in 2019 compared with China's 20 billion baht in 2018. In 2019, Board of Investment (BoI) Secretary-General Duangjai Asawaschinatachit declared that China overtook Japan and became the number one investor for the first time.[9] Japan was the second most active bidder in 2019, with investment applications valued at US$2.4 billion, followed by Hong Kong (US$1.2 billion), Switzerland (US$800 million), and Taiwan (US$700 million).[10] Hong Kong, the Netherlands, Germany, Mauritius, and the United Kingdom are also among the major investors.

[9] China was Top Investor in Thailand in 2019, official says, https://www.benarnews.org/english/news/thai/economic-investment-01162020161823, accessed on November 3, 2020.
[10] *Ibid.*

Thailand has an optimal business environment and the World Bank ranks it 26th in its ranking of countries where it is easy to do business (Doing Business Report, 2018).[11]

8.4 China–Thailand Relations

It is well known that the Chinese settlement in Thailand dates back to early periods in Thai history (Punyodyana, 1976). The earliest Chinese came and settled in Thailand through the traditional route, viz. ports of southeast China to Bangkok. This diaspora is a significant factor in conditioning the political relations between the two nations. They number around four million, of which less than one million were born in China (Wilson, 2020). At present, ethnic Chinese form one-tenth of the Thai population and China-born residents of Thailand number over half a million. Therefore, in comparative terms, the Chinese community in Thailand is as old as, or older than, that in other Southeast Asian countries.

In this context, the work of Skinner is significant. According to Keyes (2011), Skinner posited a distinction between Sino-Thai (*lūk cīn*) and ethnic Chinese living in Thailand. Although most Chinese migrants adapt to Thai culture, some continue to identify primarily as Chinese even while holding Thai citizenship.

Thailand did establish formal diplomatic relations with China in 1976 and, subsequently, the relations between the two countries became very amicable and mutually beneficial. As a result, it has become a perfect strategy for some families of descendants of Chinese migrants to accentuate their Chinese-ness, including ensuring that some family members acquire a good working knowledge of spoken Mandarin and written Chinese.

According to Chambers (2005), ever since the establishment of diplomatic relations in July 1975, China and Thailand have maintained cordial relations. President Yang Shangkun, during his visit to Thailand in June 1991, also praised Sino-Thai relations as being "close and all-weather" which would not be affected by any changes across the world or within both countries (Deng, 2020). Wilson (2020) underlines that

---

[11] Country profile Thailand, https://www.nordeatrade.com/en/explore-new-market/thailand/investment#, accessed on November 2, 2020.

political relations between Thailand and China are conditioned by significant historical, geographical, and social ties. Thailand and China are in close geographical proximity from the north and southwest areas. Zha (2020) also maintains that Thailand has maintained a stable and cordial relationship with China despite domestic political turmoil over the past decades.

8.4.1 *Thailand China: The military relationship*

Thailand and China have a healthy military and defense relationship; sometimes, this relationship is more significant than US–Thai military relations, even though Thailand was an ally of the United States prior and during the Cold War. The 1997 Asian financial crisis changed circumstances when the United States did not bail out its time-tested ally. Instead, China provided aid to Thailand and other Southeast Asian countries.

In December 2001, at a Thai and Chinese defense ministers' meeting, the two sides agreed to resume Chinese arms sales to Thailand, conduct combined military training and exercises, and institutionalized annual defense talks (Murphy, 2010). The 2006 military coup in Thailand further weakened ties with the US. However, these coups never did deter China from befriending its neighbor. In May 2007, Surayud Chulanont, then Prime Minister of Thailand and head of Thailand's interim government, signed the Joint Action Plan on China–Thailand Strategic Cooperation. This was followed by Sino-Thai combined military exercises.

In 2008, Thailand purchased Chinese-made C-802 anti-ship missiles worth US$48 million. China and Thailand also signed a Joint Action Plan, which increased bilateral cooperation in military training, military exercises, and defense industry research (Storey, 2008). Since 2007, Chinese and Thai Special Forces have conducted joint counter-terrorism exercises. In 2010, Chinese and Thai marines initiated joint drills (Hiebert *et al.*, 2014). When Thailand returned to democracy in early 2008, the country's military had increasingly diversified its sources to include the US, China, Sweden and other countries. In 2014, the Yingluck Shinawatra government was overthrown by a military coup, which brought in the Prayut Chan-o-cha regime. According to Chambers (2015), the 2014 military coup resulted in a fillip in Chinese-Thai military relations. Nanuam asserts that the Chinese military assistance has grown by a yet-unspecified amount, given Thailand's preference for Chinese military hardware; in 2015, the Thai junta tentatively agreed to pay US$1.06 billion for three

Chinese-made submarines (Nanuam and Jikkham 2015). China is also working with Thailand to enhance military cooperation in terms of more exchanges of military officers, provision of Chinese military education for Thai soldiers, and a larger Chinese role in developing Thailand's defense industry and joint intelligence cooperation.[12] Thailand's military government has inked an agreement to purchase tanks from China, and the Royal Thai Army (RTA) has formally signed a pact to buy the MBT-3000 main battle tank produced by China North Industries Corporation (NORINCO) (Parameswaran, 2016).

This contextualization is significant to underline that despite strong military ties, there have been issues in the economic relationship.

8.5 China–Thailand Economic Engagement

This section analyzes China's economic engagement with Thailand through trade, investment in BRI projects, and other economic indicators over the period 2000–2019. The Sino-Thai FTA of 2003 was also the first FTA between China and an ASEAN country.[13]

8.5.1 *Thailand and China: Trade*

In March 1978, China and Thailand signed a trade pact and an agreement on scientific and technological cooperation. The two countries also signed a protocol agreement related to the formation of a significant joint trade commission. In March 1985, during President Li Xiannian's visit to Thailand, the two countries agreed to establish a joint committee on economic cooperation and another one on promoting and protecting investment.

According to Rupanichkij (2010), Thailand has enjoyed booming trade with China. In the early 1980s, China embarked on a competition program for market shares in an increasingly friendly Thailand. In the process, a flood of consumer-oriented light manufactured goods from China appeared in Thai markets. The low-cost goods made extensive inroads into the Thai market and, for some time, benefited the local

---

[12] *The Nation*, Thailand, China agree to closer military ties during senior official's visit, April 25, 2015, http://bit.ly/1z0bGaI, accessed on January 25, 2016.

[13] Chachavalpongpun, *Reinventing Thailand*, op. cit., p. 130.

Table 8.3:   International trade of Thailand in 2019.

	Import (US$)	Export (US$)	Total trade (US$)	GDP (US$)	Trade as a % of GDP
Thailand	63,717,299	20,422,579	84,139,878	543,650,000	15.5

Source: Trade Economy, https://trendeconomy.com/data/h2/Thailand/0805, accessed on November 2, 2020.

consumers. In 1982, trade rose to US$0.46 billion, an increase of twenty times since the mid-1970s. In 1989, the trade value reached a record US$1.2 billion. Hence, China is the sixth largest trading partner of Thailand (Deng, 2020).

In October 2013, Yingluck Shinawatra and her Chinese counterpart Premier Li Keqiang signed the Memorandum of Understanding (MoU) on Deepening Railway Cooperation between China and Thailand. Under the terms of the MoU, Thailand agreed to import high-speed trains and technology from China. The China Railway Corporation would partici- pate in constructing a high-speed rail network linking Nong Khai in northern Thailand with Phachi District near Bangkok. In exchange, China offered to increase the import of Thai rice from 200,000 tons to one million tons plus 200,000 tons of Thai rubber per year (Zha, 2020). However, due to allegations of corruption, this "rice for rail" program was canceled.[14]

Table 8.3 indicates the recent trade statistics of Thailand. In 2019, total imports amounted to US$63,717,299, exports were worth US$20,422,579, and total trade as share of Thailand's GDP was 15.5%, respectively.

The Kingdom of Thailand exported a total of US$245.3 billion worth of goods globally in 2019. That dollar amount reflects a 16.4% gain since 2015 but a −1.8% decline from 2018 to 2019. Approximately two-thirds (63.2%) of Thai exports by value in 2019 went to Asian countries, while 14.6% were shipped to North America. Thailand shipped another 12.4% of its exports to Europe and 5% to Oceania, led by Australia and New Zealand.[15]

---

[14]"China Cancels Thailand Rice Deal Amid Probe", BBC, February 4, 2014, at http://www.bbc.com/news/world.

[15]Thailand's Top Trading Partners, http://www.worldstopexports.com/thailands-top-import-partners/, accessed on November 2, 2020.

Figure 8.1:   Thailand's top five export partners (US$).

Source: U.N. Comtrade database, https://comtrade.un.org/data/ (accessed on October 24, 2020).

In 2010, the main export trading partner was China (US$21.4 billion). However, in 2019, United States assumed the top position: US$31.4 billion (12.8% of total Thai exports), China: US$29 billion (11.8%), Japan: US$24.5 billion (10%), Vietnam: US$12.1 billion (4.9%), and Hong Kong: US$11.7 billion (4.8%), respectively (see Figure 8.1).

Thailand's major exports were Machinery (16.38%), Electrical Machinery & Equipment (13.8%), Vehicles (11.8%), Pearls & Precious Stones (6.38%), Rubber (6.25%), Plastics (5.44%), Mineral Fuels & Oils (3.46%), Preparations of Meat, Fish or Crustaceans (2.72%), Optical, Photographic, Medical Equipment (2.2%), and Organic Chemicals (1.88%). Thailand's export statistics show that these categories valued 67.31% of total exports in 2019. Pearls and precious stones were the top gainers among the top 10 export categories, up by 31.5% since 2018.[16]

Figure 8.2 indicates Thailand's top five import partners in 2010 compared to 2019. Thailand's main import partners in 2019 were China, Japan, United States, Malaysia, and South Korea. According to Thailand customs data, these countries accounted for 51.7% of total imports in 2019. Thailand's significant imports in 2019 were Electrical Machinery & Equipment (18.08%), Mineral Fuels & Oils (15.69%), Machinery (12.4%), Pearls & Precious Stones (5.11%), Iron and Steel (5%), Vehicles (4.47%), Plastics (3.85%), Articles of Iron & Steel (2.88%), Optical, Photographic, Medical Equipment (2.67%), and Organic Chemicals (1.8%).[17] It is evident from Figure 8.2, that China unseated Japan in 2019,

---

[16]Thailand's Top 10 Export Commodities, https://www.exportgenius.in/export-import-trade-data/thailand-export.php, accessed on November 2, 2020.

[17]*Ibid.*

Figure 8.2:   Thailand's top five import partners (US$).

Source: U.N. Comtrade database, https://comtrade.un.org/data/ (accessed on October 24, 2020).

to be Thailand's number one import partner. In terms of exports, the US was Thailand's number one partner in 2019, with China in second place.

To assess Thailand's trade with China, we compare 2010 and 2019 trade statistics. Friendship considerations have been a significant factor in the Sino-Thai trade. As is with most Southeast Asian countries, Thailand's exports to China too are primarily agricultural products, rubber and sugar. However, Thailand's challenge is to create a demand for Thai goods in China by convincing them its manufactured goods are of superior quality and worth buying (Deng, 2020). More details are provided in the next section.

8.5.2 *Chinese investments in Thailand*

Chinese investments in Thailand include (i) road, railway, and marine technology, (ii) the energy sector (energy supply, distribution, and storage), (iii) information technology, and (iv) transport and logistics.

Thailand as an investment hub: Foreign direct investment is an important component in the development of Thailand's economy. The geo-economic location, abundance of natural resources, cost-effective labor and government incentives have enabled inflows of investment. According to the UNCTAD World Investment Report 2019, FDI flows rose to US$10.49 billion in 2018, growing by 62% from the previous year, the steepest growth seen in ASEAN. This was largely due to significant inflows from Asia, led by investors from Japan, Hong Kong, and Singapore. Manufacturing, and financial and insurance activities, attract nearly 70% of all FDI inflows into Thailand. Real estate, commerce, and information and communication are key investment areas.[18]

Deng (2020) indicates that China has to rely on the ASEAN countries, including Thailand, for trade, investment, and technology transfer. Beijing is keen to attract more investments in energy, communications, and raw materials from Thailand.

8.5.3 *BRI projects*

Chinese investments constitute a mere 1% of Thailand's GDP. Evidently, Thailand receives foreign investment from several countries.

Details of the key BRI projects are discussed here.

- **Thailand–China High-speed Rail (HSR)**

This is one of the major projects of China under the BRI. After years of heated debates and unanticipated delays, bullet trains are finally coming to Thailand. One project is under construction, another is approved, and others are already being considered. However, many Thai citizens question whether or not HSR is the best idea for the country. A big reason for the concern is that both approved projects will employ Chinese HSR technology refer Map 8.1.

Thailand's first HSR line is currently under construction and is expected to open in 2023. The project is proposed to connect Bangkok with Nong Khai in northern Thailand. From Nong Khai, passengers will cross the border into Laos and board a train to Vientiane, which would transport them through northern Laos into Kunming in China. The government of Thailand is said to be providing 60% of the total funds for the project, which will consist of 181 km of elevated track, 8 km of underground track, and 2 km of surface track.[19] The HSR line has received a vast amount of criticism due to the investment of 179 million baht (CA$7.8 billion) worth of public funds.

Director of the Department of Science and Technology and I.T. Application of China's State Railway Group Co Ltd Mr. Huo Baoshi

---

[18] https://www.china-briefing.com/news/china-plus-one-series-thailand-investment-opportunities/, accessed on December 29, 2020.

[19] *Belt and Road News*, According to Railwaytechnology.com, https://www.beltandroad.news/2019/11/21/high-speed-rail-of-thailand-expected-to-be-in-operation-by-2023/, accessed on October 20, 2020.

Map 8.1:   China–Thailand HSR.

Source: https://88property.com/thai-chinese-high-speed-rail/

told the Bangkok Post "I think it is important. The project will help connect people in China and Thailand via Laos. It can help promote socio-economic development and prosperity in these two countries and across the whole Asian region. We use our experience, skills, lessons and knowledge to help other countries. I think equal cooperation is the key point".[20]

At the same time, there are sub railway lines to be built and connected to this HSR. Predicted to open in 2021, a separate new rail hub in Bangkok's Bang Sue district will replace the 103-year-old Hualamphong Station. Passengers will be able to use both HSR and the country's pre-existing railway network, which will also undergo some upgrades. However, the most significant factor is the line switch from single to dual tracks. Many project supporters assert that the speed will reduce the time it takes to transit between Bangkok's two main airports, Suvarnabhumi Airport (BKK) and Don Muang Airport (DMK), to just 20 minutes.

---

[20] Thailand–China high-speed rail expected to be operational by 2023, https://www.beltandroad.news/2019/11/21/high-speed-rail-of-thailand-expected-to-be-in-operation-by-2023/, accessed on October 20, 2020.

The line will also include U-Tapao International Airport, a military public airport that serves the cities of Rayong and Pattaya in Thailand.[21]

Upgrading the dual-track rail is estimated to have substantial economic benefits, mostly because Thailand's economy relies heavily on the production, transport, and trade of goods. However, the benefits of the Thai-Chinese HSR appear to be limited. The primary benefits will be centered on saving time for passengers compared to other transportation alternatives. An interesting estimate provided by Pechnipa Dominique Lam of the Thailand Development Research Institute states that the HSR line "would need to ferry 50,000–85,000 passengers every day for 20 years in order to pay back the costs of investment".[22] At the same time, this HSR has cabins with a capacity of 600 passengers. This would mean that the trains would have to run roughly every five to nine minutes on a 12-hour day schedule.[23]

8.5.4 *Status of the Sino-Thai rail project*

This Sino-Thai railway project is part of the proposed Pan-Asian Railway Network linking Kunming with Singapore along Vientiane and Bangkok. This line is now part of the BRI and China's HSR diplomacy. The 873 km Sino-Thai line is linked to Nong Khai and the border with Laos in the north, from the Map Ta Phut harbor in the south on the Gulf of Thailand. In April 2012, China and Thailand's governments signed a MoU on Sino-Thai railway cooperation (Lauridsen, 2019).

The first negotiations on Sino-Thai HSR line with a possible joint venture took place during the Abhisit Vejjajiva government (2008–2011). During the Yingluck Shinawatra government (2011–2014), a set of mega-projects with a total value of 2 trillion baht (US$62 billion) were listed in the Infrastructure Development Plan 2014–2020 and much emphasis was put on getting the private sector to invest through public–private partnership arrangements (Wu and Chong, 2018). Of the total planned investments, 83% were reserved for rail, of which the HSR accounted for

---

[21]Thailand–China high-speed rail expected to be operational by 2023, https://www.beltandroad.news/2019/11/21/high-speed-rail-of-thailand-expected-to-be-in-operation-by-2023/, accessed on October 20, 2020.

[22]*Ibid.*

[23]*Ibid.*

783 billion baht with double-tracking costing 403 billion (World Bank, 2014, 2015). However, according to Lauridsen (2019), the regime came up with another 2.4 trillion baht master plan for infrastructure 2014–2022, which set aside 393 billion baht for the Nong Khai–Bangkok–Map Ta Phut HSR line.[24] This was to ensure staying away from costly Chinese loans, and Thailand funded part of the project. It is interesting to note that after 30 rounds of negotiations, the Chinese have built only 3.5 km of the railway line till date.

- **Kra Isthmus Canal**

The Thai Canal, also known as Kra Canal or Kra Isthmus Canal, refers to proposals for a canal that would connect the Gulf of Thailand with the Andaman Sea across the Kra Isthmus in southern Thailand; refer Map 8.2. This provides an alternative transit route to the Straits of Malacca. It shortens the Maritime Silk Road by 1,200 km and will marginalize Singapore's influence in the region.[25] This canal, if constructed, would be 120 km long across the Kra Isthmus; the narrowest part of the Malay Peninsula in southern Thailand. While China is keen to surmount its Malacca Dilemma by building the canal, the Thai Government has yet to finalize this project. Paul Busbarat, a lecturer in international relations in the faculty of political science at Bangkok's Chulalongkorn University, said that "The EEC link to the Kra Canal, connecting the Gulf of Thailand to the Andaman Sea, is possible if the Chinese really push it".[26]

Even as Thai people are becoming averse to Chinese funding, Thailand is conducting a feasibility study of an overland bypass to the Malacca Strait, cutting across the Kra Isthmus in the country's south with a combination of road and rail projects. While a Kra canal is not among Beijing's OBOR projects, according to Ian Storey, a senior fellow of the Institute of South East Asian Studies (ISEAS), the PRC does view Thailand as "a key node in its trillion-dollar global infrastructure project" and "there are constant but unsubstantiated rumors that China might be

---

[24]Boi, 2014. *Journal of Contemporary Asia*, 135–136; interview, NESDB official, Bangkok, February 2016.

[25]Seven opportunities: Thailand and the one belt, one road initiative, https://pugnatorius.com/obor/, accessed on October 20, 2020.

[26]Thailand pushes China's belt and road despite differing visions, https://asia.nikkei.com/Spotlight/Belt-and-Road/Thailand-pushes-China-s-Belt-and-Road-despite-differing-visions, accessed on October 20, 2020.

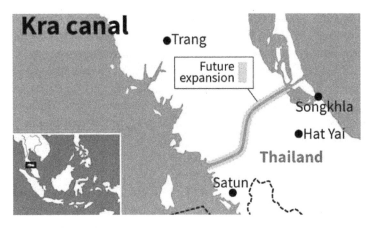

Map 8.2: Kra Isthmus Canal in Thailand.

Source: https://medium.com/@willowivyrose/what-is-the-kra-canal-thai-chinese-weapon-against-singapore-bdbaf47ab88b

interested in investing in an artificial waterway through the south of Thailand".[27]

- **Eastern Economic Corridor (EEC)**

On February 1, 2018, the Thai parliament approved the law for trade and investment in the EEC. With the EEC, Thailand hopes to develop its three provinces in eastern Thailand namely; Chonburi, Rayong, and Chachoengsao, into a leading ASEAN economic zone.[28] Collectively, these provinces occupy an area of 13,266 km², and in 2016 had an estimated population of over 2.8 million.

The zone was established on January 17, 2017, at the direction of the National Council for Peace and Order (NCPO), to promote economic integration across the Eastern seaboard. The first law of the EEC is the Eastern Special Development Zone Act of May 15, 2019. The government hopes to complete the EEC by 2021, turning these provinces into a hub for technological manufacturing and services with robust connectivity to its ASEAN neighbors by land, sea, and air. According to the data from Thailand's BoI, January 1, 2018, the EEC has attracted US$9.3 billion in

---

[27]Tom Abke, https://ipdefenseforum.com/2020/10/thailand-favoring-rail-and-road-bypass-instead-of-kra-canal-idea/, October 27, 2020, accessed on December 29, 2020.

[28]Thailand's Eastern economic corridor — What you need to know, https://www.asean-briefing.com/news/thailand-eastern-economic-corridor/, accessed on November 3, 2020.

promised FDI. The government expects US$43 billion (1.5 trillion baht) for the realization of the EEC over the next five years. This funding will come from a mix of state funds, public–private partnerships, and FDI.[29]

The Thai government has identified 15 major investment projects for the EEC. Paramount among these are the Sattahip commercial sea port, turning eastern provinces into medical, business, and tourism hubs, further development of the Map Ta Phut port, and strengthening public utilities. Much of Chinese investment is being directed to EEC projects.

- **Development of U-Tapao airport**

The U-Tapao International Airport City Project & Eastern Airport City Project also incorporate a high-speed train route linking the three major airports. That contract was signed in October 2019, between the Charoen Pokphand Group led consortium and the State Railway of Thailand (SRT). In June 2020, a 290 billion baht deal to build the Eastern Airport City Project at U-Tapao was signed; refer Map 8.3. This airport would become Bangkok's third international airport under a scheme that would link it with DMK and BKK airports. This will boost their handling capacity up to 200 million passengers annually. The project is expected to create 78,000 jobs in the aviation industry and related businesses in the first five years.[30]

For the acropolis development, the BBS Joint venture comprises Bangkok Airways, which owns 45% of the shares, BTS Group Holdings, which owns 35%, and Sino-Thai Engineering and Construction (STEC), which owns 20%. U-Tapao International Aviation Co has an initial capital of 4.5 billion baht that will increase to 9 billion baht in 2024. Bangkok Airways (BA) president Puttipong Prasarttong-Osoth said the project requires a 130 billion baht investment throughout its four phases starting from 2020 until 2055. According to Chokchai Panyayong, the project's special adviser, the four phases involve building a 157,000 square meter passenger terminal that, when fully completed in 2055, will result in the airport being able to handle 60 million passengers per year. The first phase, expected to be completed in 2024, is building a passenger terminal to handle 15.9 million passengers annually. Phase 2 will be completed in 2030.[31]

---

[29] Govt signs U-Tapao "airport city" deal, https://www.bangkokpost.com/business/1937920/govt-signs-u-tapao-airport-city-deal, accessed on November 1, 2020.
[30] *Ibid.*
[31] PTT Public Company Limited or simply PTT is a Thai state-owned SET-listed oil and gas company. PTT was founded in 1978 (as Petroleum Authority of Thailand) as a state-owned enterprise.

Map 8.3: U-Tapao–Pattaya International Airport development project.

Source: https://www.pattayamail.com/news/290-billion-baht-for-u-tapao-pattaya-international-airport-and-eastern-airport-city-project-304750

- **Expansion of Laem Chabang and Map Ta Phut seaports**[32]
PTT[31] Tank Terminal corporation and Gulf Energy Development formed a consortium. They submitted bids for the third phases of the Laem Chabang seaport (114 billion baht) and Map Ta Phut seaport (55.4 billion baht) in the flagship Eastern Economic Corridor. PTT and Gulf formed a consortium with China Harbour Engineering Corporation with an investment budget of 156 billion baht for Laem Chabang port. The project aims to raise capacity to 18 million TEU per year from 11 million TEUs. Hence, For Map Ta Phut port, another consortium plans to develop a liquefied natural gas (LNG) jetty and receiving terminal. This will transform the port, making it a regional hub for petroleum and petrochemical shipments.[33]

- **Rail infrastructure upgrading plans**
The Thai government has plans to spend more than US$21 billion (77.1 billion baht) to expand Bangkok's rail transit and train lines and build high-speed rails — with a massive US$1.3 billion hub at the

---

[32]Laem Chabang seaport is located in Chon Buri Province and Map Ta Phut seaport is located in Rayong Province.

[33]Third phase expansion of Thailand's Laem Chabang port uncertain, https://thailand-construction.com/third-phase-expansion-of-thailands-laem-chabang-port-uncertain/, accessed on November 3, 2020.

center, that could become Southeast Asia's largest train station when it opens in 2021.[34]

The Infrastructure Development Master Plan 2015–2022 targeted increasing the operating speed to 60 kph for freight and 100 kph for passenger trains. It was planned to expand the number of passenger trips from 45 to 75 million per year and freight transportation by rail from 2.5% to 5%. The Plan gives high priority to developing a double-tracked rail network that will start with diesel locomotives but later become electrified.[35] Prior to 2010, Thailand had just over 4,000 km of railway tracks, with these being mostly old and single track. The average speed of freight trains was 39 kilometers per hour (kph) with passenger trains averaging 60 kph (Pichet, 2015; Lauridsen, 2019).

Ultimately, this will benefit the entire railway network being expanded with Chinese funding.

- **Mekong River blasting project**

In February 2020, Thailand scrapped a Chinese-led project to blast rapids on the Mekong River. China had initiated a plan to dredge the Mekong River in 2001 to enable large ships to carry goods from its landlocked southern province of Yunnan to ports in Thailand, Laos, and Southeast Asia. The plan had been opposed by conservationists and communities in Thailand living along the Mekong River. They feared it would harm the environment and benefit only China.[36]

8.6 Benefits and Costs of BRI Initiatives in Thailand

The high-speed rail project, one of the key initiatives of China's OBOR, has been a non-starter from the beginning. The cascading impact of this project has been perceived on other BRI projects as well, where local communities and environment activists have prevented the military government from pushing Chinese projects. Yet, China is a key trade and

---

[34]Thailand planning US$21 billion upgrades to rail network, https://www.thenationalnews.com/business/economy/thailand-planning-21bn-upgrade-to-rail-network-1.986346#, accessed on November 3, 2020.
[35]NESDB 2016; Interview, Ministry of Transport Official, Bangkok, February 2016.
[36]Panarat Thepgumpanat, February 5, 2020, https://www.reuters.com/article/us-thailand-china-idUSKBN1ZZ1T6.

investment partner of Thailand, with Chinese companies and individuals owning several industries. Here, the benefits and costs are assessed.

8.6.1 *Benefits of BRI*

- **Infrastructure development and time-saving**

The Express Railway and other development projects in Thailand were initiated as OBOR projects as these would save travel time. This express rail line will also include U-Tapao International Airport, a military public airport that serves Rayong and Pattaya's cities in Thailand. Supporters also suggest that the line will reduce highway traffic, thus decreasing the number of accidents in a country with one of the world's highest road fatality rates.

- **Investment hub**

Thailand ranked 7th in the world according to A.T. Kearney's 2019 Global Services Location Index. *It has a rank of 27 in Ease of Doing Business according to the World Bank's 2019 Ease of Doing Business Report*. The country has six deep sea ports and two international river ports including containers, tank farms, and liquid jetties. The ports are being further upgraded. Thailand's neighboring countries are more directly linked to the route of the Silk Road Economic Belt (SREB) and the MSR. This opens significant opportunities for Thailand as Southeast Asia's investment hub.

- **Border issues, security, and defence cooperation**

As discussed, Thai-China defense cooperation has grown steadily since the 2014 coup. China has sold 50 VT-4 main battle tanks and 30 ZBL-09 armored vehicles to the RTA, and has orders to supply Thailand three S-26T submarines in an extraordinary "buy-two-get-one-free" deal worth US$1.03 billion and a US$192 million, 22,000-tonne Type 071-E Landing Platform Dock (LPD, a large amphibious landing ship). The Thai armed forces are the only Southeast Asian military to hold annual exercises with all three branches of the PLA.

According to Ian Storey (2020), Thailand's economic crisis is unlikely to lead to any decline in Sino-Thai defense cooperation for several reasons. These include: first, the sale of defense equipment necessarily brings the training and maintenance aspects embedded in the arms deals. Another reason is even more significant. Thailand is viewed by China as a geo-economic hub, lever and advertiser for its sales to other ASEAN countries. Thirdly, the Thai navy seeks to match countries' capabilities through the acquisition of inexpensive Chinese weapons and submarines.

Moreover, for defraying the cost, Thailand is sure that China will agree to defer the annual installments on the first submarine and offer a generous financing package for the second and third vessels. It may also agree to build the necessary support and maintenance infrastructure for the submarines free of charge. China may also accept a mix of hard currency and barter trade arrangements, as its strategic partner Russia does. Moreover, if the Royal Thai Air Force (RTAF) cannot find the money to exercise with the PLA, China will subsidize those exercises (as it has done with neighboring Cambodia).[37]

The above is in addition to China's conventional arms sales to Thailand and its expanding military cooperation with Bangkok. It suits China well to help Thailand's armed forces so that its dependence on the US military is reduced. Hence, China will make efforts to sell security equipment at a comparatively low price with quick delivery.

8.6.2 *Costs of BRI*

It is interesting to note that although the military, commercial, and diasporic linkages are strong between Thailand and China, the former has managed to steer clear of a debt trap. No strategic assets have been leased out to China either. Thailand has hedged its bets and balanced its interests, befriending countries both in the East and West.

- **Budget deficit and trade deficit**
The Projected Budget deficit in 2021, given the COVID-19 pandemic, is estimated at 623 billion baht, up 32.8% from the previous year.[38] However, the 2020 annual budget expenditure has been set at 3.2 trillion baht, with a revenue target of 2.73 trillion baht, resulting in a 469 billion

---

[37]ISEAS Commentary 2020/69 "Will the COVID-19 crisis affect Thai-China defence cooperation" by Ian Storey, https://www.thinkchina.sg/thai-military-deepens-engagement-china-amid-pandemic, accessed on November 16, 2020.

[38]Thailand plans bigger deficit due to COVID-19 as budget debate starts, https://ca.reuters.com/article/health-coronavirus-thailand-budget/thailand-plans-bigger-deficit-due-to-covid-19-as-budget-debate-starts-idUSL4N2E812R, accessed on November 1, 2020.

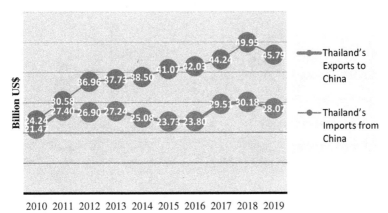

Figure 8.3:   Thailand's bilateral trade with China (2010–2019).

Source: Using UNCOMTRADE data created by the authors, https://comtrade.un.org, accessed on September 25, 2020.

baht budget deficit.[39] Prime Minister Prayuth Chan-ocha cautioned, "The Thai economy remains highly uncertain and may perform worse than forecast if the COVID-19 outbreak continues".[40] Figure 8.3 depicts Thailand's bilateral trade with China from 2010 to 2019, showing a significant trade gap between exports and imports with China. This gap has been high in recent years. In 2019, China exported goods with a value of around US$50.4 billion to Thailand, while Thailand exported merely US$28.07 billion of goods to China in the same year, giving rise to a deficit of almost US$22 billion. More recently, China has made substantial inroads into Myanmar, challenging Thailand in supplying cheap consumer goods and a lucrative smuggling trade in timber, gems, and narcotics (Deng, 2020).

- **Debt ratio**

Thailand's government debt accounted for 39.2% of the country's Nominal GDP in June 2020, compared with a ratio of 34.5% in the previous quarter. Thailand's government debt to GDP ratio data is updated

---

[39]Govt mulls extra public debt, https://www.bangkokpost.com/business/1941784/govt-mulls-extra-public-debt, accessed on November 1, 2020.

[40]Thailand plans bigger deficit due to COVID-19 as budget debate starts, https://ca.reuters.com/article/health-coronavirus-thailand-budget/thailand-plans-bigger-deficit-due-to-covid-19-as-budget-debate-starts-idUSL4N2E812R, accessed on November 1, 2020.

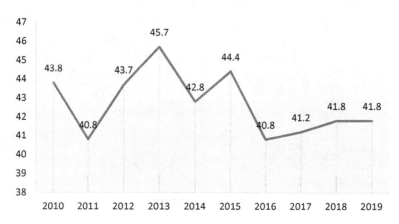

Figure 8.4:   Government debt to GDP in Thailand (2010–2019) (%).

Source: Using Trading Economics data created by the Authors, https://tradingeconomics.com/thailand/government-debt-to-gdp, country profiles, accessed on October 4, 2020.

quarterly, available from December 1997 to June 2020. This debt reached an all-time high of 39.2% in June 2020; it was only 5.7% in March 1998. In value terms, national government debt reached US$210.0 billion in August 2020.[41]

Figure 8.4 maps the debt ratio in Thailand as a share of GDP from 2010 to 2019. In 2019, debt ratio in Thailand was 41.8%, signaling a marginal decline since 2013. In the case of Thailand, unlike for other countries studied, most of its debt is home-grown. This is at 78.6% of the GDP, the third highest in Asian countries.[42] Thailand continues to steer clear of the "Chinese debt trap", till the present time.

- **Business dominant/Chinese dominant companies**
It is well known that the Chinese own at least 44% of businesses in Thailand. The Chinese also own the big conglomerates, hotels, malls and shopping plazas, and critical physical assets.

According to a BoI report, investment applications from Chinese projects in the first nine months of 2020 amounted to 45 billion baht, up

---

[41] Thailand government debt: % of GDP, https://www.ceicdata.com/en/indicator/thailand/government-debt--of-nominalgdp#, accessed on November 3, 2020.
[42] https://www.thailand-business-news.com/banking/72269-thailands-biggest-debt-trap-is-not-chinese.html, accessed on November 3, 2020.

100% from the same period last year. These Chinese investments are mainly for the rubber industry and tire manufacturing industries. Duangjai Asawaschinatachit, of the BoI, said the prolonged trade war between China and the US had prompted Chinese manufacturers to look at relocating to ASEAN countries.[43] Chinese companies' dominance in major projects cannot be avoided; Pugnatorius Ltd., a law firm sees, in particular, several implications for Thailand which could be viewed as business opportunities for foreign companies to participate in OBOR in Thailand.[44] It is for the Prayut Government to evaluate projects objectively, before committing overflows of Chinese investment.

- **Limiting investments from China into Thailand**

China is pushing for Chiang Rai to be the nodal city in North Thailand's cross-border special economic zone and logistics hub that would eliminate tariffs on goods shipped down from southwest China via the Mekong River to encourage e-commerce trade. Nonetheless, Thai stakeholders, including local government officials, argue against this proposal. In their opinion, e-commerce is of little relevance in a region that is largely devoted to agricultural production.

Dr. Chayan Vaddhanaphuti, director of Chiang Mai University's Regional Centre for Social Science and Sustainable Development said, "In Thailand, civil society and local people question government policy. So it is not easy for Prayuth. After declaring the area an SEZ, the government has not been able to secure proper investment in their plan, or carry out the infrastructure investment in electricity or water". The result of these unsettled issues is that Chinese direct investment into Thailand has so far been limited.[45]

Moreover, according to Maria Brenda Lapiz, managing director of the institutional research department at Maybank Kim Eng Securities in Bangkok, "In the BRI, mapping Thailand is missed out. This is a reason for Thailand's insistence on implementing the HSR project, despite

---

[43] Chinese factory applications to rise, https://www.bangkokpost.com/business/1782899/ chinese-factory-applications-to-rise, accessed on November 3, 2020.

[44] Seven opportunities: Thailand and the one belt, one road initiative, https://pugnatorius. com/obor/, accessed on October 20, 2020.

[45] Thailand pushes China's belt and road despite differing visions, https://asia.nikkei.com/ Spotlight/Belt-and-Road/Thailand-pushes-China-s-Belt-and-Road-despite-differing-visions, accessed on October 20, 2020.

difficulties and delays. As for Chinese investment in Thailand, many believe that is growing and the industrial estate operators also confirm this. However, we do not see evidence of this in the Board of Investment data".[46]

On the contrary, recent pledges of further investment in Thailand by Chinese companies such as Alibaba Group and Huawei suggest Sino-Thai interests are beginning to coalesce. Prayuth on his visit to China during the second BRI forum, in 2019, said that he expects more high-tech Chinese investment in the EEC going forward.

- **Environmental damage**

Due to the environmental damage, Thailand has canceled the Mekong river blasting project. This project, bordering Laos, aimed to blast and dredge parts of the Mekong riverbed to remove rapids so that it could be used by cargo ships, linking China's southwestern province of Yunnan to ports in Thailand, Laos, and the rest of Southeast Asia. This was canceled due to the opposition from local communities along the river and environmentalists, who feared it would destroy the already fragile ecosystem and would only benefit the Chinese.[47]

8.7 Impact of Pandemic on Thai Tourism

2019 witnessed 40 million tourists in Thailand. Chinese tourists are known to use their tour operators, stay in Chinese owned hotels, and use Alipay for making payments, adding little to the real economy.

Phuket is Thailand's largest island and a key tourist destination. Phuket receives the highest number of tourists from Germany, followed by China, Russia, and Australia.[48] However, as a result of the pandemic, many tour operators are struggling to stay in business without foreign travelers. Thomas Moog, who runs a German restaurant and has been offering tour services in Phuket for over 20 years, is also uncertain about the future. He said that "The pandemic is worse than the tsunami (in

---

[46] *Ibid.*

[47] Thailand nixed China's Mekong River blasting project. Will others push back?, https://sg.news.yahoo.com/thailand-nixed-china-mekong-river-095508355.html, accessed on October 25, 2020.

[48] https://www.dw.com/en/coronavirus-how-long-can-thailand-survive-without-foreign-tourism/a, accessed on November 22, 2020.

2004). Back then, we cleaned up and reopened our business. Now we have no idea when things will go back to normal".

In 2019, over 14 million travelers, including 10 million foreign tourists, visited Phuket. Somehow, the domestic tourists have kept the industry alive; however local spending cannot compensate for the slump in foreign tourism revenue. According to Phuket Tourist Association (PTA), tourism businesses in Phuket suffered a loss of 180 billion baht (€4.84 billion/US$5.72 billion) in the first six months of 2020. The government has devised a plan to attract foreign tourists, to some destinations that can effectively contain the pandemic. Without foreign visitors, the Thai economy would be severely impacted. 2020 accounts for at least US$47 billion as losses from tourism.[49]

8.7.1 *Alipay in Thailand*

Since 2017, China's Alipay cooperates with Thai commercial banks. Alipay and Thailand's Kasikorn Bank announced on September 16, 2017, that they would enhance their cooperation in promoting QR code payment in Thailand. The Thai Bank has already developed a mobile app that supports QR code payment for the Thai market. Chinese tourists can use the Alipay app to scan the QR code generated by the Kasikorn app to complete the buying with Thai sellers.[50] The majority of shops in Thailand have accepted Alipay in their businesses in Thailand.

Hence, there is abundant evidence of the Chinese forays in the Royal Kingdom of Thailand, through both economic and military engagement. Thailand's resistance to Chinese driven investments have faced a pushback from social and environmental groups resulting in stalling of key projects, ensuring that the military government does not override the concerns of Thai people.

8.8 Conclusion

The above discussion highlights the close "kith and kin" relationship between China and Thailand for generations. The Chinese are now

---

[49] Chinese factory applications to rise, https://www.bangkokpost.com/business/1782899/chinese-factory-applications-to-rise, accessed on November 3, 2020.
[50] China's Alipay cooperates with Thai commercial bank, https://www.nationthailand.com/Startup_and_IT/30326951#, accessed on November 3, 2020.

well immersed in Thai society, with Thai names and marriages with Thai women (Marwah, 2020). Hence, businesses and commercial establishments are also owned to a large extent by the Chinese. In terms of BRI projects and Chinese investment in Thailand, it is only where the interests of large sections of people are expected to be compromised that the government is forced to intervene. As in other BRI countries, details of China's investment are often not divulged to the public; in Thailand, freedom of the press has been severely constrained since 2014. Despite the apparent Sino-Thai "kith and kin" relationship, an objectivity coupled with hard bargaining traverses BRI project negotiations. Moreover, Thailand has kept its doors open for investment from other partner countries, underlining that its sovereignty will not be compromised.

It is also significant to decipher the dynamics of China's relations with Thailand in its relations with the US, given that diplomatic ties between the Kingdom of Thailand and the United States of America date back to 1818. According to Chongkittavorn (2020), Thailand–US relations reached a significant milestone in 2018 when the two countries marked the 200th anniversary of diplomatic ties. Ever since Thailand became the first Asian nation to establish ties with the United States in 1818, the two countries' bilateral relations have been tested through two centuries of global turbulence and change.

Chachavalpongpun (2011) asserts that Thailand has been strengthening its ties with China; however, it continues to hedge against the possibilities of China's aggressive posturing, as experienced by other ASEAN countries. Thailand also seeks United States' protection against any foreseeable threat that might accompany China's rise. The US also understands Thailand's strategic importance as an ASEAN member and continues engagement through the Indo-Pacific vision.

There is an alternate view as well. Given the strengthening cultural, economic, and defense relations between Thailand and China, Pavin Chachavalpongpun asserts, "For Thailand, the growing level of reliance on China leaves little room for foreign policy maneuvers. Although Thai leaders know they cannot fully trust Beijing, they have no other choices but to maintain this friendship in the absence of the United States".[51] This

---

[51] https://sr.sgpp.ac.id/post/thailand-in-the-midst-of-a-us-china-rivalry, October 22, 2020, accessed on November 16, 2020.

is despite an increasingly belligerent China stoking tensions in Thailand's neighborhood.

Yet, it can be inferred that China, as its key economic partner, in terms of the well-embedded commercial, diasporic, and business linkages, as well as the RCEP grouping, ensures that other major powers including Japan, India, and the US will have limited leverage over Thailand. Domestic tensions, which have escalated in 2020, marked by continuing protests against the military regime and the monarchy, do not make the task for the leadership any easier.

Chapter 9

China in South and Southeast Asia: Pursuit vs. Proximity

9.1 Introduction

Proximity invites immediate mutual influences that may obscure or even deconstruct China as a common category. This is regardless of China either feeling more isolated due to self-perceived vulnerability to external intrusion or being more influential as it ascends to major power status (Shih *et al.*, 2018, p. viii).

It is China's proximity to the two sub-regions of Asia that has expanded its sphere of influence; it has also pursued each of the countries for aiding its rise, for impressing upon them its willingness to provide, even before the demands come.

This **chapter has two sections**: the first brings in a micro comparative perspective of the four countries studied in the previous four chapters, through specific economic indicators, including HDI, trade, investment, and debt. The second section provides a granular analysis of the overall diversities and nuances in China's engagement with countries in South and Southeast Asia, within a more disaggregated landscape. It brings within the ambit of the discussion China's motivations and compulsions, its methods and modalities of reigning over people and polities in the region.

The critical question this chapter seeks to address is: If the path to growth-led development for the developing countries of Asia is indeed to be defined and articulated by the country's political leadership, then to what extent can external investment stimulate the impulses of growth?

Given that several countries in the region struggle to provide necessities for their population, to what extent can physical infrastructure as stadia and convention halls, or empty airports, be justified? Such unviable projects have been seen in Chinese investment, where the win–win accrues for Chinese companies and the Chinese Government, even as these remain shrouded in coercive and clandestine deals.

The following figures vividly explain the above. Here, an overall comparison of China's trade and investment with South and Southeast Asia is presented.

9.2 China's Trade Relations

9.2.1 *SAARC countries and China*

The data in Table 9.1 points to the trade advantage for China. While exports from South Asian countries increased marginally from 2010 to

Table 9.1:   Trade in goods: South Asian Association for Regional Cooperation (SAARC) and China (2001–2019).

Year	SA Countries Imports from China (US$)	SA Countries Exports to China (US$)
2001	2,943,916	937,785
2002	3,705,828	1,567,705
2003	6,168,905	2,887,913
2004	9,232,405	4,460,257
2005	15,168,992	7,713,171
2006	21,928,122	9,138,426
2007	32,452,831	10,363,599
2008	42,471,026	10,963,597
2009	39,928,510	11,572,918
2010	54,371,790	19,249,937
2011	69,033,258	18,899,883
2012	71,207,983	17,938,128
2013	69,563,846	19,714,153
2014	85,109,474	16,669,465
2015	88,851,111	12,516,213

(*Continued*)

Table 9.1: (*Continued*)

Year	SA Countries Imports from China (US$)	SA Countries Exports to China (US$)
2016	95,534,307	11,606,282
2017	108,782,193	15,338,751
2018	113,217,292	19,709,845
2019	104,686,498	20,851,306

Source: Calculations based on data from the International Trade Centre (2019), "Trade Map Database". https://www.trademap.org/Bilateral_TS, accessed on August 4, 2020.

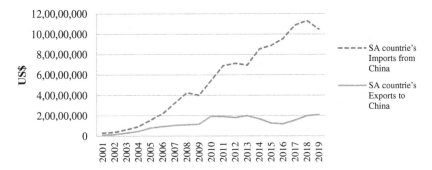

Figure 9.1: SAARC countries trade with China (2001–2019).

Source: Calculations based on data from the International Trade Centre (2019), "Trade Map Database". https://www.trademap.org/Bilateral_TS.aspx?nvpm, accessed on August 4, 2020.

2019, China's exports have risen rapidly, with these having almost doubled since 2010. The trade deficit is more than US$80 billion. Undoubtedly, the larger share of both exports and imports is that of India. It is the structural weaknesses in the countries manufacturing capabilities that trade benefits accrue disproportionately to China. This is also evident in Figure 9.1.

The data in Table 9.2 shows that in terms of value, Southeast Asia has been trading with China to a greater extent than South Asia. The overall exports from China to ASEAN countries are also three times more than that of SAARC countries. Exports from ASEAN to China are ten times more, in comparison with SAARC countries. It is interesting to note that since 2010, the trade deficit has been increasing rapidly, despite a rise in

Table 9.2: Trade in goods: Association of Southeast Asian Nations (ASEAN) and China.

Year	ASEAN Countries Imports from China (US$)	ASEAN Countries Exports to China (US$)
2001	19,436,533	16,586,727
2002	26,216,308	21,677,363
2003	32,765,646	30,752,724
2004	46,653,902	41,340,709
2005	60,275,425	52,422,400
2006	75,408,025	66,314,191
2007	94,077,339	78,527,354
2008	110,988,031	88,264,426
2009	95,987,689	81,681,873
2010	126,702,441	113,185,784
2011	155,941,551	142,853,968
2012	177,578,767	142,570,128
2013	198,361,796	153,922,918
2014	212,492,742	153,742,863
2015	218,283,515	141,290,629
2016	224,861,247	141,874,218
2017	253,956,324	185,805,600
2018	292,243,258	199,976,654
2019	333,315,860	225,456,185

Source: Calculations based on data from the International Trade Centre (2019), "Trade Map Database", https://www.trademap.org/Bilateral_TS, accessed on August 4, 2020.

exports and imports from ASEAN. Here, too, China's exports to ASEAN countries have almost doubled over the period 2012–2019, while exports from ASEAN to China have increased by about 50% over the same period. Figure 9.2 also clearly shows the above.

A comparison of the trade data points to the growing deficit in trade in favor of China for both sub-regions of Asia.

Table 9.3 and Figure 9.3 show that China's investment in South Asia is significantly higher than its investment in Southeast Asian countries in 2019.

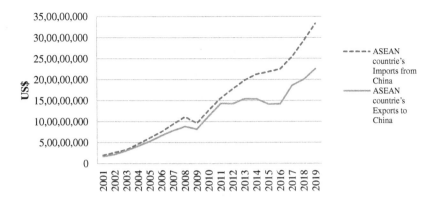

Figure 9.2:   ASEAN countries trade with China (2001–2019).

Source: Calculations based on data from the International Trade Centre (2019), "Trade Map Database", https://www.trademap.org/Bilateral_TS.aspx?nvpm=, accessed on August 4, 2020.

Table 9.3:   China's investment in South and Southeast Asia in 2019.

China's Investment	US$ Million
Investment to South Asia	18,530
Investment to Southeast Asia	11,110
Total	29,640

Sources: Using data from China Global Investment Tracker by the American Enterprise Institute and The Heritage Foundation, created by the authors.

9.3 China's Investment: Recipient Countries

Details of Chinese investment flows to countries in South and Southeast Asia have been discussed in the preceding chapters. Here, the comparison is instructive to understand the magnitude of investment that flows to different countries, indicating the disproportionate dependence of some on China from a comparative perspective.

Figure 9.4 clearly shows that in South Asia, China's investment in Sri Lanka, Pakistan, and Maldives is equivalent to 14%, 16%, and 15%, respectively, of each country's respective GDP for 2018. In Southeast Asia, the high dependence of Laos and Cambodia on Chinese investment is visible. Chinese investment in Myanmar and Thailand constitutes merely 8% and 1% of these countries' GDP, respectively.

Total Investment

- Investment to South Asia (Quantity in Millions)
- Investment to South East Asia (Quantity in Millions)

Figure 9.3: China's investment in South Asia and Southeast Asia (2019).

Sources: Using data from China Global Investment Tracker by the American Enterprise Institute and The Heritage Foundation, created by the authors.

9.4 Country-Specific Analysis: Pakistan, Sri Lanka, Myanmar, and Thailand

Here, the change in per capita incomes in real terms for the four countries is presented. Figure 9.5 shows the real GDP per capita since 2010 for Pakistan, Sri Lanka, Myanmar, and Thailand.

In terms of per capita income, it is evident that Thailand in SEA, followed by Sri Lanka in South Asia, have higher per capita incomes than Pakistan and Myanmar. It is interesting to note that Pakistan's real per capita income is virtually stagnant over the ten years. Sri Lanka and Myanmar have experienced slow growth rates; Sri Lanka's rate of growth is almost negligible from 2016–2019.

9.5 Human Development Index (HDI)

Human Development Index for these countries is shown in Figure 9.6. The situation for HDI is also revealing. HDI for Pakistan has improved marginally from 0.52 to 0.56; for Myanmar, this improved from 0.52 to 0.58; for Sri Lanka the change is from 0.75 to 0.78, though the improvement since 2013 is a mere 0.1; for Thailand it is 0.73 to 0.77. Sri Lanka and Thailand have much higher levels of human development in comparison to Pakistan and Myanmar.

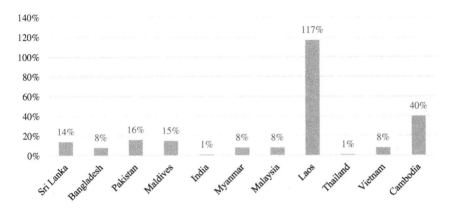

Figure 9.4:   Total Chinese investment as a % of the destination country's GDP (2018).

Source: Wignaraja *et al.* (2020). LKI calculations based on data gathered from the American Enterprise Chinese Investment Database and the IMF, World Economic Outlook Database.

Note: Cumulative investment 2006–2018/GDP of the respective country in 2018.

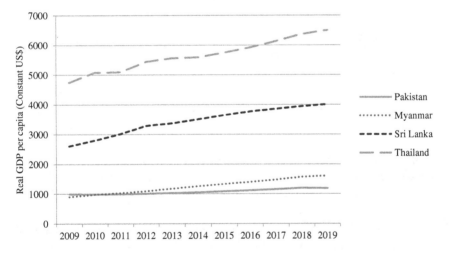

Figure 9.5:   Real GDP per capita (2009–2019): Four countries.

Source: Using World Bank WDI data, created by the Authors, https://databank.worldbank.org/source/world-development-indicators, accessed on October 1, 2020.

9.6 Government Debt

Several studies have examined the effects of high government debt on levels of growth. Cuestas *et al.* (2014) argue that government

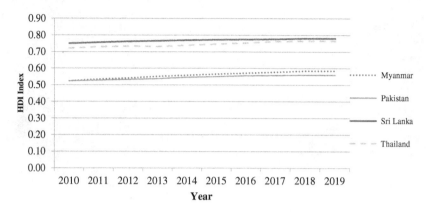

Figure 9.6:   Human Development Index of 4 countries (2010–2019).

Source: Using U.N. Human Development report data, created by the authors, http://hdr.undp.org/en/data, for 2019 data http://hdr.undp.org/en/content/2019-human-development-index-ranking, both websites are accessed on October 5, 2020.

debt-to-GDP is likely to hurt economic growth. Also, high government debt levels are likely to have nonlinear effects on growth and become relevant only after a specific threshold value. Kumar and Woo (2010), for a panel of 38 developed and emerging countries over the period 1970–2007, found that a 10% increase of public debt is associated with a 0.2% decrease of GDP growth, the impact being stronger in emerging market economies and weaker in developed ones. Kumara and Cooray (2013) find a nonlinear relationship between public debt and GDP per capita growth in Sri Lanka. The threshold level for public debt is 59.42% of GDP. Above this level, public debt makes a negative impact on GDP per capita growth.

Figure 9.7 clearly shows government debt levels as a percentage of GDP for the four countries. In Thailand, debt has been in the range of 40–45% of its GDP, in Myanmar, there is an upward shift post-2013, rising from about 37% to 50% in 2018. For Pakistan, the upward trajectory clearly shows the steep rise in government debt as a % of GDP from 63 in 2015 to 85 in 2019, thus reaching precarious debt levels, similar to Sri Lanka. As discussed above, Sri Lanka's debt level above the threshold of 60% negatively impacts the GDP growth rate. Pakistan is in a similar situation.

According to Alice Wells, as quoted in a 2020 Brookings paper, in a scathing criticism of Pakistan's unsustainable debt levels, said, "CPEC

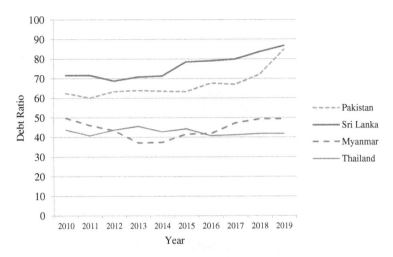

Figure 9.7:   Government debt to GDP (in %) (2010–2019).

Source: Using Trading Economics data, created by the Authors, https://tradingeconomics.com/thailand/government-debt-to-gdp, country profiles, accessed on October 4, 2020.

almost always takes the form of burdensome loans or financing with Chinese state-owned enterprises and the Chinese Government profiting. This is hardly the "peace and win–win cooperation" OBOR is supposed to facilitate". Wells's main criticisms center around the unsustainability of Chinese loans. The argument is that projects primarily use Chinese workers and supplies, and Chinese enterprises and the Chinese Government profits at Pakistan's expense. Wells also drew a sharp contrast with US investments in Pakistan, which she said help build local capacity and sustainable growth (Afzal, 2020).

9.7 Bilateral Trade with China: Pakistan, Sri Lanka, Myanmar, and Thailand

The trade imbalances are presented in Figures 9.8, 9.9, 9.10, and 9.11. Given Pakistan's near stagnant exports to China, it is evident that the crisis is more than what meets the eye.

A 2019 study by Rosbach and Aleksanyan (2019) focuses on structural weaknesses of Pakistan's trade. The study concludes that improving Pakistan's export performance remains the most relevant long-term structural challenge to alleviate the balance-of-payments constraint to sustained economic growth.

It is evident from the above figures for each of the four countries that the trade deficits vis-à-vis China have been gradually increasing. While China exported US$4,032 million of goods to Sri Lanka, Sri Lanka's exports to China were less than 400 million dollars in 2019. Hence, the imports are more than ten times in value than its exports. For Pakistan, its imports were six times as high as its exports to China. The interesting fact is that Pakistan's exports to China in value terms has been around US$2000 million or US$ 2 billion since 2011.

Figures 9.10 and 9.11 depict the trade of Myanmar and Thailand, respectively, with China. Here again it is evident that the trade balance favors China, with imports for both countries staying ahead of their exports. In Myanmar's case, the deficit has mostly remained below US$1 billion, over the period 2010–2019, the case of Thailand is different.

Thailand's trade value is much higher than that of Myanmar's. In 2019, Thailand's exports to China were about US$28 billion; in contrast, its imports were almost 46 billion, giving rise to a huge trade deficit of US$18 billion. Its interesting to note that exports declined from 2013 to 2016 in Thailand before picking up in 2017. Despite this, China's positive trade balance with Thailand makes the latter an important partner. The Prayut Chan-o-cha Government has not made efforts to reduce this deficit.

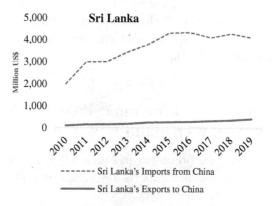

Figure 9.8:   Sri Lanka–China trade (2010–2019).

Source: Using UNCOMTRADE data, created by the authors https://comtrade.un.org, accessed on September 25, 2020.

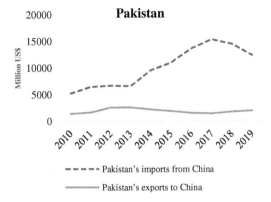

Figure 9.9: Pakistan–China trade.

Source: Using UNCOMTRADE data, created by the authors https://comtrade.un.org, accessed on September 25, 2020.

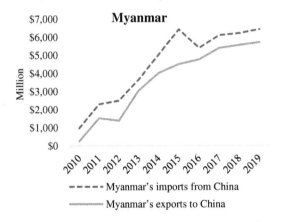

Figure 9.10: Myanmar–China trade (2010–2019).

Source: Using UN COMTRADE data, created by the authors, https://comtrade.un.org, accessed on September 25, 2020.

9.8 China's Investment in the Four Countries

China's investment in Sri Lanka, Pakistan, Myanmar, and Thailand is presented below in Figures 9.12, 9.13, 9.14, and 9.15. These have been discussed in detail in the country-specific chapters. In the comparative

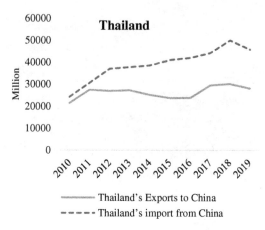

Figure 9.11:   Thailand–China trade.

Source: Using UN COMTRADE data, created by the authors, https://comtrade.un.org, accessed on September 25, 2020.

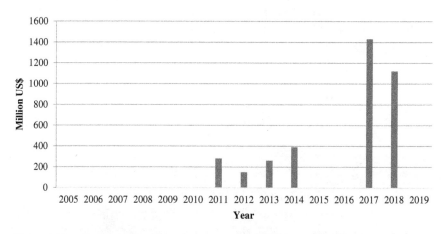

Figure 9.12:   Investment by China in Sri Lanka.

Sources: Using China Global Investment Tracker (Data compiled by The American Enterprise Institute and The Heritage Foundation) data, figures created by the Authors.

analysis, it can be seen that the highest level of inward investment has flowed to Sri Lanka in 2017 and 2018; being to the extent of US$1,430 million and US$1,120 million, respectively.

Pakistan, on the other hand, has received much higher levels of investment from China. This is shown in Figure 9.13. Over US$5 billion

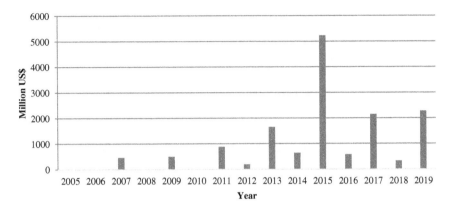

Figure 9.13: Investment by China in Pakistan.

Sources: Using China Global Investment Tracker (Data compiled by The American Enterprise Institute and The Heritage Foundation) data, figures created by the Authors.

was received in 2015 alone. More details have been shared in the country-specific chapters.

9.9 The Xi Jinping Era: Chinese Investment in South and Southeast Asia

Since the advent of Xi Jinping, China has been extending its economic influence in Asia. The report by Moody's (Kong *et al.*, 2019) has assessed that within Asia (out of China's total worldwide investment of US$614 billion), the largest investment has been in the domain of energy, with the sector accounting for almost 40% of the total funding in Asia. At 25%, spending on transport is the second-largest BRI investment component and contracts in the region.

It is important to note that the countries of South and Southeast Asia, such as Pakistan, Malaysia, Singapore, Indonesia, and Laos, are the top beneficiaries of Chinese BRI funding in Asia. Combined, they have attracted US$128 billion in investments and contracts, almost 40% of the total value in Asia. Research by Moodys (2019) shows that for every 1% increase in FDI, there is a 0.145% increase in productivity growth. An important caveat with this estimate is that different types of investments affect productivity growth in different ways. Airports and seaports will not have the same effects as highways and railroads.

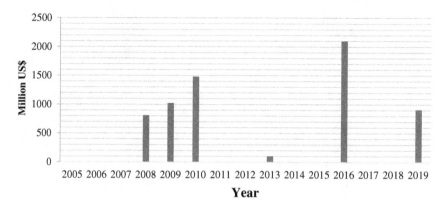

Figure 9.14:   Investment by China in Myanmar.

Sources: Using China Global Investment Tracker (Data compiled by The American Enterprise Institute and The Heritage Foundation) data, figures created by the Authors.

Nevertheless, applying this estimate to BRI investments in all four of the studied countries shows that potential productivity increases, as expected. Improved road and rail transportation, for instance, improves trade flows and reduces travel time. However, in the case of these four countries, not all investments have been for vital infrastructure.

Investment by China in Myanmar has been undertaken since 2008, with US$2,100 being provided in 2016.

In comparison, the flow of investment to Thailand has been relatively smaller, though more consistent over the years 2009–2019, with the highest amounts having been disbursed in 2014, 2018, and 2019; underlining the fact that post 2014, the changed government brought the country closer to China refer Figures 9.14 and 9.15. Table 9.4 clarifies the high levels of China's engagement in the Xi Jinping era with Pakistan, the country has received over US$10 billion over the 5 years.

To quote James Crabtree (associate professor in practice at the Lee Kuan Yew School of Public Policy in Singapore) at this juncture is significant. In his words, "Facing a crunching post-pandemic slow-down, China has far less money to splash out on expensive infrastructure. Moreover, President Xi was also facing severe political pressure on two fronts: from developing countries wanting loans canceled and from his citizens who did not want the money sent abroad that could

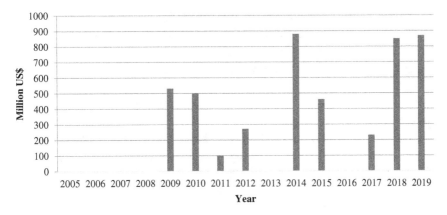

Figure 9.15:   Investment by China in Thailand.

Source: Using China Global Investment Tracker (Data compiled by The American Enterprise Institute and The Heritage Foundation) data, figures created by the Authors.

Table 9.4:   China's investment in four countries (2015–2019).

Year	Investment to Pakistan (US$ Millions)	Investment to Sri Lanka (US$ Millions)	Investment to Thailand (US$ Millions)	Investment to Myanmar (US$ Millions)
2015	5,230		460	
2016	580			2,100
2017	2,150	1,430	230	
2018	330	1,120	850	
2019	2,280		870	910
Total	**10,570**	**2550**	**2410**	**3010**

Source: Using China Global Investment Tracker (Data compiled by The American Enterprise Institute and The Heritage Foundation) data, figures created by the Authors.

be used to aid recovery at home.[1] There are already challenges emerging in the flow of investment to Pakistan. The issue is concerning the financing of Main Line 1, or ML-1, railway project, the largest in

---

[1] Majority of China's BRI projects abroad adversely affected by COVID-19 pandemic: Official, https://economictimes.indiatimes.com/news/international/business/majority-of-chinas-bri-projects-abroad-adversely-affected-by-covid-19-pandemic-official/articleshow/, accessed on November 19, 2020.

China's BRI in Pakistan. This is because Beijing is hesitant to finance it at the 1% interest rate requested by Islamabad. According to Jeremy Garlick, from the Jan Masaryk Centre of International Studies at the Prague University of Economics and Business, "Beijing does not want to say no to ML-1, it wants to appear committed in Pakistan, but at the same time it is aware of the risky environment for Chinese investments".[2]

Interestingly, many CPEC projects have not generated any economic value to Pakistan. Projects expected to enhance employment and wealth have instead been built by Chinese labor, equipment, and materials. Reports indicate that after 5 years and US$20 billion of realized investments, only 75,000 jobs have been created in Pakistan; far short of the promised 1.5 million jobs per year.

After taking a comparative perspective through key economic indicators of the four countries studied, it is also significant to provide an overview of how China's engagement with South Asia is different from Southeast Asia. Section 2 elucidates some macro aspects of the engagement with China.

9.10 China in South vs. Southeast Asia: A Macro Perspective

China is Asia's largest economy and one whose growth momentum of three decades has not failed to surprise. China has also not failed to befriend any country with its deep pockets, especially in South and Southeast Asia. While countries in South Asia, barring India, do not view China's assertiveness and power projection as a threat; there are countries in Southeast Asia who would prefer to see China as their economic partner, without its aggression in the maritime space.

There are key points of distinction between China's perceptions and China's policies in these two sub-regions of Asia.

Firstly, China's India-centric approach to South Asia has resulted in its trust deficit with India. On its part, China has defended its economic and military ties with South Asian countries as "legitimate and normal

---

[2] Saikiran Kannan, https://www.indiatoday.in/news-analysis/story/cpec-crisis-china-plays-hard-pakistan-in-debt-trap-1742696-2020-11-20, November 20, 2020, accessed on November 25, 2020.

state-to-state relations" well within the purview of the Five Principles of Peaceful Coexistence or Panchsheel. With close historical relations, Southeast Asia has been a critical area for China, where its rise has been felt most significantly. China is engaged in weaving close-knit relations bilaterally with every ASEAN country through the ASEAN plus mechanism and more recently with the signing of the RCEP in November 2020.

Secondly, boundary disputes and the Tibet issue have contributed much to defining China's South Asia policy, especially vis-à-vis India, and to shape China's relations with South Asia. It is to be noted that China has already resolved its disputed boundaries with Nepal and Pakistan, though territorial disputes with India and Bhutan are yet to be resolved. With Southeast Asian countries, boundary disputes are relatively recent. China's engagement has been both at the multilateral and bilateral level, with bilateral engagement being prioritized by China, especially as it asserts its maritime dominance over 90% of the South China Sea.

At the Sino-India border, the Himalayan crisis has seen a turning point in the bilateral relations between the two countries since April 2020, after almost four decades of relative calm. Post the pandemic, the world is witnessing a more belligerent China, demonstrating the strength of its army and navy. According to Samphel, 2020, "The only time communist China opened two fronts was in 1950 when it invaded and occupied Tibet and fought the US-led UN forces to a standstill at the present demilitarized zone between South and North Korea". In the present times, China is harassing Japan in the East China Sea, enacting laws to restrict the freedoms of the people of Hong Kong, and firing missiles across the Taiwan Strait and claiming most of the South China Sea, the SCS being disputed by many countries in Southeast Asia. On June 15, 2020, PLA troops crossed over the Line of Actual Control in eastern Ladakh, on the Sino-India border, and were repulsed by the Indian army. China is doing everything per the Tibet playbook: in the early 1950s, it occupied the Indian territory of Aksai Chin. In Ladakh and the South China Sea, Beijing hopes to apply its Tibet playbook to establish facts on the ground and water and later argue that possession is nine-tenth of the law (Samphel, 2020).

Thirdly, China's relations with South Asian countries owe much to the Beijing-Islamabad "special relationship", which is part of China's grand strategy of stimulating the South Asian security environment in its favor and providing a stimulus to its Belt and Road Initiative. This "special relationship" provides a good example of using China as a counterweight to what smaller South Asian regimes perceive as India's attempts at bullying them. It demonstrates that much like Pakistan, other South Asian countries can follow an "independent" policy and need not allow India to influence their decision-making.

Fourthly, China remains a significant economic aid donor to countries in South Asia, viz. Bangladesh, Nepal, Pakistan, and Sri Lanka. Such economic ties further strengthened through the BRI projects between China and these smaller South Asian countries, helping China in its security objectives and goals in the region. In Southeast Asia, China is a significant trading and investment partner for each of the ASEAN countries. Several bilateral FTAs and multilateral FTAs center around ASEAN, referred to as the "noodle bowl" in Asia, (ASEAN plus 3, ASEAN plus six etc.) (Marwah and Ramanayake, 2019). China's Communist Party successfully implements infrastructure development projects, whereas democratic India is often slow to act. Hence, India has often been criticized for its bureaucratic hurdles in limiting its capacity to engage with alacrity with neighbors in South Asia or adopt an invigorated "Act East" Policy with its neighbors in the East.

Additionally, independent India's conscious choice in favor of de-globalization has led to a steady dissipation of commercial connectivity with the neighbors. Delhi's new quest for autarky was not just from the global economy but also the regional one. India's economic reorientation since the 1990s and the rediscovery of regionalism brought possibilities for reconnecting with its neighbors. Delhi today is acutely aware of the need to revive regional connectivity (Raja Mohan, 2020).

India has launched several regional initiatives with its neighbors, including SAARC in 1985, BIMSTEC in 1997, MGC in 2000, BBIN in 2015. However, each of these has had limited success and traction compared with China's fast paced connectivity projects including the Lancang–Mekong cooperation, Belt and Road initiative, and now the Regional Comprehensive Economic Partnership.

Fifthly, whereas India as a result of its historical and cultural proximity and geographically positioned influence is regarded by neighbors as interfering in their domestic politics, China has deliberately ensured that it continues to use the narrative of benign abstinence from interference. In Southeast Asia, China engages with all polities and leaders, without intervening in any domestic or home-grown issues; the Rohingyas in Myanmar is one example. As shared in a discussion group on Jonathan Ward's book *China's Vision of Victory*, 'China's leaders do not ask clients to change their government system, but to squelch criticism of Chinese communism inside their borders'. Thus, the leaders of Muslim-majority countries as Pakistan pretend that their faith is not being crushed in Xinjiang. The Thai government turns a blind eye to Chinese security kidnapping dissidents inside its borders.[3]

Sixth, it is crucial to understand that historical, cultural, and geographical locations have influenced China's relations with South and Southeast Asia countries. It is evident that China's relations with South Asian countries are essentially to limit India's influence in the region and are mainly State-led; in contrast, its relations with countries in Southeast Asia are that of kith and kin as well as of shared identity and linguistic compatibility. The diasporic and historical connect implies that most SEA countries are home to large communities of Chinese. This proximity helps drive political and economic relations, foregrounded on history, geography, and culture (Marwah, 2018).

Seventh, according to Adhir Ranjan Chowdhury, 2020, China's expansionism in the region is directly proportional to the deterioration of India's relations with its neighbors. Given that India's neighbors, including Nepal, are all young emerging democracies developing new institutions, they find a growing appeal in Beijing's authoritarian paradigm than India's democratic one.[4]

K.P. Oli's regime in Nepal even initiated a border dispute with India, while at the same time maintaining silence on reports of land grabbing by China of its territory. Similarly, China's bankrolling of Duterte resulted in the latter denying the favorable verdict of the International Court of Justice in 2016.

Eighth, according to Raja Mohan (2020),[5] the problems generated by the subcontinent's great division on religious lines continue to animate the region. No amount of virtue-signaling in the name of good neighborly policy can help fix the challenges of settling boundaries, sharing river-waters, protecting the rights of minorities, and easing the flow of

---

[3] China's Vision of Victory? https://scholars-stage.blogspot.com/2019/10/chinas-vision-of-victory.html, October 19, 2019, accessed on November 19, 2020.

[4] https://indianexpress.com/article/opinion/columns/india-china-border-dispute-south-asian-countries-relationships-modi-govt-adhir-ranjan-chowdhury-6550761/, accessed on October 30, 2020.

[5] There is no happy end-state in India's relations with its neighbors, https://indianexpress.com/article/opinion/columns/tending-to-the-neighbourhood-south-asia-india-6621078/, September 29, 2020, accessed on November 17, 2020.

goods and people. The burden of the Subcontinent's history is not easily discarded. Hence, for India, despite its best intentions and friendly overtures by successive governments through neighborhood first policies, the China factor has gradually permeated the subcontinent in more ways than one.

Ninth, China influences perceptions not only through its deep pockets and personal rapport with leaders of weak polities, but also through influencing the media and academics, through its vast network of China study centers, Confucian centers, and language teaching institutions. There are five such centers in Pakistan, two in Sri Lanka, and 16 in Thailand, hosted in significant universities. Given the criticism against Confucius Institutes in various countries, the Chinese Government decided to continue with the institution, while working to optimize the "regional distribution of the Confucius Institutes, strengthen its abilities and building, and fully raise its educational standards", as reported by the Xinhua news agency.[6]

China's *Global Times*, well known for its caustic remarks, along with its propaganda machinery, more often than not is instrumental in changing the narrative. For example, when China was being ostracized for unleashing the pandemic, China was projected as the victim, not the aggressor.

Finally, according to Brahma Chellaney, the Chinese premier Xi Jinping, whose persona is being compared to that of Mao Zedong, has attempted to build a modern version of the tributary system. Chinese emperors used to establish authority over vassal states: making the latter submit to the emperor and reap the benefits of peace and trade with the empire. While the pandemic has devastated economies — both developed and developing – China will be one of the very few countries to end year 2020 with a positive growth rate of about 2% (Chellaney, 2020).

The countries of Southeast Asia in focus in our book, viz. Myanmar and Thailand, are also primary recipients of Chinese investment, though this is smaller than those in South Asia, viz. Sri Lanka and Pakistan. This presents an interesting fact, when juxtapositioned with the situation vis-á-vis trade. While Southeast Asian countries have more significant trade volumes with China, the approach appears to be more cautious in

[6] https://www.straitstimes.com/asia/east-asia/china-aims-to-optimise-spread-of-controversial-confucius-institutes, February 24, 2019, accessed on November 19, 2020.

terms of investment, especially in Myanmar and Thailand. Both these countries also seek India, Japan, and other countries as developmental partners.

9.11 Comparing CPEC of Pakistan with CMEC of Myanmar

It is important here to compare the two most significant economic corridors that China is dearly invested in. These are the CPEC in Pakistan and the CMEC in Myanmar, Gwadar, and Kyaukphyu, being critical for trade. Both these are of immense strategic significance for China. Prof. Wang Gugwu articulated in a seminar, "China is concerned about its trade through the maritime space, and hence, given the potential for its trade to be restricted through the Malacca Straits, it envisions freedom of navigation in the Bay of Bengal and the Indian Ocean through alternate routes".[7]

Hence, Myanmar's CMEC serves a similar purpose for China as Pakistan's CPEC — an avenue for strategic advantage. 80% of China's oil travels along Indian Ocean routes through the vulnerable Malacca Straits, a geography weakness, which the Chinese must surmount. This same vulnerability prompted China to choose Djibouti for its first overseas military facility, ostensibly to safeguard the sea-lines of communication through which vessels carry Chinese oil.

The objectives for these corridors are also to keep India's aspirations limited. These road, rail, and sea corridors limit India's influence in the region and help isolate India, given that CPEC flanks India to the west and CMEC flanks it to the east.

China's strategic maneuvers extend to India's Northeast state of Arunachal Pradesh and the northern Himalayas. It has stationed troops in the bordering areas at several points since April 2020. India is closely monitoring Chinese activities in the Andaman Sea and the Indian Ocean region. She is also responding by beefing up the country's security and naval defense facilities in the Andaman and Nicobar Islands offshore of Myanmar. For India, these islands are

---

[7] Wang Gungwu, in a lecture titled *Rewriting History: East and West*, on November 11, 2020, organized by the Association of Asia Scholars.

guardians of the Indian Ocean. China's chess moves in India's vicinity are not lost on anyone.[8]

9.12 Limits to Chinese Checkers

However, a pertinent question is: Can all of China's calculations and Chinese checkers obliterate its real intentions? Experts have cautioned recipient countries of China's magnanimous gestures, that the optics do not always reveal the reality.

In South Asia as in Southeast Asia, wariness of real Chinese motives is often being assessed, debated, and questioned. Often, critical voices are silenced by politicians and elites who are the stakeholders in the corrupt deals. Understandably, despite China making its forays cautiously and without upsetting the seemingly strong friendships, cracks in relationships appear. It is also well known that BRI policy facilitates FDI to countries with a weaker rule of law and less government accountability

9.12.1 *Evidence and lessons learnt*

According to Lampton, David *et al.* (2020), smaller states do have agency and can drive a hard bargain for infrastructure projects. While Thailand, is courted by all major powers because of its geo-strategic centrality in Southeast Asia, Myanmar, too, is cautious of going the Sri Lanka way. Hence, several factors/issues for pushback of project funding have been articulated by experts and media persons for Chinese BRI projects in the host countries.

a. *Security concerns* of China giving rise to a clash with the local forces: There are several examples of clashes between Chinese workers and host country security forces. One such incident happened at a CPEC site on July 21, 2020. As stated by, Srinjoy Chowdhury, "Even for the all-powerful Pakistan Army, the Chinese are unique, they are above the law. The attack, not the first of its kind, was between the Chinese laborers working on Main Line 1 of

---

[8] https://www.wilsoncenter.org/blog-post/china-myanmar-economic-corridor-and-chinas-determination-see-it-through, accessed on September 10, 2020.

the CPEC and the soldiers, who were supposed to protect them.[9] Despite China reinvigorating the CPEC with a fresh infusion of US$11 billion in July 2020, growing discord at the working levels and corruption is marring its flagship Belt and Road Initiative in Pakistan. In recent meetings between Chinese and Pakistani officials, reports of which have been leaked and seen by a leading newspaper, the Chinese side has expressed anger and frustration with Pakistan regarding lack of security. These complaints escalate to senior levels of the Pakistan army who are expected to comply with Chinese demands. Pakistan has raised an entire special security division (SSD) to protect Chinese contractors and workers along the CPEC.

The discord between the two sides has been sharp regarding the Karot hydropower project in Punjab and at the Azad Pattan project. The Chinese are unhappy about the progress and lack of security. A similar story is heard from the Kohala hydropower project. Repeated Chinese complaints have led to both the army and civilian government scrambling to accede to these demands. Disputes over the design and execution of this project have been going on since 2019. In other places, for instance, in the Matiari–Lahore road projects or even the Peshawar–Karachi road project, the Chinese contractors are not allowed free movement even in Lahore (Bagchi, 2020).

b. *Debt concerns* and the issue of control of information especially concerning CPEC, as pointed out in the Brookings report by Afzal (2020). Several experts have warned about the opacity of project funding by Beijing. As US Secretary of State Rex Tillerson opined, "Beijing encourages dependency using opaque contracts, predatory loan practices, and corrupt deals that mire nations in debt and undercut their sovereignty, denying them their long-term, self-sustaining growth" (Fernholz, 2018).

c. *Environmental and social concerns:* Several concerns related to China's dam-building activities have been reported by non-governmental organizations in the Mekong countries, resulting in protests against dam building. China has already built 11 dams on the Mekong

---

[9] https://www.timesnownews.com/india/article/exclusive-pak-soldiers-insulted-assaulted-by-chinese-labourers-working-on-the-economic-corridor/634216, August 9, 2020, accessed on November 19, 2020.

river, which passes through continental Southeast Asian countries. According to a study by Eyes on Earth, "Some of those dams have compounded the alteration of the river's natural flow, resulting in the Lower Mekong recording "some of its lowest river levels ever throughout most of the year" (Tan, 2020). There have been pushbacks from affected communities in Myanmar and Thailand.

d. *Land Grabbing:* A leading British daily has reported land grabbing and encroaching by China on territory in Bhutan, Nepal, and India. China has annexed over 150 hectares of Nepal's territory in five areas near its border.[10] The border areas in Myanmar, Laos, and Cambodia are becoming hubs of illegal Chinese activities, from casino cities to drug trade.

e. *Interference in internal politics:* While reports of the Chinese ambassador in Kathmandu having honey-trapped Nepalese Prime Minister K.P. Oli have been dismissed by Nepal's people, there is no doubt that China does engage with different stakeholders. In December 2020, the split in the largest Communist Party of Nepal and the ensuing crisis in leadership saw a Chinese delegation reach Kathmandu.

   According to the USIP report 2018, China has set aside its stated adherence to the principle of non-interference to become more proactively and assertively involved in Myanmar's peace process. It has made efforts to be directly involved in the primary conflict issues. This is evidently a result of its expanding economic footprint and the imperative to secure strategic assets including the port at Kyaukphyu, the planned special economic zone (SEZ), road, rail, and pipeline networks, *et al.*[11]

f. *Dual use of facilities as ports:* In 2015, China's state media described Kyaukpyu (Myanmar), Chittagong (Bangladesh), Colombo (Sri Lanka), and ports in the Maldives as potential industrial hubs to support PLA military operations. While the facilities at Hambantota, Gwadar, and Kyaukpyu are not being used yet by the PLA, Beijing's militarization of its human-made South China Sea facilities does have the potential to be converted into military logistic support. The vulnerability of countries as Sri Lanka, Myanmar, and Pakistan to

---

[10] https://en.akhbar1.com/nepal-land-grab-beijing-dismisses-report-as-rumour-74138. html, November, 2020, accessed on November 19, 2020.
[11] https://www.usip.org/sites/default/files/2018-09/ssg-report-chinas-role-in-myanmars-internal-conflicts.pdf, accessed on October 30, 2020.

Chinese debt traps associated with these infrastructure projects was highlighted recently by the International Monetary Fund director, who suggested how easily Beijing might tighten the financial screws to obtain strategic access (Fanell, 2019).

This issue has found fertile ground in Pakistan, too. Mir Hasil Khan Bizenjo, previously the minister of Balochistan's maritime affairs, revealed to the Senate that Pakistan would get only 9% of total revenues from Gwadar Port. The remaining 91% will go to China over the next 40 years, as per the agreement signed between them. Despite senators raising concerns over sharing assets, it is rare for the civilian institutions to get their voices heard. Moreover, CPEC is not only an economic project, but a military one, too. According to data on global military spending released by SIPRI, China in 2020 is the second-largest country for military spending after the United States, with its investments within CPEC and other BRI projects being closely followed by military bases (Marino, 2020).

g. *Viability of projects:* In addition to the above, several other issues regarding the high cost of projects have resulted in the renegotiation of projects such as the Kyaukpyu Port and the Myitsone Dam's stalling in Myanmar. In Thailand, too, the railway line project has gone through more than 30 several rounds of negotiation. In Pakistan, there have been issues centered around the low wages paid for the local workers compared to the wage rates for Chinese labor. However, voices of protest are usually silenced when the elite are involved.

h. *Issues of FTAs:* There are issues related to the signing of Free Trade Agreements as well. In the Maldives, Mr. Nasheed, who is also the leader of the ruling MDP, made it clear that the FTA with China will "not go forward" as it has to be ratified in Parliament, and said the combined private and public loans totaled more than US$3.5 billion, which must be restructured, warning that otherwise there will be a debt crisis in the Maldives by 2022 when the loans come due.

"If you are unable to restructure these projects or amend the course, I do not see a soft landing for the Maldives at present. If you lack vision or a set of principles to take things forward, then what you do becomes unsustainable", Mr. Nasheed told journalists in India, accusing China of "inflating project costs" to "debt trap" the Maldives, and compared it to the British East India Company (Haider, 2019).

9.13 Conclusion

The earlier chapters point to the fragility of governance in most BRI countries, especially in South Asia, thus enhancing their vulnerability to Chinese influence and generous dole.

Asian nations have expressed concerns about the "debt trap" caused by BRI projects. From the Maldives and Sri Lanka to Malaysia and Thailand, questions are being asked about many Chinese-driven projects' future viability (Pant, 2019). The renegotiations have been more visible in Thailand and Myanmar as compared to Sri Lanka and Pakistan, even though both Thailand and Myanmar have fraternal relations with China. One common feature in all four countries is the important role of the military and elite bureaucracy. Another is the lack of transparency in negotiating projects with the Chinese, with most information coming out of Chinese media rather than media in these countries. China's pretensions of port development catalysing opportunities for the host countries is a misreading of the tea leaves.

Chinese aid to countries in South and Southeast Asia has also been discussed in earlier chapters. However, it is significant to underline that a considerable amount of aid that goes to several countries, especially in South and Southeast Asia, remains undisclosed. This has been reiterated in the paper by Yoon Ah Oh. There is no information disaggregated by recipient country, year, sector, or flow type mentioned in China's Foreign Aid White Paper 2014. The only information that was available is that the total foreign aid was US$14 billion from 2010 to 2012 for 121 countries (Government of China, 2014; Oh, 2020). The author further adds that the Chinese Government's data problem is unlikely to be resolved in the immediate term. According to Yoon Ah Oh, within Asia, South Asia is the largest recipient of Chinese aid (39.8%), followed by Southeast Asia (30.1%) and Central Asia (17.8%). Countries in East Asia and the Pacific region (excluding Southeast Asia), represented mainly by Pacific island states, make up the smallest group, receiving 12.3%. Although South Asia ranks first as a sub-region, the largest country recipient is Cambodia, which received US$3.0 billion for the period (Oh, 2020). China's unbridled quest for domination over the maritime spaces, linking continental geographies to maritime port facilities including port cities is emblematic of its unique template for South Asia.

Most countries in these two sub-regions of Asia define their relationship with China as being driven by economic compulsions. These two sub-regions have become the epicenter of multi-billion dollar projects, which serves China's ambitions to become a resident power. For China, however, there is no dichotomy between the economic and the strategic; one must be tethered with the other! This is evident from the RCEP deal, clinched sans India, in November 2020. As Kurlantzick (2020) stated, China now presents itself as a leading protector of regional free trade, given that the United States under Trump pulled out of the Trans Pacific Partnership. Additionally, some of the United States' closest partners, like Japan and Australia, joined RCEP. This mega deal, without a doubt, helps China move the goalposts.

Chapter 10

China: A Futuristic Perspective

10.1 Introduction

The previous chapters underpin China's quest to enhance its economic footprint across South and Southeast Asia by increasing trade, achieving technological supremacy, and making territorial acquisitions. The BRI projects, aimed at realizing win–win economic benefits for both the home and host countries, have created new challenges for the host countries. Economic aspirations must be shielded and protected by security umbrellas, thus making these countries partners of the China-dominated security architecture in South and Southeast Asia.

It is also important to present a holistic understanding of China, its aspirations and ambitions, both at home and abroad, through the lens of its vision and how it is envisioned. To situate or confine China and Chineseness in any one region or dimension would not be plausible, and hence, the narrative must be all-encompassing. After all, China is engaged in the project of stitching together the disparate regions of the world.

Given that unattended and unanswered questions remain, this chapter would navigate through aspects as to how the pandemic has impacted the leadership of Xi Jinping and the Communist Party of China. Could there be any roadblocks to China's emergence as the leading power in the Asia-Pacific region and globally? What will be the fallout for global geopolitics?

Hence, the broad issues and perspectives articulated within China and its external engagement are elucidated here through:

- ➢ China's Prowess, Pathways, and Progress: Internal Dimensions
- ➢ China's External Engagement: Cooperation and Competition

10.2   China's Prowess, Pathways, and Progress: Internal Dimensions

Within this section, we briefly engage with the notion of Xi Jinping as an embodiment of Mao Zedong as well as some facets of China's contemporary challenges despite its growing economic potential.

It is important to interrogate at the outset: Is there some replication of Mao Zedong in Xi? On the occasion of the 2,565th Anniversary of Confucius's Birth, Xi Jinping underlined, "Reviewing the past generates new insight. Knowledge handed down from our predecessors has accumulated the significant understandings and experiences of the relations among man, society, and Nature".[1] A benign speech, igniting emotions of civilizational continuity, did not warrant a worldview where Xi Jinping is being seen as one who has overseen a suppression of dissent, engineered the effective demise of the "one country, two systems" arrangement with Hong Kong, filled concentration camps and detention centers with Uighurs and other Muslims in Xinjiang province, and led constitutional changes to remain President for life. US National Security Adviser Robert O'Brien stated, "Xi sees himself as Joseph Stalin's successor". Many others have compared Xi to Adolf Hitler, even coining the nickname "Xitler". But it is Mao — the People's Republic's founding father — to whom Xi bears a stellar resemblance.[2]

Even as Xi's tirades replete with allegations of those labeled as corrupt continue, he is being likened to Mao for his acquisition of absolute

---

[1] September 24, 2014, Xi Jinping's Speech in Commemoration of the 2,565th Anniversary of Confucius's Birth, by Xi Jinping http://library.chinausfocus.com/article-1534.html, accessed on November 28, 2020.

[2] Brahma Chellaney, China's five finger punch, https://www.project-syndicate.org/commentary/china-xi-resurrects-mao-five-fingers-strategy-by-brahma-chellaney-2020-07?barrier=accesspaylog, July 21, 2020, accessed on November 28, 2020.

power. Xi, as the son of one of Mao's revolutionary comrades, has a personality cult (Lovell, 2019, p. 421).

China's rise has created anxieties in other nations who worry that China's growing economic power and increasing military capabilities might threaten their interests (Hollihan and Zhang, 2016). China's altercation and heightened tensions (to coincide with the onset of the pandemic) with India since April 2020 seek to reign in what it views as a potential competitor. Shiv Shankar Menon, a former foreign secretary of India, states, "China often displays a form of great power autism, a lack of empathy or understanding of how others think and how they might react, to a greater degree than other powers do".[3]

The pandemic has witnessed China striving to salvage its reputation, from being viewed as the source of the outbreak of COVID-19, to being the benevolent power, which is not only capable of controlling the pandemic within its boundaries, but also providing aid and assistance, coupled with vaccine diplomacy to BRI partner countries.

Moreover, China's consistent applauding of its outreach and public diplomacy and propaganda has resulted in greater visibility of the Chinese largesse than that of other donors. Even as the virus continues its devastating path in Europe, the United States, and other countries, China is exploiting the crisis in an attempt to build long-lasting political weight. According to Pew Research, 2020, "relatively few think China has handled the pandemic well, although it still receives considerably better reviews than the US response".[4]

In this section, we navigate some economic aspects of BRI's sustainability, China's demographic and debt-related challenges, among others.

10.2.1 *BRI: Sustainability during and after the pandemic*

According to Ramabadran (2017), Xi continued to plug his favorite "new era" theme for economic rejuvenation, which includes raising China's per capita income to European standards by 2035, and for China to "achieve all its goals" by 2049, the centenary of the Party. Although China seems

---

[3] Shiv Shankar Menon, a special lecture on November 29, 2020.

[4] US Image Plummets Internationally as Most Say Country Has Handled Coronavirus Badly, https://www.pewresearch.org/global/2020/09/15/us-image-plummets-internationally-as-most-say-country-has-handled-coronavirus-badly/, accessed on December 1, 2020.

to be stuck in the "middle-income trap", with a per capita income of about US$8,000 in 2020, Xi continues to believe that his policies have worked. There are huge problems with bad debt and non-performing assets (NPA), given that China's growth has been propelled by the State. Ramabadran further adds, that as the tangible cost–benefit analyses of Xi's BRI are yet not visible, this appears to be more of a Maoist white elephant. With several small partner economies trapped under the pandemic's deleterious effect and the debt burden, it will not be long before this burden becomes insurmountable, even for Xi's China.

As discussed in the preceding chapters of our book, Ramabadran questions the risk assessment of Chinese loans and highlights the difficulties of assessing the costs, benefits, and successes. He even draws a parallel between the huge Soviet loans for unsustainable projects given to allies, with Xi's funding risky infrastructure investments in developing countries. The perils are that it could result in catastrophic maneuvers like the Cultural Revolution. In the final analysis, one can only hope, this wasn't Xi's "Swim in the Yangtze" moment.

Given that India was the only country in South Asia to stay away from joining China's One Belt, One Road initiative in 2013, the increasing BRI project profile in the rest of South Asia has contributed to increasing India–China tensions. Viewed from a developmental perspective, some projects have helped develop transport infrastructure and energy security, whereas others have raised concerns over "debt-trap diplomacy". The economic downturn associated with COVID-19 could add further complications to BRI projects' sustainability. Many of these projects might need redesigning and renegotiation (Gu *et al.*, 2019). At a glance, China appears to be steaming ahead. A microscopic view shows the country is going through its most difficult phase since the turn of the century.

10.2.2 *China's demographic challenge: The silver economy*

An OECD report has highlighted China's looming demographic challenge. If the current low fertility rate continues, China's population will turn to negative growth in 2027 and, by the end of the 21st century, it is predicted to decrease to 940 million (United Nations, 2010). Although China's population in 2100 will be as large as it was in 1975, the age structure will be fundamentally different. In 1975, people aged 0–14 accounted for 38.9% while those aged over 65 represented only 4.6%. However, when China's population declines to 940 million in 2100, the proportion of the below 14 age-group will drop to 15.9%, while 28.2%

would be aged over 65, which means a seriously aged population. To surmount this challenge, the three child policy was announced on May 31, 2021. Few predict that the demographic profile will be altered. Given China's low level of expenditure on social security and health infrastructure, an ageing society will throw up several additional challenges for employment (OECD Report, 2020).[5]

It is believed that this crisis could be the Achilles heel of China's stunning economic transformation over the last 40 years. The declining population could create an even greater burden on China's economy and its labor force. A decline in the working-age population would also result in a decline in consumer spending, directly impacting domestic growth impulses in China. China's demographic crisis has also been compared to Japan in the 1990s, which stalled Japan's economic progress. Some experts believe the population has already started shrinking. In a recent paper, Dr. Yi and Su Jian argue that the population contracted in 2018, the first year it has done so since the famines of 1961 and 1962, induced then by the Great Leap Forward, Mao's industrialization campaign. The researchers said inaccurate census estimates had obscured the actual population and fertility rates. "China's population has begun to decline and is rapidly aging. Its economic vitality will keep waning. It appears that the period of the demographic dividend has ended, labor costs have risen and the percentage of national savings to GDP has reduced" (Myers *et al.*, 2020).

China is also populating newly-created villages in a bid to grab land, especially in borderlands in South Asia, the latest being 150 hectares in Nepal and a Chinese village settlement created inside two kilometers of Bhutanese land (Gangadharan, 2020).

10.2.3 *China's internal reset: Dual circulation strategy*

Since May 14, 2020, the term Dual Circulation, first used in a meeting of the Communist Party Politburo, has been interpreted in various ways by other countries. According to some, it is a refocus on spurring local demand; others believe that the Chinese economy is moving toward self-sufficiency. The leadership proclaimed that the nation would "fully bring out the advantage of its large market and the potential of domestic demand

---

[5] Dr. Wenmeng Feng, OECD Report, Chapter 6, https://www.oecd.org/employment/leed/oecd-china-report-final.pdf, accessed on November 28, 2020.

to establish a new development pattern featuring domestic and international dual circulations that complement each other". It is believed that this new strategy could become a key priority in the Chinese Government's 14th five-year plan for 2021 to 2025.

According to Li Yiping, an economics professor at the Renmin University of China, the dual circulation development pattern, focused on the domestic economy, and aimed at integrating the domestic and global economies, is the right choice to not only give a much-needed boost to the Chinese economy but also revive the world economy. Frank Tang, a reporter for the *South China Morning Post*, stated that the new strategy is focused on competition and opening-up, including lowering barriers for foreign investors, a motivation to secure regional trade pacts and a supply-side structural reform of state-owned enterprises (Oya, 2020).

10.2.4 *Thousand talents program: Bringing world-class research teams to China*

It is believed that ever since the inception of China's Thousand Talents Plan in 2008, more than 10,000 overseas scientists have been invited to work in the country with highly lucrative offers. The Australian Strategic Policy Institute (ASPI) report, authored by analyst Alex Joske, notes that the overseas talent-recruitment stations have a directive broader than the Thousand Talents Plan. It starkly concludes CCP talent-recruitment programs facilitate "efforts which lack transparency; are associated with misconduct, intellectual property theft or espionage; contribute to the People's Liberation Army's modernization; and facilitate human rights abuses". What has created suspicion is that, these stations, "receive instructions to target individuals with access to particular technologies". The report notes that cases of economic espionage have been critically linked to the recruitment program. Interestingly, this report has been made public at a time of growing scrutiny of CCP involvement in cultivating and recruiting scientists and technologists from foreign countries, often through quasi-legal or even downright illegal means. The case of US professor Charles Lieber and the suicide of Zhang Shoucheng shook both the physics community as well as Silicon Valley. Excessive payments made through this program to gain access to technology secrets have come to light in the USA. That does not imply that other countries are not vulnerable (Rej, 2020).

In terms of taking strides in Artificial Intelligence, in which China is heavily invested, a study by Macro Polo states that China still lags significantly behind the US. While 29 percent of global A.I. researchers hail from China, only 11% work in China. On the other hand, 59% of A.I. researchers work in the US. With the "thousand talents program" and other similar initiatives, China aims to bridge this gap. Despite setbacks due to COVID-19 and the trade war with the US, China has persisted to develop chip manufacturing capabilities. In September 2020, China included the third-generation semiconductor industry into China's upcoming 14th Five-Year Plan (2021–2025). Several challenges limit China's ambitions to become self-sufficient in semiconductor design and manufacturing; first, the pandemic has adversely effected several industries including semiconductor manufacturing, and second, the semiconductor industry in China is generations behind the top manufacturers in the field (Pardhi, 2020).

10.2.5 *China's money matters*

A report by *The Economist*, May 7, 2020,[6] states clearly that China's Big Four Banks, viz. Bank of China, Industrial and Commercial Bank of China (ICBC), China Construction Bank, and Agricultural Bank of China, now feature among the 30 "global systemically important banks" by the Financial Stability Board. With US$40 trillion in assets, these banks that were at the third position in 2008, now surpass the assets of both America and the Euro area. However, skeptics argue that many of these are dud loans and are being reined in by the State, which owns them. Undoubtedly, Chinese banks have been engaged by their home market, where they have a 98% share.

The trend is however changing. The banks are following their clients in the industry and, given the stagnation in the home market, are inclined to move to more international operations in the future. Moreover, they fund the infrastructure under BRI projects in foreign locations. In fact, in 2020, Chinese banks supplied nearly two-thirds of all cross-border lending within emerging markets, especially within Asia and Africa. Although

---

[6]As China goes global, its banks are coming out, too, https://www.economist.com/special-report/2020/05/07/as-china-goes-global-its-banks-are-coming-out-too, accessed on December 3, 2020.

the unofficial sums are huge but unknown, it is believed that Chinese banks have lent nearly US$600 billion to 820 official BRI projects since 2013. The Big Four are unstoppable, with a total of 618 branches outside the mainland, entering into several kinds of facilities for international settlements.

For example, in January 2019, the Central Bank of Myanmar (CBM) announced allowing the Chinese Yuan as the settlement currency for international payments and transfers, aiming to develop international payment and settlement and border trade. How China is internationalizing the Renminbi through various arrangements is well known and has been written about in our earlier chapters.[7]

However, there are limits on the future of the internationalization of the Renminbi, a move toward which China embarked on soon after the 2008 global financial crisis; the Xi regime has strengthened rather than loosened capital controls.

According to Forbes senior contributor, Rapoza (2020), "The dollar is the gold standard. If the Euro couldn't overtake it, the Chinese Renminbi (RMB) sure won't. Add to the fact that many of the core economies are angry with China for lack of transparency regarding the new SARS coronavirus and it is even less likely that its key trading partners settle trade in the local currency". According to the monthly RMB Tracker by SWIFT, the global financial messaging services provider for cross-country transactions, China's currency accounted for a mere 1.85% of global transactions.[8]

Controls on outward flows of capital have also resulted from the uncertainty of domestic policies and the fear of being castigated under the anti-corruption campaign. In this fear-charged atmosphere, there is a penchant among wealthy Chinese families to move their money out of China's borders. Additionally, rising levels of debt and the slowing of the formerly rapid growth on which much lending was premised have created risks for banks. They make tightened financial controls a needed prudential measure. According to William Overholt, this implies that the renminbi's aspirations to become a top international currency are best

[7] Chinese bank promotes RMB financial express services in Myanmar, https://en.imsilk road.com/p/308567.html, September 26, 2019, accessed on November 28, 2020.
[8] China Is Nowhere Near Replacing the Dollar, https://www.forbes.com/sites/kenrapoza/2020/04/23/china-is-nowhere-near-replacing-the-dollar/?sh=6d1fc50b4dfdcal, yuan post-pandemic. April 23, 2020, accessed on November 30, 2020.

deferred for many years. He also adds that although Beijing hopes that the Belt and Road Initiative will facilitate the emergence of a China-centred blockchain settlement system that would fulfill many of the aspirations associated with renminbi internationalization, it is early to speculate about how this will evolve (Overholt, 2020).

China's alarming debt levels will also have implications for foreign investors. According to Bloomberg, Chinese companies have been piling on debt for at least a decade, which ensured that China's economy kept rising, but at a cost. The corporate debt-to-GDP ratio surged to a record 160% at the end of 2017, from 101% ten years earlier. A particular goal for Xi Jinping has been to curb China's US$10 trillion ecosystems of shadow banking (*shadow banks are financial institutions that act like banks, are not supervised like banks, and were one of the reasons for the 2008 financial crisis*). Hence, while Chinese leaders back bankruptcies for zombie firms, creditors are subject to strong-arm tactics from local governments. There is also a high risk for lenders in China, especially in the energy sector, which is considered the riskiest for investors (Zhu *et al.*, 2020).

10.2.6 *China's private sector: Reined in*

According to experts, the postponement of the Ant Group's IPO, scheduled for early November 2020, is a serious muscle flex by Chinese President Xi Jinping over Ant's founder, Jack Ma, China's second-wealthiest man. The suspension came soon after Ma made a speech at odds with the Chinese Communist Party's handling of the economy. As the fallout continues, investors are eyeing what Ant's fate means for international businesses in China's authoritarian landscape.

To briefly explain, Ant is the financial arm e-commerce giant Alibaba had begun in 2004 as the site's way to process payments. Ant's Alipay app now has more than 730 million monthly users in China who use it to pay bills, shop, and send money to friends. Ant had almost US$3 trillion in orders for its dual listing in Hong Kong and Shanghai and the IPO was viewed as the world's biggest public share sale. However, it was Jack Ma's overshooting the boundaries of China's freedom of speech when he, at the Bund conference in Shanghai on October 24, 2020, lamented that the world "only focuses on risk control, not on development, and rarely do they consider opportunities for young people and developing countries". Ma further added that financial regulators worked as a club for the elderly, which is not good for "youth" economies like China's. Ma's stake in Alibaba Group Holding, which owns a major share of Ant, fell about US$3 billion after the IPO was postponed. China's government seems to be sending a clear signal that it is not afraid to step in and cancel the party when a private company does not play by its rules. The implication is that it could deter investors who are keen to get in on the world's second-largest economy — but are not eager to toe the Communist Party line (Forde, 2020). Experts believe that with rising regulations, the Ant IPO may not again be listed till 2022. The Shanghai Gang, comprised of CCP's rebellious members who rose to prominence because of their association with Jiang Zemin while he was in Shanghai, are considered a serious threat to Xi Jinping. Hence, Jack Ma's fortunes have been clipped. "Between the rules for Ant and the $2.8 billion fine for Alibaba, the golden days are over for China's big tech firms", said Mark Tanner, founder of Shanghai-based China Skinny. "Even those who haven't been targeted to the same extreme will be toning down their expansion strategies and adapting many elements of their business to the new bridled environment".[9]

10.2.7 *China's economic miracle: Are there constraints to future growth?*

When in 1978, China's reform and opening-up began, led by Deng Xiaoping, China posted an average annual real GDP growth rate of 9.8% between 1978 and 2008. Its exports posted an annual increase of 16% on average between 1979 and 2001, and an annual growth of 27% on average between 2002 and 2008, making the country the world's top exporter.

The national savings rate increased to over 30% of GDP in the 1980s, over 40% in the 1990s, and over 50% around 2010, encouraging active investment and, at the same time, creating a huge current account surplus. Despite China's impressive growth rates, the prerequisites for growth are disappearing. The US–China trade dispute shows that it has become difficult for Beijing to maintain high growth, given its excessive dependence on exports. China's GDP per capita stands at less than US$10,000, still low compared with US$60,000 for the US and US$40,000 for Japan.

---

[9] https://www.bloomberg.com/news/articles/2021-04-13/jack-ma-s-double-whammy-marks-the-end-of-china-tech-s-golden-age, accessed on April 16, 2021.

China's rapidly aging population risks growing old before becoming rich. Since the nation cannot expect its population to grow, the only other option would be to increase its productivity. However, according to one estimate, China's total factor productivity growth rate fell from 6.1% between 1996 and 2004 to 2.5% between 2005 and 2015.

The world has applauded China for having pulled more than 800 million people out of poverty in only three decades, creating its miracle. However, high growth levels have also created new challenges including widening income inequality, a looming environmental catastrophe, and the social disruption caused by the uprooting of millions of rural immigrants now taking up residence in the expanding megacities.

China's education system has also achieved international standards. A total of 12 Chinese academic institutions have been included in the global top 100 of Quacquarelli Symonds (Q.S.). World University Rankings 2020, by Q.S. China has also made significant new investments in higher education even as it aspires to create Chinese Silicon Valleys (Xinhua, 2019).

Ever since China became a member of the WTO in December 2011, it has enjoyed huge trade surpluses and bankrolls other nations through foreign bonds. China has also moved up in the manufacturing supply chain, with China's manufacturing capabilities extending from cars, to bullet trains, and space transport vehicles. The private sector in China, though closely regulated, has extended its tentacles from acquiring land in Africa, large overseas companies, office towers and apartment complexes in New York, London, as well as making major acquisitions in the US media industries, including film studios and even theater chains. According to the authors of a World Bank Policy Paper, 2020, the allocation of a larger share of credit and investment to infrastructure and housing led to lower returns to capital, a rapid buildup in debt, and higher risks to growth. China's growth potential remains high, but its long-term growth prospects depend on reversing the recent decline in total factor productivity growth (Brandt, 2020).

10.3 China's External Engagement: Cooperation and Competition

Even as the early warning bells of the pandemic rang in China in November 2019, the leadership was in a state of denial for almost two months, till when it became impossible to negate its deleterious effects. Adopting authoritarian style lockdowns, China projected itself as being "in siege" by the global community, questioned and castigated for unleashing the pandemic. It was then that young Chinese diplomats posted in Europe, Australia, and elsewhere transformed into "wolf warriors" facilitating a narrative of China's superior governance model in disease control. These warriors also engaged themselves in vigorously defending their country's innocence through aid diplomacy to buy goodwill, diffuse charges of responsibility, and manipulate the prospects for an international investigation.

According to Mearsheimer, offensive realism is when states seek to maintain their survival (their territorial integrity and domestic autonomy) above all other goals. The pursuit of regional and global hegemony among all great powers gives rise to constant security competition with the potential for war. This is the so-called "Tragedy of Great Power Politics": security-seeking states forced to engage in conflict to ensure their security (Snyder, 2002).

Concurrently, from April/May 2020, while individuals were defending verbal and written tirades against the CCP, the Chinese PLA and PLA Navy (PLAN) flexed their muscles from the Himalayan border with India to the South China Sea.

10.3.1 *Collective response of big powers: Will China change?*

The China challenge was met by big powers' moves to strengthen security alliances among themselves; through the Quad alliance partners including USA, Japan, Australia, and India and the US-led vision of an Indo-Pacific alliance (Bitas, 2020). Questions are being raised regarding the capability of the Quad to neutralize the China threat in the Indian Ocean and the South China Sea, as the ultimate vision of China is to ensure that the United States turns its gaze away from China's backyard. Moreover, Japan's relations with China are being reset by its new Prime Minister Yoshihide Suga. For Australia, too, its economic dependence on China is well known. The Biden administration too is expected to move toward cautious engagement with China, even as Trumpism will continue in terms of making China "play by international rules". A strong and growing economic and military bilateral relationship between India and the US could concern China (Fickling, 2020). Concurrently, China–US relations will have their fallout for all economies.

Quad is emerging as a normative bulwark against China; hence, the Quad countries joining the Malabar Exercises in November 2020 has been a tactical move. The 24th edition of the naval Malabar Exercise has been held in two phases in November 2020. Phase 1 of the Exercise Malabar 20 involved the participation by Indian Navy (IN), United States Navy (USN), Japan Maritime Self Defence Force (JMSDF), and Royal Australian Navy (RAN); this commenced off Visakhapatnam in the Bay of Bengal from 03 to November 6, 2020. Phase 2 of Malabar 20 has been conducted in the Arabian Sea in mid-November 2020.

Dave Makichuk, quoting *Global Times*, citing China's response to the exercises, said the action was "an ill-intentioned attempt to corner China [and] is a hollow bluff … India's irrationality or US interference will not disrupt China".[10]

Hence, it is important to interrogate: Will China change? The answer is "highly unlikely". According to Yun Sun, with the heightened great power competition and a heightened sense of vulnerability, China is likely to grow even more defensive and counterattack any country, any media, or any individual critical of China's behavior and performance in the pandemic. It is also a war of competing narratives, competing for political systems, and a war of competing ideologies (Sun, 2020).

10.3.2 *US — China rivalry: The way forward*

Elizabeth C. Economy explains the trajectory of US–China competition and rivalry through three inflection points. According to her, these were the 2008 financial crisis, the advent of Xi Jinping in 2012, and the entry of Mr. Trump as the President of the United States in 2017. In her book *The Third Revolution* (2018), she writes, China "embraces globalization insofar as it controls the flow of ideas, as well as human and financial capital". Beijing can sustain its claim to be an anchor of globalization because the US is still seen as the chief motor of an open world. It would find itself in an exceedingly uncomfortable position if Washington was to experience a precipitous, absolute decline or institutionalize an "America First" foreign policy. Economy notes that Trump's America "may well be

---

[10] Malabar 2020: A show of force on China's doorstep, https://asiatimes.com/2020/11/malabar-2020-a-show-of-force-on-chinas-doorstep/, November 4, 2020, accessed on November 29, 2020.

taking a step back from its willingness to lead the way on addressing the world's many challenges, but China is not prepared to replace it" (Economy, 2018).

Global leadership requires a willingness to subordinate one's narrow interests for the benefit of the larger community. Contrary to Western predictions, though, growing engagement with the world has not softened its illiberal tendencies; on the contrary, they have grown considerably more pronounced under Xi. While China underlines the imperatives of economic reforms and free trade, its actions at home betray a regression from incremental marketization to statist dominance: China's state sector "continues to incur ever-higher levels of debt, consume valuable credit, and provide few new jobs", and the role of State-owned enterprises in "core sectors of the economy" has grown. This trajectory poses a dilemma for China's leaders. On the one hand, "the inefficiencies generated by non-market activity" "contribute to their political power" and "afford them the luxury of longer-term strategic investments". Though, those same inefficiencies run counter to China's professed desire for a more open global economy.

This tension — between China's growing role in globalization and its increasingly illiberal turn — also makes it a more complex strategic challenge for the US than the Soviet Union. While China is an increasingly formidable competitor in several areas, it remains an essential partner in addressing issues ranging from macroeconomic instability, cybersecurity, to climate change.

According to Ashley Tellis (2020), the US under Trump had changed its stance from viewing China as a strategic partner to a strategic competitor. The administration has challenged China in five key areas: control over the Indo-Pacific rimland, trade and the economy, China's quest for alternative technical standards, the pursuit of technological dominance, and Chinese military advancement. However, this contestation is complex due to both the close economic relationship between the US and China and the interconnectedness of global trade networks. Nonetheless, states are attempting to exploit the growing US–China competition for their benefit, avoid being penalized by it, or use each rival to protect their national interests. Tellis (2020, p. 24) argues that as Trump was convinced that the multilateral trading system was flawed; he even described the WTO as a "disaster", refused to support the appointment of new members to its appellate body, and chided the body as being "very unfair" to the United States. His conviction also resulted in pulling the United States out of the TPP and renegotiated the North American Free Trade Agreement. This created a vacuum, allowing China to respond with alacrity, to increase its influence over multilateral institutions.

With a divided mandate, given that 73 million people voted for Trump in the 2020 elections, the China challenge may not be what the Biden administration could surmount. China's vision of victory compels it to continue on its single point agenda of ascending to the number one global power. With growing economic muscle and military influence, there may be more countries gravitating toward it. It's pragmatism in wooing weak, fragile polities with a tangible matrix of offerings, is palpable in this part of the world.

With the signing of the RCEP in November 2020, China demonstrated its prowess and clinched the 15 country Economic Partnership. It is believed that China's dual circulation policy is also aimed to counter US trade protectionism and technology blockade, even as it seeks to set up a global economic and technological innovation center, rivaling that of the US. The inner circulation policy will strengthen the domestic capabilities, while at the same time channelizing initiatives meant to forge economic partnerships with Belt and Road countries. According to Shin Oya, the motivation for China's rush to adopt the dual circulation strategy is that the nation is being threatened by Washington's attempt to stop the flow of technology to Beijing, the US restricting activities of Chinese firms, and Western countries rethinking their supply chains (Oya, 2020).

There is a possibility that experts' views on the dual circulation strategy differ even in China. As the US–China conflict escalates, there is a risk, according to some, that China's focus on domestic demand could result in it striving to completely replace imports in a bid to become self-sufficient.

The strategy is a framework that could lead to a new growth model that does not depend excessively on exports or investments, based on improved productivity by resolving issues the Chinese economy encounters, including reform of State-owned enterprises and financial sector liberalization. There are voices within the US, with some urging the country to completely decouple from China, while others calling for partial disengagement in tech fields.

What are the costs of decoupling? A 2020 report by BCG highlights that, given the interdependencies in trade between the two countries, the stakes for both the United States and China are very high.

In fact, these are higher for the United States. US companies have around US$400 billion of revenue at risk in China, representing 5% of their total revenues. Although this appears relatively low, this implies a loss of almost 15% of market capitalization, or about US$2.5 trillion in value. There are seven major US industrial sectors — consumer electronics, motor vehicles and parts, aerospace, medical supplies, medical equipment, machinery, and enterprise hardware, which derive 7% to 16% of their global revenue from China. Overall, Chinese firms have three to five times less revenue exposure to the US market; only the consumer electronics, enterprise electronics, and machinery sectors rely on the US for at least 7% of revenue.

Moreover, the share of US industrial sectors that would find it hard to replace China as a finished- and intermediate-goods supplier is larger than the share of Chinese sectors that would find it hard to replace US suppliers. And more than half of the 16 US manufacturing sectors studied by the authors of the BCG study were engineering-intensive ones such as aerospace and telecom equipment that rely on China for critical components or raw materials. Except for consumer electronics and telecom equipment, Chinese industries are more self-sufficient in critical inputs (Varadarajan *et al.*, 2020).

Hence, to what extent the decoupling would take place and alternate suppliers would emerge is not easy to assess at this stage. What is certain is that in the post-pandemic phase, new investments into China would decline.

Despite confronting formidable challenges at home and abroad, Xi's China has proven masterful at conveying an aura of inexorability around its resurgence — and, it appears, at unnerving the US.

According to Pant and Karpiani, the Biden administration, with an Obama era team, could help the world oversee America's resurgence to a position of strength from which to engage China.[11]

Moreover, there is a clear indication that the United States will re-engage in United Nations agencies and multilateral institutions, ensuring that it supports the global climate and health agenda, among others.

---

[11] Seasoned faces who could aid the return of America, https://www.thehindu.com/opinion/lead/seasoned-faces-who-could-aid-the-return-of-america/article33207274.ece, November 30, 2020, accessed on November 30, 2020.

10.3.3 *The tryst with technology*

Huawei is currently on a path to become the world's biggest 5G mobile network equipment provider, but it is by no means traveling that path alone. Huawei owes its rise to Chinese industrial policies that have suppressed global competition for nearly two decades.

A report by Melanie Hart and Jordan Link, October 14, 2020,[12] points clearly to the advantages that Huawei's 5G network has in terms of being highly competitive. US intelligence agencies fear that if global networks run on Huawei equipment, Beijing could use that equipment to gather intelligence, steal trade secrets, track down and punish its critics, and potentially bring down networks to incapacitate other nations in times of crisis. The Trump administration tried to convince other nations that the manifold risks warrant banning Huawei from their 5G networks. A few countries in Europe, including Britain, France, and Slovenia, have followed the United States to restrict investments by Huawei, the Chinese telecommunications giant, while others are leaving open the possibility pushed to the background. However, there is no denying that China has established itself in this regard, due to two factors. First, the mobile network equipment market is an oligopoly with just four major vendors to choose from — none of which is a US company. Second, Beijing deploys powerful industrial policies to make Huawei equipment cheaper to deploy than the three alternatives.

For the telecom companies making network equipment purchases — and the national governments who regulate them — the security risks associated with Huawei equipment are theoretical and hard to quantify. But the cost associated with choosing an alternative vendor (Ericsson, Nokia, or Samsung) and forgoing the lucrative incentives Beijing offers to Huawei's customers are immediate and measurable. Thus far, the United States has largely overlooked the market-distorting industrial policies that Beijing uses to make Huawei a global front-runner. This must change. If the United States can successfully counter those policies to make this market more competitive, that will make the security side of the 5G challenge much easier to solve.

---

[12] There is a Solution to the Huawei Challenge, https://ap-stage.devprogress.org/issues/security/reports/2020/10/14/491476/solution-huawei-challenge/, accessed on November 28, 2020.

Beijing has been able to expand its Huawei network with inexpensive smartphones by providing direct and indirect subsidies, which reduce Huawei's operational costs, and allow it to price its products well below prices set by its competitors. The banks provide financing on easy terms, thereby making Huawei equipment cheaper to deploy at any price. Additionally, Chinese officials interfere in the International Telecommunication Union (ITU) standardization process to increase Huawei's share of the emerging global 5G standard, making Huawei equipment even harder to avoid and setting it up to extend its dominance into 6G and beyond. Together, they fuel Huawei's takeover of the global telecom market and make it difficult for the United States to convince other nations to choose a more secure option.[13]

10.3.4 *Global governance: China secures seats on many high tables*

According to Elizabeth Economy, China is concurrently "a threat to the underlying principles of globalization" and "a leading pillar of the global-ized world". Its attitude toward the postwar order, meanwhile, is selec-tively revisionist: "China is using its newfound status to shape regional and global institutions ... in some cases supporting traditional norms, while in others supplanting them". Economy notes that Beijing decided to establish the AIIB in part because of its "frustration with the inability of the international community ... to reform pre-existing international eco-nomic institutions ... to reflect more accurately China's standing in the global economy". That frustration manifests a desire to participate in the Bretton Woods institutions, not upend them.

As China's economy grew, so did its global ambitions of occupying seats at the United Nations institutional architecture's high tables. It did so not only by taking on a bigger role in institutions, but also by adver-tising its increasing influence, embarking on its mega BRI networks, creating its institutions like the AIIB, and circumventing rules to suit itself.

---

[13] There Is a Solution to the Huawei Challenge, https://ap-stage.devprogress.org/issues/security/reports/2020/10/14/491476/solution-huawei-challenge/, accessed on November 28, 2020.

Over the past several years, Beijing has systematically positioned Chinese nationals at the head of a wide range of United Nations agencies. In 2018, Mr. Zhao Houlin continued his second term as the International Telecommunication Union secretary general. He has been instrumental in helping Huawei expand its network as a 5G telecommunications equipment vendor in various countries. Chinese officials also hold key positions in the United Nations's Department of Economic and Social Affairs and the International Civil Aviation Organization.

In 2019, in the United Nations Environment Program, China launched the Belt and Road Initiative International Green Development Coalition, which develops standards and best practices around environmental protections to "ensure that the Belt and Road brings long-term green and sustainable development to all concerned countries". This is a well-thought-out strategy, since Belt and Road projects have often been criticized for their complete obscuring of environmental protections. More broadly, China has co-opted the United Nations's Sustainable Development Goals in its effort to help ensure the realization of these goals in BRI partner countries. China also collaborated with Russia to institutionalize international norms around surveillance and censorship. This also resulted in the passage of a joint United Nations cybercrime resolution in November 2019, which can equip and embolden authoritarian governments with greater authority to repress and censor political dissent online.[14]

Thus, China's advances are evident at the United Nations, where Chinese nationals now head four of 15 United Nations specialized agencies, compared with America's one. America has started to push back. It stopped China from claiming the leadership of a fifth agency, the World Intellectual Property Organization — the job went to a candidate from Singapore. But as America withdraws from bodies such as the World Health Organization, it gives China a chance to exert yet more influence (*The Economist*, 2020, p. 49).[15]

To be fair, it is important to recognize that China has extended support for the Catastrophe Containment and Relief Trust, which allows the IMF

---

[14] It's Not Just the WHO: How China Is Moving on the Whole United Nations, https://www.politico.com/news/magazine/2020/04/15/its-not-just-the-who-how-china-is-moving-on-the-whole-un-189029, Accessed on December 1.

[15] Xi's new economy. Don't underestimate it, https://www.economist.com/weeklyedition/2020-08-15, accessed on November 28, 2020.

to provide debt forgiveness for its poorest members hit by the crisis. China has also pledged to the G20 to provide debt relief for low-income countries. While this does underline the fact that China views itself as a responsible power, it reiterates its desire to be recognized as a benefactor by the low-income countries.

The IMF estimates that over two years, the world economy will suffer a dramatic loss of more than US$12 trillion. For global recovery, China's growth must be a catalyst even as its negative 6.8% real GDP growth in the first quarter transformed to positive 3.2% in the second quarter of 2020 (Geoffrey Okamoto, IMF First Deputy Managing Director Forum on National Affairs, Counsellors' Office of the State Council, September 24, 2020).[16]

10.4 Conclusion

China's deepening economic links with its continental and maritime neighbors in Asia will steam ahead if the US does not re-engage Asia with a more pragmatic economic blueprint. However, the "America First" impulse is part of the domestic political discourse across both parties. It is unclear how the Biden Presidency would reconcile renewing the pandemic-stressed US economy and simultaneously engaging Asia by offering superior terms to states than what China could. In essence, this is what the next great game will be about (Singh, 2020).

The global community should be on alert over China's actions violating international law regarding various issues including the South China Sea, the Senkaku Islands, Hong Kong, Taiwan, and the Xinjiang Uighur Autonomous Region. It is imperative to conduct partial disengagement to a certain extent in areas like technology to protect a free society. However, Oya cautions, in the event that Western countries show excessive decoupling moves toward China to maintain their employment or mercantilist intentions, China could implement the dual circulation strategy to reduce exchanges with foreign countries (Oya, 2020).

China's consistent outreach to countries in South and Southeast Asia, as has been discussed in the previous chapters, has comprised of aid, investment, flows of goods. This implies an ever-increasing Chinese

---

[16] Securing China's post-pandemic Recovery: Deepening Reforms and Pursuing Rebalancing, https://www.imf.org/en/News/Articles/2020/09/24/sp092420-securing-china-s-post-pandemic-recovery. Accessed on November 28, 2020.

footprint in terms of signature infrastructure, presence of Chinese work-force, part ownership of ports, land, assets, and enterprises, and the construction of dams on the Mekong and Brahmaputra. What has been truly amazing is the speed with which the economic footprint has per-meated the landscape and maritime space, from the South China Sea to the Indian Ocean and beyond. Concerning the four countries' case stud-ies discussed in this book, while Myanmar and Thailand seek to main-tain some elements of hedging and balancing in their economic engagement and foreign policy, Sri Lanka and Pakistan are now com-pletely under China's sway. Thailand, due to its strategic nodal location, and Myanmar as it moves toward democratization, do exhibit agency in pushing back Chinese investment. However, in Pakistan, the scope for balancing has been completely forfeited in favor of China. As Siegfried O Wolf shared with the author on August 5, 2020, Gwadar might trans-form into a high security compound, which will help China with mili-tary options in the Persian Gulf and the Indian Ocean. With Iran, it depends on how far it can use Iranian ports. More and more security forces have been built up in Baluchistan, with more and more silencing of journalists and activists — but realpolitik states that this cannot go on forever; this also depends on how Baluch militants cooperate and if Pakistan forces can quash the Baluchs.[17]

According to Bilahari Kausikan, "the current political situation in Indonesia, Malaysia, and Thailand is already tenuous. Myanmar and the Philippines" future political and policy trajectories, which face elections this year and 2022, respectively, are uncertain, and how Cambodia will evolve after Hun Sen is anyone's guess. The only ASEAN members where basic political continuity can be assumed with some confidence are Myanmar, Brunei, Singapore, Laos, and Vietnam. This is not a situation conducive to great optimism about the region's ability to optimize the potential opportunities (Kausikan, 2020).

Given the zero tolerance to criticism against the CCP leadership, sev-eral officials were purged on the grounds of corruption, etc. In the Ant Initial Public Offering case, the CCP made it crystal clear: No private company, even if it is Jack Ma, the second richest man in China, can be

---

[17] Siegfried O Wolf, in response to a question by Dr. Reena Marwah, in a webinar orga-nized by Association of Asia Scholars, on August 5, 2020.

critical of it. This rising insecurity, marked by authoritarianism and stifling of voices, reflects cracks within the Party structure.

China's growing assertiveness which has been referred to earlier, is also spilling over in its external engagement, as in the case of Australia. Even as the second and third waves of the pandemic in 2021 batters economies, and the theory of the leak from the Wuhan laboratory gains traction, is the dragon too ominous to be investigated?

In conclusion, it can be inferred that the Chinese economic power-house marches on, stringing perilous polities through a veneer of capa-bility-induced projects, laced with promises of win–win co-option. It has secured for itself strategic assets, including maritime facilities, ports, cities, connectivity and energy ventures, thereby seeping into every pore of the host country's commercial and political fabric. Nowhere is this more evident than in the porous borders of South Asia. It occupies land in Nepal, Bhutan, and India, bringing in its geographical terrain an all-encompassing vision of China's historical right. China's successful overtures in Sri Lanka through cooperation and gradual pen-etration hold the potential of converting the island nation into a geo-political battleground.

The flip side is that China is also dependent on the rest of the world for commodities, energy, and markets; and, is entangled in disputes all along with her eastern, southern, and south-eastern periphery (but not the north!). Her ethnic nationalism and authoritarianism are both a strength and a weakness. The Party is anchoring its future on nationalism as an important source of legitimacy and unity, having come to one key realiza-tion: economic growth cannot forever remain the source of its legitimacy (Krishnan, 2020).

As Elizabeth Economy asserts, China is both a pillar of the globalized world and a threat to the process of globalization. Hence, for the United States to compete with a belligerent China on the latter's terms is certainly a zero-sum game. In the long run, both the USA and Europe, with like-minded partners, must engage in harnessing China's resurgence while tempering its revisionism.

According to India's Minister of External Affairs, Jaishankar, in his book *The India Way* (2020), "The really uncharted territory that US–China frictions will take us into is that of coping with parallel universes. They may have existed before, most recently globalized Cold War. But not with the interdependence and interpenetration of the globalised era. As a result, divergent choices and competing alternatives will be based on partially shared foundations. This dilemma will be evident in a growing number of domains, from technology, commerce, and finance to connectivity, institutions, and activities". The big powers, he adds, will have to struggle with the dichotomy of such parallel existence. Countries' choices and leanings will be tested, even as they seek to maintain independent foreign policies. Even if ties between China and the West take on a more adversarial character, it is difficult to return to a strongly bipolar world. In his opinion, the landscape has now changed irreversibly. Other countries are steadily growing, through demographic dividends and technological capabilities. In his words, "We see forces at play that reflect the relative primacy of local equations when the global construct is less overbearing. The reality is that the US may have weakened, but China's rise is still far from maturing. And together, the two processes have freed up room for others".

According to John Ikenberry, "Can China's next moves be predicted?". China does not have a model that the rest of the world finds appealing, nor does it have alternative ideas for world order. The values, interests, and mutual vulnerabilities that drove the rise and spread of liberal internationalism are still alive. Crises and transformations in liberal internationalism have marked their presence over several decades of resilience. The world order is transforming and China alone is not responsible (Ikenberry, 2018).

The writing on the wall is lucid: China has won, and earlier than expected! The 2008 global financial crisis, Xiism, Trump's Presidency, and the Pandemic have together catapulted China's global ambitions to secure the number one position sooner than 2049; this could be in 2035 or earlier!

References

Abeyagoonasekera, A. (2019). *Sri Lanka at Crossroads: Geopolitical Challenges and National Interests*. World Scientific, Singapore.

Abi-Habib, M. (2018). How China Got Sri Lanka to Cough Up a Port, *New York Times*, June 25 2018, https://www.nytimes.com/2018/06/25/world/asia/china-Sri-Lanka-port.html, accessed on February 3 2020.

Afzal, M. (2020). https://www.brookings.edu/wp-content/uploads/2020/06/FP_20200615_china_pakistan_afzal_v2.pdf, accessed on November 19, 2020.

Ahmed, I. (2012). Regionalism in South Asia: A conceptual note. *Millennial Asia*, 3(1), 95–103.

AidData (2019). China's Public Diplomacy Dashboard Dataset, Version 1.0. Retrieved from http://china-dashboard.aiddata.org.

Ali, S. M. (2019). *Cold war in the High Himalayas: The USA, China and South Asia in the 1950s*. Routledge, United Kingdom.

Amiti, M. and Freund, C. (2008). *The Anatomy of China's Export Growth*. The World Bank.

APSI report (2020). Pentagon Releases Annual China Military Power Report. https://thediplomat.com/2020/09/pentagon-releases-annual-china-military-power-report/, accessed September 10, 2020.

Asia Maritime Transparency Initiative (2018). China's Reach Has Grown; So Should the Island Chains, https://amti.csis.org/chinas-reachgrown-island-chains/, accessed on August 2020.

Asian Survey (2020). 60: 2 Downloaded from http://online.ucpress.edu/as/article-pdf/60/2/323/385451/as.2020.60.2.323.pdf by guest on July 18, 2020.

Aslam, M. (2011). Impact of ASEAN-China free trade area agreement on ASEAN's manufacturing industry.

Bagchi, I. (2020). August 14, 2020, China angry with Pak over poor security for it is CPEC workers. Read more at http://timesofindia.indiatimes.com/articles how/77536341.cms?utm_source=contentofinterest&utm_medium=text&utm_campaign=cppst.

Baker, C. and Pasuk, P. (2017). A History of Ayutthaya. Cambridge University Press, United Kingdom.

Balachandran, P. K. (2018). https://www.thecitizen.in/index.php/en/NewsDetail/index/6/14251/Chinas-Soft-Power-Instruments-Funded-Confucius-Institutes-Change-Goals-To-Suit-Local-Needs--- | July 1, 2018, accessed on July 21, 2020.

Bartholomew, C., Cleveland, R., Goodwin, H. C. P., Mcdevitt, M. A., Kamphausen, R., Talent, H. J. M., ... and Lewis, K. (2019). US-China economic and security review commission.

Barua, S. (2020). China in Myanmar: An Incremental Foothold over a geostrategic hinge point, https://niice.org.np/archives/5293, accessed on October 10, 2020.

Barua, S. (2020a). The New 'New' in Myanmar-China Relationship, https://niice.org.np/archives/3147, accessed on October 10, 2020.

Basil, C. Bitas*, (2020). ASEAN amid China's Vision of the Belt and Road and the US Strategy for the Indo-Pacific: Building a strategic bridge to two great power initiatives.

Basu, K. (2013). Does economic theory inform government policy? *Millennial Asia*, 4(1), 27–39.

Bhatia, R. (2020). Myanmar's growing dependence on China, https://www.thehindu.com/opinion/op-ed/myanmars-growing-dependence-on-china/article30627576.ece, accessed on October 17, 2020.

Bhattacharya, A. (2016). Conceptualizing the Silk Road initiative in China's periphery policy. *East Asia*, 33(4), 309–328.

Bhattacharyay, B. N. (2010). Financing Asia's infrastructure: Modes of development and integration of Asian financial markets. *ADBI Working Paper No. 229*, available at SSRN: https://ssrn.com/abstract=1654255 or HYPERLINK "https://dx.doi.org/10.2139/ssrn.1654255" http://dx.doi.org/10.2139/ssrn.1654255.

Bloom, N., Draca, M., and Van Reenen, J. (2009). Did trade induce technical change? The impact of Chinese imports on innovation and information technology. *CEP Discussion Papers*, (1000).

Bloom, N., Draca, M., and Van Reenen, J. (2016). Did trade induce technical change? The impact of Chinese imports on innovation, I.T. and productivity. *The Review of Economic Studies*, 83(1), 87–117.

Blum, R., Dreher, A., Fuchs, A., Parks, B., Strange, A., and Tierney, M. (2018). Connective financing: Chinese infrastructure projects and the diffusion of economic activity in developing countries. Working Paper 64, AidData, Williamsburg, VA.

Bolesta, A. (2018). Myanmar-China peculiar relationship: Trade, investment, and the model of development. *Journal of International Studies*, *11*(2), 23–36.

Brandt, L. and Rawski, T. G. (eds.). (2008). *China's Great Economic Transformation*. Cambridge university press, United Kingdom.

Brandt, L., Litwack, J., Mileva, E., Wang, L., Zhang, Y., and Zhao, L. (2020). China's productivity slowdown and future growth potential. *The World Bank*.

Breslin, S. (2011). China and the crisis: Global power, domestic caution and local initiative. *Contemporary Politics*, *17*(2), 185–200.

Brown, M. E. (2000). *The Rise of China* (Vol. 1). The MIT Press, MIT Press, USA.

Cable, D. V. (2017). Architect of the Chinese Superpower http://www.lse.ac.uk/ideas/Assets/Documents/reports/LSE-IDEAS-From-Deng-to-Xi.pdf; 2 | LSE IDEAS Special Report, May 2017, pp. 2–4.

Cai, K. G. (2003). The ASEAN–China free trade agreement and East Asian regional grouping. *Contemporary Southeast Asia: A Journal of International and Strategic Affairs*, *25*(3), 387–404.

Campbell, I., Wheeler, T., Attree, L., Butler, D. M., and Mariani, B. (2012). *China and conflict-affected states*. January. Safer World, UK.

Careem, N. (2017). September 27, https://www.scmp.com/special-reports/business/topics/special-report-belt-and-road/article/2112980/beijings-grand-strategy.

Chachavalpongpun, P. (2011). Competing diplomacies: Thailand Amidst Sino-American Rivalry. *Southeast Asian Affairs*, *2011*(1), 306–319.

Chambers, M. R. (2005). The Chinese and the Thais are Brothers: The evolution of the Sino-Thai friendship. *Journal of Contemporary China*, *14*(45), 599.

Chambers, P. (2015). Civil-Military Relations in Thailand since the 2014 Coup, Peace Research Institute Frankfurt (2015). Stable url: https://www.jstor.org/stable/resrep14467.7.

Chaziza, M. (2016). China–Pakistan relationship: A game-changer for the Middle East? *A Contemporary Review of the Middle East*, *3*(2), 147–161.

Chellaney, B. (2020). China is Paying a High Price for Provoking India, https://www.project-syndicate.org/commentary/china-expansionism-meets-indian-resistance-in-himalayas-by-brahma-chellaney-2020-09?barrier=accesspaylog, September 23, 2020, accessed on November 17, 2020.

Chirathivat, S. (2002). ASEAN–China free trade area: Background, implications, and future development. *Journal of Asian Economics*, *13*(5), 671–686.

Chongkittavorn, K. (2020). The Thailand-U.S. defense Alliance in U.S.-Indo-Pacific Strategy, East–West Center, https://www.jstor.org/stable/resrep21071.

Christie, K. and Hanlon, R. J. (2014). Sustaining human rights and responsibility: The United Nations global compact and Myanmar. *Athens Journal of Social Sciences*, *1*(1), 9–20.

CPEC (2017–2030). Long term plan for China-Pakistan economic corridor.www. cpec.gov.pk.

Cuestas, J. C., Gil-Alana, L. A., and Staehr, K. (2014). Government debt dynamics and the global financial crisis: Has anything changed in the EA12? *Economics Letters*, *124*(1), 64–66.

Deng Xiaoping. (1984). Build Socialism with Chinese Characteristics, in (ed.) The research department of party literature, central committee of the communist party of China (1991), Major Documents of the People's Republic of China — Selected Important.

Deng, Y. (2020). Sino — Thai relations: From strategic co-operation to economic diplomacy. *Contemporary Southeast Asia*, *13*(4) (March 1992): 360–374.

Desai, M. (2005). Will India ever catch up with China? *South Asia: Journal of South Asian Studies*, *28*(2), 321–336.

Deshpande, G. P. (2010). China and the politics of Southern Asia. *Strategic Analysis*, *34*(3), 470–475.

Devare, S. T., Singh, S., and Marwah, R. (2014). ASEAN at the crossroads of regionalism: The Indonesia perspective meidyatama suryodiningrat. In *Emerging China* (pp. 58–67). Routledge India.

Devare, S. T., Singh, S., and Marwah, R. (eds.). (2014). *Emerging China: Prospects of Partnership in Asia*. Routledge, New Delhi, India.

Devonshire-Ellis, C. (2019). Will Italy Be Overrun by Chinese Workers? EU Minimum Wages Compared with China's Belt and Road Contractors', Silk Road Briefing.

Devonshire-Ellis, C. (2020). Changes in China's Purchasing and Import Trends between 2019 and 2024, https://www.china-briefing.com/news/changes-chinas-purchasing-import-trends-2019-2024/, September 2, 2019, accessed on August 20, 2020.

Dezenski, E. K. (2020). Below the Belt and Road, Corruption and Illicit dealings in China's global infrastructure, https://www.fdd.org/analysis/2020/05/04/below-the-belt-and-road/, FDD, Monograph, May 6, 2020.

Dollar, D. (2018). Is China's development finance a challenge to the international order? *Asian Economic Policy Review*, *13*(2), 283–298.

Druce, S. C., and Julay, A. H. (2018). The road to Brunei's economic diversification. *China and Southeast Asia in the Xi Jinping Era*, 139.

Dumbaugh, K. B. (2010). Exploring the China-Pakistan relationship. *Roundtable Report*.

Economy, E. (2018). *The Third Revolution: Xi Jinping and the New Chinese State*. Oxford University Press, United Kingdom.

Editor, (2020). Bangkok Post Editorial Column: April 17, 2020, accessed on July 28, 2020, https://www.bangkokpost.com/opinion/opinion/1901410/chinas-drain-on-mekong.

Eichengreen, B., Rhee, Y., and Tong, H. (2004). *The impact of China on the exports of other Asian countries* (No. w10768). National Bureau of Economic Research.

EIU Report (2019). Democracy, http://www.eiu.com/public/thankyou_download. aspx?activity=download&campaignid=democracyindex2019.

Elizabeth C. Economy (2019). The Third Revolution — Xi Jinping and the new Chinese State, OUP.

Elman, B. A. and Liu, C. H. J. (eds.). (2017). *The Global and the Local in Early Modern and Modern East Asia.* Brill, Leiden, The Netherlands.

Fairbank, J. K. (1942). Tributary trade and China's relations with the West. *The Journal of Asian Studies, 1*(2), 129–149.

Fanell, J. E. (2019). Asia rising: China's global naval strategy and expanding force structure. *Naval War College Review, 72*(1), 4.

Fei, J. (2020). https://fsi-live.s3.us-west-1.amazonaws.com/s3fs-public/east_coast_rail_line_in_malaysia_0.pdf, accessed on August 16, 2020.

Feigenbaum, E. A. (2020). Reluctant stakeholder: Why China's highly strategic brand of revisionism is more chal-lenging than washington thinks. In *China's Economic Arrival* (pp. 113–130). Palgrave Macmillan, Singapore.

Feng, W. (2020). The silver and white economy: The Chinese demographic challenge, https://www.oecd.org/employment/leed/oecd-china-report-final.pdf, accessed on November 28, 2020.

Fernando, S. N. (2010). China's relations with Sri Lanka and the Maldives: Models of good relations among big and small countries. *China Report, 46*(3), 285–297.

Fernholz, T. (2018). March 8, 2018, https://qz.com/1223768/china-debt-trap-these-eight-countries-are-in-danger-of-debt-overloads-from-chinas-belt-and-road-plans/, accessed on November 19, 2020.

Fickling, D. (2020). Biden, Like Trump, Will Deepen Integration With China. https://www.bloomberg.com/opinion/articles/2020-11-09/biden-like-trump-will-deepen-integration-with-china, accessed on November 29, 2020.

Forde, K. (2020). https://www.aljazeera.com/economy/2020/11/5/what-does-ant-groups-frozen-ipo-say-about-business-in-china, accessed on November 28, 2020.

French, H. W. (2017). *Everything under the Heavens: How the Past Helps Shape China's Push for Global Power.* Knopf: New York, USA.

Fuller, T. and Geitner, P. (2012). European Union suspends most Myanmar sanctions. *The New York Times.*

Gangadharan, S. (2020). https://stratnewsglobal.com/after-land-grab-in-nepal-china-makes-claims-in-bhutan/, September 28, 2020, accessed on November 28, 2020.

Ganjanakhundee, S. (2020). Thailand uses participatory diplomacy to terminate the joint clearing of the Mekong with China, ISSUE: 2020 No. 30, Singapore | April 17, 2020.

Ge, J. (2018). The silk road: Historical geographic background and outlooks. In *China's Belt and Road Initiatives* (pp. 1–14). Springer, Singapore.

Gilley, B. (1998). Tiger on the Brink, Jiang Zemin and China's New Elite, October 1998.

Giri, Anil. (2019). Nepal Trims Projects Under BRI from 35 to 9 at Chinese Call. https://kathmandupost.com/national/2019/01/18/nepal-trims-projects-under-bri-from-35-to-9-at-chinese-call.

Goodman, J. (2014). https://thediplomat.com/2014/03/sri-lankas-growing-links-with-china/, Jack Goodman, March 6, 2014.

Government of China (2014). Foreign Aid White Paper 2014. Available at: http://english.gov.cn/archive/white_paper/2014/08/23/content_281474982986592.htm.

Government of Sri Lanka (2017). The concession agreement for the port of Hambantota: Public-Private Partnership Hambantota Port Agreement, HIPG Pvt. Ltd and HIPS Pvt. Ltd, July 29, 2017, unpublished.

Grossman, D. (2020). https://thediplomat.com/2020/05/reviewing-vietnams-struggle-options-in-the-south-china-sea/, May 5, 2020, accessed on August 21, 2020.

Gu, J., Corbett, H., and Leach, M. (2019). 'Introduction: The belt and road initiative and the sustainable development goals: Opportunities and challenges' in Sen, G., Leach, M. and Gu, J. (eds) in The Belt and Road Initiative and the SDGs: Towards Equitable, Sustainable Development, IDS Bulletin 50.4, Brighton: IDS.

Gu, S. and Lundvall, B. Å. (2006). China's innovation system and the move toward harmonious growth and endogenous innovation. *The Learning Economy and the Economics of Hope*, 269.

Gu, Y., Wong, T. W., Law, C. K., Dong, G. H., Ho, K. F., Yang, Y., and Yim, S. H. L. (2018). Impacts of sectoral emissions in China and the implications: Air quality, public health, crop production, and economic costs. *Environmental Research Letters*, *13*(8), 084008.

Guan, A. C. (1998). Vietnam–China relations since the end of the cold war. *Asian Survey*, *38*(12), 1122–1141.

Gul, A. (2019). China: BRI investments Boost Pakistan economic structure, https://www.voanews.com/south-central-asia/china-bri-investments-boost-pakistan-economic-structure.

Guo, K., Hang, J., and Yan, S. (2018). Determinants of China's structural change during the reform era. *China Political Economy*. *1*(1), 100–119. https://doi.org/10.1108/CPE-09-2018-007.

Haider, S. (2019). Maldives negotiating China debt, says Foreign Minister: http://timesofindia.indiatimes.com/articleshow/77536341.cms?utm_source=contentofinterest&utm_medium=text&utm_campaign=cppst, accessed on October 30, 2020.

Hayes, A. (2020). Interwoven 'Destinies': The significance of Xinjiang to the China dream, the belt and road initiative, and the Xi Jinping Legacy. *Journal of Contemporary China, 29*(121), 31–45.

Hiebert, M., Nguyen, P., and Poling, G. B. (eds.). (2014). *Perspectives on the South China Sea: Diplomatic, Legal, and Security Dimensions of the Dispute.* Rowman & Littlefield.

Hillman, Jonathan E. (2018). China must play fair over BRI contracts. *Nikkei Asia Review*, February 6, 2018a, as of January 20, 2020, https://asia.nikkei.com/Politics/China-must-play-fair-over-BRI-contracts.

Hilton, I. (2013). China in Myanmar: Implications for the future. *Norwegian Peacebuilding Re. October.* https://www.files.ethz.ch/isn/172094/822f00b4d7da6439a3252789b404f006.pdf.

Hollihan, T. A. and Zhang, Z. (2016). Media narratives of China's future.

Hoontrakul P., Balding C., and Marwah R. (2014). The rise of China and India—its implications. In Hoontrakul P., Balding C., and Marwah R. (eds.) *The Global Rise of Asian Transformation.* New York: Palgrave Macmillan, https://doi.org/10.1057/9781137412362_6.

Hornby, L. and Zhang, A. (2019). Belt and road debt trap accusations hound China as it hosts forum. *Financial Times*.

Howe, Y. Y. K. and Ash, R. (2003). China's economic reform: A study with documents. In Christopher, (ed.). London, New York, NY: Routledge, Curzon, 2003.

Htwe, C. M. (2018). Myanmar successfully renegotiates debt, ownership terms for Kyaukphyu. *The Myanmar Times*, October 1, 2018, https://www.mmtimes.com/news/myanmar-successfully-renegotiates-debt-ownership-terms-kyaukphyu.html.

Hu, A. (2018). The belt and road: Revolution of economic geography and the era of win-winism. In *China's Belt and Road Initiatives* (pp. 15–32). Springer, Singapore.

Huang, C. C. (2015). Balance of relationship: The essence of Myanmar's China policy. *The Pacific Review, 28*(2), 1–22.

Human Development Report (2019). United Nations Development Programme. 2019. Retrieved December 9, 2019.

Hurley, J., Morris, S., and Portelance, G. (2018). Examining the Debt Implications of the Belt and Road Initiative from a Policy Perspective, Washington, DC: Centre for Global Development, https://www.cgdev.org/publication/examining-debt-implications-belt-and-road-initiative-a-policy-perspective, accessed February 3, 2020.

Ikenberry, G. (2018). John the end of liberal international order? International Affairs, 94(1), 7–23, https://doi.org/10.1093/ia/iix241, Published: January 1, 2018, https://academic.oup.com/ia/article/94/1/7/4762691, accessed on November 29, 2020.

Ikenberry, G. J. (2008). The rise of China and the future of the West-Can the liberal system survive. *Foreign Affairs, 87*, 23.

International Institute for Sustainable Development (2001). Global Green Standards, Manitoba, https://www.iisd.org/library/global-greenstandards. accessed February 3, 2020.

ISEAS Survey (2020). https://www.iseas.edu.sg/wp-content/uploads/pdfs/ TheStateofSEASurveyReport_2020.pdf.

Jabbar, Z. (2015). Chinese contractor puts India at ease. The Island, April 20, 2015, http://www.island.lk/index.php?page_cat=articledetails&page=article-details&code_title=123392, accessed on August 5, 2020.

Jacob, J. T. (2010). China–Pakistan relations: Reinterpreting the Nexus. *China Report, 46*(3), 217–229.

Jacques, M. (2009). *When China Rules the World: The End of the Western World and the Birth of a New Global Order.* Penguin, United Kingdom.

Jaishankar, S. (2020). *The India Way: Strategies for an Uncertain World*, Harper Collins, India.

Japan Times, Mekong (2020). https://www.japantimes.co.jp/news/2020/12/14/asia-pacific/china-dams-mekong-us-rivalry/, accessed on December 1, 2020.

Kapoor, K. and Thant, A. T. (2018). Exclusive: Myanmar scales back Chinese-backed port project due to debt fears: Official. *Reuters*, August 2, 2018, https://www.reuters.com/article/us-myanmar-china-port-exclusive/exclusive-myanmarscales-back-Chinese-backed-port-project-due-to-debt-fears-official-idU.S.KBN1KN106.

Karim, M. A. and Islam, F. (2018). *The Korean Journal of Defense Analysis*, 30(2), 283–302 ISSN: 1016-3271 print, online © 2018 Korea Institute for Defense Analyses, http://www.kida.re.kr/kjda 284.

Kartha, T. (2020). https://theprint.in/opinion/pakistan-chuckled-while-india-clashed-at-the-lac-forgot-how-china-nibbled-its-territory-too/457891/, July 10, 2020, accessed on October 10, 2020.

Kartha, T. (2020). Tara Kartha, July 10, 2020, https://theprint.in/opinion/pakistan-chuckled-while-india-clashed-at-the-lac-forgot-how-china-nibbled-its-territory-too/457891/, accessed on July 13, 2020.

Katzenstein, P. J. (2002). Area studies, regional studies, and international relations. *Journal of East Asian Studies*, 127–137.

Kausikan, B. (2020). How the coronavirus may change the geopolitics of Southeast Asia, https://www.scmp.com/week-asia/opinion/article/3076460/how-coronavirus-may-change-geopolitics-southeast-asia, accessed on November 28, 2020.

Kawashima, S. (2020). https://thediplomat.com/2020/08/japans-painful-choice-on-rcep/, August 3, 2020, accessed on August 20, 2020.

Kelegama, S. (2014). China–Sri Lanka economic relations: An overview. *China Report, 50*(2), 131–149.

Keyes, C. (2011). G William skinner and the study of Chinese in Thailand and the study of thai society, paper presented at a workshop on "The Legacy of G. William Skinner's Field Research: China and Southeast Asia", University of Washington.

Khanna, P. (2016). *Connectography: Mapping the Future of Global Civilization*. Random House, Broadway in Manhattan, USA.

Kiik, L. (2016). Nationalism and anti-ethno-politics: Why 'Chinese Development' failed at Myanmar's Myitsone Dam. *Eurasian Geography and Economics*, *57*(3), 374–402.

Kim, Y. (2020). Is China Spoiling the Rules-Based Liberal International Order? Examining China's rising institutional power in a multiplex world through competing theories. *Issues & Studies*, *56*(01), 2050001.

Kobi, M. (2016). *Constructing, creating and contesting cityscapes: A socio-anthropological approach to urban transformation in Southern Xinjiang, People's Republic of China*. University of Berne.

Koga, K. (2018). *The Chinese Journal of International Politics*, ASEAN's evolving institutional strategy: Managing great power politics in South China Sea Disputes, Oxford. 49–80, doi: 10.1093/cjip/pox016.

Kong, V., Cochrane, S. G., Meighan, B., and Walsh, M. (2019). The belt and road initiative–six years on. *Moody's Analytics*, 3.

Krishnan, A. (2020). China's nationalist turn under Xi Jinping. https://www.thehindu.com/opinion/op-ed/chinas-nationalist-turn-under-xi-jinping/article32655108.ece, accessed on November 25, 2020.

Kristof, N. D. (1992). The rise of China. *Foreign Affairs*, *72*, 59.

Kulczuga, A. (2013). A Taste of Freedom: Burma's Guarded Optimism. World Affairs, March/April, 32–40.

Kumar, M. and Woo, J. (2010). Public debt and growth. *IMF Working Papers*, 1–47.

Kumar, S. (2007). The China–Pakistan strategic relationship: Trade, investment, energy and infrastructure. *Strategic Analysis*, *31*(5), 757–790.

Kumar, S. (2018). India-China-Nepal triangular relations. *International Journal of Science and Research (IJSR)*, *9*(4), 477–478.

Kumar, S. (2020). China's revisionism versus India's status quoism: Strategies and counter-strategies of rivals in doklam standoff. *Jadavpur Journal of International Relations*, *24*(1), 73–100.

Kumara, H. and Cooray, N. S. (2013). Public debt and economic growth in Sri Lanka: Is there any threshold level for pubic debt. *Economics & Management Series, EMS-2013–2022). Minamiuonuma: IUJ Research Institute, International University of Japan.*

Kundu, S. (2018). Deciphering the Pauk Phaw* between Myanmar and China. *China Report*, *54*(3), 341–353.

Kurlantzick, J. (2020). https://www.cfr.org/blog/rcep-signing-and-its-implica-tions, November 16, 2020, accessed on November 20, 2020.

Kwan, C. H. (2007). China Shifts from Labor Surplus to Labor Shortage — Challenges and opportunities in a new stage of development, accessed on July 23, 2020.

Lakatos, C. and Walmsley, T. (2012). Investment creation and diversion effects of the ASEAN–China free trade agreement. *Economic Modelling, 29*(3), 766–779.

Lama, M. P. (2017). Renegotiating alternative integration model in the SAARC. *International Studies, 54*(1–4), 82–105.

Lama, M. P. (2020). The Chinese trishul in South Asia. Updated: July 12, 2020, accessed on July 12, 2020, https://www.hindustantimes.com/analysis/the-chinese-trishul-in-south-asia/story-qUKiiJBi66Dx6QtD6aQtTJ.html.

Lampton, D. M. Selina, H., and Cheng-Chwee, K. (2020). *Rivers of Iron: Railroads and Chinese Power in Southeast Asia*, University of California Press, USA.

Lampton David M, Selina Ho, *Cheng-Chwee Kuik, Rivers of Iron: Railroads and Chinese Power in Southeast Asia*, University of California Press, USA.

Lauridsen, L. S. (2019). *Drivers of China's Regional Infrastructure Diplomacy: The Case of the Sino-Thai Railway.*

Lee, K. (2013). Schumpeterian analysis of economic catch-up: Knowledge, path-creation, and the middle-income trap. Cambridge University Press.

LePoer, B. L. (1989). *Thailand: A Country Study*. Federal Research Division, Library of Congress.

Li, L. (1998). The China miracle: Development strategy and economic reform. *Cato Journal, 18*(1), 147.

Li, C. and Char, J. (2015). *China-Myanmar Relations Since Naypyidaw's Political Transition: How Beijing Can Balance Short-term Interests and Long-term Values*. Singapore: S. Rajaratnam School of International Studies.

Liao, J. (2020). The rise of the service sector in China. *China Economic Review, 59*, 101385.

Lim, Ida. (2019), https://www.malaymail.com/news/malaysia/2019/11/24/chinas-ambassador-says-will-teach-chinese-tourists-to-behave-properly-in-ma/1812805, November 24, 2019.

Lintner, B. (2019). *The Costliest Pearl: China's Struggle for India's Ocean.* Oxford University Press.

Lintner, B. (2020). China flips the electoral script in Myanmar, https://asiatimes.com/2020/05/china-flips-the-electoral-script-in-myanmar/, accessed on November 16, 2020.

Lohani, M. P. (2014). Involving China through Asian Integration: A Nepalese Perspective. *Emerging China: Prospects of Partnership in Asia*, 256.

Lord, A. (2016). Citizens of a hydropower nation: Territory and agency at the frontiers of hydropower development in Nepal. *Economic Anthropology, 3*(1), 145–160.

Lovell, J. (2019). *Maoism: A Global History*, Penguin, Random House, UK.

Lubin, D., Chua, J., Kalisz, P., Morse, E. L., Revilla, E., Kit, W. Z., Cowan, D., *et al.* (2018). *China's Belt and Road at Five: A Progress Report*. New York: Citi GPS.

Luthi, A. J.-L., (2020). A road, a disappearing river and fragile connectivity in Sino-Inner Asian borderlands. *Political Geography*, *78*, 102122, Elseiver.

Mações, B. (2019). *Belt and road: A Chinese world order*. Oxford University Press, United Kingdom.

Madhani, A. (2012). Obama administration eases Burma sanctions before visit. USA Today.

Mahbubani, K. (2020). Has China won?: the Chinese challenge to American primacy, Hachette UK.

Mahbubani, K. (2020). Has China won: The Chinese challenge to American primacy, Public Affairs, USA.

Malik, M. (2020). One Belt One Road: Dimensions, Detours, Fissures, and Fault Lines, in *What China Wants*, vol. 13, no. 5, May/June 2018, Asia-Pacific Center for Security Studies, Honolulu, Hawaii, USA, accessed June 14, 2020.

Mardell, J. (2020). China's economic footprint in the Western Balkans. *Asia Policy Brief, Bertelsmann Stiftung*.

Mardell, J. (2020). The BRI in Pakistan: China's flagship economic corridor, https://merics.org/en/analysis/bri-pakistan-chinas-flagship-economic-corridor, accessed on September 10, 2020.

Margolin, J. L. (2014). China–Singapore cyclical relations in the longue durée: Some lessons for the future. *Emerging China: Prospects of Partnership in Asia*, 228.

Marino, F. (2020). https://www.thequint.com/amp/story/voices/opinion/china-pakistan-economic-corridor-beijing-islamabad-imran-khan-government-xi-jinping; November 19, 2020, accessed on November 20, 2020.

Marks, D. and Zhang, J. (2019). Circuits of power: Environmental injustice from Bangkok's shopping malls to Laos' hydropower dams. *Asia Pacific Viewpoint*, *60*(3), 296–309.

Marks, D. and Zhang, J. (2019). Circuits of power: Environmental injustice from Bangkok's shopping malls to laos' Hydropower Dams. *Asia Pacific Viewpoint*, *60*(3), 296–309. doi: 10.1111/apv.12242.

Marwah, R. (2018). 8: China studies in South and South East Asia: A comparative perspective through Sri Lanka and Thailand. *China Studies in South and Southeast Asia: Between Pro-china and Objectivism*, 193.

Marwah, R. (2018). RCEP: More Than a Trade Deal — OpEd, https://www.eurasiareview.com/05072018-rcep-more-than-a-trade-deal-oped/, accessed on July 25, 2020.

Marwah, R. (2020). Book review: Bertil Lintner. *The Costliest Pearl: China's Struggle for India's Ocean*, *56*(4).

Marwah, R. (2020). *Reimagining India-Thailand Relations: A Multilateral and Bilateral Perspective*. World Scientific, Singapore.

Marwah, R. and Ramanayake, S. S. (2019). The development Trajectories of Thailand and Sri Lanka: A comparative analysis. *Millennial Asia, 10*(3), 395–416.

Marwah, R. and Singh, S. (2013). *Interview*, http://www.china-studies.taipei/act02.php 2nd, March 2, 2013, Dhaka.

Mathai, K., Gottlieb, G. Hong, G. H. Jung, S. E., Schmittmann, J., and Yu, J. (2016). China's changing Trade and the implications for the CLMV economies, https://www.imf.org/external/pubs/ft/dp/2016/apd1601.pdf, p. 40, IMF.

Mathai, M. K., Hong, G. H., Jung, S. E., Schmittmann, J. M., and Yu, J. (2016). *China's Changing Trade and the Implications for the CLMV*. International Monetary Fund.

Mathew, S. D. and Skidmore, D. (2019). The AIIB in the liberal international order. *The Chinese Journal of International Politics, 12*(1), 61–91.

Mauss, M. (1966). *The Gift London*, Routledge, 2002 (first edition 1954).

Medina, A. F. (2020). https://www.aseanbriefing.com/news/asean-overtakes-eu-become-chinas-top-trading-partner-q1-2020/, May 15, 2020, accessed on July 27, 2020.

Ministry of Finance Sri Lanka (2019). National policy framework, vistas of prosperity and splendour-summary, Colombo, http://www.treasury.gov.lk/documents/10181/791429/FinalDovVer02+English.pdf/. accessed February 5, 2020.

Mishra (2019). https://www.orfonline.org/expert-speak/young-bhutans-opinion-on-its-mega-neighbours-57215/ Shreya Mishra, November 1, 2019, accessed on July 9, 2020.

Mohanty, M. (2013). Xi Jinping and the Chinese Dream'. *Economic and Political Weekly*, 34–40.

Moody's Analytics (2019). https://www.moodysanalytics.com/-/media/article/2019/belt-and-road-initiative.

Moodys (2019). The Belt and Road Initiative — Six Years On, by Veasna Kong, Steven g. Cochrane, Brendan Meighan, and Matthew Walsh, https://www.moodysanalytics.com/-/media/article/2019/belt-and-road-initiative.pdf, accessed on November 20, 2020.

MoPIT (Ministry of Physical Infrastructure and Transportation) (2016). Five Year Strategic Plan 2073–2078 (2016–2021). Kathmandu: Government of Nepal.

Mulvad, A. M. (2019). Xiism as a hegemonic project in the making: Sino-communist ideology and the political economy of China's rise. *Review of International Studies, 45*(3), 449–470.

Murphy, A. M. (2010). Beyond balancing and bandwagoning: Thailand's response to China's rise. *Asian Security, 6*(1), 1–27.

Murton, G., Lord, A., and Beazley, R. (2016). "A handshake across the Himalayas:" Chinese investment, hydropower development, and state formation in Nepal. *Eurasian Geography and Economics*, *57*(3), 403–432.

Murton, G. and Lord, A. (2020). Trans-himalayan power corridors: Infrastructural politics and China's belt and road initiative in Nepal, *Political Geography*, *77*, 102100.

Myers, S. L., Wu, J., and Fu, C. (2020). China's looming crisis: A shrinking population, https://www.nytimes.com/interactive/2019/01/17/world/asia/china-population-crisis.html, accessed December 1, 2020.

Nanuam, W. and Jikkham, P. (2015). Thailand, China bolster military ties as U.S. relations splinter. *Bangkok Post, 6*.

Nayar, B. R. (2004). The geopolitics of China's economic mMiracle. *China Report, 40*(1), 19–47.

NDRC (2015). https://www.uschina.org/sites/default/files/NDRC%202015.03.pdf, accessed on September 12, 2020.

Nye Jr, J. S. (2015). *Is the American century over?* John Wiley & Sons.

OECD Report (2020). Chapter 6, https://www.oecd.org/employment/leed/oecd-china-report-final.pdf, accessed on November 28, 2020.

Oh, Y. A. (2020). Chinese development aid to Asia: Size and motives. *Asian Journal of Comparative Politics, 5*(3), 223–234.

Outbound Chinese Tourism and Consumption Trends (2017). https://www.nielsen.com/wp-content/uploads/sites/3/2019/05/outbound-chinese-tourism-and-consumption-trends.pdf, accessed on July 24, 2020.

Overholt, W. (2020). Renminbi internationalisation deferred, https://www.omfif.org/2020/05/renminbis-limited-internationalisation/, accessed on November 30, 2020.

Oya, S. (2020). What China's 'dual circulation' strategy means for the world, https://www.japantimes.co.jp/opinion/2020/11/03/commentary/world-commentary/china-dual-circulation-strategy/, accessed November 28, 2020.

Panditaratne, D. (2020). 'China's Commercial and Military Presence in the Indian Ocean: A Perspective from Sri Lanka', Proceedings from CNA conference on 'Views of China's Presence in the Indian Ocean Region' on 17–18 June 2019, forthcoming.

Pant, H. V. (2019). Read more at https://www.deccanherald.com/opinion/in-perspective/bri-delhi-has-shaped-discourse-729981.html, accessed on April 22, 2019.

Parameswaran, P. (2016). Thailand to buy battle tanks from China agreement inked with Beijing for MBT-3000s, https://thediplomat.com/2016/05/thailand-to-buy-battle-tanks-from-china/.

Pardhi, M. (2020). *How China Plans to Further its Technology Ambitions — A Snapshot from Semiconductor Industry*, https://icsin.org/blogs/2020/10/, accessed December 1, 2020.

Pattanaik, S. S. (2019). India's policy response to China's investment and aid to Nepal, Sri Lanka and Maldives: Challenges and prospects. *Strategic Analysis*, *43*(3), 240–259.

Perlez, J. and Huang, Y. (2017). Behind China's $1 trillion plan to shake up the economic order. *The New York Times, 13*.

Pichet, K. (2015). Thailand's Rail Transport Infrastructure Development Strategy 2015–2022, http://www.otp.go.th/uploads/tiny_uploads/PolicyPlan/1-Policy Plan/M-MAP2/25600629-PDF1-Dr.Pichet.pdf.

Porter, A. and Low, A. M. (1999). *The Oxford history of the British Empire: The nineteenth century* (Vol. 3). Oxford University Press, England.

Punyodyana, B. (1976). The Chinese in Thailand: A synopsis of research approaches. *Philippine Sociological Review*, 57–61.

Raja Mohan, C. (2020). Putting sovereignty back in global order: An Indian view. *The Washington Quarterly*, *43*(3), 81–98.

Ramabadran. (2017). https://economictimes.indiatimes.com/blogs/et-commentary/xi-jinping-more-mao-zedong-than-deng-xiaoping/, accessed on November 2020.

Rand, J. (2015). Understanding FDI spillover mechanisms, *Learning to Compete Working Paper*, Washington, DC: The Brookings Institution, https://www.brookings.edu/blog/africa-in-focus/2015/11/19/understanding-fdi-spillover-mechanisms/, accessed on August 4, 2020.

Rapoza. (2020). https://www.forbes.com/sites/kenrapoza/2020/07/27/the-dollar-is-a-sword-of-damocles-over-china/?sh=56dd3e91371f, accessed on November 2020.

Rastogi, V. (2017). https://www.aseanbriefing.com/news/aseans-free-trade-agreements-an-overview/, accessed on August 20, 2020.

Reid, A. (1993). *Southeast Asia in the Age of Commerce 1450–1680: Volume 2: Expansion and Crisis*.

Rej, A. (2020). China's Science Talent-Recruitment Program Draws Fresh Attention, https://thediplomat.com/2020/08/chinas-science-talent-recruitment-program-draws-fresh-attention/, accessed on November 28, 2020.

Rosbach, K. and Aleksanyan, L. (2019). Why Pakistan's economic growth continues to be balance-of-payments constrained.

Rupanichkij, P. (2010). Overview of the Thai economy in 2010.

Russel, D. R. and Berger, B. H. (2020). Weaponizing the belt and road initiative. *The Asia Society Policy Institute*, New York, https://www.brookings.edu/articles/chinas-digital-services-trade-and-data-governance-how-should-the-united-states-respond/, accessed June 14, 2020.

Russell, D. and Berger, B. H. (2020). *Weaponizing the Belt and Road Initiative*, The Asia society policy institute, September 2020, USA.

Rutnam, E. (2018). Navy strengthens presence in and around Hambantota Port, *The Morning*, October 21, 2018, http://www.themorning.lk/hambantota/, accessed January 9, 2020.

Sahoo, P. (2013). Economic relations with Bangladesh: China's ascent and India's decline. *South Asia Research, 33*(2), 123–139.

Samphel, T. (2020). September 11, 2020; https://www.hindustantimes.com/books/review-the-end-of-an-era-india-exits-tibet-by-claude-arpi/story-PJt6Xuogi8B0w8dBKQLb6H.html, accessed on November 15, 2020.

Sampson, M. (2019). The evolution of China's regional trade agreements: Power dynamics and the future of the Asia-Pacific. *The Pacific Review*, 1–31.

Santasombat, Y. (2015). *Impact of China's Rise on the Mekong Region*, Palgrave Macmillan US, p. 2.

Schwaag Serger, S., Benner, M., and Liu, L. (2015). Chinese university governance: Tensions and reforms. *Science and Public Policy, 42*(6), 871–886.

Setiono, B. (2016) Interviewee, Matsumuro — February 29, 2016, http://www.china-studies.taipei/act02.php.

Sharma, B. P. (2019). Belt and road: Overview of developing countries like Nepal. *China and the World, 2*(03), 1950016.

Sheu, J. B. and Kundu, T. (2018). Forecasting time-varying logistics distribution flows in the One Belt-One Road stra-tegic context. *Transportation Research Part E: Logistics and Transportation Review, 117*, 5–22.

Shi, Z., Manomaivibool, P., and Marwah, R. (eds.). (2019). *China Studies in South and Southeast Asia: Between Pro-China and Objectivism*. World Scientific Publishing Company Pte. Limited, Singapore.

Shih, C., Manomaivibool, P., and Marwah, R. (eds.) (2018). Introduction, China Studies in South and Southeast Asia, pp. i–xvii, World Scientific, Singapore.

Siddiqa-Agha, A. (2001). *Pakistan's Arms Procurement and Military Buildup, 1979–1999: In Search of a Policy*. Springer.

Siddique, A., Selvanathan, E. A., and Selvanathan, S. (2012). Remittances and economic growth: Empirical evidence from Bangladesh, India and Sri Lanka. *Journal of Development Studies, 48*(8), 1045–62.

Singh, G. (2019). *Belt and Road: A Chinese World Order: Bruno Macaes*. Hurst and Company, London, 2018. pp. v+ 203. Notes. Pb.£ 20.

Singh, S. (2016). Interview — Ms. Lily Wangchuk, Bhutan in an interview on June 4, 2016, http://www.china-studies.taipei/act02.php.

Singh, S. W. (2020). On the economy, don't disengage with China | Opinion https://www.hindustantimes.com/analysis/on-the-economy-don-t-disengage-with-china/story-Er5AOSLoDjS7bqTcB3ffEI.html, July 28, 2020, accessed on July 28, 2020.

SinhaRaja, (2012). Interviewee: Dr. SinhaRaja Tammita-Delgoda Interviewer: Dr. Shard Soni Date: March 22, 2012, http://www.china-studies.taipei/act02.php.

Skinner, G. W. (1957). Chinese assimilation and Thai politics. *The Journal of Asian Studies, 16*(2), 237–250.

Small, A. (2015). *The China Pakistan axis: Asia's new geopolitics*. Random House India.

Small, A. (2019). *The China Pakistan Axis: Asia's new geopolitics*. Random House India.

Snyder, G. H. (2002). Mearsheimer's world — offensive realism and the struggle for security: A review essay. *International Security*, *27*(1), 149–173.

Son, J. (2019). Laos and Cambodia: The China dance. *By Johanna Son, Reporting ASEAN*, https://www.reportingasean.net/laos-cambodia-china-dance/; September 29, 2019, accessed on July 12, 2020.

Soni, S. K. (2018). China–Mongolia–Russia economic corridor: Opportunities and challenges. *China's Global Re-balancing and the New Silk Road*, 101–117.

Storey, I. (2008). China and Thailand: Enhancing military-security ties in the 21st century, https://jamestown.org/program/china-and-thailand-enhancing-military-security-ties-in-the-21st-century/, accessed on October 26, 2020.

Stuart-Fox, M. (2004). Southeast Asia and China: The role of history and culture in shaping future relations. *Contemporary Southeast Asia: A Journal of International and Strategic Affairs*, *26*(1), 116–139.

Suhartono, M. (2020). China limited the Mekong's flow. *Other Countries Suffered a Drought*, https://www.nytimes.com/2020/04/13/world/asia/china-mekong-drought.html, accessed on August 15, 2020.

Sun, Y. (2013). *Chinese investment in Myanmar: What lies ahead?* Stimson Center.

Sun, Y. (2020). http://www.theasanforum.org/chinas-wolf-warrior-diplomacy-in-the-covid-19-crisis/, May 15, 2020, accessed on November 29, 2020.

Tambunan, T. (2006). Is ASEAN still relevant in the era of the ASEAN-China FTA? In *APEA Conference*.

Tan. (2020). https://www.cnbc.com/2020/04/28/china-choked-off-the-mekong-which-worsened-southeast-asia-drought-study.html, accessed on November 20, 2020.

Tangredi, S. J. and French, H. W. (2019). Everything under the heavens: How the past helps shape China's push for global power. *Naval War College Review*, *72*(1), Article 12, https://digital-commons.usnwc.edu/cgi/viewcontent.cgi?article=7879&context=nwc-review.

Tellis, Ashley J. (2020). The Return of U.S.-China Strategic Competition in Strategic Asia 2020, in (Tellis, A., Szalwinski A., and Wills, M. (eds.) U.S.-China Competition for Global Influence, National Bureau of Asian Research (NBR), USA.

Than, T. M. M. (2006). Myanmar: Challenges galore but opposition failed to score. *Southeast Asian Affairs*, *2006*(1), 181–207.

Thanme, C. (2020). State transformation and uneven development across Southeast Asia's cross-border special economic zones. *Journal of Political Science Review*, *6*(1) 29–67.

The Economist (2020). Trade without trust: How the West should do business with China.

Tisdell, C. (2009). Economic reform and openness in China: China's development policies in the last 30 years. *Economic Analysis and Policy*, *39*(2), 271–294.

Tongzon, J. L. (2005). ASEAN-China free trade area: A bane or boon for ASEAN countries? *World Economy*, *28*(2), 191–210.

USIP report (2020). Myanmar: Casino cities run on blockchain threaten nation's sovereignty, https://www.usip.org/publications/2020/07/myanmar-casino-cities-run-blockchain-threaten-nations-sovereignty, accessed on October 6, 2020.

Varadarajan *et al.* (2020). https://www.bcg.com/publications/2020/high-stakes-of-decoupling-us-and-china, accessed on November 2020.

Vaughn, B. (2005). East Asian summit: Issues for congress. *Congressional Research Service*, Library of Congress.

Vaughn, B. and Morrison, W. M. (2006). China-Southeast Asia relations: Trends, issues, and implications for the United States. Library of Congress Washington DC Congressional Research Service.

Wang, Gungwu. (1995). The Southeast Asian Chinese and the development of China. In Leo Suryadinata, (ed.). Southeast Asian Chinese and China: The Political-economic Dimension. Singapore: Times Academic, pp. 12–30.

Wang, H. (2019). China's approach to the belt and road initiative: Scope, character and sustainability. *Journal of International Economic Law*, *22*(1), 29–55. https://doi.org/10.1093/jiel/jgy048.

Wang, Y. and Yao, Y. (1999). *Sources of China's economic growth, 1952–1999: incorporating human capital accumulation*. The World Bank.

Wagner, C. (2016). The role of India and China in South Asia. *Strategic Analysis*, *40*(4), 307–320.

Wani, A. (2020). Pakistan: Govt report uncovers corruption in CPEC projects, https://www.orfonline.org/research/pakistan-govt-report-uncovers-corruption-in-cpec-projects-66801/, accessed on September 24, 2020.

Wattanapruttipaisan, T. (2003). ASEAN-China Free Trade Area: Advantages, challenges, and implications for the newer ASEAN member countries. *ASEAN Economic Bulletin*, *20*(1), 31–48.

Weerkoon, D. and Jayasooriya, S. (2019). Commentary: Sri Lanka's debt problem was not made in China, https://www.channelnewsasia.com/news/commentary/sri-lanka-debt-port-borrowing-problem-not-made-in-china-11309738#:~:text=Commentary%3A%20Sri%20Lanka%27s%20debt%20problem%20wasn%27t%20made%20in,situated%20along%20key%20shipping%20routes%20%28Photo%3A%20AFP%2FLAKRUWAN%20WANNIARACHCHI%29, accessed on August 7, 2020.

Wignaraja, G., Panditaratne, D., Kannangara, P., and Hundlani, D. (2020). Chinese investment and the BRI in Sri Lanka. Royal Institute of International Affairs.

Wignaraja, G., Panditaratne, D., Kannangara, K., and Hundlani, D. (2020). Chinese investment and the BRI in Sri Lanka, *Asia Pacific Region*, https://www.chathamhouse.org/sites/default/files/CHHJ8010-Sri-Lanka-RP-WEB-200324.pdf.

Wignaraja, G., Tyson, J., Prizzon A., and Willem te Velde, D. (2020). Asia in 2025, *Report*, London: Overseas Development Institute, https://www.odi.org/publications/11202-asia-2025-development-prospects-and-challenges-middle-income-countries, accessed on August 3, 2020.

Wilson, D. A. (2020). China, Thailand and the spirit of Bandung. *The China Quarterly*, *30* (April–June 1967), pp. 149–169.

Wishnick, E. (2012). There goes the neighborhood: Afghanistan's challenges to China's regional security goals. *The Brown Journal of World Affairs*, *19*(1), 83–100.

Wolf, M. (2019). The future might not belong to China. *Financial Times*, January 1, 2019.

Wolf, S. O. (2020). Challenges towards the implementation and functioning of the CPEC, in *The China-Pakistan Economic Corridor of the Belt and Road Initiative* (pp. 93–123). Springer, Cham.

Wolf, S. O. (2020). *The China-Pakistan Economic Corridor of the Belt and Road Initiative*. Springer International Publishing, Switzerland.

Womack, B. (2012). Asymmetry and China's tributary system. *Chinese Journal of International Politics*, *5*(1), 37–54.

Woodworth, M. D. (2018). Landscape and the cultural politics of China's anticipatory urbanism. *Landscape Research*, *43*(7), 891–905.

Workman, D. (2019). *Myanmar's Top 10 Exports*, http://www.worldstopexports.com/myanmars-top-10-exports/, accessed on October 7, 2020.

Wu, S. S. and Chong, A. (2018). Developmental Railpolitics: The political economy of China's high-speed rail projects in Thailand and Indonesia. *Contemporary Southeast Asia*, *40*(3), 503–526.

Wu, Y. (2004). *China's Economic Growth: A Miracle with Chinese Characteristics* (Vol. 6). Routledge.

Xinhua. (2019). http://www.xinhuanet.com/english/2019-05/02/c_138028976.htm, accessed on November 2020.

Xuetong, Y. (2001). The rise of China in Chinese eyes. *Journal of Contemporary China*, *10*(26), 33–39.

Yan, J. (2018). The belt and road initiative in Southeast Asia. *China's Belt and Road Initiative (BRI) and South-east Asia*, 4–9.

Yang, H. and Zhao, D. (2015). Performance legitimacy, state autonomy and China's economic miracle. *Journal of Contemporary China*, *24*(91), 64–82.

Yasmin, L. (2019). India and China in South Asia: Bangladesh's opportunities and challenges. *Millennial Asia*, *10*(3), 322–336.

Yeh, Emily Ting. (2013). Taming tibet: Landscape transformation and the gift of Chinese development. Ithaca, NY: Cornell University Press.

Zha, W. (2015). Personalized foreign policy decision-making and economic dependence: A comparative study of Thailand and the philippines' China policies. *Contemporary Southeast Asia*, *37*(2), 242–268. Retrieved December 29, 2020.

Zhu, N., Bu, Y., Jin, M., and Mbroh, N. (2020). Green financial behavior and green development strategy of Chi-nese power companies in the context of carbon tax. *Journal of Cleaner Production, 245*, 118908.

Zhu, X. (2012). Understanding China's growth: Past, present, and future. *Journal of Economic Perspectives, 26*(4), 103–124.

Index

A

a century of humiliation, 148
Achilles heel, 271
ADB, 46
ADMM-Plus, 176
Afghanistan, 58
AFTA, 213
agreements, 155
agriculture, 10
AidData, 42
airports, 251
Aksai Chin, 255
Alexander, 83
Alibaba, 70, 173
Alibaba Group, 234
Alibaba Group Holding, 276
Alipay, 24
All-Weather Strategic Cooperative
  Partnership, xi
Amu Darya, 64
AmYu, 185
Andaman, 259
Andaman Sea, 224
anti-corruption, 32
APEC forum, 48
Arabian Sea, 57
Arakan Army, 202

arms sales, 216
artificial intelligence, 273
Arunachal Pradesh, 75
ASEAN, viii, 181, 212
ASEAN Economic Community, 152
ASEAN Regional Forum (ARF), 176
Asian financial crisis, 30
Asian Infrastructure Investment Bank
  (AIIB), 20
Asia-Pacific, x
Aung San Suu Kyi, 180
automotive, 213
axis, 55
Azad Pattan Hydel Power, 101
Azad Pattan project, 261

B

Bactrian, 83
Balochistan, 92
Bandaranaike Kumaratunga,
  Chandrika, 117
Bandung, 165
Bangkok, 215
Bangladesh, 84
Bay of Bengal, 57
BBIN, 58, 256
BCB blockchain, 206

BCIM, 58
Beijing, 68, 71
Belt and Road Initiative, viii
beneficiaries, 251
Berlin Wall, 30
Bhutan, 67
bin Mohamad, Mahathir, 39, 167
BIMSTEC, 58, 181, 256
blockchain settlement system, 275
Bloomberg, 275
Boao Forum for Asia, 71
borderlands, 271
Borneo, 167
boundary disputes, 255
Bretton Woods, 46
BRI, 211, 217
British, 54
Buddha, 74
Buddhist, 114, 172
Burma, 179
Burmese Communist Party, 180

C
18th Communist Party Congress
    (CPC), 2
Cambodia, viii, 42
Casino, 206
Ceylon, 115
charm offensive, xii
Chavalit Yongchaiyudh, 212
Chen Hai, 192
China, 44
China-centric, 31
China Communications Construction
    Company, 192
China Development Bank, 44
China Harbour Engineering, 125
China–Indochina Peninsula
    Economic Corridor (CIPEC), 188
China–Maldives Friendship Bridge,
    71
China–Pakistan Economic Corridor
    (CPEC), 37

China Power International (CPI), 193
China Railway Eryuan Engineering,
    191
China–Singapore Free Trade
    Agreement (CSFTA), 171
China's South Asia policy, 255
Chinese, 211
Chinese characteristics, 6
Chinese dream, viii
Chinese-run banana plantations, 201
Chittagong, 262
Chittagong port, 65
Chonburi, 225
Clinton, Bill, 30
CLMV, 150
CMEC, 188
CMIM, 45
code, 174
cold war, 54, 211
Colombo, 119, 121, 262
Colombo City Project, 78
Colombo Outer Circular, 124
colonial, xi
Communes, 30
Communism, 55
conduct, 174
confidence-building measures
    (CBMs), 177
conflicts, vii
Confucian centers, 258
Confucius classrooms, 41
Confucius institutes, 41
connectivity, 55, 174
Connectography, 55
continental, 57
contracts, 251
convention hall, 72
cooperative security, 177
cost–benefit analyses, 270
counter-terrorism, 216
COVID-19, 269
cryptocurrencies, 206
Cultural Revolution, 9, 30

D

Dalai lama, 55
Dali, 191
dam-building, 162
debt, 239
debt burden, x, 44
debt rate, 106
democracy, 63
democratization, x
demographic, 269
Deng Xiaoping, 6, 31
development assistance, 32
Diamer Bhasha Dam, 101
digital, 35
Digital Free Trade Zone Initiative, 168
disruptions, 85
Djibouti, 259
Doklam, 75
donor, 32
dual circulation, 271
Duangjai Asawaschinatachit, 214
Dutch, 114
Duterte, 257

E

earthquake, 73
EAS, 176
Ease of doing business index, 61
East Coast Rail, 167
Eastern, 127
Eastern seaboard, 225
East Pakistan, 84
ECRL, 167
EEC, 224
energy, 18
energy insecurity, 73
entrepreneurs, 109
environmental, 109, 234
Environmental and Social Impact Assessments, 190
Environmental Impact Assessment, 137

ethnic, 180
ethnic Chinese, 215
Eurasia, 39
European colonialism, 149
exchange rate, 110
exercises, 216
exile, 75
Export–Import Bank, 44
exports, 30, 186
export structure, 14
extremism, 56
Eyes on Earth, 160

F

Faisalabad, 41
Fa Xian, 76, 116
FDI, 18, 156, 214
financial, 73
Financial Action Task Force (FATF), 112
financial crisis, 212
financing, 110
Fincy, 206
Five Principles, 71
footprint, x
four modernizations, 8
Free Trade Agreement (FTA), 119, 153
French, 148

G

5G technology, 27
G-20, 25
Galle Trilingual inscription, 116
gambling cities, 164
GDP, 181, 213
genocidal intent, 183
geopolitics, x
gift, 79
Gilgit-Baltistan, 98
Global Climate Risk Index 2019, 204
Global Competitiveness Index (GCI), 60

globalization, 1
Gotabaya Rajapaksha, 116
governance, 43
Great Leap Forward, 30
growth rates, 8
Guandong, 30
Gulf, 85, 224
Gulf Cooperation Council, 110
Gwadar, 90

H
Hambantota, 78, 121
Hamid Karzai, 63
Hanban, 41
Han Chinese, 182
harmonious socialist society, 31
Hasan Abdal–Raikot, 98
HDI, 239
health, 35
Himalayan, 255
Hinduism, 83
Hong Kong, 70, 148
HSR, 221
Huawei, 234
Huawei technologies, 22
Hu Jintao, 31, 72
Hulhumalé Phase II, 71
humanitarian, 73
humanitarian intervention, 4
human rights, ix, 184
Human Rights Council, 113
Hun Sen, 164
Hunza territory, 76
hydropower projects, 193

I
IMF, 112
impact assessments, 191
imperial, 54
Imran Khan, 104
India, 54
Indian Ocean, ix, 55, 71, 188

Indochina, 211
Indo-Pacific, 236
infrastructure, viii
institutions, 32
International Court of Justice, 257
internationalization, 274
International Labor Organization, 12
Internet, 60
intra-ASEAN trade, 152
investment, 17, 69, 156, 239
investor, 214
Iqbal, 84
Irrawaddy, 179, 188
ISEAS Survey 2020, 164
Islam, 83, 167
Islamic radicalism, 87

J
jade, 185
Jakarta, 165
Jammu, 84
Japan, 2, 24, 127, 214
Japanese, 148
Japanese professor, 185
Jiang Zemin, 30, 31
Jinnah, 84
junta, 180

K
K2K rally, 58
Kachin, 185
Kachin Independence Organisation,
   182
Kalpitiya peninsula, 136
Kandy, 114
Kanpiketi town, 196
Karachi, 112
Karakoram Highway, 76
Karen State, 196
Karnaphuli River, 66
Karot hydropower, 261
Kashgar, 76

Kashmir, 84
Kashmir conflict, 98
Kathmandu, 262
Katunayake, 121, 124
Kautilyan, 83
Kazakhstan, 39
Kelaniya, 41
Khunjerab Pass, 80
King Chulalongkorn, 148
kingdoms, 147
kinship, 183
kith and kin, ix
KKH Project, 98
Kohala hydropower, 101
Kokang, 203
Kolkata, 58
Kra Isthmus, 224
Kunming, 58
Kyaukpyu, 183

L
Ladakh, 255
Laem Chabang, 227
Lahore, 99
landlocked, 58
language teaching institutions, 258
Laos, viii
Lao Tzu, 34
Laukkai township, 196
laying low, 31
LDCs, 58
Liberation Tigers of Tamil Eelam
  (LTTE), ix
Lintner, 68
Lobsang Sangay, 75
Lotus Tower, 121
Lumbini, 74

M
1MDB, 167
Macau, 148
Macedonian, 83

Macro Polo, 273
Malacca dilemma, 224
Malacca Straits, 166
Malay Peninsula, 224
Malaysia, 39, 212
Maldives, 60, 70
Mali, 188
Mandalay, 191
Mandarin, 211
MANPADS, 202
Mao, 30
Mao Zedong, 1
Map Ta Phut, 224, 227
Maritime Silk Road, viii, 224
Mattala, 78
Mattala International Airport, 127
Mauritius, 70
Mauryans, 83
McMahon Line, 55
Mekong, 234
Mekong conservationist, 162
Mekong river blasting, 234
Mekong River Commission (MRC),
  160
MGC, 256
Middle East, ix
middle-income trap, 270
Middle Kingdom, vii, 148
military, ix, 180
military training, 216
Ming, 116
ML-I, 99
Mong La, 196
Moodys, 251
multilateral, 176
Muse-Mandalay railway, 194
Muslim, 83, 114
Myanmar, ix
Myanmar Times, 190
Myawaddy, 196
Myitkyina district, 197
Myitsone dam, 188

N
Nathu la, 80
National League for Democracy, 180
National Rejuvenation, 32
Naypyidaw, 183, 202
NCPO, 225
neighborhood, 55
Nepal–China trans-Himalayan Multi-Dimensional Connectivity Network, 73
networks, 180
neutralism, 180
New Yangon City, 188, 192
Nicobar Islands, 259
Non-Aligned Movement, 181
Nong Khai, 221
non'-interference, ix
Norocholai, 121
Northeast region, 59

O
ODI, 36
Oli, K. P., 74
oil refinery, 66
Olympics, 71
Opium Wars, 147

P
Pacific Ocean, 166
Padma Multipurpose Bridge, 66
Pakistan, ix, 55
Pakistan Occupied Kashmir, 57
Panchsheel Agreement, xi
pandemic, 27, 255
Paracel Islands, 173
partner, 220
patent, 21
Pattaya, 223
pauk-phaw, 183
Payra port, 66
peaceful co-existence, 71

pearl, 71
People's Bank of China (PBOC), 25
periphery diplomacy, 37
Persian, 85
Pew Research, 269
Phuket, 234
PIA, 76
PingPong diplomacy, 77
Politburo Standing Committee, 2
population, 212
port, 18, 112
Portuguese, 148
Post-Cold war, 173
poverty, 30
PPP, 212
Prayut Chan-o-cha, 216
President, 31
programmatic, xi
public debt, 134
Purchasing Power Parity, 181
Pyidaungsu Hluttaw, 196

Q
Quadrilateral Security Dialogue, 174

R
Rail Project, 191
Rajapaksha, Mahinda, ix, 116
Rakhine, 184
Rama V, 148
rapprochement, 77
Rasuwagadhi, 73
Rayong, 223, 225
Razak, 167
R&D, 3
refugees, 182
Regional Comprehensive Economic Partnership (RCEP), 16, 255
Renminbi (RMB), 25, 274
respondents, 131
RMB, 80

RMB tracker, 274
Rohingyas, 183, 256
royal family, 211
Rubber-Rice, xii
Ruili, 191

S
SAARC, xi, 55
salami slicing, 70
Samsung, 175
scholarships, 57
scientific development, 31
seaports, 251
sectoral, 10
security problem, 108
Serendib, 114
service sector, 12
SEZ, 196
Shan, 191
Shanghai Cooperation Organization,
  20
Sheikh Hasina, 65
Shenzhen Special Economic Zone, 35
Shigatse–Lhasa–Shanghai railway, 80
Shin Kawashima, 155
Shweli-Muse Core Zone, 196
Siam, 149
Sikkim, 75
Silk Road, 5, 35
Silk Road Economic Belt, viii
Singapore, 70, 212
Singapore Holdings, 70
Sinhalese, 114
Sinocentric, vii, 147
Sino-globalization, 38
Sinohydro Corporation, 125
Sino-India war, 55
Sinosure, 105
Sino-Thai, 216
Sino-Thai Engineering and
  Construction (STEC), 226
Sino-Thai free trade agreement, 172

Sino–US rapprochement, 171
SIPRI, 263
Sir Syed Ahmed Khan, 83
Sirisena, Maithripala, 77, 116
Skinner, 215
solar panels, 69
Sonadia Island, 65
Song Ching Ling's, 76
South Asia, 54
South China Sea, 164
Southeast Asia, viii
Southeast Asia (SEA), 147
Soviet Union, 54
Sri Lanka, ix, 190
Sri Lankan Tamils, 115
State Law and Order Restoration, 185
State-Owned Enterprises (SOE), 3
Strait of Hormuz, 92
strategic cooperative partnership, 77
string of pearls, 57
successor, 268
Suki Kinari, 101
summit, 55
super power, viii
sustainability, 270
Swim in the Yangtze, 270
Swiss Challenge, 192

T
Taiwan, 30
Tamil, 114
Taprobane, 114
Tatmadaw, 202
technology, 21
terrorism, ix
Thailand, ix, 224
Thailand–China High-speed Rail,
  221
Thailand Development Research,
  223
Thai Special Forces, 216
Thein Sein, 188

Thilawa, 197
tianxia, vii
Tibet, 255
Tibetan Government, 75
Tibetans, 63, 71
timber, 197
tourism, 213
Tourism Minister Prasanna
    Ranatunga, 127
tourists, 23, 158
township and village enterprises
    (TVEs), 30
TPP, 48, 155
trade war, 26
trading partners, 186
Treaty of Amity and Cooperation,
    176
tributary, vii
trilateral highway, 206
troops, 64
troubled transactions, 99

U
U Set Aung said, 190
Uighur Muslims, 39
United Kingdom, 46
United States, viii, 31, 64, 236
UNSC, 173
USA–Pakistan, 85
USIP report, 206
US National Security Adviser, 268
U-Tapao International Airport, 223
U Thein Sein, 194

V
vaccine diplomacy, xiii
vassal state, 112
Vejjajiva, Abhisit, 223
veto power, 177

victory, ix
Vietnam, 148

W
Waingmaw township, 201
walking on two legs, 31
Wang Yi, 199
Wangchuk, Lily, 68
water diplomacy, 160
Weerakoon, Dushni, 125
West Pakistan, 84
white elephant, 270
Wilpattu National Park, 136
win–win, 267
WIPO, 21
wolf warrior, 28
workers, 98
World Bank, 8
World Economic Forum, 48
World Trade Organization (WTO), 2,
    30, 45
World War II, 54

X
Xie Chuntao, 33
Xi Jinping, viii, xi, 192
Xinjiang, 64, 268
Xitler, 268
Xuan Zang, 76

Y
Yangon Project Bank, 192
Yatai New City, 206
Yingluck Shinawatra, 223
yuan, 38
Yunnan province, 182

Z
Zheng He, 70, 116

CPSIA information can be obtained
at www.ICGtesting.com
Printed in the USA
LVHW011350260921
698752LV00002B/236